The State in India 1000 – 1700

OXFORD IN INDIA READINGS

Themes in Indian History

GENERAL EDITORS

- C.A Bayly
- Basudev Chatterji
- Muzaffar Alam
- Romila Thapar
- Neeladri Bhattacharya

THE STATE IN INDIA 1000 – 1700

Edited by

HERMANN KULKE

DELHI
OXFORD UNIVERSITY PRESS
CALCUTTA CHENNAI MUMBAI
1997

Oxford University Press, Great Clarendon Street, Oxford OX2 6DP

Oxford New York
Athens Auckland Bangkok Calcutta
Cape Town Chennai Dar es Salaam Delhi
Florence Hong Kong Istanbul Karachi
Kuala Lumpur Madrid Melbourne
Mexico City Mumbai Nairobi Paris
Singapore Taipei Tokyo Toronto
and associates in
Berlin Ibadan

Oxford India Paperbacks 1997

ISBN 0 19 564267 8

Typeset by Rastrixi, New Delhi 110070
Printed in India at Pauls Press, New Delhi 110020
and published by Manzar Khan, Oxford University Press
YMCA Library Building, Jai Singh Road, New Delhi 110001

Contents

General Editors' Preface

This series focuses on important themes in Indian history, on those which have long been the subject of interest and debate, or which have acquired importance more recently.

Each volume in the series consists of, first, a detailed Introduction; second, a careful choice of the essays and book-extracts vital to a proper understanding of the theme; and, finally, an Annotated Bibliography.

Using this consistent format, each volume seeks as a whole to critically assess the state of the art on its theme, chart the historiographical shifts that have occurred since the theme emerged, rethink old problems, open up questions which were considered closed, locate the theme within wider historiographical debates, and pose new issues of inquiry by which further work may be made possible.

Since the 1940s, the revaluation of the nature of the state has been a major preoccupation of history and the human sciences worldwide. Neo-Marxist writing has stimulated a debate on the extent to which the state was independent of the interests of the ruling classes. Concurrently, liberal historiography, anthropology and sociology have investigated state formation, the relations between pre-modern states and kinship, and the legitimization of state power through patterns of religious and cultural practice.

Pre-colonial India provides a unique testing ground for such debates, providing examples of forms of statehood which vary from little more than ritual overlordship, through military fiefdoms, to highly complex and relatively centralized empires. Though colonial officials were aware of some of this variety, the Eurocentric preoccupations of many contemporary historians and the belief of others that the state in India was always on the point of being overwhelmed by 'caste' and 'brahminism' deferred serious consideration of these issues until after Independence.

Now, however, as Professor Kulke demonstrates in his introduction, several basic models of Indian state forms have been isolated. While the rather uninflected notion of 'centralized empire' still dominates the literature, alternative models of 'Indian Feudalism', the 'segmentary state' and the 'patrimonial state', amongst others, have given rise to productive if sometimes ill-tempered debates. It is hoped that this volume will encourage scholars to consider further models which will integrate ideological discourses and patterns of production into the study of the Indian state. Further volumes, on the Mughal state and its decline, have been planned within this series.

Acknowledgements

The editor and the publishers would like to thank the following for permission to include the present articles in this volume.

RAM SHARAN SHARMA, 'How Feudal was Indian Feudalism', from *The Journal of Peasant Studies*, vol. 12, 2/3, 1985, pp. 19–43, published by Frank Cass, London. (Special issue, *Feudalism and Non-European Societies*, ed. by T.J. Byres and Harbans Mukhia.)

HARBANS MUKHIA, 'Was There Feudalism in Indian History?', from *The Journal of Peasant Studies*, vol. 8, 1981, pp. 273–310, published by Frank Cass, London.

BURTON STEIN, 'The Segmentary State: Interim Reflections', from Collection *Puruṣārtha*, vol. 13, 1991, pp. 217–88, *From Kingship to State. The Political in the Anthropology and History of the Indian World*, edited by J. Pouchepadass and H. Stern. Éditions de l'École des Hautes Études en Sciences Sociàles, Paris.

JAMES HEITZMAN, 'State Formation in South India, 850–1280', from *The Indian Economic and Social History Review*, vol. 24, 1987, pp. 35–61, published by Sage, New Delhi/London.

BRAJADULAL CHATTOPADHYAYA, 'Political Processes and the Structure of Polity in Early Medieval India: Problems of Perspective', Presidential Address, Ancient India Section, from *Proceedings of the Indian History Congress*, 44th Session, Burdwan 22–24 December 1983.

HERMANN KULKE, 'The Early and the Imperial Kingdom: A Processural Model of the State in Early Medieval India' (revised and translated version of the paper 'Frühmittelalterliche Regionalreiche: Ihre Struktur und Rolle im Prozess staatlicher Entwicklung in Indien'), from *Regionale Tradition in Südasien*, edited by H. Kulke and D. Rothermund, 1985, pp. 77–114, Wiesbaden, Franz Steiner-Verlag.

M. ATHAR ALI, 'Towards an Interpretation of the Mughal Empire', from *Journal of the Royal Asiatic Society of Great Britain & Ireland*, 1978, pp. 38–49, published by the Royal Asiatic Society of Great Britain & Ireland, London.

STEPHEN P. BLAKE, 'The Patrimonial-Bureaucratic Empire of the Mughals', from *Journal of Asian Studies*, vol. 39, 1979, pp. 77–94, published by Association for Asian Studies, University of Wisconsin, Milwaukee.

SURAJIT SINHA, 'State Formation and Rajput Myth in Tribal Central India', Presidential Address, Section of Anthropology and Archaeology, 49th Indian Science Congress, Cuttack 1962, from *Man in India*, vol. 42, 1962, pp. 35–80, published by The Manager, Man in India, Ranchi.

Chapter One

Introduction: The Study of the State in Pre-modern India

HERMANN KULKE

I

In the broader context of Indian history, the period between AD 1000 and 1700 witnessed a transition from great regional kingdoms to the emergence of a centralized state formation under the Delhi Sultanate and the Mughals. At the same time, the extension of statehood into the tribal hinterland and its stepwise integration into the process of state formation increased considerably. Due to the wide spectrum of state development as well as the various conceptual or ideological approaches of historians, the study of the state in India between 1000 and 1700 has become one of the most controversial issues in contemporary Indian historiography. Various scholars, and in some cases 'schools', have come forward with different approaches and conceptual models to define the Indian state and its key features, e.g. the degree of central authority and/or local autonomy; and the role of religious institutions (e.g. *agrahāra* Brahmin villages and temples) as indicators of political fragmentation and segmentation, or as instruments of the extension of central political authority. The present volume does not intend to solve any of these controversial issues. On the contrary it intends to raise relevant questions through the introduction and critical evaluation of various and often contradictory conceptual models of the pre-modern Indian state.

At the moment there exist at least five distinct models of state formation and of the state in India between 1000 and 1700. Listed according to their date of origin, these models are:

1. Marx's notion of *oriental despotism* and the *Asiatic mode of*

production. This concedes to the 'unchanging' state a strong central coercion for external warfare and internal exploitation of the village communities. In order to increase agrarian surplus the central bureaucracy took charge of large-scale irrigation projects.

2. The *Indian historiographical model* of a rather unitary, centrally organized and territorially defined kingdom with a strong bureaucracy.[1]

3. The Marxist-influenced model of an *Indian feudalism*, of a decentralized and fragmented feudal state which however presupposes the existence of an earlier rather strong state weakened through the feudalization of society.

4. The model of the *segmentary state*, which allots the early medieval state in India a position on a continuum of governance formation between the tribal 'stateless' form of government and a patrimonial state.

5. The *patrimonial state*, which depicts the Mughal empire as a household-dominated patrimonial-bureaucratic empire rather than a highly structured bureaucratically administered state.

6. Besides these different models, a number of recent contributions to the debate on the pre-modern Indian state show a reluctance to accept any of these models. A distinct denominator of this group of studies is their focus on integrative processes and structural developments *within* a given state system. These studies will be dealt with at the end of this Introduction.

The existing models depict the state in medieval India as a strong and centralized state (1, 2); or as a kingdom which was a weak and decentralized successor to an earlier strong and centralized state (3); or as a state which has not yet reached the position of a strong and centralized state (4); or as a state with a strong patrimonial administration at its centre which it was able to extend temporarily beyond its core area through increased military and administrative control (5). The models thus ascribe to the state in pre-modern India very different positions on a continuum of governance formation.

[1] No generally accepted name of this model has yet been found. Various designations are used in this context, e.g. 'bureaucratic' (Heitzman, see below), 'unitary' (Spencer 1983: 7), 'imperial' (Shulman 1985: 19) or 'conventional' (Stein 1975b). K.A.N. Sastri is often quoted for having spoken of a 'Byzantine royalty' of the Cholas under Rājarāja I, although he had clearly limited his statement to an '*almost* Byzantine royalty' (1955: 447). The term 'Indian historiographical model' is used here, as the overwhelming number of early and of contemporary 'conventional' contributions of Indian historians are depicting the pre-modern Indian state in the line of this model.

Among these concepts the anthropologically derived *segmentary state* model concedes to the Indian state (except its core area or dynastic *Stammland*) the least extent of centrally administered political control, although it was not a 'state *sans* politics'. But in the course of its development 'from below' (or 'from within' its central segment) the segmentary state did not develop methods of political integration beyond ritual sovereignty.

According to the *Indian feudalism* model, state formation after the Gupta period had a decisively negative character since the many small kingdoms and principalities emerged in a protracted process of fragmentation 'from above' at the cost of former larger political entities. The degree of political control of the 'feudal state' outside its dynastic *Stammland* depended largely on the specific stage of its development. Initially, after its forcible foundation, its political profile is assumed to have been higher than in the segmentary state but it decreased in the course of its further development through a continuous process of 'loss of men and means' due to the massive increase of land grants and subinfeudation.

The concept of the *patrimonial-bureaucratic state* of late medieval India concedes a much higher political profile to the pre-modern state in India. Even though basically still facing similar structural problems as the two former models, as for instance the lack of political integration and ubiquitous centrifugal tendencies, the patrimonial-bureaucratic state was able to increase its surplus appropriation considerably through a new system of land assignment and thus develop new and temporarily successful administrative and military methods to cope with these problems.

The Marxist model of the *Asiatic mode of production* depicts the Indian state as a strange hermaphrodite juxtaposing of the unchanging world of rather unstratified, communally landowning village societies and the absolute power of the 'Oriental despot'. Both levels are seen as connected rather one-sidedly through the craving of the court for agrarian surplus, which it tried to increase through large government-sponsored irrigation projects. In the context of Indian historiography the concept of the Asiatic mode of production is certainly the most controversial and at the same time the least seminal conception. In has to be regarded as the outcome of nearly 2500 years of occidental prejudice against an alleged Oriental despotism and of Marx's understandably poor knowledge about pre-British and particularly pre-Mughal India. It entered modern Indian historiography only rather recently in the context of an inner-Marxist controversy as to whether Marx and his 'reinterpreters' up to Stalin were right to exclude pre-modern Asia, and in particular India, from the orthodox Marxist modes of production of slave and feudal societies, and to postulate a special Asian mode of production. Particularly since Indian Marxist historians, too, vehemently deny the existence of an Asiatic mode of production in India, it should be allowed to pass away peacefully—without however being entirely forgotten.

The *Indian historiographical model* places the state in medieval India in the final position of a continuum of pre-modern state formation. It depicts the early medieval ('Hindu') state and the post-1200 late medieval ('Muslim') state likewise as polities headed by a strong ruler, equipped with an efficient and hierarchically organized central administration based on a religiously legitimated monopoly of coercion in a (more or less) clearly defined territory. Historians who follow this model sometimes tend to interpret early theoretical treatises (e.g. the *Arthaśāstra*) and eulogistic late medieval Arab and Persian chronicles of India as sources for their description of the actual structure of the state and the position of its ruler. Moreover, a hierarchy of centrally controlled bureaucratic levels of administration in the whole state is inferred from chronologically and spatially widely scattered early medieval epigraphical evidence. The same appears to be true with many writings on the Delhi Sultanate and the Mughal Empire as monolithic, centrally administered states. Problems of continuous growth and the decline of early and late medieval states are often considered as an effect of mere military conquest or dynastic history rather than as structural issues. This 'imperial model' emerged particularly during the time of the Indian freedom movement when, at the height of British Imperialism, Indian historiography became a major ideological prop of the national claim that classical Indian culture and civilization had produced political and social institutions which were equal if not superior to those of their imperial masters. In a period of early communal assertiveness the imperial model of Indian historiography also served, however, as an ideological prop to assert the respective roles of early medieval ('Hindu') and late medieval ('Muslim') states in pre-modern Indian history. Today, therefore, some Indian historians regard the communalist overtones of this model as potentially dangerous for contemporary India because it unduly projects the glory of two competing 'Golden Ages' into the Middle Ages, which in turn were then destroyed by Central Asian and European invaders, respectively (S. Settar 1982).

The juxtaposition of these two lists following two different principles of order of the existing state models, i.e. one according to the dates of their development and one according to the degree of central coercion the respective models concede to the Indian state, clearly reveals that the earliest two models depicted the pre-modern state as a very strong institution. More recent theories on the other hand agree that the pre-modern state in India was only lightly bureaucratized, although there is no agreement about the *degree* of political fragmentation or segmentation on the one hand, and temporally or spatially fluctuating unitary tendencies within these states on the other. But most recent contributions to this debate, particularly those which either stress patrimonial-bureaucratic aspects of the medieval state or which do not subscribe to any of the above models, tend to outline the Indian pre-modern state with chronologically and spatially differentiated degrees of centralization. In this context, the model of the patrimonial-bureaucratic state in medieval India is of particular relevance. On the one hand it clearly poses this state much nearer to the first two models and their respective states. With its administrative, fiscal and military abilities, the patrimonial state may indeed come quite near to the 'imperial' or 'conventional' model and to Max Weber's sultanism (as an extreme form of patrimonial authority), which shows certain similarities with Marx's Oriental Despotism. But on the other hand, the patrimonial-bureaucratic model clearly stresses the fact that the patrimonial state still remained in its essence a rather fragile institution as it depended strongly on the personal ambitions and abilities of its ruler and his capability to cope with the various autonomous and centrifugal forces of his state. Even though Max Weber's model may refer to a state similar to those of the first two models, there is an important difference. Whereas Marx's Oriental Despotism and the conventional Indian model depict an allegedly unchanging strong state, Weber emphasizes its precarious and often even weak position, which was only temporarily overcome through the personal abilities of rulers and their administrative measures. Moreover, a patrimonial-bureaucratic state depended strongly on the appropriation of additional surplus (e.g. through levy on trade), which however could never be taken for granted.

The following introductory remarks emphasize the more recent models 3, 4 and 5, i.e. the feudal, segmentary and the patrimonial models, but also refer to other studies on the Mughal state, and conclude with a few remarks about some conceptualizing contributions outside these models (6).

II

The concept of Indian feudalism, doubtless the most controversial issue of modern Indian historiography, is of relatively recent origin. In 1956 Daniel Thorner was still right when he concluded his contribution to R. Coulborn's comparative study on *Feudalism in History* with the remark: 'there is no single work solely devoted to feudalism in India; nor is there even a single article on the place of feudalism in the historical evolution of India' (Thorner 1956: 133). D.N. Jha (1979) and Irfan Habib (1974) have shown that the discussion on Indian feudalism began with the heated and protracted Marxist debate on Marx's concept of the Asiatic Mode of Production (AMP)—'the unfortunate thesis that Marx had once propounded' (I. Habib 1974: 38). The expulsion of the AMP from official Soviet Marxism is too well known to be discussed here in detail.[2] However,

> during the sixties we have been privileged to witness the curious phenomenon that in spite of the general inability of Asian Marxist scholars to recognize the existence of the Asiatic mode of production,[3] certain Marxists of Western European countries have begun to insist that they know better and have 're-opened' the debate on the subject among themselves. . . . The essential purpose in the attempted restoration of the Asiatic Mode is to deny the role of class contradictions and class struggles in Asian societies, so as to establish that the

[2] Irfan Habib admits: 'The last word was said on that matter by Stalin in his classic essay on Dialectical and Historical Materialism, 1938. Much though this may be mourned as a mechanical application of a "standard unilinear" scheme for the whole world, there is no doubt that it provided significant stimulus for fruitful Marxist work in the sphere of Indian History' (I. Habib 1974: 40f). However, even Habib maintains in his works that the sequence of the four (orthodox) modes of production 'cannot contain in its chain all the primitive and class societies that have existed nor can there be any universal order of succession' (p. 44). In his scornful paper 'Against Feudalism' Ashok Rudra even stated: 'The truth is that Indian feudalism is a product of the Stalinist revision of Marxism. Rejection of the Asiatic Mode of Production and the substitution in its place of Indian feudalism was canonized during Stalin's time, after some vigorous debates in which many important scholars fought valiantly against the idea of feudalism' (Rudra 1981: 2145). The feudalism debate, however, entered Indian historiography only after Stalin's death!

[3] It is difficult to decide to what extent this 'inability' was confirmed by the 'official Soviet Indology' (Habib 1974: 41) and the fact that the AMP had been 'banned by Stalin from public discussion in the Soviet Union' (D.N. Jha 1987: 25). Moreover, it is not unlikely that the official textbook *Political Economy*, published in 1954 by the Academy of Science of the Soviet Union, also influenced the early discussions on Indian feudalism in the mid-fifties.

entire past history of social progress belongs to Europe alone (I. Habib 1974: 39f).[4]

The understandable dislike of Indian Marxist historians of the notion of the unchangeableness of Asiatic societies and of Oriental Despotism, 'both derived from the concept of AMP', led to the 'theoretical emancipation of Indian [Marxist] historians from Marx's loosely knit construct of the AMP' (D.N. Jha 1979: 3) and to an acceptance of the Marxist periodization of European and world history as 'a hypothesis for the analysis of the historical evidence' (ibid.). It is necessary to mention this Marxist background of the concept of Indian feudalism at the very outset of this volume as Indian historiography still suffers unduly from this heritage. Whereas Marxist historians who have made 'the main contribution to the study of Indian feudalism' (V.K. Thakur 1989: 1) tend to neglect contradicting evidence, non-Marxist historians usually abhor the idea that some aspects or even periods of Indian social and state formation may depict traces of feudalism. However, one should keep in mind that feudalism is neither a Marxist nor an European monopoly, as Max Weber and Marc Bloch have shown.[5]

It is not without a touch of irony that exactly in the same year that Thorner had been unable to detect a 'single work devoted to feudalism in India', D.D. Kosambi published two articles on the development of feudalism in India and Kashmir (Kosambi 1956b and c). Moreover, in 1956 appeared Kosambi's famous *An Introduction to the Study of Indian History.* Its two separate chapters on 'feudalism from above' and 'feudalism from below' may be regarded as the first conceptual definition of Indian feudalism.[6] Only two years after Kosambi's contribution to the

[4] V.K. Thakur, too, remarks 'that this formulation (APM) entirely suited the political requirements of the imperialist historians' (Thakur 1989: XXVI). Sometimes one feels the urge to ask whether there was a conspiracy between these imperialist historians and Marx.

[5] In a short chapter at the end of his *Feudal Society,* Bloch concluded: 'Feudalism was not "an event which happened only once in the world." Like Europe—though with inevitable and deep-seated differences—Japan went through this phase. Have other societies also passed through it? And if so, what were the causes, and were they perhaps common to all such societies? It is for future works to provide the answers. I should be happy if this book, by suggesting questions to students, were to prepare the way for an inquiry going far beyond it' (M. Bloch, *Feudal Society,* London, 1961, p. 447).

[6] 'Feudalism from above means a state wherein an emperor or powerful king levied tribute from subordinates who still ruled in their own right and did what they liked within their own territories—as long as they paid the paramount ruler . . . By feudalism

concept of Indian feudalism, R.S. Sharma began to publish articles on the origins and development of feudalism in India.[7] In 1965 these articles, enlarged and supplemented by new studies, came out in his book entitled *Indian Feudalism*, which became the standard work on Indian feudalism, and as such the focal point of an ongoing debate which continues.

According to Sharma, a major cause of feudalism in India was the ever-increasing number of land grants to Brahmins and religious institutions since the early centuries AD and later also to government officials. Their endowment with more and more immunities (*parihāra*), e.g. freedom from taxation and from inspection by royal officers, and with royal prerogatives, e.g. jurisdiction and collection of fines, led to the emergence of a class of landed intermediaries.[8] They encroached on communal village land and slowly reduced villagers to serfdom. This development was partly caused and further aggravated by a decline of urbanism and interregional, particularly international, trade,[9] and as a result of this decline, there was a paucity of coins in the post-Gupta period.[10] Politically, this development

---

from below is meant the next stage [since the Delhi Sultanate] where a class of landowners developed within a village, between the state and the peasantry, gradually to wield armed power over the local population' (Kosambi 1956a: 294).

[7] R.S. Sharma (1993) is right to point out that his first paper appeared in 1958 and not 'a decade later' than Kosambi's first contributions, as stated by B. Stein in his 'Interim Reflections'.

[8] In a recent study, however, Om Prakash of Allahabad University arrives at the conclusion that 'there is hardly any valid ground to infer the existence of a landed aristocracy of chiefs and officials from these grants', and that these grants meant a loss of revenue for the state (Prakash 1988: XI).

[9] The question of 'Urban Decay in India' (Sharma 1987) and its impact on the emergence of feudalism in India is one of the most controversial issues of the feudalism debate (see below).

[10] The 'paucity of coins' in early medieval India is yet another controversial issue. See e.g. B.D. Chattopadhyaya, *Coins and Currency Systems in South India, c. A.D. 225–1300* (Cambridge, 1969), and D.C. Sircar, *Early Indian Numismatic and Epigraphical Studies* (Calcutta, 1970). For south-east Bengal, M.R. Tarafdar furnished evidence of coins issued from the sixth to about the eleventh century (Tarafdar 1978). In a recent comprehensive study J.S. Deyell gives a regionally and temporarily highly differentiated picture of the degree of monetization in early medieval north and north-western India which, however, does not allow us to speak of a dearth of coinage. Instead he concludes that the changing degrees of monetization suggest an 'economic model (which) might be one in which different stages of enfeudalization or capital development coexisted in the medieval period and where change and progress were not uniformly distributed from kingdom to kingdom' (Deyell 1990: 245).

was characterized by a continuous process of fragmentation and decentralization, caused 'by the widespread practice of granting big and small territories to vassals and officials who entrenched themselves territorially and ended up as independent potentates' (Sharma 1965: 159).

Already in December 1964, a few months before the publication of his magnum opus R.S. Sharma conducted a special symposium at the Centre of Advanced Study in Ancient Indian History and Culture at the University of Calcutta. During this seminar Sharma's theories were thoroughly discussed. They met with a fairly wide consensus among the participants,[11] but also with some contradictions,[12] and evoked D.C. Sircar's famous verdict against Indian feudalism. In a paper entitled 'Landlordism Confused with Feudalism' Sircar postulated that 'feudalism is a misnomer in the early Indian context' (1966: 62). Sircar's main argument against the applicability of any concept of feudalism to early medieval India is the undeniable scarcity of evidence for service tenure against the overwhelming majority of land grants to Brahmins and religious institutions.[13] 'The majority of the numerous charters discovered all over the country record grants of land to gods and Brahmanas without stipulating any obligation of the donees to the donors. Obviously, the priestly class was the most unsuitable for rendering services of the feudal type' (p. 58). In the narrow context of the European model of early feudalism this argument is certainly correct. But, as has been shown elsewhere, in early medieval India Brahmins often fulfilled exactly this role (Kulke 1982: 247), though with means different from their contemporary feudal counterparts in Merovingian and Carolingian Europe.

Except for an irritatingly schoolmasterish review by R. Coulborn,[14] the debate on Indian feudalism appears to have calmed down considerably over the following years.[15] Thus for instance in 1967 D.N. Jha, a student

[11] e.g. B.P. Mazumdar (1966) and B.N.S. Yadava (1966).

[12] e.g. S.K. Maity (1966).

[13] In 1969, however, Sircar accepted the *amara* system of Vijayanagara as a feudal relation (see below).

[14] R. Coulborn accepted the existence of feudalism in India, but points out that landgrants to Brahmins 'cannot be described as feudal in any sense or on any pretext' (Coulborn 1968: 358). According to Coulborn the major cause of India's emerging feudal relation was foreign invasion, particularly by the Huns and the Gurjaras.

[15] In a general account of the debate Rothermund designates Brahmins as the 'first agents of feudalism' and agrees that 'these relations can very well be described in term of feudalism if the cultural differences are taken into account' (Rothermund 1970: 168f).

of R.S. Sharma and today one of the prominent proponents of the concept, published his Ph.D. thesis without any reference to feudalism.[16] The discussion gathered momentum again in the early seventies. A strong impetus came from B.N.S. Yadava's study of northern India during the twelfth century. Published in 1973, it has to be regarded, after Kosambi and Sharma's works, as the third major contribution to Indian feudalism. In many ways, it is a consequent and consistent follow-up of Sharma's study. Thus, Yadava endeavours to provide new and much needed evidence for an increasing practice of land-grants to military officers during the post-Gupta period and for restrictions on the mobility of peasants.[17] Moreover, he follows the Marxist model when, for instance, he stresses the development of productive forces (e.g. iron implements) and the collapse of the imperial state of the Guptas, and the influence of these factors on the emergence of feudalism in India.[18] But Yadava also pays more attention to different concepts of feudalism than earlier Indian historians. In this regard his quotation of Marc Bloch's 'fundamental features of European feudalism' is of particular importance (Yadava 1973: 178). It shows that the influence of Bloch's monumental work *Feudal Society* (the English translation was published in 1961) appears to have partly replaced Marx's works as a major conceptual framework of Indian feudalism.[19] Perhaps under the influence of Bloch, as well as Weber whom Yadava quotes in this context (p. 178f), Yadava shifted the emphasis of his studies on Indian feudalism slightly towards the political sphere of feudalism. For him the term *sāmanta* (often translated as 'vassal' or 'tributary chief') became 'the

[16] D.N. Jha, *Revenue System in Post-Maurya and Gupta Times* (Calcutta, 1967).

[17] As regards service-assignments, B.D. Chattopadhyaya draws attention to the fact that they post-date the assumed genesis of feudal polity (Chattopadhyaya 1983: 6). For secular grants see also L. Gopal (1965: 26).

[18] However he too warns against a 'simplistic assumption of the universal applicability of any law of history' (Yadava 1973: 176).

[19] The only ones of Bloch's 'fundamental features of European feudalism' (Bloch, p. 446) emphasized by the 'Indian Feudalism School' were apparently subject peasantry, widespread service tenement and fragmentation of authority; whereas the other characteristics (i.e. supremacy of a class of specialized warriors, ties of obedience—called vassalage—within the warrior class and survival of other forms of associations) were not taken into account. D.N. Jha moreover draws attention to 'a striking similarity' between Pirenne's reconstruction of the origins of feudalism in Europe and Kosambi and Sharma's attempt to explain its beginnings in India (D.N. Jha 1987: 31). Mukhia (see below) even regards Sharma's early notion of Indian feudalism 'almost as a carbon copy of the Pirennean version of the rise and decline of feudal economy in Western Europe'.

key word of Indian feudalism' (p. 136).[20] Originally signifying independent neighbouring chiefs and rājas, the sāmantas, since *c.* 600, rose to prominence at the central royal courts as defeated and reinstalled feudatories and court officials. Because of their emergence

> the conception of empire tended to lose sight of the territorial aspect. The tributary relationship together with personal loyalty, which loosely bound together the sāmantas and the paramount lords, came thus into prominent relief, and the latter became far removed from the people. The establishment of empire meant only the extension of the tributary system on a large scale. Such empires or tributary superstructures naturally lacked solidarity, stability and real political unity (Yadava 1973: 157).

It is interesting to note the 'structural nearness' of certain aspects of this model of the early Indian statehood to B. Stein's definition of the political sphere of the segmentary state (see below).

In the year 1974 two commemoration volumes for D.D. Kosambi were published as tribute to the 'father of scientific Indian history'.[21] Remarkably, Kosambi's concept of the two stages of feudalism from above and from below was not taken up by the various contributors to these volumes; apparently his unorthodox concept had found no acceptance among Indian Marxist historians.[22] This impression is confirmed by another important publication of the same year, namely the first volume of the journal *The Indian Historical Review.* Published by the Indian Council of Historical Research and edited by R.S. Sharma and V. Jha, it became in a way the mouthpiece of the Indian Feudalism School.[23] The

[20] The development of the institution of the sāmantas was studied by L. Gopal (1963) and K. Gopal (1964). The issue of their role in early medieval state formation is taken up by B.D. Chattopadhyaya, and by me in the present volume.

[21] R.S. Sharma and V. Jha (1974) and D.D. Kosambi Commemoration Committee (1974).

[22] This is particularly remarkable in the case of the Introduction by R.S. Sharma and V. Jha (1974). D.N. Jha's anthology of papers on Indian feudalism (1987) includes two of Kosambi's papers which, however, do not deal with his concept of the 'two feudalisms'. Athar Ali argues that Kosambi's feudal system 'was obviously on rather obscure ground' (Athar Ali 1993). In his contribution to the present volume Mukhia remarks that Kosambi's 'fresh outline' for the study of Indian feudalism 'was unfortunately found inadequate by some other historians' (see also R. Thapar 1992).

[23] The first volume of the *Indian History Review,* however, also contained a few dissenting votes, e.g. 'A note on R.S. Sharma's Ideas on Indian Feudalism' by Surendra Gopal et al. (vol. I, 1974, pp. 441–4) and particularly B.D. Chattopadhyaya's study, 'Trade and Urban Centres in Early Medieval North India' (1974, see below).

first number of its first volume contains three articles by R.S. Sharma on 'Indian Feudalism Retouched' and related subjects (Sharma 1974a–c). Other articles of this volume give a fairly comprehensive overview of those subjects, which meanwhile have been taken up in connection with Indian feudalism studies.[24] These as well as other articles published during the following years proceeded on similar lines, as had been shown by R.S. Sharma, and in a slightly modified form by Yadava. They enlarged the available evidence, particularly through regional case studies, but paid little attention to theoretical issues and controversies. One of these important issues, which now came into the focus of the discussion, was the question of alleged urban decay and decline of trade in the post-Gupta period, particularly after B.D. Chattopadhyaya published an article in 1974 questioning this major prop of the concept of Indian feudalism. This issue had apparently remained unsolved even at the empirical level.[25]

In 1979 and 1980 the issue of Indian feudalism suddenly stood in the limelight of a large audience when three presidential addresses of the Indian History Congress were delivered on this subject. At the fortieth session of the Indian History Congress at Waltair University in December 1979 D.N. Jha read 'Early Indian Feudalism: A Historiographical Critique' in the section on Ancient India. Harbans Mukhia addressed the section on Medieval India with a controversial paper, 'Was there Feudalism in Indian History?' At the forty-first session of the Indian History Congress in Bombay, B.N.S. Yadava delivered yet another presidential address in the section on Ancient India, this one on 'The Problem of the Emergence of Feudal Relations in Early India'. During these years, clearly, Indian feudalism had become the major issue in early India's historiography.

After having again refuted Marx's concept of the Asiatic Mode of Production, Jha fully supported in his address the Marxist concept of Indian feudalism and demanded: 'What needs to be adequately appreciated is the fact that Indian Marxist historiography, opposed to the British view of the Indian past, has used the European model of feudalism

24 These articles of the first issue of *IHR* pertain to 'Art under Feudalism in India' (D. Desai), 'Emergence of Brāhmaṇas as Landed Intermediaries in Karnatak' (M. Liceria), 'Immobility and Subjection of Indian Peasantry in Early Medieval Complex' (B.N.S. Yadava) and 'Tribalism to Feudalism in Assam' (A. Guha).

25 B.D. Chattopadhyaya (1974, 1986), Sharma (1973, 1987), Champakalakshmi (1979, 1986), V.K. Thakur (1981, 1987).

to explain social change in India from the middle of the first millennium' (D.N. Jha 1979: 8). But he also pointed out that

there has been in the past few years some realisation of the theoretical weakness of the explanation of feudal developments only in terms of foreign trade, whose decline, to a large extent, depended on factors external to the Indian situation. . . . It is this theoretical impasse which has recently led to a rethinking on the part of the exponents of the Indian feudal model from the vantage point of the internal social contradictions (p. 6).[26]

Jha, therefore, following what had already been done in an article by Yadava (1979), elaborates on the concept of the Kaliyuga as a period of allegedly sharp class antagonism.[27] According to this new Indian Marxist interpretation it was this antagonism of class struggles which led to the emergence of the feudal order.[28] Later on, in the same way, social crisis and the resurgence of trade and urbanism around AD 1000 caused the weakening of the feudal order in India. On the other hand, Jha rightly observed that 'the areas where the land grant economy first made its appearance were on the periphery of the regions with firmly entrenched brahmanical orders and had thus nothing to do with the social crisis and decadence reflected in the idea of Kaliyuga' (p. 7). With this statement Jha in fact questions one of the main props of the orthodox Marxist explanation of the origins of Indian feudalism.

In his Presidential Address of 1980 Yadava adopted a more critical tone when he stated that the study of Indian feudalism 'has yet to achieve greater theoretical sophistication in historical analysis'. He based his arguments primarily on the evidence from late classical and early medieval literary sources—e.g. early treatises on horoscopy of the *jyotiḥśāstra* and *dharmaśāstras* and their commentaries—which have 'undoubtedly the potentiality of providing additional bits of evidence' for the subjection of

[26] According to V.K. Thakur the 'alleged antagonism between feudalism and external trade stems from an over-reliance on the works of Henri Pirenne' (1989: 84).

[27] To my understanding, the Kaliyuga does not reflect a social crisis or even class-struggles, but a crisis of the Brahmanical worldview (and perhaps of their social status) due to the rise of local and often foreign rulers who were not yet fully integrated into the *varṇāśrama* system.

[28] As regards the so-called 'Kaivarta rebellion', which R.S. Sharma interprets as a case of class struggle, Swapna Bhattacharya points out that it was primarily a power struggle between the emerging elite of the Kaivartas and the Pālas who tried to recover their control over Varendra (S. Bhattacharya 1985: 64f). For a general criticism of alleged class struggles in early medieval India, see also Om Prakash (1992: 167ff).

peasants by landlords through non-economic coercion. But even though he tried to present new evidence on the subjection of the peasantry, forced labour and restriction on mobility, he admitted that the feudal mode of production was not as strong in India as in medieval Europe, because in India 'it is found to have been interlocked and to have coexisted with the non-feudal elements' (p. 56). With regard to the feudal nature of India's political structure, however, he observed 'in essence a marked resemblance to that of Western European feudalism' (p. 57).[29]

Whereas D.N. Jha and B.N.S. Yadava in their respective Presidential Addresses had tried to reconcile the notion of Indian feudalism with Marxist and European concepts even more than R.S. Sharma, in 1979 Harbans Mukhia questioned the very existence of this alleged Indian feudalism. Although Mukhia's essay is reproduced in this volume, it is advisable to lay stress on a few of his major arguments for the sake of the debate.

After a thorough analysis of various notions of European feudalism, he points out that European feudalism emerged from changes at the base of society, whereas in India the establishment of feudalism is attributed by its protagonists primarily to state actions in granting land. 'It is, indeed, a moot point whether such complex social structures as feudalism can be established through administrative and legal procedures' (Mukhia 1981: 286).[30] Mukhia also questions several other essentials in the concept of Indian feudalism. Where Sharma and Yadava noticed the peasantry's *dependence*, he perceives increasing *exploitation* and points out that forced labour in India was in its essence 'an incidental manifestation of the ruling class's political and administrative power rather than a part of the process of production' (p. 32). Similarly, he doubts that serfdom was a dominant feature in medieval India. Another important point of Mukhia's argument is his statement that the high fertility of India's soil permitted the Indian peasant to subsist at a much lower level of resources than his European

[29] In this regard Yadava stresses again the sāmanta system ('the consolidation of their domination and lordship over the peasantry proved to be the bedrock of Indian feudalism, 1980: 24). For an interesting comparison between Pāla land grants and contemporary German 'feudal' documents, see S. Bhattacharya (1982; 1985: 104ff).

[30] See Om Prakash for a contradicting interpretation of land grants, which 'appear to have a linkage with state policy [and state economy] of imperial expansion' (1988: XI). Elsewhere it has been pointed out that during the process of early state formation the Brahmins might have acted as pace-makers of royal authority and coercion and its legitimation, rather than as agents of feudalization (Kulke 1982: 247).

counterpart. He therefore argues that, partly caused by this factor, 'Indian history has been characterized predominantly by the free peasantry (in the economic rather than legal sense)' (p. 286). According to Mukhia these characteristics of the agrarian history of medieval India—a high fertility of land, a low subsistence level and a free peasantry—therefore 'also explain the relative stability in India's social and economic history' (p. 292),[31] or a 'kind of equilibrium . . . which facilitated the state's appropriation of the peasant's surplus in conditions of relative stability' (p. 293). After reading all this it comes as no surprise to find that Mukhia concludes his address thus: 'it is difficult to see the logic of such a comparison in the ancient and medieval periods when it might only persuade us to ask questions which have so little relevance to our history' (1981: 310, note 225). Mukhia lectured again on his theses at Erasmus University in Rotterdam and at Sorbonne University in Paris before republishing his address in the *Journal of Peasant Studies* in 1981. His outright rejection of this concept of Indian feudalism evoked a bitter feud among scholars. The impact of his criticism cannot be explained only by his arguments. It stems to a large extent from the fact that the criticisms came right from the centre of leftist and Marxist scholarship.[32]

In 1985, after several years of intensive preparation, a special issue of the *Journal of Peasant Society* on 'Feudalism and Non-European Societies' was edited by T.J. Byres and H. Mukhia. Here a number of renowned scholars came forward with critical evaluations of Mukhia's theses in the context of Asian history. R.S. Sharma, Irfan Habib, Burton Stein and Frank Perlin's papers pertain to India, as does Mukhia's response to his critics. Through the publication of this volume and its contributions the question of an Indian feudalism was, for the first time, taken up at an international level. In its broader context the major issue of this intellectual endeavour was the question: 'if not the Asiatic mode and if not feudalism, then, within a Marxist analysis, what?' (Byres 1985: 2).[33] In his contribution 'How Feudal was Indian Feudalism?', which is reproduced

31 A similar argument is brought forward by Om Prakash in his criticism of the Indian feudalism model (1992: 178f).

32 In this regard it has to be mentioned that B.D. Chattopadhyaya's Presidential Address of the year 1983 also emerged from the Centre of Historical Studies at Jawaharlal Nehru University in New Delhi. The more recent controversial debate thus appears to have been taken over to a large extent by historians of JNU and Delhi University.

33 In his Introduction, Byres remarks moreover that 'the issue considered is essentially one that lies within the Marxist discourse' (p. 3).

in the present volume, R.S. Sharma 'enters a spirited and eloquent defence of the feudalism notion in orthodox Marxist terms', as Byres says in his Introduction. Sharma's paper may have to be regarded as the final comprehensive interpretation of the prevailing concept of Indian feudalism. Although this concept has been modified in details by the contributions mentioned above, it is still primarily based on Sharma's notion, as described in his book *Indian Feudalism*, published more than twenty-five years ago.

Irfan Habib's exposition ('Classifying Pre-Colonial India') modifies his earlier rejection of the AMP. He points out that Marx was right that 'Indian society merited analysis on the basis of its own specific features' (Habib 1985: 45) when he distinguished the pre-colonial Indian economy from the feudal formation of Western Europe. On the other hand he points out that Marx's 'simultaneous relegation of it to a vast Asiatic system seems questionable' (p. 46). He also questions the justification of designating India's pre-colonial formation as feudal on the basis of its ability to generate by itself the elements of capitalism. Moreover, he emphasizes that the breakdown of a pre-colonial formation had consequences very different from those of the feudal crisis in Europe. Habib, therefore, instead of speaking of feudalism, prefers the term 'medieval Indian system—for such is the name I would give it until a better one is offered' (p. 49). Burton Stein welcomes Mukhia's deconstruction of the concept of Indian feudalism as it does not fit the South Indian socio-economic formation, 'in which peasant production and property was dominant' (Stein 1985: 61). But Stein complains that Mukhia refrained from defining the type of state that would be theoretically and empirically congruent with 'free peasantry'. Stein also refutes several of Mukhia's arguments. Thus, 'the "relative stability" of agrarian history was engendered, not by fertile soils and low subsistence need, but by historically evolved and localised form of co-operation among people with a high degree of social differentiation and with a level of living which, in general cannot be considered low' (p. 59). It is interesting that Stein's paper corresponds markedly with Irfan Habib's arguments. Stein too sees in Marx's 'largely discredited' AMP a 'profound perception which ought not to be lost, or consigned to the dustbin of historiography' (p. 83). But instead of postulating a single Asiatic Mode of Production, Stein thinks of 'a great number of different formations', and in the case of India of 'yet some unspecified "medieval Indian social formation" ' (p. 83).

In response to his critics, Mukhia admits that Sharma's article (also reprinted in the present volume) marks 'a search for a genuinely "Indian" variant of feudalism' (1985: 235). But he says that Sharma's model still does not take sufficient notice of the considerable technological and economic growth in the early medieval period. Moreover, it does not provide any help on how to characterize the five or six centuries between the decline of feudalism and the beginning of India's colonization—'a sad comment on the lack of rigour in the concept of Indian feudalism' (p. 288). However, in view of Sharma and Stein's criticism he admits that his notion of free peasantry 'had probably been overstated', yet is unwilling to abandon the notion altogether. As regards Stein's criticism that he did not define the type of state which was congruent with his notion of a 'free peasantry', Mukhia stresses that the state 'remained by and large uninvolved with the process of production. Its coercive power was therefore never rooted in the production system' (p. 245).

The latest comprehensive publications on Indian feudalism are a compilation of articles of the Indian Feudalism School edited by D.N. Jha (1987), and V.K. Thakur's *Historiography of Indian Feudalism* (1989). In the same way as Sharma's article of 1985 (reproduced in the present volume) contains a comprehensive depiction of his notion of Indian feudalism, Jha's anthology gives a fairly impressive account of the various feudalism studies which, meanwhile, have been taken up by the Indian Feudalism School and its adherents.[34] However it does not contain any new attempts to reassess the concept in view of Mukhia's challenge. On the contrary, in his Introduction, which is in fact a revised version of his Presidential Address (1979), Jha vehemently rejects Mukhia's notions and blames him for 'bringing in through the back door the concept of AMP and even legitimizing, under a radical camouflage, the perception of pre-colonial Indian society as stagnant' (p. 18).[35] Thakur's *Historiography*

[34] Stein's remark in his 'Interim Reflections' that 'the feudal concept has never been seriously tested against the claims inherent in it nor has it been elaborated in a significant way' appears to be only partly correct. The volume edited by Jha shows that the concept was tested against its inherent claims—in some cases quite critically, e.g. by N. Karashima (1983) and Tarafdar (1978). However, Stein's statement that the concept itself has not been elaborated systematically appears to be still correct, despite D.N. Jha's Introduction (1987) and Sharma's contribution (1985). See also K.M. Shrimali's most recent summary of the debate in his appendices to volume IV of *A Comprehensive History of India* (1992: 728–39 and 758–72) and in his Presidential Address (1994).

[35] The heat of this debate and the ideological dust it has been stirring up can be

of Indian Feudalism, too, is a rather orthodox attempt to reject Mukhia's thesis and its 'faulty premise of the absence of a dependent peasantry' (Thakur 1989: 30), as well as B.D. Chattopadhyaya's findings (1974) on a continuation of urbanization and trade in early medieval India (Thakur 1989: 59ff). On the basis of his own interpretation of the evidence Thakur states, in full agreement with Sharma, that the interrelated substratum components of a decay of urban economy and the subjection of the peasantry 'underline the validity of the model of Indian feudalism as an appropriate tool of analysis' (p. 89). Most recently, Chattopadhyaya observes an 'inflation' of the concept and complains that 'the construct of Indian Feudalism has begun to acquire a stereotyped image, particularly in its failure to accommodate long-term dynamics of change in Indian history' (B.D. Chattopadhyaya, 1995).

III

Burton Stein's model of the segmentary state in South Indian history has to be regarded as the second major conceptual contribution to contemporary medieval Indian historiography. His 'Interim Reflections' of 1991 (reproduced in the present volume) has a fairly long prehistory. It began in 1956, with the publication of A.W. Southall's anthropological study of Alur society in Eastern Africa (Southall 1956), wherein Southall formulated his concept of the segmentary state. However his concept appears to have remained unnoticed by students of Indian history till 1971, when R.G. Fox referred to it at some length in his Rajput studies as a possible model of pre-modern North Indian states, without however pursuing the hypothesis any further (Fox 1971).[36] In 1956, too, when Stein was still working for his Ph.D. thesis on the Tirupati temple (Stein 1958), B. Subbarao's socio-cultural geographical study of ancient and medieval India appeared as another important component of Stein's future concept.

---

imagined from this kind of remark by Jha (1987, e.g. his notes 33, 66, 67) and by V.K. Thakur (1989, e.g. p. 27).

[36] According to Fox, in North India states are segmentary in two ways, i.e. the central authority does not have primary responsibility for many local decisions and local political institutions are based on a segmentary lineage system (Fox 1971: 56f). In 1977 he added that 'central authority and regional kin group interweave to form a state wherein kinship organizes local administration' (1977: XIV).

Subbarao distinguished between 'areas of attraction', 'areas of relative isolation' and 'tribal areas or areas of isolation' as a major feature of India's historical development (Subbarao 1956).[37] At a series of workshops in 1963 and 1964 on land control and social structure in India, Stein came forward with his seminal study on 'Integration and the Agrarian System of South India' (Stein 1969). Strongly influenced by Subbarao he elaborated his concept of 'nuclear areas of corporate institutions', which became a basic element of his interpretation of South Indian history. The core components of these nuclear areas were 'the *brahmadeya*, or Brahman-controlled circle of villages, and the *periyanāḍu* or a Sat-Sudra-controlled extended locality' (1969: 180).[38] Situated mainly in the fertile drainage basins of the major rivers and in the coastal districts of the Coromandel coast of South India, they all shared a set of characteristic features. 'All contained a set of highly autonomous, self-governing institutions, Brahman and Sat-Sudra settlements, caste and occupational assemblies, and religious bodies, which were linked to other similar institutions in other nuclear areas; all maintained some relationships with the Chola rulers to whom some tribute went and with whom joint looting expeditions were carried out' (1969: 188). On the basis of his structural analysis Stein came to the conclusion that in the 'absence within that system of any persistent administrative or power structure . . . the political system may best be described as a multicentred system' (1969: 186). Another major point of Stein's new interpretation of the Chola state, which differs strongly from the conventional 'imperial' interpretation of its statehood, is the question of revenue or surplus transfer from these autonomous nuclear areas to the royal centre. Although Stein at one point admitted that 'the nuclear areas of Chola times were responsible for transmitting at least a small share of their resources to the Chola treasury', a few lines later he points out that 'the single overarching nuclear area institution which seemed to be capable of commanding the resources of all such bodies was the *periyanāḍu* assembly. As for the nuclear areas and

[37] Southall and Stein distinguish between the central, intermediate and periphery 'zones' or 'levels' (see below).

[38] Following Subbarayalu ('The nadu is the very key to political geography of the Chola country' 1973: 19) Stein later shifted the emphasis from *periyanāḍu* to *nāḍu* as the structural key element of the Chola state (Stein 1977: 43, 1980: 91ff). For a criticism of the concept of supra-local integration through the emergence of *periyanāḍu* assemblies, see R. Champakalakshmi (1982: 419).

the Chola warriors, the transfer of resources appears to be of minor importance, except that the Chola rulers drew from the rich agricultural land around the capital of Tanjore, itself a nuclear area. For the most part, however, "royal" income came from looting expeditions against neighbouring peoples' (1969: 186).[39] Stein therefore concluded that 'the nuclear area as a centre of power within the South Indian political system was *the central element of that system* until the thirteenth century' (p. 185, my emphasis).

These detailed quotations from Stein's earlier work show that Stein had formulated most of the core components of his own concept several years before he redefined his own findings on the basis of Y. Subbarayalu's new and apparently concurrent material as well as in the light of Southall's concept of the segmentary state. In 1973 Subbarayalu's *Political Geography of the Chola Country* was published (Subbarayalu 1973), and this, according to Stein, 'provides an impressive extension of our understanding of Chola history and the importance of the hundreds of locality units (*nāḍu*) upon which Chola society was founded' (Stein 1977: 35). Subbarayalu's detailed study of the political geography of the Chola state, and particularly his mapping of the hundreds of *nāḍu* appears to have strongly influenced and confirmed Stein in his intention to define his own interpretation of the Chola state in the light of Southall's segmentary state model.[40] Stein introduced his own concept of 'The Segmentary State in South Indian History' in the same year at a conference held at Duke University on 'Realm and Region in Traditional India'. The papers of this conference were published only in 1977 (Stein 1977). Three years later there appeared Stein's magnum opus, *Peasant State and Society in Medieval South India.* In this he elaborated his concept in the broader context of South Indian history, from the Pallava to the Vijayanagara period (Stein 1980).[41]

[39] The 'politics of plunder' is another major controversial point of the debate on Chola statehood. See particularly W.G. Spencer 1976, and for a criticism of it, A. Wink (1990: 318ff).

[40] For a more detailed inclusion of Subbarayalu's analysis, see Stein, chapter III, 'Peasant Micro Regions: The *Nadu*' (Stein 1980: 90–140).

[41] As Stein's contribution to the present volume does not repeat the basic elements of his interpretation of Southall's concept, a short quotation from Stein's book may be given here for a better understanding of the debate. '(1) In a segmentary state sovereignty is dual. It consists of actual political sovereignty, or control, and what Southall terms "ritual hegemony" or "ritual sovereignty". These correspond in the Indian usage to *kṣatra* and

In regard to Stein's concept of the state in medieval South India, and in particular of the Chola state, several propositions are of particular relevance. Thus there existed a clear distinction between three levels or 'zones' (Southall), i.e. the central, the intermediate and the peripheral. Only in the central zone, the 'core domain of the Cholas', was their actual political control undisputed, whereas in the intermediate and peripheral zones political control faded off gradually into mere ritual sovereignty.[42] Moreover, local territories did not constitute administrative regions of the centre, nor can local administrators be definitely construed as bureaucratic officials of the centre. Inscriptions had primarily the function of distributing the standardized message of great kingship to all places of the realm. Inscriptions have therefore to be taken as evidence of ritual sovereignty rather than actual political control, a difference that, according to Stein, is fundamental. Yet the persons who were distributing the royal message 'were involved in the system of ritual sovereignty which converted a congeries of local political systems into a segmentary state' (1977: 16).[43] Stein elaborates both in his article and monograph on the fundamental importance of the royal Śiva cult as 'the overarching ideological element which makes these units segments of a whole' (1977: 18). Other constituent features of the segmentary state model are complementary oppositional elements within each segment, e.g. the right-hand and left-hand division (*valaṅgai-idaṅgai*) of the caste system, between

rājadharma respectively. (2) In the segmentary state there may be numerous "centres" of which one has primacy as a source of ritual sovereignty, but all exercise actual political control over a part, or segment, of the political system encompassed by the state. (3) The "specialized administrative staff"—what in some unitary states would be called "the bureaucracy"—is not an exclusive feature of the primary centre, but is found operating at and within the segments of which the state consists. (4) Subordinate levels, or "zones" of the segmentary state may be distinguished and the organization of these is "pyramidal". That is, the relationship between the centre and the peripheral units of any single segment is the same—in reduced form—as the relationship between the prime centre and all peripheral focuses of power . . . In the Indian context this principle is expressed in the terms "little kingdoms" and "little kings" to describe a local ruler whose "kingly" authority is that of any great king, but more limited in scope' (Stein 1980: 274).

42 The problem of distinguishing between actual 'political control' and 'ritual sovereignty' (Stein) or 'political sovereignty' and 'ritual suzerainty' (Southall 1988: 52) is reconsidered by Stein in his 'Interim Reflections'. See also H. Kulke (1982: 248ff) and Dirks (1987: 404) and Sharma (1993).

43 In 1985 he went even a step further when he argued that 'the Chola state existed as a state only as the hundreds of *nādus* of its realm recognized the overlordship, the ritual sovereignty, of Chola kings' (1985d: 394).

peasants and (low caste) artisans, and between caste populations and tribal elements within the society as a whole. These oppositional elements prevented the Chola society from collapsing into a 'fragmented system approximating statelessness' on the one hand, or being 'transformed into a more unitary kingdom' on the other (Stein 1977: 42).[44] Another basic characteristic of the *nāḍu* segment is, according to Stein, its 'shared ethnicity' (1977: 14).[45]

Whereas in his first article of 1977 Stein had applied his concept of the segmentary state primarily to the Chola state, in his monograph of 1980 he extended it to Vijayanagara too.[46] The latter state appears to be particularly resistant to a clear definition of its statehood, for it has brought forth an astonishingly wide range of different interpretations of its polity. These include its conventional definition as an empire, K.A.N. Sastri's interpretation of it as 'a military confederacy of many chieftains co-operating under the leadership of the biggest among them,'[47] and the interpretation of it as a feudal state by A. Krishnaswami (1964) and others,[48] this last being a definition which once even D.C. Sircar appears to have partly accepted.[49] In his monograph, Stein considered Vijaya-

[44] Stein also points out that the balanced or complementary opposition 'may have conceded to a chief a degree of executive authority (Stein 1980: 271). See also H.J. Maynard, 'Influence of the King upon the Growth of Caste' in: *Journal of the Panjab Historical Society*, 6 (1917), pp. 88–100.

[45] Elsewhere Stein argues that 'the essential governmental significance of the *nadu* was its ethnic coherence' (Stein 1980: 109). Dirks (1987: 32) agrees in general with the notion of the 'shared ethnicity' of the *nāḍus* ('all the more convincing in the light of ample modern-day ethnographic evidence'). Subbarayalu, however, to whom Stein had referred in this respect (Stein 1977: 35, note 52), recently admitted that on the basis of new evidence he has to 'modify my previous statement that the nadu itself was an ethnically cohesive territory' (1989: 5). V. Ramaswamy, too, argues strongly against the notion of ethnic and administrative coherence of the *nādus* (Ramaswamy 1982: 309f); see also Champakalakshmi (1982).

[46] Stein contributed an article on Vijayanagara to the *New Cambridge Economic History of India* (1982) and wrote a separate volume on Vijayanagara for the New Cambridge History of India (1989).

[47] Nilakantha Sastri, *Sources of Indian History with Special Reference to South India* (London, 1964), p. 79. In his *A History of South India* (Madras, 1958, p. 297) Sastri even argues that 'Vijayanagara was perhaps the nearest approach to a war-state ever made by a Hindu kingdom'.

[48] More recently K. Naik, for example, speaks of Vijayanagara as an 'amalgamation of feudalized segments' (1982: 363).

[49] Stein (1980: 377, note 16) points out that Sircar's comparison of the *amara* tenure with feudal obligations (Sircar 1969: 17) is substantial different from Sircar's earlier view

nagara, despite 'significant discontinuity' and changes in the system which existed under the Cholas, 'as a continuation of the earlier segmentary state' (Stein 1980: 380). But already a few years later he began to attach considerably greater importance to changes which occurred during the Vijayanagara period. For this reason Stein regarded 'that kingdom not as the end of an age but as the precursor of a South Indian society which is evolving toward that society encountered by the first generation of British administrators in the late eighteenth century. I call this later society of South India "patrimonial"' (Stein 1985b: 73). Influenced by Frank Perlin, who speaks of the emergence of a semi-bureaucratic organization (1981: 276), and particularly by Stephen Blake's paper on 'the Patrimonial-Bureaucratic Empire of the Mughals' (see below), Stein came forth with his new interpretation at two conferences in Heidelberg (1985b) and Wisconsin (1985c) in July and November 1983, respectively. As features which distinguished Vijayanagara from its medieval predecessors, Stein emphasizes Vijayanagara's greatly increased martial character. This was based on new technological innovations of its age and in the so-called *nāyaṅkāra* system, on commerce and long-distance trade, on urbanization associated with temples, and on Vijayanagara's ability to increasingly derive its revenue from customs and trade.[50] Whereas in his first lecture on 'transition to patrimonial systems' Stein had interpreted these new features of Vijayanagara as still 'proto-patrimonial elements' (1985b: 81), he appears to have gone a step further in his second lecture. Here he defines the period between 1450 and 1550 as a 'major period break . . . demarcating a new era in South Indian history' (1985c: 43); and for the case of Krishnadevaraya's age he even used Max Weber's term 'sultanism' as 'a special ("extreme") case of patrimonial authority' (1985c: 41). In a volume of the New Cambridge History of India—Stein's most recent contribution to the history of Vijayanagara—however, he reasserts that the term segmentary state 'in broad terms is still considered valid', for

(Sircar 1966). For a detailed criticism of the issue of feudalism in Vijayanagara see Stein (1980: 374–8).

50 See also R. Palat's important articles (1986, 1987) in which he stresses the increased efficiency of the Vijayanagara state to appropriate agrarian surplus, in some cases between two-thirds and three-fourth. This hitherto unknown exploitation in South India led to agrarian unrest and popular revolts (1986). This unrest appears to have been partly quelled by re-allocation of land and cash to temples and sectarian leaders (A. Appadurai 1978: 62).

Vijayanagara too (Stein 1989: 10).[51] As a major reason for thinking of the Vijayanagara kingdom as a segmentary state he points out that the supersession of local chiefs was not yet accomplished by the Rayas of Vijayanagara, despite their strenuous efforts (1989: 145).[52]

The introduction of the segmentary state concept within the field of South Indian history, as well as the debate on its validity, may have to be regarded as the most important contribution to South Indian historiography since K.A.N. Sastri's publication of his great work on the Cholas. Regardless of whether one agrees with the concept or not, it initiated a debate which led to a new and urgently needed conceptualization of South Indian history and to a hitherto unknown awareness of its structural problems. A major advantage of this new development is an integrated study of the socio-economic and political structures and religious movements of the medieval state in South India, thus overcoming the compartmentalization and 'dynastification' in conventional historiography (Stein 1975b).[53] Accordingly, positive reactions to Stein's concept stress its 'appropriateness as an alternative model to the unitary state model' (Spencer 1983: 7),[54] or praise it even as 'an immensely powerful deconstructive

51 In a more recent paper Perlin, too, dissociated himself at least partly from the patrimonialism concept when he restricted the usage of 'the term "patrimonialism" to characterize the general behavioural features which I see influencing social organizations. None of these should be confused with Weber's applications, nor with those of Burton Stein. In order to avoid confusion I have provisionally renounced these more general usages' (Perlin 1985: 444).

52 The extension of the segmentary model to Vijayanagara brought Stein back to his studies of South Indian temples (1958, 1959, 1961), which had played only a minor role in his earlier papers on South Indian history (1969, 1975b). After having published a special issue of the *Indian Economic and Social History Review* on South Indian temples in 1977, which included an important contribution by Arjun Appadurai ('the interpretation of royal authority over temple as a form of conquest is a process whose understanding we owe principally to Arjun': Stein in the present volume), Stein included the great temples and their sectarian leaders as a major issue into his segmentary model in South India (1980: 439–69); see also A. Appadurai 1978; Carol Appadurai-Breckenridge 1985b; and their jointly published paper 1976; and R. Palat 1986.

53 This new dimension of recent historical studies of medieval South India becomes evident when one looks, for instance, at the papers of Heitzman (1987) and Subbarayalu (1982, 1989). However, one has to keep in mind that Subbarayalu himself had contributed considerably to this new historiographical development through his earlier studies on the historical geography of Tamilnadu (1973) and, together with N. Karashima and B. Sitaraman, through the comprehensive epigraphical analysis of the Chola inscriptions (Sitaraman 1976).

54 David Ludden, too, regards Stein's description of the system as segmentary

tool' (Dirks 1987: 403) against conventional models. And David Shulman, while writing on 'the elusive king in the transformational state' admits that 'there is no doubt that this model is far more accurate than the older "imperial" one developed by Nilakantha Sastri' (Shulman 1985: 19), an assessment which is also followed by G. Berkemer (forthcoming). Dirks and Shulman, however, also admit that the segmentary model cannot fully explain certain aspects of state development in South India.[55]

Stein seems to have anticipated and perhaps even invited stronger reactions against his application of Southall's concept to South Indian history when he wrote: 'The concept of the segmentary state, drawn from African material and adapted to early Indian society, may produce a certain, predictable culture shock generally, and, for students of South Indian society, especially' (1977: 49). The debate began after the publication of the monograph in late 1980, and with its wider circulation in India with several reviews.[56] During the following years a fairly large number of articles on state formation in early medieval India appeared with special reference to Stein's segmentary state concept. Thus, a special issue of *Studies in History*, edited by R. Champakalakshmi and published by the Centre of Historical Studies of the Jawaharlal Nehru University, contained, besides Ramaswamy's review, two articles by Y. Subbarayalu (1982) and myself (Kulke 1982), respectively; and in December 1983 B.D. Chattopadhyaya delivered an important Presidential Address at the Indian History Congress. These contributions were followed by a critical review of recent concepts of state formation in India and South East Asia by S. Subrahmanyam (1986), Heitzman's article on state formation in early medieval South India (1987), A. Southall's rethinking on the segmentary state in Africa and Asia (1987), Subbarayalu's renewed critical evaluation of Stein's concept (1989), and R.S. Sharma's attack against the concept as a whole (1993). Although Stein's 'Interim Reflections' is essentially a reply to his critics, and while B.D. Chattopadhyaya's and J. Heitzman's papers, too, are reproduced in the present volume, a few general remarks on the present debate and references to some of its details

'appropriate, even more so because, despite Chola imperial expansion, the whole of the system was never unified under one state' (Ludden 1985: 204).

55 Dirks (1987: 403f) and Shulman (1985: 20).

56 J.F. Richards in *Journal of Asian Studies*, 42 (1980), p. 1008, D.N. Jha (1981), R. Champakalakshmi (1981, 1982), K.R. Hall (1982) and V. Ramaswamy (1982).

(which are not fully covered by these two articles and Stein's reply) are necessary.

The debate on the segmentary state in Indian history may be ideologically less burdened than the debate on Indian feudalism,[57] but it is certainly not less controversial. Two major points of the controversy between Stein and his critics refer to the degree of administrative centralization of political power achieved by the Cholas and to the question whether the four hundred years of Chola rule can be treated structurally as a single unit. In contrast to Stein,[58] most of his critics[59] emphasize the astonishing structural changes during the eleventh century when the Cholas succeeded in establishing and maintaining direct political control over their considerably extended core area through an impressive and well-organized central administration.[60] In this regard Subbarayalu's

57 An exception is D.N. Jha (1981: 74f) who compares the concept of peasant economy and society with the writings of the 'neo-populist Russian economist A.V. Chayanov, resurrected and strengthened in the West by several scholars who prefer to use it as a substitute for the Marxist theory of mode of production'. Where Stein observes Brahmin-Vellala alliance, Jha emphasizes social cleavage and class struggle under the Cholas, and therefore he subscribes to the 'growing understanding of the medieval South Indian state as feudal' (p. 92). But, on the other hand, he criticizes Stein for his conclusion that the Chola state was not unitary and centralized (p. 89), a feature that would not fit a feudal model.

58 It is particularly difficult to follow Stein's interpretation of the Chola state under its two great rulers Rājarāja I and his son Rājendra when he writes that the segmentary state 'is perhaps best exemplified by the Chola state of Rājarāja the Great and his son, Rājendra. This and other South Indian states of the medieval period were integrated primarily by the symbolic or ritual sovereignty which attached to the king, not by the effective power possessed by him' (1980: 46; repeated by Stein in his contribution to T. Raychaudhuri and I. Habib 1982: 34). In a personal communication Mukhia raised another interesting point: 'My own discomfort with *Peasant State and Society* is that it draws away from the State one of its defining elements: coercive power. If, in an agrarian society, peasantry pervades both the state and society, then who is coercing whom. This is not so much a critique of the notion of Segmentary State as of Peasant State, though the two are coterminous in Stein's conception.'

59 An exception is G.W. Spencer, who points out that Rājarāja's construction of the greatest temple of contemporary India at Tanjavur, 'far from representing the self-glorification of a despotic ruler, was in fact a method adopted by an *ambitious ruler to enhance his very uncertain power*' (Spencer 1969: 45; my emphasis).

60 A. Wink stresses that in the eleventh century the Chola state 'was going through a rapid transformation which did affect its basic constitution' (Wink 1990: 319). Arasaratnam raised the question whether ritual sovereignty would be 'sufficient to explain the relatively long periods of "imperial" rule, especially of the Pallavas and the Cholas' (1984: 112).

paper on the Chola state (1982) is particularly revealing. Thus, for instance, he concludes on the basis of his epigraphical analysis that from about AD 1000, i.e. from the middle of Rājarāja I's through the reign of Kulottuṅga I, 'inscriptions are bewilderingly silent about the chiefs which were, it seems, replaced by officials' (1982: 270).[61] Moreover it is significant that the disappearance of these chiefs coincided with the establishment of the *vaḷanāḍus* as superimposed and centrally controlled revenue units,[62] and with the establishment of *maṇḍalas* (administrative 'districts') which 'incorporated the adjoining chiefly territories besides of course their core territory' (p. 273). Furthermore, Subbarayalu contrasts the statistically clearly recognizable rise of the number of official title holders[63] and the standardization of taxation[64] on the one hand and the disappearance of chiefly troops during this period on the other.[65]

In his article on 'the Cōḷa state' (1982: 295ff) Subbarayalu reproaches Stein for treating the Chola rule as a single historical unit and for applying the segmentary concept to the whole period. He suggests instead to divide, for analytical purposes, their four hundred years of rule into four periods, i.e. the formative period before 985, the ['imperial'] period of expansion and consolidation from 985 to 1070, the period of gradual revival of chiefly rulers from 1070–1178, and the time of their full emergence and the disintegration of the Chola kingdom from 1178 to 1270.[66] On the basis of this analysis Subbarayalu concludes that 'the segmentary idea can be applied to the first phase, with its communal property, large vestiges of tribal society and small kingdoms.[67] The imperial phase witnessed

[61] Berkemer (1991: 196) observes exactly the same replacement of 'little kings' through officials in Kalinga under the Ganga king Vajrahasta V (1035–1070).

[62] Champakalakshmi reproaches Stein for evading the *vaḷanāḍu* as an important piece of evidence for the centralizing efforts of the Cholas (Champakalakshmi 1982: 417).

[63] In this regard Subbarayalu complains that Stein 'does not concede any possibility of distinguishing "officials" from chiefs' (1982: 299).

[64] 'There prevailed a sort of regular tax transfer' (Subbarayalu 1982: 299); see also Shanmugan (1987).

[65] However, Subbarayalu agrees with Stein that 'government officers were only temporary intruders into the village, mainly for collecting taxes, not permanent village officers' (p. 293) and that judicial proceedings remained local in nature (p. 294).

[66] This periodization was first introduced by N. Karashima and B. Sitarama (1972).

[67] Dirks, too, appears to accept the segmentary model in a regional context of newly emerging polities 'where we can see direct links between the segmentary structure of lineages, subcastes and castes on the one hand and the emerging structure of the pre-colonial old regime state on the other' (Dirks 1987: 153f).

growth of private property, well stratified society and a powerful monarchy. Subsequently a sort of feudalization followed along with the decline of kingly power. The segmentary concept is inappropriate and inadequate for these two later phases' (p. 301).[68]

Heitzman's present paper, too, is impressive in demonstrating 'the progressive replacement of more arbitrational, occasional administrative policies by those involving direct penetration into local economy.' He concludes his statistical analysis with this cautious statement: 'The general tendency seen in the variables of royal activity, official presence, and important taxation favours a period of increasing central dominance from at least 1000 to 1150, as more "segmentary" or "feudal" political organizations succumbed to royal dominance.' In his study of the *nagaram*, the 'local merchant community', K.R. Hall comes to similar, though in some cases slightly divergent, conclusions. He, too, detects 'a move toward centralization' (Hall 1980: 196; 1982: 394). But he appears to be more sceptical than Subbarayalu and Heitzman about the success of these royal efforts when he interprets the continuous existence of private merchant armies as 'a basic flaw' in the Chola system as it reflects the inability of the Cholas 'to guarantee the safe transit of commercial goods within their domain' (1980: 193). He agrees with Champakalakshmi (1982) and Subbarayalu (1982) that the establishment of the *vaḷanāḍus* under Rājarāja I, and particularly their reconfirmation under Kulottunga I, has to be interpreted as an act of bureaucratic centralization. But the establishment of these tax units has also to be understood as an attempt by these strong Chola monarchs 'to circumvent *nāḍu* hostility to the Cōḷa rulers' centralizing efforts' (1980: 200; 1982: 407f). And moreover he comes to the interesting conclusion that the *periyannāḍus* have to be recognized as 'a creation of the cultivators themselves in order to defend their interests against the centralizing activities of the Cōḷa monarchs' (p. 203). He therefore postulates a very direct connection between the decreasing references to *vaḷanāḍus* in local epigraphy and the corresponding increase in references to *periyannāḍus* under the late Cholas (p. 204).

Understandably, the early comments and criticisms of the segmentary state came mainly from scholars of South Indian history. However, in December 1983 B.D. Chattopadhyaya took up the issue in the broader

[68] N. Dirks complains that Stein's model does not facilitate the detailed analysis of change or variations in the Indian state (1987: 404).

context of early medieval India in a separate section in his presidential address (1983, section V: 14–19). His criticism of the concept of ritual sovereignty and of defining the state as a 'ritual space' ('state sans politics'), relegating different foci of power to the periphery instead of analysing their transformation into vital components of the political structure of an 'integrative polity'—both these and other points are taken up by Stein in his 'Interim Reflections' and need not be repeated here.

The same is true with Stein's reaction to a more recent contribution to the segmentary state debate. In 1987 Southall, being 'surprised as well as complimented' at Fox's and Stein's application of his African model to Rajput and South Indian history, decided to reverse the compliment in an article on the 'Segmentary State in Africa and Asia', thus also 'reformulating my own idea by learning from Stein's refinement of the model for India' (Southall 1987: 53). Southall's paper does contain helpful clarifications of his model, for instance by even more strongly emphasizing the distinction between 'ritual suzerainty' and 'political sovereignty' and by some remarks about the limitations of its applicability to Indian history, particularly in the context of Rajput history.[69] Moreover, while being confronted again with the anthropological sources of his impressive model of Alur society, it becomes clear that from the Indian point of view one has to distinguish clearly between the model as such and the society from which it was derived. Whereas a direct comparison between the pre-state society of the Alurs and South Indian society under the Cholas, particularly in the *nāḍu* regions, appears to be irrelevant if not nonsensical, the concept of the segmentary state as a theoretical model may well be of considerable heuristical value in India too, even for more complex societies than the Alurs'. Thus, for instance, Southall's distinction between ritual suzerainty and political sovereignty certainly has some bearing on our understanding of the state in early medieval India, even

69 Southall mentions in this regard two points, first, the agnatic segmentary lineages do not extend to the very top of the Rajput system at the central state level (p. 71), second, the Rajput rulers were segmentary rulers only within a vastly larger state—the Mughal Empire (p. 69). As Southall himself even speaks only of a 'surface similarity' between the Alur and the Rajput segmentary systems (p. 71) and in view of Fox's extremely meagre definition one may perhaps give up completely the idea of a Rajput segmentary system. In this context it is worth mentioning that Fox, while introducing Stein's segmentary state article in the volume edited by himself (Fox 1977: XIV), did not elaborate on his own concept any more. Stein takes up this issue at some length in his 'Interim Reflections'.

though not in a mutually exclusive way, as still postulated by Southall.[70] Stein, who initially had also argued in favour of a clear distinction between these two spheres of authority (Stein 1977), is now 'convinced, that lordship for Hindus always and necessarily combined ritual and political authority' (see below). Although it has been argued elsewhere (Kulke 1982: 254) that in traditional societies ritual sovereignty is part of a genuine policy rather than a 'ritualized substitute' of it,[71] the distinction nevertheless maintains its heuristic value. If not 'misused' it is in fact one of the 'powerful deconstructive tools' against the conventional 'unitary' interpretation of pre-modern states in India.

It is extremely difficult to follow Southall in another point of argument, when he assumes that the Rajput and Chola politics were 'expressions of the Asiatic mode of production' (1987: 65). Having agreed with Fox and Stein in their definition of the Rajput and Chola politics as segmentary states, he suddenly also accepts Kathleen Gough's controversial definition of the Chola state in terms of the Asiatic Mode of Production (Gough 1981). He tries to solve this obvious contradiction by concluding that the notion of 'the segmentary state does not belong to any specific mode of production' (Southall 1987: 79). This completely unexpected and to my mind untenable jumbling of different or even contradicting concepts may have to be regarded as a further attempt at rescuing the AMP, but in the Indian context it certainly means an unnecessary burden to the segmentary state debate. Even Stein admits that Southall's reformulation poses empirical difficulties for him and assumes that Southall's position 'confuses conceptual levels'. His 'Interim Reflections' appear to be partly a rectification of his own notion of the segmentary state *vis-à-vis* Southall's reformulation.

Southall's juxtaposition or even partial equation of alleged Indian segmentary states with the AMP also provoked R.S. Sharma's sharp reaction against the segmentary model as a whole and its application to Indian history in particular (Sharma 1993). Sharma's lengthy essay is

70 Southall suggests to 'define the segmentary state as one in which the spheres of ritual suzerainty and political sovereignty do not coincide. The former extends widely towards a flexible changing periphery. The latter is confined to the central, core domain' (1987: 52). The last two sentences, however, do have this heuristical value and remind us of S.J. Tambiah's 'galactic state' (1976).

71 'Perhaps "ritual sovereignty" was a means to implement political power' (Hall 1982: 409).

primarily a dispute with Southall and his expositions about Indian history. He begins his deliberations with calling into question the heuristic value of a single anthropological field study for historical research in a very different society, although he assures us that this objection has nothing to do with an alleged Indian racism against a comparison with African societies. Sharma then very soon comes to his main concern, i.e. the rejection of the segmentary state as a valid concept for Indian history in general (and the Rajput and Chola history in particular) and of its association with the Asiatic and even feudal model of production.[72] The thread of his argumentation is the existence of various socio-economic and political changes during the Middle Ages in India. A major cause of these changes was an enormous increase of land grants. According to Sharma, it led to the emergence of a rich landholding class intermediating between state and peasants—a class which has neither a place in Southall's segmentary notion of Alur society nor in Marx's Asiatic Mode of Production. The increase of landed intermediaries and their appropriation of administrative and juridical regalia caused a decrease of directly controlled 'state land' and a weakening of the central administrative apparatus and its hold over the countryside. All this led, according to Sharma, to qualitative changes in the economy and the nature of the state which, in the Indian case, as one may expect 'may best be described as feudal' (p. 94).[73] He therefore rejects Southall's suggestion to substitute the notion of segmentary society for the feudal or Asiatic mode because this raises insoluble conceptual and empirical problems. And to the same effect as has earlier been argued by Mukhia (1981: 310, note 225) and Stein (1991) in regard to the validity of Indian feudalism, Sharma asks in regard to Southall's segmentary state model: 'how does our understanding improve if we apply a blanket label to social formations?' (p. 95).

IV

Whatever may be the outcome of future debates about possible structural changes in early medieval India, there has always been wide agreement among historians that the establishment of the Delhi Sultanate and the

72 'The model of the feudal mode of production . . . is a segmentary system of lords and vassals owning rent-producing landed estates. . . . ' (Southall 1988: 78).

73 See above for D.N. Jha's (1981) similar statement.

Mughal empire initiated a new phase of state formation in Indian history. Being initially classical conquest states, their rulers had to establish their authority in, and control over, their newly conquered territories through a sharing of the spoils with their followers and, at the same time, keeping these followers under control. The main instrument for the implementation of this policy were territorial assignments (*iqtā'*) on a temporary basis and the frequent transfer of the holders (*muqti'*) of these assignments. Fifteen hundred years after the Mauryas, the Delhi Sultanate was capable of producing under Alauddin Khalji the first and most sincere—though again only temporarily successful—attempt to centralize systematically the administration of the far extended core region of the state. The efficient system of simultaneously appropriating a sizeable part of the peasant's surplus and distributing it to members of the ruling elite[74] soon began to influence contemporary states outside the Sultanate, e.g. Vijayanagara[75] and Orissa.[76] The greatly improved assignment of *jāgīrs* in a highly elaborate rank (*manṣab*) system under the Mughals has to be regarded as the culmination of pre-modern state administration in India. But the administrative efficiency of the *manṣabdāri* system did not remove its structural weakness: a strictly enforced temporariness of the *jāgīr* assignments led to a nearly unlimited exploitation of peasants, and thus to agrarian unrest and social crisis;[77] whereas the heritability of territorial assignments was bound to lead sooner or later to a fragmentation of political authority, as was the case in the reorganization of the *jāgīr* assignment under Feroz Shah. The crucial structural weakness of the Delhi Sultanate and even of the Mughal empire was the fact that, despite their greatly improved military power and administrative efficiency and (as a result of both) more clearly defined territoriality, they still remained at their core extended patriarchal and thus patrimonial systems.

Whereas previous generations of British and Indian historians had regarded the establishment of foreign Muslim rule and the step-by-step

74 I. Habib, in T. Raychaudhuri and I. Habib (1982: 68ff).

75 R.A. Palat even states that the *iqtā'* system 'was adopted *mutatis mutandis* by the Vijayanagara emperors as the *nāyaṅkara* system'.

76 S.K. Panda was able to trace altogether 39 'governors' (*parīkṣa*) of Kaliṅga under the Gaṅga dynasty between 1271 and 1426. Between 1376 and 1405 altogether 16 *parīkṣas* administered Kaliṅga for an average of about two years! (Panda 1986: 77ff and 1993).

77 This 'Irfan Habib thesis' appears to be generally accepted, though not as the only cause of the decline of the Mughal Empire.

political unification of the Indian subcontinent under its authority as the major indicator of change, modern historians emphasize structural changes as major parameters of this development. These new studies had begun with W.H. Moreland's pioneering works, culminating in his *Agrarian System of Moslem India* (1929), and were followed by studies like K.M. Ashraf's *Life and Conditions of the People of Hindustan* (1935) or I.H. Qureshi's *Administration of the Sultanate of Delhi* (1942). Important new contributions on the Delhi Sultanate came from Mohammad Habib (1974) and K.A. Nizami (1974, 1985) particularly in the form of their jointly published monumental work on the Delhi Sultanate as volume 5 of the *Comprehensive History of India* (1970). After the publication of J.N. Sarkar's monumental opus on the Mughals a number of detailed and more critical studies about the economic and social foundations of the Mughal state and its decline were published since the late fifties and during the early sixties . Prominently among them figure Satish Chandra's *Parties and Politics at the Mughal Court 1707–1740* (1959),[78] Irfan Habib's *Agrarian System of Mughal India* (1963), Athar Ali's *Mughal Nobility under Aurangzeb* (1966) and more recently the first volume of *The Cambridge Economic History of India* (T. Raychaudhuri and Irfan Habib 1982). These works produced a series of fascinating studies of the ethnic and social stratification of the ruling elites, of the agrarian system, its surplus production and appropriation, the emergence of mercantile communities, and the socio-economic reasons which led to the decline of the empire. These works break important new ground in our knowledge of the socio-economic fabric of the Mughal state (S. Chandra 1976).

The present volume contains two articles on the Mughal state. Athar Ali's 'Towards an Interpretation of the Mughal Empire' is a revised version of his Presidential Address at the Indian History Congress of 1972 which attempts to locate the Mughal state in Indian history between advanced traditional and early modern statehood. Stephen Blake's 'Patrimonial-Bureaucratic Empire of the Mughals' aims at a conceptualization of the Mughal state on the basis of Max Weber's theory of the patrimonial state.

The question whether the Mughal Empire has to be regarded 'either as the most successful of the traditional states [in India] or as an abortive quasi-modern polity' (A. Ali) has been asked time and again since Bernier's 'Travels in the Mogul Empire'. Athar Ali approaches the solution

[78] Of particular relevance is the Introduction of Satish Chandra's work.

of this problem through a distinction between traditional but highly developed and rationalized elements of Mughal authority and new means of domination introduced by the Mughals from outside. As regards the traditional means Athar Ali distinguishes between administrative, ideological, and socio-structural spheres. Based on the continuing survival of the administrative framework of the Delhi Sultanate, particularly on the land revenue assessment of the Sūr regime, the Mughal government derived its strength from Akbar's systematization of the administration. The creation of the *manṣabdāri* system, the further systematization of the *jāgīr* land-revenue assignment and his 'largely successful attempts to make the entire administrative structure of one *ṣūba* into the exact replica of the other, with a chain of officers at various levels ultimately controlled by the ministers at the centre, gave identity to Mughal administrative institutions irrespective of the regions where they functioned'. Apart from 'this immense work of centralization and systematization' Athar Ali sees a new stress on the 'absoluteness of sovereignty'. This second prop of Mughal authority was based on religious and ideological traditions prevailing in contemporary India and the Muslim World, particularly in Central Asia and Iran. Their blending with Akbar's rationality created the hitherto unknown absoluteness of sovereignty which, however, did not solve the problem of 'spiritual authority in his relations with non-Muslim subjects'. The third sphere of structural changes was, according to Athar Ali, the creation of a composite nobility by the Mughals in order to remove their dependence on the Muslim nobility. In this field Athar Ali is able to make use of the extensive studies which he and his colleagues of the Aligarh School conducted on the composition of the Mughal nobility and its changes. In the present paper Athar Ali stresses even more strongly than in his other publications (Athar Ali 1966) the 'unvarying nature of the proportions shared by the various elements' of the nobility which was upset only slightly through the inclusions of the Marathas and Deccanies after Aurangzeb's expansion into the south.

But as Athar Ali rightly points out these 'causal factors' of the greatness of the Mughal Empire did not have 'a directly modern origin'. Aspects of early modernity emerged neither from traditions prevailing in sixteenth-century South Asia nor from the contemporary Muslim World but from their contacts with the Western World of early modern Europe. Athar Ali exemplifies these new influences and their impact on Mughal statehood by the influx of silver 'an economic by-product of the Age of

Discovery' and by the importance of artillery for the Mughal state. Both fields are known to have strengthened the development of modern statehood in Europe and should have shown the same capacity in the Mughal state, particularly as the Mughals had access to detailed information about Europe and its powers. But in India these potential 'modernizers' did not lead to the emergence of an early modern state. According to Athar Ali they were instead used to strengthen the traditional culture and system of sovereignty. The Mughal state was therefore 'essentially the "perfection" of a medieval polity, made possible by certain early modern developments'. In a Marxian context Athar Ali concludes that although the developments led to a stability and power hitherto unknown in Muslim history in South Asia, the Mughal society and state did not 'resolve the new contradiction inherent in the existence of a medieval polity in a world advancing towards modernity'

Athar Ali's differentiating attempt to assign to the Mughal state its place in Indian history is a clear departure from earlier—mainly British colonial—writings and from more contemporary national and often communalist statements. But in regard to the place of Mughal statecraft in the above mentioned successive stages of state formation, Athar Ali, too, assigns to the Mughal state an extremely high position and thus follows to a considerable extent the Indian historiographical model of the pre-modern state in India whereas other historians of the Aligarh School and related scholars tend to treat the Mughal state and its inherent structural defects more critically (e.g. Satish Chandra, Irfan Habib and Tapan Raychaudhuri). More recently the high profile of Mughal statecraft, particularly the alleged degree of centralization of administration and its standardization throughout the Empire has been questioned. Thus, for instance, M. Alam and S. Subrahmanyam criticize in a forthcoming paper on state-building under the Mughals the 'picture of unremitting centralization' and emphasize instead the 'persistence of differences from region to region, rather than centrally imposed uniformity'. Chetan Singh, too, argues in favour of a 'regionalization of the administrative functionaries' of the Mughal state in seventeenth-century Punjab (C. Singh 1988: 317). In a recently published paper Athar Ali takes up the gauntlet against these 'revisionalistic approaches' and defends his definition of Mughal polity as a centralized polity 'geared to systematization and creation of an all imperial bureaucracy' (A. Ali 1993: 710).

Stephen Blake (1979) admits in the Introduction to his paper that the studies of Athar Ali and Satish Chandra 'break important new ground' but criticizes that 'neither has looked into the impact of his work on the conventional model of the Mughal state' and points out that so far 'no complete model of this traditional state was presented'. In this context he refers particularly to Athar Ali's above mentioned study. In view of the many analytical books and articles written on the Mughal state since Moreland and in particular by the Aligarh School such a statement seems exaggerated. But it is no exaggeration to state that Blake's article meets the requirements of such a comprehensive model to a very large extent. In fact, his article and his attempt to evaluate the validity of Weber's concept of patrimonialism in the Indian context may even have to be regarded as the third major contribution to a conceptualization of the pre-modern state in India—after Sharma and Stein's introductions of their respective concepts of feudalism and the segmentary state to Indian history. Whereas these latter concepts pertained mainly to early medieval India, Blake's concept of the patrimonial state refers to the Mughal empire, the final stage of state development in pre-modern India. But, as has been pointed out earlier, it may have some bearing on earlier Indian states, too.

Blake's concept of patrimonial bureaucracy is based on Max Weber's monumental work *Economy and Society*,[79] which contains several chapters on patrimonialism. Weber defines gerontocracy and primary patriarchalism as the two most elementary types of traditional domination. Both are characterized by the complete absence of a personal (*patrimonial*) staff:

> The decisive characteristic of both (these elementary types) is the belief of the members that domination, even though it is an inherent traditional right of the master, must definitely be exercized as a joint right in the interest of all members[80] . . . Patrimonialism and, in the extreme case, *sultanism* tend to arise whenever traditional domination develops and administration and a military force which are purely personal instruments of the master (EaS, 231).

Whereas in primary patriarchalism authority was regarded as a communal right, in patrimonialism it appears as a personal right. Here the ruler appropriates and exploits his power like any other economic asset. A major

79 Max Weber, *Economy and Society, an Outline of Interpretative Sociology.* Translated and edited by Guenther Roth and Claus Wittich (Berkeley: University of California Press, 1978).

80 In this sense the pre-Balban period of the Delhi Sultanate was still characterized by these elementary types of domination.

structural feature of patrimonial domination is the fact that the administrative staff in turn appropriates peculiar powers and the corresponding economic assets. Moreover, patrimonial domination is characterized by its permanent confrontation with local authorities.

> Within the patrimonial structures the independence of the local powers may vary widely, ranging from officials attached to the patrimonial household to tributary princes and to divisional rulers who are dependent merely in name. The continuous struggle of the central power with the various centrifugal local powers creates a specific problem for patrimonialism when the patrimonial ruler, with his personal power resources—his landed property, other sources of revenue and personal loyal officials and soldiers—confronts not a mere mass of subjects differentiated only according to sibs and vocations, but when he stands as one landlord (*Grundherr*) over other landlords who as local honoratiores wield autonomous authority of their own (EaS, 1054f).[81]

Weber referred quite frequently, although only very cursorily, to Mughal India and the Delhi Sultanate as patrimonial states in *Economy and Society*, and rarely to the Mauryan empire in his *Religion of India*. But he avoided outlining a comprehensive model of the states in India in terms of his patrimonialism concept. This stands, as J. Rösel rightly remarked, 'in complete contrast to Weber's study on Confucianism and Taoism where he devotes nearly a hundred pages to an exhaustive analysis not only of the structure but also of the emergence of the Chinese patrimonial state' (Rösel 1986: 139). Obviously Weber's interest in India was confined mainly to its religions.[82] Blake's attempt to define a concrete historical state in India in Weberian terms as patrimonial-bureaucratic is thus also a pioneering work in the context of Weberian studies. In his summary Blake concludes that a careful reading of major documents of the Mughals, e.g. the *Ā'īn-i Akbarī*, not only reveals the weakness of the

81 'The patrimonial ruler cannot always dare to destroy these autonomous local powers. However, if the ruler intends to eliminate the autonomous honoratiores, he must have an organization of his own which can replace them with approximately the same authority over the local population. Otherwise a new stratum of honoratiores comes into being with similar pretensions—the new leaseholders or landowners who take the place of their native predecessors' (EaS 1055). Whereas the Brahmin grantees in early medieval states never assumed this role of an 'administrative organization', the *manṣabdārs* played exactly this role—as long as the Mughal rulers were able to enforce the temporariness of their jāgīr assignments.

82 W. Schluchter (ed.), *Max Webers Studie über Hinduismus und Buddhismus. Interpretation und Kritik* (Frankfurt 1984).

established interpretation but shows as well the remarkable congruence between the state Akbar organized and the patrimonial-bureaucratic empire analysed by Weber: 'In its depiction of the emperor as a divinely-aided patriarch, the household as the central element in government, members of the army as dependent on the emperor, the administration as a loosely structured group of men controlled by the Imperial household, the travel as a significant part of the emperor's activities, the *Ā'īn-i Akbarī* supports the suggestion that Akbar's state was a patrimonial-bureaucratic empire.'

Although there still seems to be a general reluctance among Indian historians to concern themselves with Weber's concept of patrimonialism,[83] its validity in the late medieval Indian context appears to become more and more accepted among Western scholars. An important consenting vote came in 1984 from Peter Hardy at a conference held near Frankfurt on Max Weber's view of Islam, to which he contributed a paper on Islamic patrimonialism under the Mughals. In his paper, which he himself regards as a companion to Blake's article, Hardy elaborates, deploying Weber's model, most particularly on the aspect of personal authority of the emperor, his various devices to cope with opposing and centrifugal local authorities, and on the role of extra-patrimonial officers, i.e. Brahmins and Kayasthas. On the basis of his analysis Hardy concludes that the Mughal empire exemplified a typical patrimonial state throughout its history. In view of the strong dependence of the imperial system on the nobility and its abilities J. Richards, too, agrees that 'one might well term the empire a patrimonial-bureaucratic system' (1993: 59). As has already been mentioned, Stein, while 'reapproaching Vijayanagara' (1985c), was directly influenced by Perlin and by Blake's attempt to introduce Weber's concept to Indian history. Most recently, Noboru Karashima too appears to have accepted Stein's interpretation at least

83 The main obstacle is certainly the so-called 'Weber thesis' of his 'Protestant Ethic and the Spirit of Capitalism' which rejects any possibility of a transformation of patrimonial capitalism ('portfolio capitalism', Subrahmanyam and Bayly 1988) to 'rational capitalism' in Asia and particularly India. In India this thesis may be left to the same fate as Marx's Asiatic mode of production. However this objection should pertain only to his *Collected Essays in Sociology of Religions* but not to his *Economy and Society* with its long delineations on feudalism, patrimonialism, etc. But it is particularly this portion of Weber's writings that is suspected to be used by non-Marxist historians as a substitute of Marx's theory of modes of production. For a criticism of the use of Weber's concept as yet another 'foreign' model in the context of Indian history, see S. Subrahmanyam (1986) and M. Alam and S. Subrahmanyam (forthcoming).

partly: 'to see the Vijayanagara period as the transition to "patrimonial" systems . . . as more understandable' (1992: 5). He even concludes that it may apply to periods prior to that of Vijayanagara. G. Berkemer similarly defines the South Indian state system of the fourteenth to sixteenth centuries as a phase of transition towards a patrimonial order and detects 'a trend towards a patrimonial structure' already in the core area of the 'imperial Cholas' of the eleventh century (Berkemer, forthcoming).

Another important contribution came from Rösel, who tried to answer the question of how far the concept of patrimonial power might prove useful for the further study of Indian history,[84] without however specifying himself to a particular period or state to which Weber's concept may apply. But his concluding definition of Weber's notion of the patrimonial state confirms Blake's and Hardy's attempts to define the Mughal empire as a patrimonial state and Stein's view which places Vijayanagara in a transitional position from the segmentary state to patrimonialism. And what holds good for Vijayanagara is certainly applicable to the Delhi Sultanate,[85] and, even though no detailed study has yet been undertaken, perhaps also to the 'imperial' Cholas in the eleventh century.

[84] In this context one quotation from Rösel's interpretation of Weber's theory of patrimonialism may illustrate the usefulness of a further study of this question: 'The patrimonial state is characterized by the fact that it leaves the most important stratum of traditional intermediaries out of its spheres of control. Based on a small number of subordinate and often better trained groups of state personnel than in occidental feudalism, patrimonial power concentrates its interests on those spheres that are structurally akin as well as indispensable to its chances of control. A high degree of control over specialized administrative functions, personnel and territories implies a concentration of control on limited amounts of space, functions and social groups that are indispensable for the stability and growth of the patrimonial state: control over the network of roads and cities, over their specific functions like manufacture, trade and money-lending, and over their specific groups like traders, bankers or ship owners. This limited sphere of influences is structurally akin to the possibilities of patrimonial control, and control over these spheres is the prerequisite for stability and growth of patrimonial power: only this urbanized sphere generates those taxes, materials, luxury items, credit facilities, specialized procedures, information and skills that are indispensable for the recruitment, training, movement and control of more specialized state personnel' (Rösel 1986: 140).

[85] In his recent thesis Conermann (1993: 183f) comes to the conclusion that the Delhi Sultanate under Muhammad Ibn Tuqluq exhibits nearly all features of patrimonial rule. However, due to the prevalence of *iqṭā* it was still based on prebendalism.

V

Besides these major concepts of the state in pre-modern India within contemporary historiography, there exists a considerable number of 'non-aligned' contributions which emphasize processes of state formation rather than the state as a given entity. Four of these are included in the present volume: J. Heitzman's 'State Formation in South India 850–1280', B.D. Chattopadhyaya's 'Political Processes and the Structure of Polity in Early Medieval India', my own 'Processural Model of Integrative State Formation in Medieval India', and S. Sinha's 'State Formation and Rajput Myths in Tribal Central India'. One common denominator of these papers, as their titles reveal, is the process of state formation or, more precisely, the analysis of political processes and the integrative structure of polity in medieval India. Various aspects of these and related studies have already been dealt with in connection with the above evaluation of the concepts of Indian feudalism and particularly of the segmentary state. Therefore short evaluations of these contributions may suffice in this Introduction.

A common issue of all these studies is their emphasis on changes in the political structure, though none of them follows a clearly evolutionary paradigm. Whereas the models of Indian feudalism and of the segmentary state restrict political change mainly to aspects of fragmentation and the segmentation of political authority, the authors of these studies perceive political changes through centralization and integration. Even though these changes tended to be restricted to certain periods and regions and regularly relapsed (usually during dynastic crisis), they normally did not fall back into the *status quo ante.* Thus a certain degree of structural change survived these dynastic changes. A major cause of this continuous though not uninterrupted process may be the emergence and gradual development of a social category or parameter which Chattopadhyaya calls 'state society'. It emanated horizontally from the central dynastic nuclear area and implied the transformation of 'pre-state polities into state polities and thus the integration of local polities into structures that transcended the bounds of local polities' (Chattopadhyaya 1983: 10).[86] This integrative development was likewise based on, and accompanied by, a series of processes, e.g. an

[86] For an interesting study on the integration of the Rajpûts into the Mughal state see N. Ziegler (1978).

extension of the agrarian society through peasantization of tribal groups; the improvement of trading networks; an expansion of caste society ('jatification'); the emergence and spatial extending of ruling lineages by processes called 'Kshatriyaization' (Kulke 1976) or 'Rajputization' (S. Sinha); interspersing the dynastic 'domain' (*Stammland*) and increasingly its hinterland with a network of royally patronized religious institutions (Spencer 1969, Kulke 1978, Heitzman 1991) and land assignments to 'officials'; 'greater penetration of the royal will into local arenas of power' (Heitzman); and never ending though rarely successful attempts to centralize administrative functions, particularly revenue collection, etc.

Although these measures rarely led to a full annexation ('provincialization') of the conquered hinterland, they nevertheless affected the structure of the pre-modern state considerably in at least two ways. First, the dynastic nuclear area came under increasingly bureaucratized direct political control of the central dynasty. Second, the politically controlled nuclear area expanded through a double process of attraction and socio-economic and political integration into its hinterland, thus creating an 'extended core region' (Kulke), as a considerably larger 'state territory' than the original dynastic nuclear area had been.[87] The frontier of 'graded political control' was thus extended considerably into the 'intermediate zone', the conquered hinterland of the pristine nuclear area.

In this regard the role of the *sāmantas*, the erstwhile autonomous neighbouring chiefs and rajas, and their integration in and emergence at, the central court is of particular relevance. Chattopadhyaya regards their 'political integration as a counterpoint to the decentralized polity of the feudal model' and as 'a keynote of early medieval polity'. As we have seen, Yadava too emphasized that the term *sāmanta* is 'the key word of Indian feudalism' (1973: 136).

As has already been pointed out in connection with criticisms of the segmentary state model, another major issue in various papers is the attempt to analyse the structural dynamics of extension and contraction

[87] The *mandala* 'divisions' created by the Cholas in the eleventh century are indicators of this extension of the initial nuclear area into an extended core region although they were in no way fully annexed to the royal central nuclear area or 'domain'. Only a few such studies have been undertaken on other great regional kingdoms of medieval India, e.g. on Bengal (B.M. Morrison 1970 and S. Bhattacharya 1985) and Orissa (Panda 1986 and Kulke 1982). One important contribution to these studies would be a comparative analysis of the respective core regions of the Chālukyas of Aihole, the Rāshtrakūtas, and the Chāḷukyas of Kalyani.

of central administrative measures. Subbarayalu's paper on the Chola state (1982) and Heitzman's contribution to the present volume on state formation in South India are particularly revealing in this regard. Thus Heitzman's analysis shows a remarkable increase of local involvement through royal orders and a greater concentration of tax-collecting power in the hands of superior agencies as well as a decline of the importance of cesses collected and officially controlled by village administration.[88] In the context of the attempt to conceptualize the Chola state, one statement by Heitzman is especially worth mentioning. He speaks of a 'floating body' of loyal honourable men as performers of tasks for the royal family. These 'fit the pattern of household staff rather than a ramified administrative organisation. Investigation of these "official" terminologies reveals little indication of a ramified bureaucratic system for ruling the Chola state, but rather an "extended court" peopled by high-ranking associates of the king, including the creatures of the king.' According to this depiction of its central administrative body, the Chola state fits apparently very well with Weber's model of a patrimonial bureaucracy.

Another major topic of various recent studies is the role played by religious institutions in the process of state formation. The importance of religions in India's Middle Ages was of course well known to previous generations of historians. However, in their conventionally 'compartmentalized' histories, religion was usually treated separately in appendix-like chapters of the dynastic histories rather than as an integral part of socio-political developments. A new awareness of the importance of religious institutions for state processes is at least partly due to R.S. Sharma and Burton Stein who, for the first time, emphasized the important role of these institutions in their respective state models. But in the feudal model, land grants to Brahmins and temples played a politically rather negative role in the process of feudal fragmentation of political authority; and in the segmentary model temples and Brahmin *agrahara* villages strengthened the localized 'segmentary' structure of the state and its ritual sovereignty.[89] Whereas these models operated mainly with various types

[88] Heitzman, however, also rightly admits in his present paper that 'the centrality of the state control is less visible in the more outlying study areas'.

[89] In a personal communication, Stein emphasized 'that the linkages among shrines in South India in which bhakti worship is practised had the effect in South India of enhancing or raising the salvational credentials of local shrines with respect to those great shrines to which they are linked' (Kulke 1982: 263).

of donations to Brahmins known from innumerable inscriptions and their impact on society, the new non-aligned studies are more concerned with the great 'sacred places as the focus of political interest'—as H. Bakker's recently edited book is entitled. Under the influence of bhakti folk religions and pilgrimage many of these places have become veritable temple cities since the beginning of the second millennium AD. Accordingly there was a clear shift of royal patronage from 'rural' Brahmin villages to urban temple complexes and temple cities. This development had a very direct and deep impact on the development of late medieval kingship ideology (and, in particular, on royal legitimation) and on political integration of the great regional kingdoms and their regional cultures.[90] Accordingly, these studies pertain to various aspects of these medieval socio-religious developments, e.g. religious and socio-political integration through religious networks (Preston 1980, Kulke 1984, C. Appadurai-Breckenridge 1985, Durga and Reddy 1992),[91] royal legitimation and expansion of royal influence through patronage of temples (Spencer 1969, Kulke 1978a, U. Singh 1990), and royal intervention in local temple management through the patronage of sectarian leaders (A. Appadurai 1978). Other studies emphasize the role of the temple as a central 'state archive' (Berkemer 1991b), as a promoter of agrarian extension (Stein 1959/60) and as 'one of the first indications of a centralized and uniform fiscal institution' (Heitzman 1991: 51)—and as such as a central institution of 'political economy' (C. Appadurai-Breckenridge 1985). All these studies confirm the existence of 'ritual policy' and 'ritual sovereignty' as an important partial aspect of genuine policy rather than a substitute of it.

Another broad spectrum of studies pertains to the proliferation of the medieval state system into its hinterland with its various intermediate and peripheral zones often interspersed with pockets of less complex ('tribal') societies. Whereas conventional historiography regards the 'imperial' extension of the state into its hinterland as its main cause, more recent studies emphasize socio-economic and cultural processes as major reasons of the emergence of the *sāmantacakra*, the circle of chiefs, princes and

90 This aspect is particularly stressed by my contribution in the present volume.

91 'Temples may be seen as the institutional intersections of two distinct axes of interrelation. Temples permitted, what may be conceived as a *horizontal* interrelation with connected centers to peripheries in the agricultural landscape, at the same time, as they (or more properly the gifts to them) facilitated the *vertical* interrelation of higher and lower levels of the political system' (C. Appadurai-Breckenridge 1985: 63).

little kings, who surrounded the medieval kingdoms. These processes operated at two levels. First, as the emergence of formerly tribal chiefs to Hindu rajas, and second, as the fission or secession of 'officials', local honoratiores and tributary chiefs. The former process has been described by Surajit Sinha, in his seminal paper (reprinted in the present volume) as 'Rajputization';[92] the latter is known from Dirks' studies on the 'little kings'.[93] Both processes have a lot in common as they were operating in the hinterland of the core region of the medieval kingdoms and were directly influenced by the cultural values of these centres. But there exists one important difference. Rajputization pertains primarily to the social process 'how the equalitarian primitive clan-based tribal organization [and its elite] has adjusted itself to centralized, hierarchic, territorially oriented political developments' (Sinha).[94] Rajputization thus refers to social mobility through an *imitation* of cultural values imported from the outside, whereas 'little kings' emerged from within the state system through an *appropriation* of cultural and political roles.[95] Even though Rajputization normally had its origin outside the medieval kingdoms and the little kings initially emerged at the cost of the central authority, both processes played

92 See also his Introduction to an anthology of papers on *Tribal Politics and State Systems* (S. Sinha 1987). This volume contains several important contributions to different processes of state formation in tribal eastern and north-eastern India.

93 See also S. Subrahmanyam's and D. Shulman's recent study on 'The Men who would be King?' (1990).

94 In his more recent study S. Sinha (1987: XIV) emphasizes agrarian extension as a major cause of this development in tribal areas when he stresses 'a significant correlation between the degree of surplus generated through appropriate technological innovations and the level of functional differentiation, stratification and centralization of a polity.'

95 The rise of 'little kings' in South India is described by Dirks as follows: 'These developments were encouraged by forces above and outside the locality as well as being outgrowths of local political developments. Chiefly groups and individuals emerged out of a context in which local authority and decision making were vested in locality assemblies first by mobilizing their local resources to secure protection rights and then by being conspicuous donors to temples, charities, and Brahmin communities. Their control over the resources necessary for such beneficent activity was steadily intensified by the transfer of protection rights from locality assemblies to these chiefs. The chiefs gradually acquired more generalized rights than had initially been awarded to them in their position as patikkaval ["protection"] chiefs. Some of these additional rights had to do with the honors accorded the chiefs; others had to do with their control over military followers and their communities. It was through this process that palaiyakkarars ["little kings"] began to dominate south Indian society and polity at the local level' (N. Dirks 1987: 154).

an important role in the proliferation of the state system at the local level. Throughout history,[96] the realignment of these newly emerging local forces led to new political configurations at the regional level.[97]

VI

Looking back at the various and often contradicting models[98] of the pre-modern state in India and their critics, one wavers between the statements of two great historians of early medieval India. In his *Vikramāṅkadeva Caritam* Bilhaṇa compares his critics with camels looking merely at the numerous thorns in the pleasure-garden of his writing.[99] Kalhana on the other hand recommends to the readers of his *Rājataraṅgiṇī* the 'sentiment of resignation' (*śānta*) after having 'pondered over the sudden appearance of living beings [or in our case, concepts] that last for a moment only.'[100]

However, before following Kalhaṇa's advice too quickly, we have to keep in mind that these different concepts do reflect in a way the great variety of successive and often coexisting state systems which India produced during its long history.[101] And there is yet another point which requires some clarification. In several cases reviewers questioned the value of a concept which raises more questions than it answers. To my mind, the value of the various debates on these concepts lies in the very fact of their raising controversial questions. Accordingly, they are likely to produce controversial answers. Questioning, and not the repeated

96 Whereas Sinha and Dirks restricted their respective studies mainly to late medieval India, Berkemer (1991) has shown that the emergence of little kings is a typical feature in Kalinga since the mid-first millennium AD. For Orissa, see also Kulke (1978b).

97 In this context A. Wink's controversial *fitna* ('sedition', 'rebellion') concept appears to be valid when he writes 'sedition was the means of establishing sovereignty', or 'the state organized itself around the conflict which was endemic in the hereditary zamindari and watan rights' (1984: 288).

98 In regard to K.A.N. Sastri's and Burton Stein's interpretation of the Chola state, Shulman remarks: 'The two views are so radically at odds that it is difficult to believe that they were constructed on the basis of the same epigraphical evidence' (1985: 19).

99 *Bilhaṇa's Vikramāṅkadevacaritam* (I, 29), translated by S.C. Banerji and A.K. Gupta (Calcutta, 1965).

100 *Kalhaṇa's Rājataraṅgiṇī* (I, 23), translated by M.A. Stein (repr. Delhi, 1961).

101 The state in ancient India and its models have not been dealt with in this volume; see particularly R. Thapar, *From Lineage to State* (Bombay, 1984) and idem, 1980 and 1981.

reconfirmation of established interpretations, will always have to remain the essence of historical research.[102] Thus, Sharma's introduction of the feudalism concept to Indian history is as much a keystone in modern Indian historiography as Mukhia's Presidential Address which questions its existence. The same is true with Stein's application of the segmentary model to Indian history and the subsequent attempts to question its validity.

Whatever the results of future research, the debates on the most controversial concepts of contemporary Indian historiography, i.e. the concepts of Indian feudalism and the segmentary state, have proved to be particularly fruitful. These debates led for the first time to a critical evaluation of several important aspects of medieval Indian history. It was through Sharma's theory of Indian feudalism that the conventional, purely religious explanation of land grants to Brahmins was replaced by his widely accepted socio-economic interpretation—even though one may not agree with his conclusion that these caused the emergence of feudal relations. Similarly, the study of issues like social crisis, peasant rebellion, urban decay and demonitarization in the post-Gupta period, which previously had little or no impact at all on conventional historiography, got a new impetus through the feudalism debate. The same is true with regard to Stein's segmentary model. Important questions like tax transfer within medieval kingdoms, the socio-economic roles of Brahmin *agrahāra* villages and of the great temple cities of the South, the controversial issue of ritual sovereignty and the distinction between different spatial zones of political authority in medieval kingdoms—all have become, only recently, major issues of contemporary historical research. This, too, is at least partly a consequence of the still ongoing debate on the segmentary model.

In a critical evaluation of the prevailing models of state formation in India and South East Asia, Subrahmanyam observes a strange cleavage between the Indian state models of North and South India. North India allegedly has 'all the characteristics of a glittering patrimonial-bureaucratic empire while, once south of the Godavari, state forms become segmentary, diffuse and decentralized' (1986: 359). Future research will have to clarify whether or to what extent these differences are real or influenced by the

[102] This statement however does not exclude the necessity of a 'spirited and elaborate defence' of the concepts as shown by R.S. Sharma and Burton Stein in their respective contributions to the present volume.

respective state models. Subrahmanyam's observation therefore draws our attention to the crucial problem that conceptual models sometimes may lead to the *reconstruction* of its object (according to the parameters of its model) rather than to its *interpretation*. Subrahmanyam moreover notices 'the dependence of the historiography on received models', particularly from Europe,[103] and to a more limited extent from Africa (1986: 375) and complains of 'the failure to develop adequate Asianist models' (p. 357). This objection is certainly noteworthy. Indian history could provide itself 'emic' models and institutions, e.g. the *maṇḍala* concept of the Arthaśāstra,[104] castes, *sāmantas* and *jāgīrs*, etc. which could form the basis for a future Indian model. Perhaps this would be an 'as yet unspecified "medieval Indian social formation"', as suggested by Stein (1985: 82), or perhaps Habib's 'Indian medieval system'. However, before such a model is elaborated, a number of crucial questions, which the prevailing models have raised for the first time, require further clarification. The fruitful debate about certain key institutions of medieval Indian society and their conceptual meaning may therefore have to continue for rather a long time yet.[105]

103 This is also Wink's major criticism of the Indian feudalism model (Wink 1990: 221ff).

104 The *maṇḍala* concept has very recently entered the debate on the pre-modern state in Southeast Asia with S.J. Tambiah's 'Galactic Polity' (*World Conqueror and World Renouncer*, Cambridge, 1976, pp. 102–58), and O.W. Wolters' *History, Culture, and Region in Southeast Asian Perspectives* (Singapore, 1982), p. 16ff; see also Jan Wisseman Christie, 'Negara, Mandala, and the Despotic State: Images of Early Java', in: *Southeast Asia in the 9th to 14th Centuries*, D.G. Marr and A.C. Milner (eds) (Singapore, 1986); C. Higham, *The Archaeology of Mainland Southeast Asia* (Cambridge, 1989) (chapter III: The development of *maṇḍalas*, pp. 239–320), R. Hagesteijn, *Circles of Kings, Political Dynamics in Early Continental Southeast Asia* (Dordrecht-Holland, 1989); S. Chutintaranond, 'Mandala, Segmentary State and Politics of Centralization in Medieval Ayudhya', in: *Journal of the Siam Society*, 78 (1990), 89–100.

105 In a personal communication Chris Bayly made valuable comments after having read a draft of this Introduction. Thus, he suggests a 'further model [which] might stress that the state was neither centralised nor decentralised, but something which depended on its ability to arbitrate between contending local groups, tribes, classes etc., i.e. its strength was not so much an essential feature but a reflection of the nature of the society it was trying to govern.' Furthermore he asks whether there exists 'a kind of *shahbandar* port-king model of the sort which we have in south east Asia: e.g. the Zamorins of Calicut etc.?' And moreover he rightly wonders if 'Tambiah's galactic polity model [although developed for South East Asia] shouldn't receive attention.' (See previous note.)

Chapter Two

How Feudal was Indian Feudalism?

RAM SHARAN SHARMA

Several scholars have questioned the use of the term feudalism to characterize the early medieval socio-economic formation in India.[1] But the points raised by Harbans Mukhia[2] deserve serious attention. He rightly suggests that unlike capitalism feudalism is not a universal phenomenon. But in my view, tribalism, the stone age, the metal age and the advent of food producing economy are universal phenomena. They do indicate some laws conditioning the process and pattern of change.

Tribalism is universal and continues to be followed by different forms of state and class society. Tribal society has many variations. It can be connected with any of the modes of subsistence such as cattle pastoralism, other types of pastoralism, hoe agriculture, plough agriculture, etc. Agriculture requires co-operation and settlement at one place, and creates a lasting base for the tribal set-up. Many tribal societies practise shifting

[1] D.C. Sircar, *Landlordism and Tenancy in Ancient and Medieval India as Revealed by Epigraphical Records*, Lucknow, 1969. Also see *Journal of Indian History*, 44, 1966, pp. 351–7; 51, 1973, pp. 56–9; *Journal of Ancient Indian History*, 6, 1972–73, pp. 337–9; D.C. Sircar (ed.), *Land System and Feudalism in Ancient India* (Calcutta, 1966), pp. 11–23. Irfan Habib discusses 'Indian Feudalism' in *The Peasant in Indian History*, Presidential Address, The Indian History Congress, 43rd Session, Kurukshetra, 1982.

[2] 'Was There Feudalism in Indian History?', *The Journal of Peasant Studies*, vol. 8, no. 3, April 1981, pp. 273–310. In this paper the whole medieval period is discussed, but I will confine myself primarily to early medieval times (5th to 12th century), about which I have some idea. My task has been made easy because Dr Mukhia's criticisms have been effectively met by B.N.S. Yadava in *The Problem of the Emergence of Feudal Relations in Early India*, Presidential Address for Ancient India Section of the Indian History Congress, 41st Session, Bombay, 1980. In a similar address delivered at the 40th Session of the IHC held at Waltair in 1979, D.N. Jha anticipated and answered many of these objections in *Early Indian Feudalism: A Historiographical Critique*. Also see Suvira Jaiswal, 'Studies in Early Indian Social History', *Indian Historical Review*, 6, 1979–80, 18–21.

cultivation or swidden cultivation. But an advanced type of agriculture produces substantial surplus and creates dents in tribal homogeneity. Conditions emerge for the rise of classes based on status and wealth and above all for the large-scale exploitation of the bulk of the kinsmen by a few people on top. In such a situation the tribal system gets corroded.

Similarly, although the tribal society is organized on the principle of kinship, this organization could have large variations. Some form of organization, inherited from the band society needed for hunting, fishing, etc. is developed further at the tribal stage. Production efforts need co-operation and division of labour. But in the horticultural stage this could be on a matriarchal basis, and in the plough agricultural stage on a patriarchal basis. Co-operative production could also be based on a combination of the two, and in fact could rest on an organization based on all kinds of kinship combinations and permutations. Marriage practices and laws of 'property' inheritance may differ from one tribal society to another, and may differ even among members of the same tribe. In some kin-ordered communities elders arrange the marriage of their kinsmen in order to exercise some authority on them. In other communities privileged elders are concerned with regulating the marriages of only close kinsmen so that their social identity is maintained; the mass of the ordinary kinsmen is left free to marry and reproduce as it chooses to. But, inspite of these variations, tribal society has been found on a universal scale. Therefore the concept of tribe is useful even for an understanding of the social formations contained in written texts.

It is not necessary to posit the diffusion of tribal society although this may have taken place in certain cases. Although feudalism does not seem to be as universal as tribalism, in the Old World it was undoubtedly more widespread than the slave system. The concept of the peasant society is still in a nebulous state. But if the peasant society means a system in which the priests and warriors live on the surplus produced by peasants, augmented by the activities of the artisans, such a society existed in a good part of the Old World. Tribalism, the 'peasant society' or the slave system could have originated due to internal and/or external factors. Similarly it is not necessary to think in terms of the diffusion of the feudal system, although this happened in certain cases. For instance, the Norman Feudalism in England was a result of the Norman Conquest.

But there could be enormous variations in tribal society, as also in the nature of feudal societies. It is rightly stated by Marx that feudalism 'assumes different aspects, and runs through its various phases in different orders of succession'.[3] But certain universals remain the same. This is admitted even by critics of Indian feudalism who think of the variants of feudalism.[4] Feudalism has to be seen as a mechanism for the distribution of the means of production and for the appropriation of the surplus. It may have certain broad universal features, and it may have certain traits typical of a territory. Obviously land and agricultural products play a decisive role in pre-capitalist class societies, but the specificities of land distribution and the appropriation of agricultural products differ from region to region. It cannot be argued that what developed in pre-capitalist Western Europe was the same as in India and elsewhere. Historical laws, as far as they are known, do not work in this manner nor could one say that feudalism was the monopoly of Western Europe. It is not possible to have a clear-cut formula about feudalism. The most that one could say about the universal aspect of feudalism would be largely on the lines of Marc Bloch and E.A. Kosminsky.[5] Feudalism appears in a predominantly agrarian economy which is marked by a class of landlords and a class of servile peasantry. In this system the landlords extract surplus produce by social, religious or political means, which are called extra-economic methods. This seems to be more or less the current Marxist view of feudalism, which considers serfdom, 'scalar property' and 'parcellized sovereignty' as features of the West European version of the feudal system. The lord–peasant relationship is at the heart of the matter, and the exploitation of the estate by its owner, controller, enjoyer or beneficiary is its essential ingredient. Apart from these basic universal aspects feudalism may have several variations. The particularities of the system in some West European countries do not apply to the various types of feudalism found in other areas. For example, evidence of peasant struggles against landlords in other countries has not been produced in sufficient degree. Similarly artisanal and capitalist growth within the womb of feudalism seems to be typical of the West European situation where

[3] Marx-Engels, *Pre-Capitalist Socio-Economic Formations* (Moscow, 1979), p. 23.

[4] Mukhia, p. 310, fn. 225. In the discussion on variants Indian feudalism is seen as a distinct possibility.

[5] Kosminsky's views based on Marx and expressed in his *Studies in the Agrarian History of England in the Thirteenth Century* (Oxford, 1956), are summarized and discussed in Barry Hindess and Paul Q. Hirst, *Pre-Capitalist Modes of Production* (London, 1975), pp. 222–3, cf. pp. 234–5.

agricultural growth and substantial commodity production created major structural contradictions. The nature of religious beneficiaries, who appropriated a major portion of land, also differs from country to country. Thus the Church owned a substantial amount of land in Portugal. Buddhist and Confucian establishments controlled land in Korea. Buddhist monasteries were also important in eastern India. Temples emerged as estate-owners in South India, and many brahmanas enjoyed a similar position in the upper and middle Gangetic basin, Central India, the Deccan and Assam. In north India religious grantees did not have to pay taxes to the state although they fulfilled other obligations. But in south India in many cases they had to pay taxes. Non-religious landed intermediaries also appear in different forms in various parts of India and outside the country. In certain parts of the country, for example, in Orissa, we find tribal chiefs being elevated to the position of landlords. In other parts many administrative officials enjoyed land taxes from the peasants. But inspite of these variations the basic factor, namely the presence of a controlling class of landlords and a subject peasantry, remained the same in early medieval times and did not change until the sixteenth century when the central authority became stronger.

Again the degree of the servility of the peasants to the landlords differed from region to region, as also the composition of the cultivating class. The development of agriculture, handicrafts, commodity production, trade and commerce and urbanization created conditions for differentiation in the ranks of the peasantry. The peasants who produced more than their subsistence requirements could buy their freedom by payment of money in lieu of labour service provided such a practice was favoured by the state and a reasonable extent of market economy was available. Peasants could also be reduced to a state of further penury and rich peasants could grow at their cost. But where such developments did not take place, a more or less homogeneous peasantry continued. However, different farming techniques and the nature of the soil affected agricultural yields and created variations.

Similarly, peasants could be compelled to work as serfs on landlords' farms in addition to working on their own farms. This was a common practice in western Europe. But serfdom should not be considered identical with feudalism.[6] It was after all a form of servility, which kept the

[6] Marx considers tenants to be an object of feudal exploitation. According to him, the

peasant bound to the soil and made him work on the farm of his lord. The peasants who were compelled to pay heavy rents in cash and kind to the landlords or were required to provide both rent as well as labour were as servile as those who supplied only labour. The degree of servility is different if a peasant has to bear allegiance only to the landlord. If he has to be loyal to both the state and the landlord, it becomes a case of double servility or of divided loyalty. But the fundamental point at issue is the subjection of the peasantry, and this subjection is found in all the situations referred to earlier. There is no doubt that this was a characteristic feature of the early medieval Indian social structure.

It is argued that the peasant in medieval India enjoyed autonomy of production because he had 'complete' control over the means of production.[7] What is the significance of owning the means of production? Do the fruits of production stay with the peasant or are these substantially siphoned off by the landlord? How does this appropriation become possible? What is the mechanism that enables the landlord to appropriate the surplus? Is it merely because of his control over the means of production or is it because of his coercive power? Is it extracted through an ideological weapon, such as the peasant's belief that he is duty bound to pay? The latter ideology that the landlords are the parents of the peasants[8] is reminiscent of the tribal outlook. But this idea may have been further fostered by the priestly landlords in medieval times. At present I will not try to answer all these questions but take up the problem of the distribution of the resources of production in early medieval India.

Obviously land was the primary means of production. But if we think in terms of exclusive control over land by one party or the other it becomes extremely difficult to understand the distribution of land. It should be made clear that in early medieval times, in the same piece of land, the peasants held inferior rights and the landlords held superior rights. Peasants may have possessed land, labour, oxen, other animals and agricultural implements. But we have to ascertain how effective was his 'control' over

---

feudal lord differs from the bourgeois in that he 'does not try to extract the utmost advantage from his land. Rather he consumes what is there and calmly leaves the worry of producing to the serfs and tenants'. Marx-Engels, p. 20. In the 1880s Engels also concluded that serfdom is not solely a 'peculiarly medieval-feudal form', ibid., p. 23. This implies that the feudal formation could have other features.

7 Mukhia, pp. 275, 290–1, 293.

8 I owe this to Ranajit Guha.

the means of production. Did other conditions such as taxes, forced labour and constant interference by beneficiaries who were ever present, make the peasant's control really operational? The peasant class was like the proverbial hen that lay the golden eggs, and so the peasants were allowed to stay alive and multiply themselves, but were not given effective control over the means of production.

In fact land grants leave no doubt that the landlord enjoyed a good measure of general control in the means of production. Why did the landlords claim various types of rents from the peasants and how could they collect the rents? Clearly they did so on the strength of royal charters which conferred on them either the villages or pieces of land or by imposing various types of taxes. Why did the king claim taxes? Formerly the king claimed taxes on the ground that he afforded protection to the people. In early medieval law books it is stated that he claimed taxes on the ground that he was the owner of the land.[9] Numerous epithets indicate that the king was the owner of the land in early medieval times.[10] By a charter he delegated this royal authority to his beneficiary who then claimed taxes. The king was called *bhūmidaḥ* or giver of land. It was repeatedly said that the merit of giving land accrues to him who possesses it.[11]

Generally the early charters gave the beneficiary usufructuary rights. But the later charters granted such concessions as rendered the beneficiary the de facto owner of the village land. The donated village/villages constituted his estate. For example, the beneficiary was entitled to collect taxes, all kinds of income, all kinds of occasional taxes, and this 'all' (*sarva*)[12] was never specified. Similarly, he was entitled to collect proper and improper taxes,[13] fixed and not fixed taxes,[14] and at the end of the

[9] The king is called *bhūsvāmin* by Kātyāyana, a lawgiver of about the sixth century (P.V. Kane, ed., verse 16).

[10] R.S. Sharma, 'From Gopati to Bhūpati' (A review of the changing position of the king), *Studies in History*, II (2) 1980, pp. 6–8.

[11] *vasya yasyu yudū bhūmiḥ, tasya tasya tadā phalam*, D.C. Sircar (ed.), *Select Inscriptions Bearing on Indian History and Civilisation*, vol. I (University of Calcutta, 1965) (abbrev. as *Sel. Inscr.*), bk III, no. 49, line 26.

[12] The terms used are *sarvoparikarakarādānasametaḥ*, *sarvakarasametaḥ*, *sarvakara-visarjitaḥ*,.see Balchandra Jain, *Utkīrṇa-Lekha* (Raipur, 1961), pp. 56–7. The terms *samastapratyāya* and *sarvāyasameta* also occur (Sharma, *Indian Feudalism*, 2nd edn, p. 100). Also see *sarvādānāsaṃagrāhya*, *Epigraphia Indica*, V, no. 5, line 14.

[13] R.S. Sharma, *Indian Feudalism*, 2nd edn, pp. 98–100.

[14] The phrase used is *niyatāniyatasamastādāya*, all specified and unspecified dues.

list of taxes the term 'et cetera' (*ādi, ādikam*)[15] was used. All this added enormously to the power of the beneficiary. These extraordinary provisions could serve as a self-regulating mechanism as and when production increased,[16] but they could also interfere with the expansion of production. Some provisions clearly give superior rights to the beneficiary in the land of the peasants. For instance, the land charters of Madhya Pradesh, northern Maharashtra, Konkan and Gujarat in Gupta and post-Gupta times empowered the beneficiary to evict the old peasants and introduce new ones; he could assign lands to others. A similar provision occurs in Coḷa charters. But it is taken to mean that the beneficiary had the right to vary the rates of taxation and impose additional dues and services in later Coḷa times.[17] In any case all such concessions leave no doubt that the beneficiary was armed with superior rights in land, which was actually occupied by the cultivator. Most grants after the seventh century AD gave away the village along with the lowland, fertile land, water reservoirs, all kinds of trees and bushes, pathways and pasture grounds. In charters from eastern India the village was granted along with mango trees, *mahuā* (Bassia latifolia) and jack-fruit trees and various other agrarian resources. Cotton, hemp, coconut and areca-nut trees are also given away in grants, but this happened mostly after the tenth century when cash crops assumed importance. Such provisions connected the agrarian production directly with the beneficiary and, more importantly, transfered almost all communal agrarian resources to him. Since the peasant did not have free access to various agrarian resources his autonomy in production was substantially crippled. Plough agriculture depended entirely on the use of cattle. What a peasant possessed was not sufficient to feed the cattle. For this purpose continued unrestricted use of the common pasture resources was essential. But the grant of these resources to the beneficiary created a difficult situation for the peasant for several restrictions were imposed on the use of the common pastures. The beneficiary could appropriate the best pasture grounds for his own cattle, could allocate the resources

---

Epigraphia Indica, XII, no. 36, line 12.

[15] *Epigraphia Indica*, XXIX, no. 7, line 42; Jain, p. 52.

[16] Mukhia rightly postulates that the village potentates would be the first to notice the rise in productivity and the first to demand a greater share in the peasant's produce, p. 309, fn. 214.

[17] R. Tirumalai, *Land Grants and Agrarian Reactions in Coḷa and Pāṇḍya Times* (University of Madras, 1987), p. 31.

to peasant families on certain conditions or even bar their access to the grazing fields as a measure of coercion. It has to be appreciated that the free exercise of agrarian rights can make a household unit effective in production, but until recent times powerful landlords effectively stopped the weak and helpless peasants from exercising such rights. Of course the caste system was also responsible for this situation. The untouchables did not have access to public tanks, wells, etc. Even if they possessed bits of land how could they function independently in production?

Most charters asked the peasants to carry out the orders of the beneficiaries.[18] These orders would relate not only to the payment of taxes which were concerned with the fruits of production but would also relate to the means and processes of production. In a way the blanket authority to extract obedience from the peasant placed him at the mercy of the beneficiary. It implied general control over his labour power which undoubtedly is an essential ingredient of the means of production. This labour could be used either in the fields cultivated by the peasant or in those directly managed by the beneficiary. The beneficiaries could insist on having certain types of produce for their ostentatious and unproductive consumption, and with all the seignorial rights that they possessed they could compel the peasants to produce those cereals or cash crops which they needed.

The law books of Yājñavalkya, Bṛhaspati and Vyāsa specify four graded stages of land rights in the same piece of land. Thus we hear of the *mahīpati*, *kṣetrasvāmin*, *karṣaka* and the sub-tenant of leaseholder.[19] It is important that the medieval jurists understood *svāmitva* in the sense of ownership and *svata* in the sense of property, and this was considered to be a significant distinction in Hindu law.[20] The *svāmin* therefore could be equated with the landed beneficiary and the *karṣaka* or the *ksetrika* with the rent-paying tenant peasant. Multiple, hierarchical rights and interests in land, which was the chief means of production, can be inferred even from Gupta land sale transactions. These transactions mention the interest of not only the king but also that of the local administrative body (*adhikarana*) dominated by powerful men; beneficiaries and the rights of

[18] The phrase *ājñāśravaṇavidheyībhūya* is common in north Indian grants.

[19] The point has been discussed in R.S. Sharma, *Indian Feudalism*, 2nd edn (Delhi, 1980), pp. 38–9.

[20] The distinction is brought out clearly in P.N. Sen, *The General Principles of Hindu Jurisprudence*, Tagore Law Lectures, 1909 (University of Calcutta, 1918), p. 42..

the occupier of the plots are also mentioned.[21] Of course in several Gupta transactions no occupier is mentioned, and it further appears that money for the purchase of the land is paid not only to the adhikaraṇa but also probably to the occupier. These typical land transactions are found in Bangladesh. But in the grant system which became widespread in post-Gupta times the local adhikaraṇa disappeared, and was generally not consulted in matters of land grants.

Hierarchical control over land was created by large-scale subinfeudation, especially from the eighth century onwards.[22] This appears in both north and south India. At one stage under the Coḷas there were as many as five grades in its landed hierarchy. It consisted of the king on top followed by the assignee and then the occupant who leased land to the sub-occupant who finally got it tilled by the cultivating tenant.[23] Subinfeudation gave rise to a hierarchy of landlords, different from the actual tillers of the soil. Such a process seems to be in line with a significant generalization made by Marx about feudalism. According to him, 'feudal production is characterized by division of soil amongst the greatest possible number of sub-feudatories'.[24]

The peasantry was divested more and more of its homogeneous and egalitarian character. Many indications of unequal distribution of land in the village are available. We hear not only of brāhmaṇas but also of the chief brāhmaṇa, *mahattama, uttama, kṛṣivala, karṣaka, kṣetrakara, kuṭumbin* and *kāruka,* land endowed brāhmaṇas and *agrahāras.* We also hear of *kṣudra prakṛti* or petty peasants, and of Meda, Andhra and Caṇḍāla. It is obvious that certain people in the villages had a greater share in the sources of production and apparently possessed more than they could manage directly. Such people got their lands cultivated by petty peasants either through lease holding, sharecropping or the system of serfdom. We have therefore no means of establishing that most of the peasants living in villages were in 'complete' control of the means of production.

Terminological studies throw an interesting and revealing light on the relation of the peasant to the land in early India. The English term

21 *Sel. Inscr.*, bk III, nos 16, 18, 19, 41, 42, 43, etc.

22 Sharma, *Indian Feudalism,* 2nd edn, pp. 73–5, 185–7.

23 R. Tirumalai, *Land Grants and Agrarian Reactions in Coḷa and Pāṇḍya Times* (University of Madras, 1987), p. 60.

24 Marx-Engels, *Pre-Capitalist Socio-Economic Formations,* p. 22.

peasant, which literally means rustic or countryman, can be translated into *jānapada*, which means an inhabitant of the countryside. That the janapada or the territorial unit formed by the countryside was considered to be a source of revenue is well known. Among the other qualities of a janapada are those of possessing active peasants capable of bearing taxes and fines (punishments).[25] Oppression of the peasantry led to revolt (*janapada-kopa*), a term used in the *Arthaśāstra* of Kauṭilya.[26] Curiously the term janapada is not much in use in medieval Sanskrit literature although it occurs in early medieval inscriptions. In medieval times *jana* came to mean a dependent who was valued for his labour power. Thus he could be a servile peasant. What is more significant, in several Indo-Aryan dialects of Bihar the term means field labourer. In practice some of these labourers are given small patches of land to earn their subsistence. This practice is apparently a survival of the medieval system according to which jana or field workers were possessed by and transferred to landed magnates, as can be inferred not only from inscriptions but also from works on horoscopy.[27] This would show that the tribal jana with an egalitarian ethos was reduced to almost a serf.

The terms for the peasant used in medieval texts, and particularly in inscriptions, signify the change in the nature of the peasant's relation to the land he cultivated. From the age of the Buddha to the advent of the Gupta period tax-paying vaiśyas continued as an omnibus order, comprising mostly peasants. However, by early medieval times they were reduced to the position of the śūdras, who in spite of having acquired peasanthood, continued to bear the hallmark of servitude.[28] *Gahapati*, literally head of the household, was the term used for the landowning peasant in early Pāli texts[29] typical of the middle Gangetic plains which witnessed the rise of the first large states. He seems to have enjoyed substantial autonomy in his unit of production. But the term almost

25 . . . *sadaṇḍakarasahaḥ karmaśīlakarṣakò balīśasvāmyavaravarṇaprāyo janapadasampat. Arthaśāstra* (of Kauṭilya), R.P. Kangle's edn, VI.1.

26 *AŚ*, 1. 13. The term *prakṛtikopa* or revolt of the subjects is used in V.6 and VII.6.

27 B.N.S. Yadava, *The Problem of the Emergence of Feudal Relations in Early India*, p. 7, contains several references to the acquisition of *jana*.

28 R.S. Sharma, *Śūdras in Ancient India*, 2nd edn (Delhi, 1980), ch. VII.

29 The term used is *kassaka gahapati*, 'cultivating family head', *Aṅguttara-Nikāya* (Pali Text Society, London), i, pp. 239–40. But *gahapati* in the sense of substantial peasants is used in Pāli texts at many places.

disappears in land grant inscriptions. Gahapati or *gṛhapati* becomes the village headman in later texts.[30] A clear term for the peasant is *kṣetrika* or *kṣatrin*,[31] which means controller of land, but even this is sometimes understood as an agriculturist or cultivator in later texts and lexicons. From kṣetrika in Assamese is derived *khetiyaka*,[32] which means cultivator or husbandman, who was not necessarily the owner of the field. A common term used for the peasant in many grants, especially in those from eastern India, is *kṣetrakara*,[33] which literally means cultivator. The term *seti* in Marathi is probably derived from it,[34] and does not always mean the owner of the land. Some other terms used in inscriptions are karṣaka[35] and *kuṭumbin*.[36] The term kuṭumbin gives some indication of an autonomous peasant family, but it occurs mainly in early land records from eastern India and Madhya Pradesh. In later grants from eastern India it is replaced by kṣetrakara or karṣaka. In Gujarat and Rajasthan the *kuṭumbika* lost his status, for he was sometimes transferred to the beneficiary along with the land.[37] According to Yājñavalkya (*c.* AD 300) the karṣaka is a mere cultivator in the service of the landowner or kṣetrasvāmin, whose field lay under the general control of the king (*mahāpati*).[38] In the Candella grants in eastern Madhya Pradesh the *karṣaka* was made over to the assignee along with the village.[39] Land grants also use the term *hālika*[40] or ploughman. Sharecroppers are called *ārddhika*, *arddhasīirika* or *ardhasīrin*. In literature the word *kīnāśa* is also used.[41] Evidently these terms have nothing to do with control over land. The term *kisan*, now so common in India, is derived from *Kṛśāna* or one who ploughs. The

30 s.v. *griha*, Monier-Williams, *A Sanskrit-English Dictionary* (Oxford, 1951).

31 R.L. Turner, *A Comparative Dictionary of the Indo-Aryan Languages* (Oxford, 1973), no. 3736.

32 Ibid.

33 R. Mukherji and S.K. Maity, *Corpus of Bengal Inscriptions Bearing on the History and Civilization of Bengal* (Calcutta, 1967), no. 18, line 45; no. 22, line 46; no. 28, line 52; no. 30, line 48; no. 36, line 36; no. 37, line 32.

34 Turner, no. 3736.

35 Mukherji and Maity, no. 47, line 50.

36 Ibid., no. 7, line 3; no. 9, line 3 (p. 59).

37 Sharma, *Indian Feudalism*, 2nd edn, pp. 188–9.

38 Ibid., p. 38.

39 Ibid., p. 188.

40 Ibid., p. 98, fn. 3, p. 99.

41 It is taken in the sense of a ploughman. See B.N.S. Yadava, *The Problem of the Emergence of Feudal Relations in Early India*, p. 25.

word *kṛṣīvala*[42] or cultivator is also frequently used in medieval texts. The term *lāṅgalopajīvin* or one who lives by ploughing is used in the *Bṛhat Saṃhitā*.[43]

A review of the terms used for the peasant in medieval inscriptions and literature fails to present the peasant's image as a controller of land. On the other hand we have such technical terms as *bhoktā, bhogī, bhogika, bhogijana, bhogapati, bhogapatika, bhogikapālaka, bhogirūpa, mahābhogī, bṛhadbhogī, bṛhadbhogika*, etc. used generally for those who enjoyed landed property.[44] Here I have not taken into account many other terms connected with *rājā, rāṇaka, sāmanta, maṇḍaleśvara*, etc. who were powerful landed intermediaries. The contrast between the two types of terms is obvious. Some people were meant for cultivating land and some for enjoying the fruits of production although in this category people did not share the surplus equally. There is nothing to show that the peasants who produced were in firm and independent control of their holdings. And finally there was the state symbolized by the king, whose general authority over land was recognized by numerous epithets used for him in early medieval records.[45]

It has been stated earlier that there were superior and inferior rights over the same piece of land,[46] but the common phrase 'means of production' was not used in that context. It may be added now that the practice of granting a village along with all the possible taxes and impositions and with all its resources created a kind of feudal property in contrast to peasant property and communal rights. This new phenomenon was troublesome to medieval jurists and law commentators, who found neither sanction nor a precedent in the early law books. Therefore Vijñāneśvara, the famous author of *Mitākṣarā*, which enjoyed authority in a large part of the country in legal matters, propounded the principle of the popular recognition of property. He and his followers, including Mitra

[42] s.v. *kṛṣīvala*, Monier-Williams.

[43] B.N.S. Yadava, *The Problem of the Emergence of Feudal Relations in Early India*, p. 32.

[44] Sharma, *Indian Feudalism*, 2nd edn, pp. 12–13, 216.

[45] These terms are *avanīśa, avanīndra, kṣitipati, kṣitēndra, kṣitīśa, kṣiteradhipa, pārthiva, pṛthivīpati, pārthivendra, pṛthivīnātha, bhūpa, bhūpati, bhūbhuj, bhūmipa, bhūmīśvara, mahīpa, mahīpati, mahīpāla, mahīndra, mahāmahendra, urvīpati, vasudhādhipa, vasudheśvara, sāmanta-bhūmīśvara*, etc. R.S. Sharma, 'From Gopati to Bhūpati, *Studies in History*, II (2), 1980, p. 8 with fns. 81–2.

[46] R.S. Sharma, *Indian Feudalism* (Calcutta, 1965), ch. IV.

Miśra, maintained that property has its basis in popular recognition without any dependence on the Śāstras.[47] Commenting on a passage of Gautama,[48] Haradatta, in about the twelfth century, expressed a similar view. According to him, even a short-term enjoyment of *bhūmi*, which is explained as a cultivated field (*kṣetra*) and orchards, gardens, etc. (*ārāmadikā*), confers property rights on the person.[49] Short-term enjoyment probably means a period of less than ten years.[50] The complexities caused by the superimposition of new rights on the means of production hitherto effectively controlled by the peasants, also because of their free access to various village resources, baffled medieval jurists who had to recognize the multiplicity of rights over the same piece of land. 'The Indian jurists took it for granted that the incidents of particular manifestations of ownership might differ, while the *svatva* (rights)[51] of the king, the svatva of the landowner, the svatva of the tenant-farmer, and in an extreme case, even the svatva of the mortgagee in possession (as against a trespasser) were all comprehensible under the single term of property.'[52] It has been shown that in law as well as in actual practice these rights were graded. In the Indian context one could therefore talk of the varying degrees of control over land and not of exclusive rights of either the landlord or the peasant. But the grants show an increasing tendency to establish the superior rights of the landlord at the cost of both the king and the peasantry so much so that ultimately assignments were converted into virtual estates.

47 P.N. Sen, *The General Principles of Hindu Jurisprudence, Tagore Law Lectures*, 1909 (University of Calcutta, 1918), pp. 42–3, 46. The theory of popular recognition, which gives preference to unwritten laws, is known as *laukika svatvavāda* (ibid., p. 42). Several logicians such as Guru, Kumārila Svāmí and Pārthasarathi Miśra, who interpreted the Dharmaśāstras according to the canons of *mimāṃsā* also supported the popular recognition theory. Jimūtavahana, Dhāreśvara, etc. supported the śāstric view (ibid., p. 42). The difference does reflect conflicting claims to land control in early medieval times.

48 *Gautama Dharmasūtra* (Varanasi, 1966), II.3.36. The passage reads *paśu bhūmistrīṇāmanatibhogaḥ.*

49 *alpenāpi bhogena bhoktuḥ svaṃ bhavati.* Comm. on Gautama, II.3.36. This interpretation covers cattle and women slaves. It is interesting that a ten-year limit of enjoyment is set for acquiring ownership over the property of others in several cases by the commentator. Comm. on Gautama, II.3.34–35.

50 Comm. on Gautama, II.3.34–35.

51 *Svatva* should be taken in the sense of property rights, as has been done by P.N. Sen, p. 42.

52 J.D.M. Derrett in *Bulletin of the School of the Oriental and African Studies*, vol. XVIII, p. 489.

More effective control over the means of production accrued in cases of the transfer of land plots to beneficiaries. Many big plots of land in Vidarbha and Maharashtra were assigned to gods and brāhmaṇas under the Vākāṭakas and also under the Raṣṭrakūṭas. For example, 8000 *nivartanas* of land were granted to one thousand brāhmaṇas by Pravarasena.[53] Similarly, 400 nivartanas of land were granted to a single brāhmaṇa.[54] Again, the same measure of land was granted to a god.[55] Further, 2052 nivartanas of land were granted to brāhmaṇas.[56] We learn from earlier authorities that in the Deccan 6 nivartanas were considered to be sufficient to maintain the family of a brāhmaṇa comprising 5 to 8 members. But such large stretches of land could not be cultivated by the brāhmaṇa beneficiaries themselves. Even if labour was available in a brāhmaṇa family for cultivating smaller pieces of land, the members would not actually cultivate it because of social inhibitions. But, more importantly, grants of large plots introduced an element of direct control by the beneficiaries over the means of production.

An important factor which gave the beneficiaries general control over the means of production was the conferment of seignorial rights on them. The charters authorized the beneficiaries to punish people guilty of ten offences,[57] including those against the family, property, individual persons, etc., and to try civil cases.[58] Further, royal officers were not allowed to enter their territory[59] and cause any kind of obstruction in their functioning.[60] All these were as good as manorial rights, and could even enable the beneficiaries to force the peasants to work in their fields. It would appear that the right to try cases on the spot involving the imposition of fines could seriously interfere with the process of production. It is therefore obvious that the political and judicial rights, which were non-economic rights, helped the beneficiaries to effectively exploit estate peasants economically. This may have been a successful way of governing the vast

53 V.V. Mirashi, *Inscriptions of the Vākāṭakas, Corpus Inscriptionum Indicarum*, vol. V, Ootacamund, 1955, no. 6, lines 19–20.

54 Ibid., no. 12, lines 20–1.

55 Ibid., no. 13, lines 22–3.

56 Ibid., no. 14, lines 22–32.

57 Sharma, *Indian Feudalism*, 2nd edn, p. 3; the common term used is *sadaṇḍadaśāparādhaḥ*.

58 Ibid., the term *abhyantarasiddhi* is used.

59 Ibid., p. 2.

60 *Sel. Inscr.*, bk III, no. 62, lines 21–2.

population because the perpetrators of crime could be dealt with immediately. At the same time these non-economic rights served to enforce the general economic authority of the beneficiaries over both the means and the processes of production. It may further be noted that in many cases the beneficiaries were empowered to adopt any means of enjoying the benefits accruing from the villages, and the term used for this was *sarvopāya-saṃyuktam.*[61] They were also authorized to enjoy the fruits of production at their own free will. If we carefully examine the phrase *sambhogyā yavadichchā kriyāphalam*[62] it would mean that the donee could even intervene in the process of production. If a person is entitled to enjoy the fruits of production at his discretion, he may develop a natural tendency to control the process (*kriyā*) itself on which the nature and the amount of yield depend. Sometimes whatever belonged to the village (*svasaṃbhoga sametaḥ*) was to be enjoyed by the beneficiary.[63] He was also granted the village along with all its products (*sarvotpattisahitaḥ*).[64] The Candella charters from eastern Madhya Pradesh name the crops that were produced in the donated villages. It is also probable that the peasant could not alter the pattern of crops but whether or not it was so, the interest of the landed beneficiary in the means and process of production is very evident. It would be extraordinary for the beneficiary not to keep an eye over the resources, processes and fruits of production in such cases.

It is not clear how the peasants were provided with agricultural implements. The charters authorized the beneficiaries to enjoy all that was hidden under the earth. This would amount to giving mining rights to the beneficiaries. It is well known that the mining rights belonged exclusively to the king. The king may have acquired this monopoly at the initial stage as the head of the tribe or the community, but once this exclusive control over iron and other minerals passed into the hands of the beneficiaries, they would be in a position to control the supply of agricultural implements to the peasants. But in pre-feudal times the big landowners did not have such rights. Mining rights belonged to the king who symbolized the community, and the peasants probably did not experience difficulties in procuring agricultural implements.

61 Mukherji and Maity, *Corpus of Bengal Inscriptions*, no. 47, line 62.

62 Ibid., line 63.

63 Ibid., no. 46, line 22.

64 *Epigraphia Indica*, V, no. 20, line 54. The village, situated near Nagpur, was granted by Kṛṣṇa III in 940–41.

Not only were the successors of the king and the people in power asked to observe the terms of the grants[65] but also all those who would upset the grants were threatened with the use of force.[66] In some warnings corporal punishment (*śarīradaṇḍam*) is clearly mentioned.[67] The threat to use force is contained mostly in grants from Madhya Pradesh, Maharashtra, Andhra and Karnatak, and the earliest example is found in a Pallava grant of the fourth century from Guntur district. In addition, the opponents of land grants were threatened with all kinds of curses. The idea that a peasant was the complete master of the means of production is also belied by the philosophical teachings found at the end of most grants. The grants underline the instability of life with regard to not only death but also to the fickleness of fortune. The concept of the fickleness of fortune (i.e. mobility of Lakṣmī) is mainly derived from the frequent transfer of control over the means of production from one person to another. Ideology and rituals were used for indoctrinating producers in ancient times also. Through ideology, rituals and administration, the priests and warriors regulated production and distribution in pre-feudal times, but now they acquired an effective control of the means of production which was the land. Initially the beneficiary would claim state-sanctioned dues from the peasants but in course of time his claims would be made so comprehensive that due to his local presence and delegated administrative powers, he could begin to treat the donated village as his estate. Clearly the peasants had to reckon with the control of the donee over the village resources.

The real problem therefore is not to demonstrate the autonomy of peasant production which in any case was drastically curtailed in the land grant areas. It is more worthwhile to examine the position of the peasant population working in the land grant areas and that of similar people working in the non-land grant areas in medieval times.[68] Since references

[65] D.C. Sircar (ed.), *Select Inscriptions Bearing on Indian History and Civilization*, vol. I (University of Calcutta, 1965) (abbrev. as *Sel. Inscr.*), bk III, no. 49, lines 18–28; no. 50, lines 15–23.

[66] . . . *sadaṇḍanigrahaṃ karisyāmaḥ*. This phrase is found with slight variations in many charters. Ibid., no. 61, II. 22–4; no. 62, II. 32–4; no. 64, II. 21–4; no. 65, II. 39–41; no. 67, II. 24–5.

[67] Ibid., no. 67, II. 24–5.

[68] In the context of a slave society it is held that if 20 per cent of the people are engaged in production as slaves, it should be considered a slave society. Five such societies have been identified. Keith Hopkins, *Conquerors and Slaves* (Cambridge, 1978),

to palm-leaf (*tālapatra*) and birch-bark (*bhūrjapatra śāsanas*) charters even for religious purposes are found in Assam and Madhya Pradesh it is likely that many such grants were issued in favour of both religious and secular parties. We learn how these *patra* grants were burnt and replaced by copper plate charters in Assam[69] and Madhya Pradesh.[70] Another major problem is to identify and plot on maps the donated villages as well as other villages or plots of land region-wise within a short time span (say within half a century or so). I have shown earlier that in the donated villages the beneficiaries enjoyed superior authority over the means of production. Donated fields, many of them very large in area, were without doubt directly and completely controlled by the beneficiaries, who manipulated the production resources and processes. How this influenced the course of production in 'free' villages has to be investigated.

It is argued that landed beneficiaries were mainly concerned with the problem of surplus collection. But the question of surplus collection/distribution cannot be viewed in isolation from that of the pattern of production. In a feudal system of production there was the lord's share called rent, in labour and cash/kind, and this was coupled with a patron–client system of distribution, primarily between the peasant and the landlord. For surplus collection superior rights in the land of the peasants became the precondition. The more the produce, the greater was the surplus collection. In pre-Gupta times the surplus was mainly collected by the agents of the state in the form of taxes, or by priests in the form of gifts. A few landowners working with the help of slaves and hired labourers existed in the age of the Buddha. We hear of state farms in the *Arthaśāstra* of Kauṭilya. But state control could operate only in small areas. By and large the settled part of the country had independent peasant units of production and was also blessed with a market economy. However, the market economy was not strong enough to enable rich landowners to invest capital in new enterprises and work for profits which would eventually lead them on to the path of capitalism. At best a millionaire such as Anāthapiṇḍika would purchase land for donation to the Buddha. Payment in cash could be made for the sale of cereals and for the purchase

pp. 99–100. But the qualitative place of slaves or other categories of servile people in the total mode of production deserves equal consideration.

[69] D.C. Sircar, *Indian Epigraphy* (Delhi, 1965), p. 97, fn. 2.

[70] Balchandra Jain, *Utkirṇa-Lekh* (Raipur, 1961), no. 3, II. 6–11, p. 8.

of petty commodities by the peasants. Generally in pre-feudal times the priests, warriors and administrators were entitled to the surplus in the form of taxes and gifts for services rendered, but a good part of these payments was made in cash. Peasant units of production first appeared in the age of the Buddha and not in post-Maurya times. Slave labour was neither preponderant nor negligible in production. Large holdings, including state farms, were worked by slaves and hired labourers in the middle Gangetic plains, and big landowners were swamped by peasants. The vaiśya, who was almost identical with the peasant, was the principal taxpayer. His counterpart in the Buddhist idiom was a peasant householder who contributed to the increase in cereal production and paid taxes to the state (*gahapatiko kārkārako rāsivaḍḍhako*). Thus the peasant units of production functioned more or less effectively in pre-Gupta times. But after that the authority of the peasants over these units diminished because of landed beneficiaries and because of the dwindling of trade and urbanism. In India the problem of the rise of the landed magnates is not connected with 'the decomposition of the slave mode of production' but with the decreasing control of the peasant over his unit of production coupled with his restricted access to the communal agrarian resources. As will be shown later, overtaxation and imposition of forced labour by the state created problems which called for new remedies.

Historical examples show that the fight for a share in the produce definitely affects production. This is true even of capitalist societies in which such fights eventually lead to structural changes. In early medieval times beneficiaries demanded a larger share of the produce because of their superior rights over the land. Since the object of the grants was to maintain the beneficiaries and provide their requirements either for the purpose of worship or for domestic consumption, the peasants could be compelled to produce those cereals which were required by the donee.

If a part of the product is placed at the disposal of the grantee, what is the difference between enjoying the means of production, that is land, and the fruits of production? Land does not mean anything without its products. There is a medieval saying that whoever seizes land rich in crops (*sasyasamṛdhāṃ vasundharām*) is guilty of a great sin. Surplus was collected not only after production but also in the course of production. On-the-spot collection and quick administration was the most effective way of managing a large population.

On the basis of the land charters we can say that in the donated areas the landed beneficiaries enjoyed general control over production resources. Of course they did not enjoy specific control over every plot of land that the peasant cultivated. But there is nothing to question their control over the plots of lands that were directly donated to them by the king, sometimes along with the sharecroppers[71] and weavers and sometimes along with the cultivators.[72] This raises the problem of serfdom. It is thought that feudalism was identical with serfdom, and there seems to be an assumption that serfdom was the only potent method of exploiting the peasants. It may be very effective, but other forms of servitude imposed on the peasantry were equally effective. After all what is the essence of serfdom? In this system small farm units are attached to big farm units, and the two are interdependent for purposes of production. Big farms are directly managed by manorial magnates but are cultivated by those who possess small plots. Therefore serfdom means giving more surplus labour for less surplus produce. But in the Indian context surplus produce is extracted more through the general control exercised by landed intermediaries than by the employment of serfs. A serf also occupies some land and provides his family with subsistence. But he not only pays rent in cash or kind for exploiting his unit of production but also spends extra hours labouring on the field of his lord. The extra yield which accrues from these extra hours of labour does not necessarily stay with the cultivator. On the other hand it enables him to pay more rent in cash or kind to his lord.

It has been argued that serfdom is an incidental feature in the case of India.[73] But the evidence cited so far would show that it is more than incidental.[74] In any case if the landlord gets his share without reducing too many people to serfdom, what basic difference does it make to him or to the social pattern. In both systems the landlord is concerned with extracting his share; in both the cultivator is a dependent peasant, exploited by his landlord; and in both the social structure is beset with the

[71] *Sel. Inscr.*, bk III, no. 65, II. 38–9.

[72] Ibid., no. 61, 1.15.

[73] Mukhia, p. 286.

[74] R.S. Sharma, *Indian Feudalism*, 2nd edn (Delhi, 1980), pp. 19, 31, 40–3, 56, 60, 67–8, 99–101, 109, 195–8; B.N.S. Yadava, *Society and Culture*, pp. 164–9; 'Immobility and Subjection of Indian Peasantry in Early Medieval Complex', *The Indian Historical Review*, 1, 1974, 18–27. A good deal of evidence can be obtained from G.K. Rai, *Involuntary Labour in Ancient India* (Allahabad, 1981), but the passage from Vātsyāyana's *Kāmasūtra* (V.5.5) is inaccurately construed and translated.

contradiction between the landlord and the actual tiller. A beneficiary may not have possessed big plots of land, but he may have possessed too many plots which made management difficult. In fact laws regarding the partition of land became effective in Gupta and post-Gupta times[75] and they may have contributed to the fragmentation of land. The fragmentation of land is also indicated by epigraphic sale transactions found in Bangladesh.[76] Therefore if a landlord possessed too many plots, tenanting and sharecropping would be more convenient than getting the land cultivated by serfs.

It is held that because soil in India was very fertile there was no scope for the rise of serfdom or forced labour.[77] But we have indications of forced labour in the middle Gangetic basin where the soil is most fertile. Till recent times poor tenants, belonging to the lower castes, were forced by upper caste landlords to work in the fields at meagre wages.[78] Peasants were compelled to plough the land of the landlords and do various kinds of odd jobs for them in other fertile areas. This is known as *harī* and *begārī* in the whole of the Gangetic basin area. The medieval term harī is *halikākara*,[79] and for *begārī viṣṭi*, from which *beṭh-begārī* is derived. The Pāla charters found in Monghyr, Bhagalpur, Saharsa and Nalanda districts, all part of the middle Gangetic plain, mention the term *sarvapīḍāparihṛta*. This means that the peasants were subjected to forced labour and oppression, and when a village was transferred to a beneficiary he became entitled to these advantages without the interference of the state. Forced labour may have originated in less populated areas but not necessarily in less fertile parts. In any case once its usefulness was recognized it spread to more populated parts.

Feudalism flourished in paddy producing areas. Paddy production requires 50 per cent more man hours than does wheat production. According to a popular saying in Patna and Gaya districts in Bihar, wheat cultivation can be undertaken even by a widow, who represents an image of helplessness in the countryside. Evidently wheat cultivation requires less labour and barley cultivation even less. Therefore at the time of paddy

75 Sharma, *Indian Feudalism*, 2nd edn, pp. 118–19.

76 Ibid., p. 49.

77 Mukhia, pp. 286, 289, 303, fn. 124.

78 This was the case in north Bihar until the abolition of the Permanent Settlement.

79 Y.B. Singh, 'Halikākara: Crystallization of a Practice into a Tax', Paper presented to the 43rd Session of the Indian History Congress, Kurukshetra, 1982.

transplantation there would be scarcity of labour; and it would be necessary to take on forced labour. The term *sotpadyamānaviṣṭi* is used frequently[80] and has been translated to mean the use of forced labour as the occasion demands. But since the term qualifies donated land or a donated village, it might mean the labour generated or produced by the village in future.[81] This was a significant development in a good part of the country. It would imply that besides customary sources of forced labour new sources could be exploited by the beneficiaries according to their needs. Unfortunately these sources are not specified in medieval records. That there were various types of forced labour is clear from the use of the term *sarvaviṣṭi*[82] in many land grants, particularly in Vākāṭaka grants. These many types may have included the use of labour in the fields in central and western India. However in northern India *viṣṭi* meant the right to compel the rural population to construct forts, roads, etc., and to help the authorities in transport, *vetti* is frequently mentioned in south Indian charters. At present in parts of north Andhra Pradesh around Srikakulam vetti stands for bonded labourers who are forced to do all kinds of agricultural operations and various types of ancillary and odd jobs. Vetti may signify a similar practice in parts of the peninsula in medieval times also. The evidence from the *Skanda Purāṇa* produced by B.N.S. Yadava leaves little doubt that hundreds of people were compelled into forced labour which was evidently meant for production in medieval times.[83] Hence serfdom cannot be dismissed as an incidental feature.

If serfdom is understood to mean the compulsive attachment of the peasants to the soil, it prevailed in good part in Madhya Pradesh, eastern India, Chamba and Rajasthan. In many cases the charters clearly transfer the peasants, artisans and even traders to the beneficiaries.[84] In most charters the villagers and peasants are asked to stay in their villages and carry out the orders of the beneficiaries. This fact of the immobility of peasants and artisans has not been contested by anybody so far. However it is argued that even if these people had been allowed to move, what

80 Sharma, *Indian Feudalism*, 2nd edn, pp. 99–100.

81 The term *utpatsyamāna* would suit this interpretation better, although even *utpadyamāna* means the same thing. I owe this suggestion to R.C. Pandeya. Palaeographically there is very little difference between the two terms.

82 *Sel. Inscr.*, bk III, no. 61, line 19; no. 62, line 28.

83 *Society and Culture in Northern India*, pp. 164–6.

84 Sharma, *Indian Feudalism*, 2nd edn, p. 188 with fn. 6.

purpose would it have served? If such a view is taken then what is the point of underlining the absence of serfdom in the Indian context? After all in conditions of serfdom a peasant is tied to his piece of land and when that piece of land is transferred the peasant is automatically transferred. This practice prevailed widely in early medieval times. Nevertheless, peasants were not widely engaged in agricultural operations in the fields of their landlords. If it is argued that peasants were not employed in production but in building forts, roads, temples and other structures, we may say that all such grandiose projects were undertaken by the landed aristocracy, chiefs and princes to strike awe in the hearts of the people. Image building was an important exercise, and it could be of great indirect help in collecting taxes and presents from the peasantry. Some measures, such as building of roads, could be eventually useful from the point of production. The employment of forced labour therefore did not depend on the fertility of the soil but on the realization of its usefulness by the landlords. There is no doubt that the rural aristocracy led an ostentatious and luxurious life with much lavish consumption. Although we cannot measure the rising expectations of the landlords there are indications of an increasingly luxurious style of living.

The practices of forced labour, sharecropping and leasing of the land were promoted and supported by social norms. The law books ask the brāhmaṇas not to take to the plough. It appears that the upper caste people could not transplant paddy.[85] Naturally, even in a small holding which could otherwise be managed by family members, such people would need to employ forced labour or give out their land on a sharecropping basis. In such a case it is immaterial whether the soil is less or more fertile, for at any rate labour would have to be drafted from outside the family unit. Lack of labour power and plenty of land create conditions for introducing an element of compulsion. But this can happen only in

[85] The passage *paṅkiśaḥ paṅktiśo bhṛtyaiḥ vinyaset samabhūmike* (verse no. 431) occurs in the context of paddy transplantation in the *Kāśyapíyakṛṣisūkti*, ed. Gy. Wojtilla, *Acta Orientalia Academiae Scientiarum Hung.*, vol. 33 (2), 1979, 209–52. The frequent use of the term *kṛṣívala* for the peasant shows that the text belongs to some paddy producing area either in south India or some other part of the country, and contains much medieval material. Verse no. 450 speaks of the employment of agricultural labourers in weeding operations: *tṛṇakoṣṭhān nirasyatha paṅktiśaḥ paṅktiśaḥ kramāt, bhṛtyavargaiḥ, praty ahaṃ va vairicchedaḥ prasasyate.* If we look at the survival of the transplantation practice, it would appear that labour was used for this purpose by the upper caste people in medieval times.

a particular socio-economic formation. We have lack of labour in socialist and even capitalist countries, but that does not necessarily lead to forced labour.

The idea that the gap between the labour potential of a family and the land that it has leads to feudal conditions may be far from true. Under-utilization of labour capacity may not necessarily produce a demand for such labour in the form of forced labour. This labour can also be invested in auxiliary crafts in response to agricultural and domestic demands. But, what is more important, if the needs of the landlord are met otherwise through rents and presents, why should he assume direct and onerous responsibility for cultivation and mobilize labour power for that purpose? At present we have no means to measure the needs, demands and expectations of the landlords, which may vary region-wise and period-wise. These needs could easily be met by the landlords because of the provisions of the charters empowering them to depart from customary and established taxes and impose new levies and new forms of forced labour.

It is repeatedly stated that no new mode of socio-economic formation can emerge as a result of political, administrative and judicial measures;[86] this does not take into account the fact that the colonial system in India owed its origin largely to such measures. The king in ancient India symbolized state authority, and the state was backed by priests and warriors who lived on the surplus produced by the peasants and augmented by the artisans. This kind of state and society appeared in the age of the Buddha. It continued to function more or less smoothly till the third century AD. But many passages in the epics and the Purāṇas speak of a kind of social crisis heralded by the advent of the Kali age. These passages are ascribed to the second half of the third century AD and the beginning of the fourth century AD. They depict a state of affairs in which rural people were oppressed with taxes and forced labour.[87] The oppressions of the state coupled with the havoc caused by natural calamities created a state of chaos, and the lower orders, particularly the Vaiśyas and the Śūdras, refused to perform the functions assigned to them. The peasants

[86] Mukhia, pp. 274, 286.

[87] The Kali passage in the Cr. edn of the *Mahābhārata* (III. 188. 71) amended by me on the basis of the Gita Press edn reads: *nirviśeṣā janapadā karaviṣṭibhirarditāḥ*. Apparently taxes (*kara*) affected the Vaiśyas and forced labour (*viṣṭi*) the Śūdras.

also refused to pay taxes.[88] The *Manu Smṛiti*, the *Śānti Parva* and other texts suggested two measures to overcome this social crisis. One was the use of force or *daṇḍa*, which is glorified in these texts. The other was the restoration of the *varṇāśrama-dharma* which was considered to be the bedrock of the class-divided and state-based society.

D.N. Jha points out that around the end of the third and the beginning of the fourth century land grant inscriptions do not appear on any scale in the Gangetic plains,[89] which were the oldest areas to have settled habitation in historical times. However they do so in eastern Madhya Pradesh, in Vidarbha in Maharashtra, in Andhra Pradesh and in northern Tamil Nadu. I believe that the social crisis involving a struggle between the priests and warriors on the one hand and the lower orders on the other first took place outside the Gangetic zone in the areas which were less civilized. The description of the Kali age in the Purāṇas may be applied to the peripheral areas because the Puranic writers, whose dynastic genealogies stop in the early third century AD were familiar with them. For example the Purāṇas mention south Kosala in which land grants appeared in the fifth century. The Maghas, who ruled in the second and the third centuries AD between Bandhogarh in Madhya Pradesh and Fatehpur in Uttar Pradesh with Kauśāmbi as the centre of their power, are mentioned in the Purāṇas; they are also associated with south Kosala.[90]

Similarly the region of Vidarbha, which abounds in Vākāṭaka grants in the fourth-fifth centuries AD, is often mentioned in Kalidāsa's *Mālavikāgnimitra*. The Sātavahana rule lasted in this area until AD 285,[91] which corresponds to the period to which the description of the Kali era is assigned. Archaeologically almost all the Sātavāhana settlements excavated so far in Vidarbha and elsewhere disappeared in the middle of the third century AD or a little later. A decline in long-distance trade was an important cause, but the possibility of internal social conflicts cannot be ruled out. Unquestionably the Purāṇas were very well acquainted with the Andhra-*bhṛtya* or *jātīya* Sātavāhana rulers whose numbers are usually given as thirty. In the second century Gautamīputra Śātakarṇi is credited

[88] R.S. Śharma, 'The Kali Age: A Period of Social Crisis', S.N. Mukherjee (ed.) *India, History and Thought, Essays in Honour of A.L. Basham* (Calcutta, 1982), pp. 186–203. Also see *Śūdras in Ancient India*, 2nd edn (Delhi, 1980), pp. 233–9.

[89] Introduction in D.N. Jha (ed.), *Feudal Social Formations in Early India* (Delhi, 1987).

[90] A.M. Shastri, *Early History of the Deccan* (Delhi, 1987), ch. X.

[91] Ibid., p. 12 and ch. IV.

with having put an end to the four varṇas,[92] which shows that the varṇa system prevalent in Maharashtra was occasionally disrupted. It is significant that the Īkṣvākus, Pallavas, Viṣṇukuṇḍins, Vākāṭakas and others, who emerged from the ruins of the Sātavāhana state, made land grants on a wide scale and generally claimed to have established *dharma*, which means the varṇa system in the existing context.

The term *ādi dharma-mahārāja* is applied to Vindhyaśakti I; his son Pravarasena I is referred to as only *dharma-mahārāja*. These titles appear in the inscriptions of the fourth and fifth centuries, though the two kings, the father and son, ruled in the second half of the third century.[93] The title of dharma-mahārāja was also adopted by the Pallavas[94] who ruled in south Andhra and north Tamil Nadu. In the backdrop of the social upheaval the epithet would indicate the obligation of the king to establish and uphold the varṇa system which had been upset by the Kali conflict. More importantly, the Vākāṭaka and other rulers of Central India and the peninsula appear committed to the removal of all those ills which had afflicted the social system on account of the advent of the Kali age. The term *kaliyuga-doṣāvasannadharmodharaṇanityasaṃnaddha*[95] is very meaningful. Such terms as suggest efforts to restore the social order occur in Vākāṭaka land grants and in those of some central and peninsular grants in the fourth to the sixth centuries.

Thus it would appear that internal social conflicts, as evident from the description of the Kali age in the Purāṇas, appeared in the peripheral areas where the varṇa system was not so well established and the tribal egalitarian spirit was still strong. Indoctrination over a much longer time span may have prevented the peasants and others organized on varṇa lines in the old, settled areas of the Gangetic plains from rising in revolt against the state and the social order. Probably the earliest Puranic description of the Kali age refers to the situation after the end of the Sātavāhana rule in Maharashtra and the adjoining areas.

Although the use of force and the restoration of the varṇa system[96]

92 *Sel. Inscr.*, vol. I, bk II, no. 86, line 6.

93 Ibid., bk III, no. 59, lines 4–5.

94 Ibid., no. 66, line 1.

95 Ibid., line 13.

96 Ibid., no. 50, line 10. The phrase *varṇāśrama-dharmasthāpanā-nirata* or similar epithets occur in several land grants of the fifth-sixth and later centuries. For examples see R.S. Sharma, *Aspects of Political Ideas and Institutions in Ancient India* (Delhi, 1968), pp. 160–1.

were recommended and also attempted these measures alone could not cope with the critical situation. Since it became difficult to collect taxes it was not possible to run the state and to pay the priests, the administrators, the army and numerous officials. Apparently, as an alternative, the practice of land grants, which was not unknown in early times, was adopted on a wide scale in a major part of the country, particularly from the fourth-fifth century AD onwards. Therefore there is an indication of a crisis in production relations, which may not be unconnected with changes in the mode of production. The fact cannot be discounted that trade[97] and urbanism[98] suffered a distinct decline, and the absence of gold coins for three centuries between the seventh and the tenth centuries and the paucity of other types of coins[99] are well known. There is practically

[97] In addition to the material presented regarding the decline of trade in my *Indian Feudalism*, 2nd edn, chs. I & III, further evidence appears in B.N.S. Yadava, *Society and Culture in Northern India in the Twelfth Century*, pp. 270–5. Speaking of early medieval Bengal M.R. Tarafdar says: 'The period between the eleventh and thirteenth centuries shows distinct signs of the decay of trade and urban centres, a process which must have started earlier'. ('Trade and Society in Early Medieval Bengal', *Indian Historical Review*, 3, January 1978, p. 282). However in western India trade shows revival in this period (V.K. Jain, 'Trade and Traders in Western India', Ph.D. thesis, Delhi University, 1983); this seems to be the case with south India also (Kenneth R. Hall, *Trade and Statecraft in the Age of the Colas*. I postulate decline of trade mainly in the seventh–tenth centuries (New Delhi, 1980).

[98] B.D. Chattopadhyaya in 'Trade and Urban Centres in Early Medieval North India', *Indian Historical Review*, 1, 1974, pp. 203–19 doubted the decline of urbanism, but in 'Urban Centres in Early Medieval India', *Situating Indian History. For Sarvapalli Gopal*, Sabyasachi Bhattacharya and Romila Thapar (eds) (Delhi, 1986), pp. 8–33, he postulated a 'third urbanization' which presupposes de-urbanization in Gupta and post-Gupta times. Almost all Sātavāhana towns decay and disappear after the third century AD. A.H. Dani informs me of a similar fate of the Kuśāṇa towns in Pakistan, and the Soviet archaeologist V. Masson tells me that five central Asian urban centres of around the first to the fourth centuries AD become either villages or castles afterwards. Some recent books such as those of O.P. Prasad, *Decay and Revival of Urban Centres in Medieval South India* (New Delhi, 1986) and B.P.N. Pathak, *Society and Culture in Early Bihar* (New Delhi, 1988), discuss de-urbanization in different parts of the country. R.N. Nandi convincingly shows that many of the decaying towns were converted into *tīrthas* or places of pilgrimage in early medieval times. 'Client, Ritual and Conflict in Early Brāhmanical Order', *Indian Historical Review*, 6, 1979–80, pp. 100, 103–9. For a detailed review of the archaeological and other types of evidence see R.S. Sharma, *Urban Decay in India (c. 330–c. 1000)* (New Delhi, 1987).

[99] R.S. Sharma, 'Indian Feudalism Retouched' (review paper), *Indian Historical Review*, 1, 1974, 320–30. For additional evidence regarding the paucity of coinage, see M.R. Tarafdar. This point has been elaborated further in my two lectures on 'Paucity

no indication of the use of slaves in production. All these are presages of change in the methods and relations of production. Hence the production system as a whole was afflicted with certain maladies, which compelled the state to convert land/land revenues into a general mode of payment for religious and administrative services. The grant system relieved the state of the heavy responsibility of getting taxes collected from all over the countryside by its agents and then of disbursing them in cash or kind. On the other hand, priests, warriors and administrators were asked to fend for themselves in the villages that were assigned to them for their enjoyment. The system also relieved the state of the responsibility of maintaining law and order in the donated villages which now became almost the sole concern of the beneficiaries. Therefore it would be wrong to assume that political, administrative and judicial measures, which created new property relations in land, were undertaken by the state entirely on its own.

The social crisis apparently led to the withdrawal of slaves from production, and the provision of land for them as tenants and sharecroppers. This explains to a good extent the elevation of Śūdras to peasanthood and their participation in rituals. It seems that landowners converted Śūdra labourers into peasants and themselves became landlords living on rents. The substantial *gahapatis* of the age of the Buddha probably turned landlords. That the village headman tended to become a landlord has already been indicated,[100] although the causes of this transformation need investigation.

The new socio-economic formation that emerged as a result of the appearance of a class of landlords and of a subject peasantry had its own limitations. The peasants were accustomed to give certain taxes and services to the state, and if the demands of the beneficiary were confined to those claims, in normal times, routine payments could continue. But the beneficiary would impose proper and improper taxes as well as fixed and unfixed taxes, would collect 'all kinds' of taxes, and, what is worse, would make additional impositions which were covered by the term *ādi* which meant etc. In certain areas they could also introduce new forms of forced labour. Besides, all communal and agrarian resources hitherto enjoyed by the peasants were transferred to the landed beneficiaries who

of Metal Money in India' (c. 500–c. 1000) delivered in the Indian Museum, Calcutta, in 1989 (unpublished).

100 Sharma, *Indian Feudalism*, 2nd edn, pp. 41–2.

were always present on the spot. This situation caused constant conflict between those who claimed rent on the strength of their royal charters and the others who claimed immunity on the basis of customary and immemorial rights which would certainly be known to the local people but because of their illiteracy would not be shown in black and white. Hence there was bound to be constant friction, tensions and struggles between the landed beneficiaries and the servile peasantry. This could lead to litigations between the beneficiaries, and also between the beneficiaries and the peasants.[101] Due to the common practice of land grants and the enormous advantages derived from them the brāhmaṇas forged many charters (*kūṭaśāsana*) and claimed villages as their own on that basis. But there were so many valid charters that conflicts between the landlord and the peasant were always a possibility. In order to settle this conflict Nārada, Bṛhaspati, the *Agni Purāṇa* and other authorities give the final authority to the royal charter in the case of a dispute. They lay down that if there is a conflict between the religious right (*dharma*), contract right (*vyavahāra*), customary right (*carita*) and the right derived from the royal charter (*rājaśāsana*) the royal charter will override all the other sources of the law or authority.[102]

But it seems that the overriding power of the royal charter did not work in all cases. We have the case of the Kaivartas, a fishing and cultivating community in Bangladesh, who rose against Rāmapāla in the eleventh century AD. They fought with bamboo sticks riding on buffaloes. So powerful was their revolt that two dozen vessels had to be mobilized by Rāmapāla in order to put down this rebellion. This is an important example of a peasant revolt.[103] The possibility of a clash is also indicated in some Bengal grants which mention the term *karṣaṇavirodhi sthāna*.[104] At least two grants take pains to show that they do not clash with the existing cultivating rights of the peasants. Therefore the possibility of a clash between the peasants and the incoming beneficiaries is clearly visualized. Similarly in many grants from Madhya Pradesh and Maharashtra, the people are warned that if they try to upset the grant in any manner

[101] In 1214 a temple in Karnataka claimed the land of its neighbours, but the local authorities decided against the temple. S. Sethar and G.D. Sontheimer (eds) *Memorial Stones* (Dharwad, 1982), p. 303.

[102] R.S. Sharma '*Rājaśāsana*: Meaning, Scope and Application', *Proceedings of the Indian History Congress*, 37th Session, Calicut, 1976, pp. 76–87.

[103] R.S. Sharma, *Indian Feudalism*, 2nd edn (Delhi, 1980), p. 220.

[104] Mukherji and Maity, *Corpus of Bengal Inscriptions*, no. 6, line 18; no. 7, line 19.

they will be punished with force.[105] This point is stated repeatedly[106] in many inscriptions. In some cases this threat is directed towards royal officials, but mostly it is a general threat meant for everybody. Again, in the texts of this period, *brahmahatyā*, that is the killing of brāhmaṇas, is considered to be a great sin and it occurs in many Purāṇas. Why did the murder of a brāhmaṇa become so important in early medieval times? Apparently it was because of his becoming a landed beneficiary and therefore an oppressor. If we look at the distribution of hero stones in Karnataka and other parts of south India it would appear that some of them are found in the *agrahāra* areas.[107] This would again suggest that there was open friction between the beneficiary of the agrahāra and the peasants living there. In the case of Karnataka R.N. Nandi has collected certain evidence which suggests some kind of collaboration between the brāhmaṇas and the peasants in the beginning but open conflict between the two later on.[108] D.N. Jha refers to several instances of conflict between the peasants and the beneficiary landlords in Coḷa inscriptions, particularly after 1000.[109] The nature of peasant protests have also been discussed by me.[110]

Although we can see and visualize polarity between the central state and smaller states, between various types of beneficiaries and between landed magnates and the cultivator, the human factor operating in these polarities does not come out clearly in our sources. It is thought that the peasant's independent control over his process of production prevented acute social tensions.[111] But as shown earlier, this control was more dependent than independent. The multiplication of the existing units of production in new areas could obviate occasions for open conflicts leading to changes. But in good measure the seeming stability was promoted by other factors which were closely linked with the system of production,

105 *Sel. Inscr.*, bk III, no. 61, lines 22–4.

106 Ibid., no. 62, lines 32–4; no. 63A, lines 21–4; no. 67, lines 24–5.

107 S. Settar and Günther D. Sontheimer (ed.), p. 223.

108 *Growth of Rural Economy in Early Feudal India*, Presidential Address, Ancient India Section, Indian History Congress, 45th Session (Annamalai University, 1984).

109 D.N. Jha, Section I: Ancient India Presidential Address, *Early Indian Feudalism: A Historiographical Critique*, Indian History Congress, 40th Session (Waltair: Andhra University, 1979), p. 18.

110 R.S. Sharma, 'Problems of Peasant Protest in Early Medieval India', *Social Scientist*, vol. 16, no. 9, September, 1988, pp. 3–16.

111 Mukhia, p. 293.

especially with production relations. First the caste system with its features of hierarchy and superiority, not to speak of untouchability, provided ritualistic and ideological sanction for the production and distribution system. The Śūdra peasant castes proliferated in medieval times. Although the peasants were exploited in a more or less similar manner, endless caste divisions undermined their solidarity. Ritualistic distinctions distorted the reality of exploitation.

It appears that the *jajmānī* system developed in the early medieval period, and was part of a more or less self-sufficient economy. At the end of harvesting, on the threshing floor, portions of paddy were given to the gods, brāhmaṇas, rulers and various kinds of labourers, indicated by the term *bhṛtyavarga-poṣaṇam.*[112] The brāhmaṇas, who controlled many 'estates', played a crucial ideological role in penetrating the consciousness of the peasantry and making them behave as they wanted them to. Some medieval religious reform movements apparently sought to improve the status of those who really produced and suffered, but these movements were manipulated to contain the conflicts and ease the tensions; they could not rouse the peasantry to retaliate. In certain parts of the country the survival of bonds of kinship also helped to keep people together. This may be particularly true of Rajasthan and the Himalayan areas. Classes with conflicting interests were kept together through the performance of *pūjā, japa, vrata, tīrthayātrā, saṃskāra* and *prāyaścitta* as well as through prospects of heaven and hell. The all-pervasive influence of astrology (*jyotiṣa*) and of the doctrine of Vedānta reconciled the people to their lot. These types of factors brought people of opposite interests together.

It is held that lack of 'concentrated social effort' blocked changes in the means, methods and relations of production.[113] We may not have much idea about the social effort, but we can certainly identify significant changes in the mode of production in early medieval times. This period was undoubtedly an age of larger yields and agrarian expansion.[114] It is possible to count hundreds of states, particularly in those areas which had never witnessed the rise of full-fledged states. A state presupposes an assured source of income which would enable it to maintain a good

112 Gy. Wojtilla (ed.), *Kāśyapīyakṛṣisūkti*, verses 491–2.

113 Mukhia, p. 292. However this statement is qualified by the phrase 'change completely' (ibid.).

114 R.S. Sharma, *Urban Decay in India* (*c. 300–c. 1000*), ch. x.

number of managerial staff. This would not be possible unless the agrarian base was strong enough to pay for the priests, officers, soldiers, etc.

Urban contraction was an important cause of the dissemination of technology in rural areas. Western India provides many examples of the migration of town-dwelling brāhmaṇas to the countryside where they were donated land by the ruling class.[115] Backward regions would benefit from the better knowledge of agriculture of the beneficiaries. Agriculture would also benefit from the ready availability of artisans who migrated from decaying towns.

Several texts on agriculture such as the *Kṛṣiparāśara* in the north and Kamban's book in the south were composed in early medieval times. Kāśyapa's *Kṛṣisūkti*, though found in the south,[116] could be set in a paddy-producing area either in the north or the south. The *Vṛkṣa Āyurveda* of about the tenth century recommends recipes for treating diseases affecting plants.[117] Apart from special attention being given to horses,[118] which were in great demand by the chiefs and princes for their cavalry and personal use, animal husbandry improved because of advances made in the treatment of cattle disease.[119] In addition, detailed instructions regarding agriculture appear in the *Bṛhat Saṃhitā* of Varāhamihira, the *Agṇi Purāṇa* and the *Viṣṇudharmottara Purāṇa*.[120] Three crops, first mentioned by Pāṇini, were known widely[121] and better seeds were produced.[122] Mateorological knowledge, based on observation, was of an advanced nature in the *Kṛṣiparāśara*. The knowledge of fertilizers improved immensely, and the use of compost was known.[123] Some other innovations in agricultural techniques are worth noting. The *bṛhadhala*

115 R.S. Sharma, *Urban Decay*, Appendix I.

116 Gy. Wojtilla (ed.), *Kāśyapiyākṛṣisūkti, Acta Orientalia Academiae Scientiarum Hung*, 33 (2), 1979, pp. 209–52. The usual term for cultivator in this text is *kṛṣīvala*, which occurs in early medieval texts and inscriptions. Most of the material in this work probably belongs to medieval times, and its core is placed in the eighth-ninth centuries (Wojtilla, tr., ibid, 39 (1), 1985, p. 85, fn. 1.

117 D.M. Bose et al. (eds), *A Concise History of Science in India*, p. 362.

118 Ibid., p. 255.

119 Ibid., pp. 363–4.

120 Ibid., pp. 358, 361, 363. The *Agni Purāṇa* belongs to the ninth–tenth centuries. The *Viṣṇudharmottara Purāṇa* is attributed to the eighth century.

121 D.M. Bose, et al., pp. 356–61.

122 Ibid., pp. 358–9.

123 Ibid., pp. 358–60.

or big plough mentioned in a tenth century inscription from the Ajmer[124] area may have been an important instrument in breaking difficult soil in certain parts of the country. Equally advantageous to agricultural processes may have been the use of the pounder, which was in use in Pāla times.[125]

More importantly, irrigation facilities were expanded. The law books lay down severe punishments for those who cause damage to tanks, wells, ponds, embankments, etc.[126] The construction of a *vāpī* (step well) became very popular in Rajasthan and Gujarat. Its importance is also underlined in the work of Kāśyapa.[127] V.K. Jain has prepared a map in which he has shown the distribution of vāpīs in western India in the eleventh-thirteenth centuries.[128] Vāpīs of the tenth and eleventh centuries are also found in good numbers in the Mehrauli area of Delhi. It is interesting to note that the term vāpī is derived from the Sanskrit root *vap* which means 'to sow'. Clearly step wells were meant for irrigating the fields, but they would be equally useful for supplying drinking water and also for irrigating gardens. Further, the use of the *araghaṭṭa* or the Persian wheel had become widespread in the ninth-tenth centuries, particularly in Rajasthan. The *Kṛṣisūkti* of Kāśyapa prescribes that the machine for lifting water (*ghaṭī yantra*) is to be operated by men, oxen or elephants.[129] The use of the term *arahaṭṭiyanara* in a lexicon of the twelfth century shows that certain persons were employed to work the water-wheel.[130]

Of course the use of iron implements attained a new peak in this period. The *Paryāyamuktāvālī*, a medieval lexicon whose manuscripts have been found in West Bengal and Orissa, mentions as many as half a dozen types or grades of iron.[131] Above all, iron artefacts were manu-

124 B.P. Mazumdar, 'Industries and Internal Trade in Early Medieval North India', *JBRS*, XLV–XLVI, 1979–80, p. 231.

125 Discovered in the Pāla stratum of Taradih and reported orally to me by A.K. Prasad.

126 These texts belong to the early centuries of the Christian era. See R.S. Sharma, *Perspectives in Social and Economic History of Early India* (New Delhi, 1983), pp. 158–9.

127 Gy. Wojtilla (ed.), pp. 219–20.

128 'Trade and Traders in Western India' (unpublished Ph.D. thesis, University of Delhi, 1983).

129 Gy. Wojtilla (ed.) verses 167–8. The *ghaṭi-yantra* operated by oxen is considered to be the best, that by men to be the worst, and that by elephants to be of middling quality.

130 B.N.S. Yadava, *Society and Culture in Northern India in the Twelfth Century*, p. 259.

131 The text was edited by T. Chowdhury in *JBRS*, vol. 31, 1945 and vol. 32, 1946.

factured in plenty. They were used as beams for holding the roof and also as memorial pillars which evidently was a non-utilitarian purpose. Several pillars, including the Mehrauli pillar in Delhi, were erected to mark the conquest of victorious princes.

The increase in the number of varieties of cereals including rice, wheat and lentils as well as in fruits, legumes, vegetables, etc. is striking. These can be inferred not only from the Amarakośa but more so from the *Paryāyamuktāvalī.*[132] According to the *Śūnya Purāṇa* more than fifty kinds of paddy were cultivated in Bengal.[133] It would thus appear that the introduction of new crops, expansion of irrigation facilities and innovation in agricultural techniques contributed to the growth of agriculture.

It appears that agriculture and agrarian settlements in the Middle Ages received special attention from the rulers, landed beneficiaries and immigrant artisans. The knowledge of irrigation techniques, paddy transplantation, preparation of fertilizers, weather conditions based on observations, various kinds of cereals as well as some other aspects of agriculture was systematized and diffused in various parts of the country.

Apart from the foundation of numerous states the various medieval texts suggest an enormous increase in agricultural production. Therefore agricultural technology in terms of a single major break may not be striking,[134] but the overall effect of various measures and improvements seems to have been substantial. However, a mere increase in production may lead neither to stability nor to structural changes. For this, certain other conditions including the rousing of consciousness may be needed.

The earliest ms. used by him belongs to 1851–62. Composed by Haricaraṇasena, the text is based on the *Paryāyaratnamālā* of Mādhavakara (*JBRS*, vol. 31, 1945, Introduction, p. i). Since it is strikingly indebted to Amara in chs. 22, 23 (ibid.) and since potato and tobacco are not mentioned in it, it seems to be pre-Mughal. The synonyms for iron and other metals are found in ch. (*Varga*) 6 (*JBRS*, 1945).

132 T. Chowdhury, ch. 18 (*JBRS*, 31, 1945, pp. 31–3) speaks of twenty-four types of *śtmbīsukadhānyagaṇa* (p. 33), but the varieties, when counted, come to nearly 110 types of cereals including wheat, barley, lentils, etc. Ch. 19 (ibid., pp. 33–4) speaks of ten types of *śālidhānya* (transplanted paddy) and nineteen types of *tṛṇaśālidhānya* (untransplanted paddy), but, on counting, the various types of paddy and allied cereals come to nearly sixty-four.

133 T.C. Dasgupta, *Aspect of Bengali Society*, pp. 249–50 quoted in B.N.S. Yadava, pp. 258–305 fn. Yadava has cited several other pieces of evidence, pp. 258–9.

134 Mukhia, p. 292.

FEUDAL VERSUS SEGMENTARY

Burton Stein's latest views have some bearing on the current debate. He states that 'notwithstanding its distinguished paternity by D.D. Kosambi in the middle 1950s and R.S. Sharma a decade later the feudal concept has never been seriously tested against the claims inherent in it, nor has it been elaborated in any significant way'.[135] Here something is wrong with the chronology. I sent my *Origins of Feudalism in India (circa* AD 400–650) for publication in early 1957, and it appeared in 1958[136] and not 'a decade' after Kosambi's work 'in the middle 1950s'. Incidentally, after 1956, when his *An Introduction to the Study of Indian History* was published, Kosambi wrote two valuable papers on feudalism in 1959.[137] That 'the claims inherent' in the feudal concept have been both 'tested' and significantly 'elaborated' will be amply borne out by the papers, including mine, found in D.N. Jha (ed.), *Feudal Social Formation in Early India*, Delhi, 1987. Since then several other publications have discussed new dimensions of the subject. The feudal model is being fruitfully applied to the study of art, religion, caste system, language and literature of medieval times. Yet the concept of Indian feudalism is called a 'convenient residual position'. If it means an unaccountable position, it will continue to be so as long as the coiner of the phrase refuses to take in to account the work done on the subject. How I wish a serious scholar would not shut his eyes to relevant publications of not only the last three decades but even earlier.

Feudalism is denounced as an 'article of left historiographical faith'. But the present paper is in response to the criticisms of Mukhia, who is considered a leftist. I also know of a few other similar critics. To attribute feudalism to leftism betrays an appalling ignorance of the work of reputed researchers such as Devangana Desai, Lallanji Gopal, N. Karashima, T.V. Mahalingam, Dasharatha Sharma and B.N.S. Yadava,[138] who by no

135 'The Segmentary State : Interim Reflections', Seminar on State Formation in the Pre-Colonial South India, Jawaharlal Nehru University, New Delhi, 1989.

136 *Journal of the Economic and Social History of the Orient*, I, 1958, pp. 297–328.

137 'Indian Feudal Trade Charters', *JESHO*, vol. 2, 1959, pp. 281–93; 'Origins of Feudalism in Kashmir', *The Sardhasatabdi Commemoration Volume*, Asiatic Society of Bombay, *JASB*, new series, vols 31–32, 1959, pp. 108–20.

138 Devangana Desai, *Social Dimensions of Art in Early India*, Presidential Address, Section I, Indian History Congress, 50th Session (Gorakhpur University, 1989); Lallanji Gopal, *Economic Life of Northern India (c.* AD *700–1200)* (Banaras, 1965); N. Karashima,

means can be labelled as 'leftists'. They have applied the feudal analogy fully or partly to the Indian state and society of different regions and periods. The declamation of the feudal concept in the Indian context has become an obsession with some western historians who cannot extricate themselves from the colonial constructs on Indian history presented in a new garb. The importance of kin, caste, religion, symbolism, segmentation, etc. is overemphasized and any comparison with the west European experience to bring out historical specificities and universalities is frowned upon. Some western historians and Indologists underline the role of decentralization in early Indian history and assert that Indian rulers were merely the masters of roads, towns and capitals and not of the hinterland. They do not consider the feudal framework for analysis although it could explain the mechanism through which rent was collected from the rural population and remitted as revenue by the feudal lords to the central treasury in medieval times.

Stein imagines that Indian feudalism is seen by its exponents only in the context of feudatories found everywhere in pre-modern India.[139] If he cares to go through relevant writings he will discover that those who emerged as landlords either on their own or through assignments made by the central authority constituted the crucial component in the feudal structure. The payment of tribute by the feudatories to the central power depended on its strength, which consequently determined the extent of the local exploitation of the peasants. If the tribute was regular the peasant would be taxed more; if it was occasional he would be taxed less. But the landlords superimposed upon the peasants became regular exploiters, whose presence was indispensable for controlling the land as well as the peasants who cultivated it. The feudal infrastructure explains the nature of the state and all the other superstructural elements such as art, religion, culture, etc. Feudatories played a supplementary role in the whole system.

Following Southall, Stein adds that 'comparisons with, and even borrowing from Europe had been acceptable, even eagerly sought whereas

'Nayakas as Lease-holders of Temple Lands, *JESHO*, vol. 19, 1976, pp. 227–32; *South Indian History and Society* (Delhi, 1984), Introduction; 'Nayaka Rule in the Tamil Country During the Vijayanagara Period', Seminar on State Formation in Pre-Colonial South India, Jawaharlal Nehru University (New Delhi, 1989) (unpublished), T.V. Mahalingam, *South Indian Polity*, revised edn (Madras); Dasharatha Sharma, *Early Chauhan Dynasties*, second edn (Delhi, 1975); B.N.S. Yadava, *Society and Culture in Northern India in the Twelfth Century* (Allahabad, 1973).

139 Stein.

merely structural comparison of Indian and African forms gives offence to many Indians'.[140] Here he not only ignores the importance of comparative study in history but also the fact that European history has been taught in India for nearly two hundred years; the colonial masters never introduced any African history except that of ancient Egypt or Africa's partition in the 1880s. Indian historians have been influenced by western writings on European history but they are not attracted by such constructs as the one on the segmentary state. The use of anthropology including the African anthropology for explaining historical processes is a comparatively recent phenomenon, and yet it is used by Indian historians in the study of ancient India.[141] Therefore to say that many Indians feel offended by such an exercise is wilful distortion. I very much hope that such allegations are not intended to prejudice the Africanists and educated Africans against Indian scholars, though such an effect is perhaps unavoidable.

In his enthusiasm for building a model, Stein propounded the distinction between ritual sovereignty and actual political control in the context of the Coḷa 'segmentary' state. But the myth of the ritual sovereignty of the Coḷas as distinct from actual political authority exercised by its different local centres (segments) of power was exploded by several scholars, and now it has been wisely abandoned by its expounder. He is 'now (1989) convinced' that 'the distinction is incorrect' and that political authority forces a lord 'to foster . . . ritual actions and services'.[142] Since I happen to be older I reached this conclusion in 1954.[143]

The 'segmentary' supporters may feel happy in their make-believe world. The test of a theory or its refutation lies in the nature of the

140 Ibid.

141 Romila Thapar, *From Lineage to State* (Delhi, 1984); Suvira Jaiswal, 'A Survey of Research in Social History of Ancient India', in R.S. Sharma (ed.), *A Survey of Research in Social and Economic History of India* (Delhi, 1986); K.M. Shrimalu, *Religion, Ideology and Society*, Presidential Address, Ancient India Section, Indian History Congress, 49th Session (Dharwad: Karnataka University, 1988); R.S. Sharma, *Origin of the State in India*, Department of History (Bombay: Bombay University, 1989).

142 Stein.

143 'Superstition and Politics in the *Arthaśastra* of Kautilya', *Journal of Bihar Research Society*, vol. XL, 1954, pp. 223–31. In his work on medieval Orissa Hermann Kulke rejects religion as a substitute for political authority; on the contrary he sees it as a promoter of political power ('Fragmentation and Segmentation versus Integration: Reflections on the Concepts of Indian Feudalism and the Segmentary State in Indian History', *Studies in History*, vol. IV, no. 2, 1982, p. 254).

supporting evidence. The attempt to project the 'segmentary' as a model for the early Indian state and society has proved to be abortive. Almost every segment of the segmentary concept has been examined and dismissed.[144] In the process the study of Indian feudalism has been enriched empirically and conceptually. In exposing the hollowness of the segmentary and similar untenable formulations on Indian history, Indian as well as other historians have done valuable work to rebut the colonialist historiographical dogmas that the Indians were always ruled by despots, that they were always absorbed in the problems of their spiritual lives, that they were not concerned with material life, and so on.

Concluding Observations

Feudalism in India was characterized by a class of landlords and by a class of subject peasantry, both living in a predominantly agrarian economy marked by a decline in trade and urbanism and by a drastic reduction in metal currency. The superior state got its taxes collected and authority recognized by creating a number of inferior power blocs or even states (that is, landed priests, *maṭhas, vihāras, basadis,* temples, *agrahāras, brahma deyas,* etc.) who generated the necessary social and ideological climate for this purpose. Unlike the European system most of the power structures within the state did not have to pay taxes. West European feudal lords granted land to their serfs in order to get their own occupied land cultivated. But Indian kings made land grants to get the taxes (surplus) collected. In their turn the grantees collected rents from their tenant peasants who could be evicted and even subjected to forced labour.

The critics of Indian feudalism posit the presence of either a peasant society or peasant control over production resources in medieval times. Both cases could suggest a kind of egalitarian, classless society with prominent tribal traits. There is a tendency, open or concealed, to resurrect

---

[144] R. Champakalakshmi, *IESHR,* vol. XVII, nos 3 and 4, 1983, pp. 411–26; D.N. Jha, 'Validity of Brāhmaṇa-Peasant Alliance and the Segmentary State in Early Medieval South India', *Social Science Probings,* vol. 4, no. 2, June 1984, pp. 270–95; R.N. Nandi, M.G.S. Narayanan, 'Review Article: South Indian History and Society', *Tamil Civilization,* vol. 3, no. 1, 1985, pp. 57–91; Vijaya Ramaswami, *Studies in History,* vol. 4, no. 2, 1982, pp. 307–19; Kesavan Veluthat, 'Power Structure of Monarchy in South India (*c.* AD 600–1300)', Ph.D. thesis of the University of Calicut, 1989.

the Asiatic mode and even oriental despotism in a new incarnation. Fortunately on the basis of sound logic and solid empirical evidence the latest full-length study on the subject by Brendan O'Leary convincingly shows that the Asiatic mode cannot be applied to the Indian experience.[145] In my view, during medieval times, the major part of the Indian subcontinent was marked by the strong presence of a surplus-consuming class which lived off the labour of a subject peasantry on the strength of its superior agrarian authority buttressed by ritualistic and ideological mechanisms. In this context the concept of class may be reconsidered. The position of class may be located in the overall system of production. If a class means a category composed of those who either exclusively control the means of production or those who are completely deprived of such control, such a thing can happen only in a full-fledged capitalist system. The application of such a concept to pre-capitalist societies is riddled with difficulties, for even in the feudal society of western Europe the serf enjoyed day-to-day control over his share of the means of production.[146] In such a society class is best seen in the context of the unequal distribution of the surplus, which was eventually given a lasting basis by the unequal distribution of the means of production and strengthened by ideological, ritualistic and juridical factors. The social structure is identified by the nature of the class which dominates it. Ecological factors influence the development of material culture but do not determine the form and nature of the social structure. Several countries have similar climatic conditions but dissimilar social structures. Therefore to attribute such structural phenomena as the absence of serfdom or the longevity of peasant autonomy to the carrying capacity of the soil is to ignore the potentialities of social dynamics.

[145] *The Asiatic Mode of Production* (Basil Blackwell, 1989). See particularly chs VII and VIII.

[146] Yadava, *The Problem of the Emergence of Feudal Relations in Early India*, p. 46, fn. 1, draws attention to the position of the serf as stated by E.J. Hobsbawm on the basis of Karl Marx: 'The serf, though under the control of the lord, is in fact an economically independent producer', *Karl Marx: Pre-capitalist Economic Formations* (London, 1964), p. 42.

Chapter Three

Was There Feudalism in Indian History?

HARBANS MUKHIA*

To discuss a problem such as 'Was there feudalism in Indian History?' one should, in fairness, begin by defining one's terms. What, in other words, is feudalism? Unfortunately the answer to this simple question varies with the historian who makes the attempt.[1] If there is no universally

* *Centre for Historical Studies, Jawaharlal Nehru University, New Delhi.* *An earlier version of this paper was first read as the Presidential Address to the Medieval India Section, Indian History Congress, Fortieth Session, at Waltair, in December 1979. It was later discussed at three seminars respectively organized by the School of Social Sciences, Jawaharlal Nehru University, New Delhi; Department of History, Erasmus University, Rotterdam; and Society for the Study of Feudalism, Sorbonne, Paris.* *I was fortunate enough to receive written and oral comments from Maurice Aymard, Guy Bois, Barun De, Irfan Habib, R.H. Hilton, Iqtidar Alam Khan, Frank Perlin, Burton Stein and Immannuel Wallerstein; it is a privilege to acknowledge my debt of gratitude to them all.*

[1] Marc Bloch's classic description of the fundamental features of European feudalism is well-known everywhere: 'a subject peasantry; widespread use of service tenement (i.e. the fief) instead of a salary, which was out of the question; the supremacy of a class of specialized warriors; ties of obedience and protection which bind man to man and, within the warrior class, assume the distinctive form called vassalage; fragmentation of authority—leading inevitably to disorder; and, in the midst of all this, the survival of other forms of association, family and state, of which the latter, during the second feudal age, was to acquire renewed strength', *Feudal Society*, tr. L.A. Manyon, Chicago, 1964, p. 446. To Joseph R. Strayer and Rushton Coulborn 'Feudalism is primarily a method of government, not an economic or a social system, though it obviously modifies and is modified by the social and economic environment', 'The Idea of Feudalism' in R. Coulborn (ed.), *Feudalism in History* (Princeton, 1956), p. 4. For Henri Pirenne feudalism was a 'closed estate economy' where production was largely for consumption and trade was practically absent, *Economic and Social History of Medieval Europe*, tr. I.E. Clegg (London, 1958) (first published 1936), pp. 7–12. Even historians sharing a common analytical methodology, namely Marxism, have understood feudalism in various ways.

applicable definition of feudalism, there is an objective reason for it, which has critical significance for our argument: feudalism was not a world-system; capitalism was the first world-system.[2] It follows therefore that there is no universally applicable abstraction of feudalism as there is of capitalism. When we speak of capitalism in its abstract form, as a generalized commodity production where labour itself is a commodity,[3] we do so because of our awareness that all of humanity was, during the nineteenth and twentieth centuries, subjected to the force of this production system through different stages of antecedent developments. Feudalism, on the other hand, was, throughout its history, a non-universal, specific form of socio-economic organization—specific to time and region, where specific methods and organization of production obtained.[4]

It is necessary to lay stress on this point here, for it is lost sight of when feudalism is defined as a system based on 'non-economic compulsion' or as a 'redistributive world system' or in even more general terms as an agrarian economy with a fairly cohesive ruling class siphoning off

---

Thus, whereas Paul Sweezy's concept of feudalism is virtually akin to that of Henri Pirenne's, in R.H. Hilton (ed.), *The Transition from Feudalism to Capitalism* (London, 1976), pp. 33–56 and 102–8, Maurice Dobb equates it with serfdom, *Studies in the Development of Capitalism*, revised edition (London, 1963), reprint 1972 (first published 1946), pp. 35–7; for Perry Anderson it was 'the specific organization in a vertically articulated system of parcellized sovereignty and scalar property that distinguished the feudal mode of production in Europe', *Lineages of the Absolutist State* (London, 1977) (first published 1974) p. 408.

In the Indian context R.S. Sharma characterizes the period between AD 300 and 1200 as feudal when he finds most features of west European feudalism having developed here, *Indian Feudalism c. 300–1200* (Calcutta, 1965), pp. 1–2, 7, 16, 52–3, 63–4, 154, 158, 271, etc. S. Nurul Hasan, on the other hand, calls medieval India feudal even though she 'did not have *any* of the characteristics of western European feudalism', *Thoughts on Agrarian Relations in Mughal India* (New Delhi, 1973), p. 2, (emphasis added).

[2] Clearly other pre-capitalist universal categories such as 'stone age', 'bronze age', etc. do not stand in the same class as a highly organized mode of production with an advanced social organization.

[3] Karl Marx and F. Engels, *Selected Works*, vol. I (Moscow, 1969), pp. 160–2.

[4] Cf. the perceptive remark of Jean Suret-Canale: '*By its very nature*, capitalism, as well as being one of the great stages of human progress, also assumes a universal value, destroying or reducing to the status of residual survivals, the previous modes of production. *A fortiori*, such universality appertains to socialism. But one cannot project this universality of the last two stages of social development on to the history which precedes them', cited in Marian Sawer, *Marxism and the Question of the Asiatic Mode of Production* (The Hague, 1977), p. 208 (emphasis original).

the agrarian surplus through the use of overt or covert force.[5] These definitions seek to identify an entire social and economic structure in terms of the political or juridical basis of the exploitation of the primary producer, the peasant; they do not take into account the totality of the production system. They seek to identify a mode of production by merely referring to the relations of exploitation. Secondly, these definitions are so broad as to cover all pre-capitalist systems in one sweep, for all pre-capitalist societies were characterized by primarily agricultural production, unequal division of property and non-economic coercion by the ruling class which appropriated the peasants' surplus in a variety of forms—rent (in labour, cash or kind) or revenue or in the form of servile or bonded labour. The use of the term 'feudal' in such a broad sense fails to demarcate the specifics of the feudal social and economic organization

[5] Thus Maurice Dobb, equating feudalism with serfdom, explains the latter term as a type of exploitation that is enforced and perpetuated through 'so-called "extra economic compulsion" in some form', *Capitalism, Development and Planning,* New York, reprint 1970, pp. 2–3. R.H. Hilton also accepts the equation of serfdom with 'non-economic compulsion', though he does not define feudalism as the equivalent of serfdom, Hilton, ed., *Peasants, Knights and Heretics,* Cambridge, 1976, p. 4. 'Redistributive world system' is Immannuel Wallerstein's term. This world system is 'based on a mode of production wherein a surplus is extracted from agricultural producers normally in the form of tribute to sustain an imperial (or state) bureaucracy at a given level of consumption', 'From Feudalism to Capitalism—Transition or Transitions?' *Social Forces,* vol. 55, no. 2, December 1976, p. 281, n2. This term is as general as 'non-economic compulsion' or 'pre-capitalist society', and is therefore hardly superior to it.

S. Nurul Hasan understands feudalism to mean a primarily agrarian economy where the surplus is appropriated by a 'fairly closed' ruling class through both non-economic coercion and the role played by it in agricultural as well as the subsidiary handicrafts production, *Thoughts,* pp. 1–2.

Perry Anderson has sharply criticized universalist definitions of feudalism, which, with suitable modifications, would equally appertain to different regions of the medieval world, *Lineages,* pp. 401–12. His criticism arises from the assumed similarity of the 'infrastructure' of economies in different parts of the pre-capitalist world, economies that are imprecisely defined by and large in terms of 'large landownership with small peasant production, where the exploiting class extracts the surplus from the immediate producer by customary forms of extra-economic coercion—labour services, deliveries in kind, or rents in cash—and where commodity exchange and labour mobility are correspondingly restricted', ibid., p. 401. He suggests that since '*all* modes of production in class societies prior to capitalism extract surplus labour from the immediate producers by means of extra-economic coercion . . . pre-capitalist modes cannot be defined *except* via their political, legal and ideological superstructures, since these are what determine the type of extra-economic coercion that specifies them. The precise forms of juridical dependence,

from the pre-feudal ones in Europe and from other, non-European, medieval social and economic systems.[6] It therefore does not explain much.

I shall, in the following pages, try to establish these demarcating lines by suggesting the specificity of feudalism to western Europe between the fifth or the sixth century and the fifteenth century. Feudalism also developed in its classic form in eastern Europe between the sixteenth and the eighteenth century and possibly in Japan during the Tokugawa regime

---

property and sovereignty that characterize a pre-capitalist social formation, far from being merely accessory or contingent epiphenomena, compose on the contrary the central indices of the determinate mode of production dominant within it', ibid., p. 404 (emphasis original). Anderson himself defines feudalism, as we have noted earlier, as the specific organization of the seigneurial and serf classes 'in a vertically articulated system of parcellized sovereignty and scalar property that distinguished the feudal mode of production in Europe', ibid., p. 408. Quite apart from the problem with defining a mode of production (even a pre-capitalist one) in terms of the politico-legal specifics, into which we need not go here, Anderson has unnecessarily accepted the notion of similarity between the 'economic infrastructures' of different medieval regions. The similarity exists only when the definitions are wide, and therefore futile, enough to cover all of these economies (definitions such as 'non-economic coercion'); in fact the histories of these medieval regional economies have followed quite divergent paths even when they were all primarily agrarian economies and even when surplus was extracted through non-economic compulsion in all of them. Japan's feudalism is the only one outside Europe the genuineness of which is accepted by most analysts from Kari Marx to Marc Bloch to Anderson himself, although even there divergent opinions have not gone unrecorded. See Karl Marx, *Capital*, vol. I (Moscow, 1954), p. 718n.; Marc Bloch, *Feudal Society*, pp. 446–7, 452; Perry Anderson, *Lineages*, pp. 413–17, 435–61. Frances V. Moulder on the other hand suggests that certain similarities in the political structure between Tokugawa Japan and European feudalism notwithstanding, Japan's history was closer to China's than Europe's, *Japan, China and the Modern World Economy: Towards a Reinterpretation of East Asian Development c. 1600 to 1918* (Cambridge, 1977), pp. 25, 71–90.

In India the chief protagonists of an 'Indian feudalism' seek to establish the system's kinship with its European counterpart not so much in terms of the 'economic infrastructure' as in politico-juridical and ideological terms in consonance with unequal social distribution of property, though they make do with a simple, rather than a fanciful, language. See R.S. Sharma, *Indian Feudalism* and 'Problem of Transition from Ancient to Medieval in Indian History' *The Indian Historical Review*, vol. 1, no. 1, March 1974, pp. 1–9; B.N.S. Yadava, *Society and Culture in Northern India in the Twelfth Century* (Allahabad, 1973). Prof. R.S. Sharma's persuasive scholarship has indeed inspired a large body of literature on Indian 'feudalism' written along the lines suggested by him.

6 Thus is S. Nurul Hasan able to use the terms 'feudal' and 'pre-capitalist' as synonyms: 'the Mughal system was feudal and pre-capitalist in character', *Thoughts*, p. 3.

in particular. I am, however, constrained to leave these regions out of the discussion in this paper, hopefully without causing much harm to my argument. Since western Europe always provides the reference-point for any discussion of feudalism in India, or, for that matter, elsewhere, I shall also attempt a comparison between medieval western Europe and medieval India. The focus of this comparison will be on the respective conditions of labour which are determined by interaction between nature and social organization and which, in turn, determine the dominant characteristics of a social formation.

I

Feudalism, like other social formations before or after it, was a transitional system. As such it stood mid-way in the transition of the west European economy from a primarily slave-based system of agricultural production[7] to one dominated by the complementary classes of the capitalist farmer and the landless agricultural wage-earner, but in which the free peasantry also formed a significant element. It is necessary to suggest here that the term 'free peasant' as used in this paper is not concerned with the legal freedom of the peasant to alienate his proprietary rights in land or implements or the usufruct of his land; it is even less concerned with the absence of legal restriction on the peasant's mobility. Legal restrictions on the alienation of land acquire social significance only in the context of a fairly developed land market, just as legal restrictions on a peasant's mobility become important only if there is a developed labour-market so that the peasant, by being made immobile, is deprived of a competitive price for his labour. In the absence of these features of developed land

[7] There are, of course, divergent opinions regarding the primacy of slavery in the economy of Graeco-Roman Antiquity. A.H.M. Jones and R.H. Hilton believe that the ancient economy was dependent on the majority of small independent peasants rather than large latifundia cultivated by slaves. See Jones, 'The Economic Basis of Athenian Democracy', *Past and Present*, no. 1, Feb. 1952, pp. 13–31, and Hilton, *Bond Men Made Free: Medieval Peasant Movements and the English Rebellion of 1381* (London, 1973), p. 10. M.I. Finley, on the other hand, suggests the ratio of slaves to free citizenry at around 3 or 4:1 in the fifth or fourth centuries BC, precisely the period Jones is concerned with, 'Was Greek Civilisation Based on Slave Labour?', *Historia*, VIII, 1959, pp. 58–9 cited in Perry Anderson, *Passages from Antiquity to Feudalism* (London, 1974), pp. 22–23n. Anderson himself suggests a ratio of 3:2 after considering various other estimates, ibid.

and labour markets—which, indeed, characterized the era of the rise of capitalism and were thus bound to be absent earlier—not all the legal freedoms would make much difference to the fate of the peasant. The economic, rather than the legal, significance of the term 'free peasant' therefore denotes a peasant who, quite independently of his social or juridical status, earns his and his family's subsistence off his own (including his family's) material resources and labour. In other words, he (or his family) does not render labour to any one else either in the performance of labour service (for purposes of production) or for wages. This does not, of course, exempt him from the obligation to part with his surplus produce in the form of taxes to the state, or, on its behalf, to its officials. Nonetheless, he retains complete control over the process of production on his land through his (and his family's) labour[8] and is assured of a relatively more certain, though perhaps no higher level of, subsistence[9] than peasants who are 'unfree'.

As slavery became an increasingly uneconomic element in the production process of late Graeco-Roman Antiquity,[10] the European slaves, freedmen and, for reasons of growing insecurity, allodialists with varying resources were transformed into different strata of dependent peasantry.[11] This transformation never succeeded in eradicating social and economic

[8] This is essentially how Marx had understood the term, *Capital*, vol. III (Moscow, 1971), pp. 804, 807.

[9] 'Subsistence' as a Marxian concept includes 'the maintenance and reproduction of the producer', Marx, *Capital*, vol. I, p. 512. Clearly subsistence needs would vary from region to region according to the climate and from class to class according to custom. They would also vary with time as nature's productive capacity is utilized more fully. But in any pre-socialist society, given the class division, they are likely to approximate more closely to 'the natural wants imperatively calling for satisfaction' (ibid.) at the lower ends of society than at the middle and higher ends.

[10] M.I. Finley, *The Ancient Economy* (London, 1973), pp. 85–7; Marc Bloch, *French Rural History*, tr. Janet Sondheimer (London, 1976), p. 68; Bloch, 'The Rise of Dependent Cultivation', M.M. Postan (ed.), *Cambridge Economic History of Europe*, vol. I, 2nd edn (Cambridge, 1966), p. 248; Georges Duby, *Early Growth of European Economy: Warriors and Peasants from the Seventh to Twelfth Century*, tr. Howard B. Clarke (New York, 1974), p. 40 (hereafter *Warriors and Peasants*); Perry Anderson, *Passages*, pp. 18, 25–8, 79, 82.

[11] Marc Bloch, *Feudal Society*, pp. 171–3; Bloch, 'The Rise of Dependent Cultivation', pp. 255–6; Bloch, *French Rural History*, pp. 72–4, 76–7, 85–90; Georges Duby, *Rural Economy and Country Life in the Medieval West*, tr. Cynthia Postan, London, 1968, pp. 33–5; Duby, *Warriors and Peasants*, pp. 88–9; R.H. Hilton, *Bond Men Made Free*, pp. 33–5; Perry Anderson, *Passages*, p. 149.

differences within the class of peasants;[12] nor were the allodialists completely eliminated from any region in any period.[13]

With slavery becoming increasingly unproductive and the capitalist farmer, along with the landless agricultural worker co-existing with free peasant economy still to develop a long way in the future, the feudal economy came to be characterized by an intermediate and transitional feature which formed the core of the feudal mode of production in its early phase: in the early feudal economy the peasant, irrespective of his social or juridical condition, came to acquire certain hereditary rights for the use of land and other resources even when they belonged to the lord; on the other hand, his and his family's labour potential was always in excess of the resources on which it could be fully expended. In general, as Georges Duby has put it, with the exception of a stratum of the class of allodialists, the area of arable land cultivated by the tenanted manses, varying greatly in size, 'was always less than the amount of land which in theory corresponded to the physical capacity of a peasant family'.[14] One could perhaps add that this would be equally true of small peasant families, legally free but economically dependent on the sale of their labour to supplement their income from the land and that the limitation of resources would include agricultural implements and draught animals, in addition to land.

This hiatus between the labour potential of a peasant family and its resources (used for production) appears to have constituted the distinctive characteristic of the feudal mode of production in its formative stages; it enables us to distinguish the feudal mode of production from the slave and the capitalist modes in Europe[15] and from other medieval economies

[12] Marc Bloch, *Feudal Society*, p. 180; G. Duby, *Warriors and Peasants*, p. 40, 87–8, 90–1; Perry Anderson, *Passages*, p. 148; R.H. Hilton, *Bond Men Made Free*, pp. 42–4.

[13] Marc Bloch had once argued that in England, where feudalism was much more thoroughgoing because of being imposed from above after the Norman Conquest, the spread of the manor completely wiped out all traces of allodial property, *Feudal Society*, pp. 187–9, 244, 248. More recently it has been suggested that feudal land tenures, along with other feudal institutions, had developed in England before the Conquest which only accentuated their further development, while features of the pre-feudal past continued to exist as subsidiary elements; see J.O. Preswich, 'Anglo-Norman Feudalism and the Problem of Continuity', *Past and Present*, no. 26, Nov. 1963, pp. 39–57.

[14] G. Duby, *Rural Economy*, pp. 33–5, 40.

[15] Maurice Dobb did make this distinction in terms of unfreedom of the serf as the reflection of a property relation which asserted itself as a direct relationship between

in different regions of the world.[16] The agrarian economy of the ancient Graeco-Roman region depended largely on the separation of the producer from the means of production under conditions of slavery facilitating the appropriation of his entire labour by the owners of the latifundia. Capitalist agriculture, on the other hand, is characterized by the separation of the producer from the means of production under conditions of a wage labour-market, so that surplus value is appropriated by kulaks through the sale of the produce. Co-existing with it, though far from being its rival, is free peasant production with regional and temporal variations. In the feudal system in its classic form, the producer is neither completely separated from the means of production, nor is he an independent economic being. Indeed, it is via this intermediate feature that the western European economy effected its transition from slavery to capitalism. This feature formed the objective basis of the appropriation of the peasants' surplus labour by the feudal lords primarily for purposes of agricultural production.

Non-economic coercion by the feudal lords, then, consisted of a system of exploitation of the structured labour surplus, or excess of the labour potential of the peasant family over its resources. This hiatus formed the basis of the availability of labour for the cultivation of the

---

rulers and servants, *Studies*, p. 35. This distinction hinges on the juridical basis of unfreedom rather than on the economic basis, though it does have economic 'content' as Dobb asserted. More important, while the equation of feudalism with serfdom may faithfully describe the numerical preponderance of serfs in the production system, the bi-polar division between lords and serfs excludes from its purview the vital multi-polar tensions which were leading the feudal society on to hectic growth, and, ultimately, to its decline. Dobb's bi-polar division of feudal society explains feudalism's decline in terms of impoverishment of the peasantry owing to the lord's demand for more revenue; this explanation assumes a static level of production. In fact, feudalism declined owing to its tremendous onward march. For a detailed review of Maurice Dobb's argument, see Harbans Mukhia, 'Maurice Dobb's explanation of the Decline of Feudalism in Western Europe—a Critique', vol. VI, nos 1–2, July 1979–Jan. 1980, pp. 154–84.

We have already commented on Perry Anderson's delimitation of west European feudalism's specificities, which, indeed, are such that pre-thirteenth century early medieval India, at least, can find herself comfortably placed there much against Anderson's will.

[16] China is another major region of the world which is said to have had its feudalism, beginning with the Chou dynasty in about 1050 BC. The distinguished Chinese historian, Wu Ta-k'un has, however, questioned the validity of the concept of Chinese 'feudalism', 'An Interpretation of Chinese Economic History', *Past and Present*, no. 1, Feb. 1952, pp. 1–13.

lord's demesne through forced labour or, marginally, hired labour. This form of coercion became part of the conditions of labour and subsistence, and hence far more effective than any amount of overt force. The dependence of the entire peasantry (including the serfs, but barring a stratum of allodialists) on the lords was thus structured in the production process, for the lord controlled, even if only partly, the use of labour-time for production on the peasant's manse.

This view of feudalism based on *the structured dependence of the entire peasantry on the lords* (with the only exception of the crust of independent allodialists) enables us to take into account the dynamism of feudal society and to understand its development during the eleventh, twelfth and thirteenth centuries and its decline in the fourteenth century as the culmination of peasant resistance generated in the course of daily toil in the fields during the preceding centuries. For this dynamism was also structured in the hiatus between the peasant family's labour power and its productive resources.

For the surfeit of labour power of the peasant family and the lord's demand for it were not quite symmetrical. In a system of agricultural production based on an intensive use of labour (including the wastage of labour in traversing vast fields), where the returns on labour were abysmal and where the period available for agricultural operations was brief, the input or withdrawal of even small amounts of labour made considerable difference to output, whether on the lord's demesne or the peasant's own manse. This resulted in a struggle between the lord and the peasant to push the limits of the surfeit labour in one or the other direction. This silent class struggle occurred in the actual process of tilling the soil.[17] If the lord imposed rigorous supervision over the peasant's toil, the peasant responded with inertia and deception and had on his side the merciful incompetence and corruptibility of the supervisory staff. If the lord endeavoured to exact labour beyond the time that the peasant could spare from the cultivation of his own land, the peasant was also constantly on the watch for opportunities to steal from the lord's time and devote it to his own manse. Such opportunities were not rare, particularly at the peripheries of the manor where supervision was less rigorous, or wherever the peasant's manse might lie adjacent to the demesne.[18]

[17] F.L. Ganshof and A. Verhurlst, 'France, the Low Countries and Western Germany', *Cambridge Economic History,* pp. 314–15.

[18] G. Duby, *Warriors and Peasants,* pp. 89–90, 94–5.

The labour-intensive nature of agricultural production was conditioned by a number of factors. The chief constraint upon medieval European agriculture was the lack of manure.[19] The implements used were relatively primitive,[20] and even the draught power of the animals was under-used owing to defective methods of harnessing them;[21] this limited the period for which land was under the plough. All these factors necessitated extensive cultivation, and the seeds had to be spread out on the field, the deeper fertility of which remained unutilized. Extensive cultivation in turn meant wastage of labour in traversing long distances on the field itself and from the nucleated village settlements to the outlying fields.[22]

Thus in the few weeks available for actual cultivation there was great demand for manual labour on which agricultural practices were so heavily dependent.[23] This might perhaps explain the relative stability of village settlements in western Europe during the eighth, ninth and tenth centuries,[24] for agricultural operations at every level, from the lord to the humble peasant, required a stable supply of labour.

This great demand for manual labour in turn conditioned some other aspects of early feudal society; labour services were so organized as to place the heaviest burden on those with least resources—those who had nothing else to give except labour with bare hands.[25] It is in this context that the question of population also assumes a peculiar complexity. For medieval Europe, in what Marc Bloch has called the 'first feudal age', was both over- and under-populated at the same time. It was over-populated during the larger part of the year when peasants had little to do and had to subsist off the forest products such as wild fruits, honey and wild animals and were periodically wiped out by famines;[26] but during the brief period

[19] Charles Parain, 'The Evolution of Agricultural Technique', *Cambridge Economic History*, pp. 133–4, 145–6; Marc Bloch, *French Rural History*, p. 25; G. Duby, *Rural Economy*, pp. 24–5; Duby, *Warriors and Peasants*, p. 169.

[20] Charles Parain, pp. 128–9, 148–57; G. Duby, *Rural Economy*, pp. 17–21; Lynn White Jr., *Medieval Technology and Social Change* (London, 1973) (first published 1962), pp. 41–3, 53.

[21] Charles Parain, pp. 144–5; Lynn White, pp. 59–60.

[22] Marc Bloch, *Feudal Society*, pp. 60–1; G. Duby, *Rural Economy*, pp. 6, 14.

[23] G. Duby, *Rural Economy*, p. 18; Charles Parain, pp. 129–31, 152–3, 157–9.

[24] G. Duby, *Rural Economy*, pp. 6–7, 14–15.

[25] Marc Bloch, *French Rural History*, pp. 72–4; G. Duby, *Rural Economy*, pp. 40–2; R.H. Hilton, *Bond Men Made Free*, pp. 61, 85–6.

[26] G. Duby, *Rural Economy*, pp. 12–15; G. Duby, *Warriors and Peasants*, pp. 78–83.

when agricultural operations were to be carried out there was an acute scarcity of labour.[27]

If this scarcity were to be overcome, it would be necessary to make more intensive use of soil-fertility and to forge some labour-saving devices. West European society as a whole was thus poised for technological development with a direct bearing on agriculture.[28]

The centuries after AD 1000 witnessed technical development which related primarily to implements and agricultural practices; manuring remained almost as meagre as earlier. Most of the tools and techniques that spread widely in western Europe during the first three centuries of the second millennium AD had been known to Europe in theory or practice for varying lengths of time, though their application had been very limited. Only in this period did conditions evolve for their wide social acceptance.[29] On the whole this era was marked by a 'technical dynamism'.[30]

Agricultural progress in these centuries, particularly in the twelfth and thirteenth centuries, following the use of better implements and practices and a more effective use of human and animal labour, led to a phenomenal rise in the productivity of land and labour. The seed:yield ratio which stood at 1:1.6 or at best at 1:2.5 during the ninth and tenth centuries became 1:4 during the thirteenth century.[31] The magnitude of this advance can be assessed from the fact that a rise in the ratio from 1:2 to 1:3 would double the amount of food available for consumption. This continued to be the average ratio until the sixteenth century in many regions of western Europe and in some of them even up to the nineteenth century.[32]

Indirectly, following a rise in the productivity of land, the size of

27 G. Duby, *Rural Economy*, pp. 38–9, 48–9.

28 Marc Bloch and G. Duby have argued that the incentive for technological development came from the lord's estates. See Bloch, 'Mediaeval Inventions' in his *Land and Work in Medieval Europe*, tr. J.E. Anderson, London, 1967, p. 182 and Duby, *Warriors and Peasants*, pp. 95–6, 177, 229–30. For the suggestion that the society as a whole created this development, see Harbans Mukhia, 'Maurice Dobb's Explanation' pp. 165–7.

29 Perry Anderson, *Passages*, p. 183.

30 Lynn White, p. 88.

31 G. Duby, *Rural Economy*, pp. 25–7; 103; C. Parain, p. 125; Lord Beveridge, 'The Yield and Price of Corn in the Middle Ages', in E.M. Carus-Wilson, ed., *Essays in Economic History*, vol. I (London, 1966) (first published 1954), pp. 15–16.

32 G. Duby, *Rural Economy*, p. 102.

holding necessary to maintain a peasant family declined sharply from about a hundred acres a manse on an average in the ninth century to anywhere between twenty and thirty in the thirteenth century.[33] While the ninth century was characterized by the existence of full manses, in the twelfth century the quarter manse had become the standard unit of a tenure.[34]

A reduction in the size of the holding minimized the wastage of labour in agricultural production; the rise in productivity on the other hand stimulated the growth of population. The availability of greater amounts of food (and particularly vegetable proteins) as a result of agricultural progress allowed population to grow at the lower ends of society where scarcity of foodgrains and proteins was a constraint on reproduction. The relative decline in the frequency and intensity of famines during the first three centuries after 1000 assisted in population growth at the peasants' level; later on, during the fourteenth century, when food again became scarce and famines resumed their dismal visitations with customary ferocity, it was at the peasants' level that death took its largest toll.[35] Life expectancy also appears to have risen from about 25 years in the Roman Empire to 35 in England in the thirteenth century.[36] However, the problem of the growth or decline of population is not related merely to the productivity of land; the uncertainty of production, and, even more important, the unequal distribution of produce (and resources in general) played a more decisive role.[37]

At any rate, even though the benefits of the rise in productivity were differentially distributed, the rural poor also shared in it and were assured of a certain amount of secure nutrition; this was not a negligible impetus

33 R.H. Hilton, *Bond Men Made Free*, p. 28. The manse comprised the amount of land necessary to maintain one household at subsistence level; it therefore differed from region to region according to soil-fertility and the customary subsistence needs of the peasant family unit. See Robert Latouche, *The Birth of Western Economy*, tr. E.M. Wilkinson (London, 1961), p. 82 and A. Gurevich, 'Representations of Property during the High Middle Ages', *Economy and Society*, vol. VI, no. 1, Feb. 1977, p. 8.

34 G. Fourquin, *Lordship and Feudalism in the Middle Ages*, tr. Iris and Lytton Sells (London, 1976), p. 168.

35 G. Duby, *Rural Economy*, pp. 294–5.

36 R.S. Lopez, *The Birth of Europe* (London, 1967), p. 398, cited in Perry Anderson, *Passages*, p. 190.

37 E.A. Kosminsky suggests, in passing, the significance of the unequal distribution of property in feudal society in this context, 'The Evolution of Feudal Rent in England', *Past and Present*, no. 7, April 1955, p. 22.

to human multiplication. Duby has noted that the influx of men to the towns during the centuries of agricultural progress originated in villages with more generous harvests.[38] There is a consensus among historians that between 1000 and 1300 there was a considerable growth of population.[39]

Many of these developments—diminution in the amount of land necessary to provide subsistence to a peasant family, the more effective use of soil-fertility through better tools and techniques, the rise in population—caused extensive land reclamation in Europe, starting hesitantly in the late tenth or early eleventh century and reaching its peak in the second half of the twelfth century. In the thirteenth century it began to taper off and was gradually replaced by increased pastoral activity.[40] Initially it was the peasants who reclaimed land in search of lessening their encumbrances.[41] Group-migration from old villages notwithstanding, the consequence of the land-reclamation movement was individualization—both of the holdings and cultivation.[42] Individualization was also reflected in the break-up of the large kinship groups into nuclear family units.[43]

[38] G. Duby, *Warriors and Peasants*, pp. 198–9.

[39] J.C. Russell, *Late Ancient and Medieval Populations* (Philadelphia, 1958), pp. 102–13; Russell, 'Population in Europe', in Carlo M. Cipolla, ed., *The Fontana Economic History of Europe* vol. I (London, 1972), pp. 39–40; M.M. Postan, *The Medieval Economy and Society* (London, 1975) (first published 1972), pp. 35–6; J.Z. Titow, 'Some Differences Between Manors and their Effects on the Condition of the Peasant in the Thirteenth Century', *Agricultural History Review*, vol. X, no. 1, 1962, pp. 1–2; Maurice Dobb, *Studies*, p. 47; Marc Bloch, *French Rural History*, p. 16; Duby, *Rural Economy*, pp. 119–22.

[40] G. Duby, *Rural Economy*, pp. 81–7; Duby, *Warriors and Peasants*, pp. 199–210.

[41] Hermann Aubin, 'The Land East of the Elbe and German Colonization Eastwards', *Cambridge Economic History*, pp. 455–6; E. Miller, 'The English Economy in the Thirteenth Century: Implications of Recent Research', *Past and Present*, no. 28, July 1964, p. 33; Patricia Croot and David Parker, 'Agrarian Class Structure and Economic Development', *Past and Present*, no. 78, February 1978, p. 39; G. Duby, *Warriors and Peasants*, pp. 201, 208.

[42] B.K. Roberts, 'A Study of Medieval Colonisation in the Forest of Arden, Warwickshire', *Agricultural History Review*, vol. XVI, 1968, p. 102; Leopold Genicot, 'Crisis: From the Middle Ages to Modern Times', *Cambridge Economic History*, pp. 733–4; Ganshof and Verhurlst, pp. 297–8; G. Duby, *Warriors and Peasants*, p. 205.

[43] Marc Bloch, *Feudal Society*, pp. 137–41; Joan Thirsk, 'The Family', *Past and Present*, no. 27, April 1964, pp. 117–22. Laslett, however, is reluctant to accept the notion that changes in family structures correspond to social transformations, *The World We Have Lost*, cited in Hans Medick, 'The Proto-Industrial Family Economy: The Structural

The movement for land reclamation was soon taken over by the lords and it became far more organized.[44] There was, however, a distinction in the condition of peasants on the two types of land reclaimed. On the piece cleared by himself, the peasant had a greater autonomy and therefore lighter burdens; on the lord's reclaimed land, on the other hand, the peasant's dependence and burdens were greater, though in comparison to peasants in the old villages they were substantially lighter.[45]

The conditions of labour in the west European countryside had changed. As the productivity of land rose with the introduction of relatively capital-intensive technology, the price of land and implements also rose; on the other hand, the demand for manual labour declined. Consequently, the burden of forced labour now shifted from bare manual work to work with a plough-team;[46] it shifted, in other words, from the lowest rung of society to a rung or two above it. The peasant also, seized by the legitimate desire to raise more produce from his own land, became increasingly reluctant to render labour service.[47] Thus unpaid labour was once again becoming an uneconomic proposition in west European history, as it had earlier become under slavery. On the other hand, the growing peasant population made labour available in the expanding labour-market. It was thus that the process of 'commutation' of forced labour into payments in cash and kind started. There was, besides, the process of 'enfranchisement' whereby the dependent peasant purchased his freedom ('the franchise') off the lord. Indeed, the lords encouraged commutation and enfranchisement, for these brought them ready incomes, whereas they could hire in the expanding labour-market such labour as they required for the cultivation of their estates. The peasant, for his part, also welcomed commutation or enfranchisement.[48] Payment

---

Function of Household and Family During the Transition from Peasant Society to Industrial Capitalism', *Social History*, vol. I, no. 3, October 1976, pp. 292–3.

44 G. Duby, *Warriors and Peasants*, pp. 205–8.

45 G. Duby, *Rural Economy*, p. 77.

46 Ibid., pp. 115–16, 207–8.

47 Ibid., pp. 207–8, 263–4; Lynn White, *Medieval Technology*, p. 65. Andrew Jones argues that labourers' perquisites had to be created in England during the thirteenth and fourteenth centuries to obtain speedy and efficient use of customary labour, 'Harvest Customs and Labourers' Perquisites in Southern England, 1150–1350; the Corn Harvest', *Agricultural History Review*, vol. XXV, 1977, p. 14.

48 Marc Bloch, *French Rural History*, pp. 106–12; G. Duby, *Rural Economy*, p. 208; Duby, *Warriors and Peasants*, pp. 91–2.

of a fixed amount of cash or kind in rent, wherever it was so fixed, would enable him to devote more attention to his own manse and he would be the exclusive beneficiary of increased production or higher prices. Franchise would permit him to become independent once and for all, so that he could look after his land or migrate to places where he would obtain the highest price for his labour. However, some caution is called for in assessing the progress of commutation and enfranchisement. These did not proceed in a linear progression; there were many reversals along the way.[49] Nonetheless the peasant's burdens were definitely lightened.

Commutation and enfranchisement made a differential impact on the different strata of feudal lords. Whereas the seigneurs[50] still had various sources of their income intact—the right to mint coins, the administration of justice[51] which was being increasingly used to collect fines, the establishment of 'monopolies',[52]—the smaller lords with no seigneurial authority had increasingly to shift to new forms of subsistence. They took to cultivating the demesne with their own, and hired, labour

49 M.M. Postan, 'The Rise of a Money Economy', in Carus-Wilson (ed.), vol. 1, p. 7; R.H. Hilton, 'Freedom and Villeinage in England', in Hilton (ed.), *Peasants, Knights and Heretics*, p. 181; P.D.A. Harvey, 'The English Inflation of 1180–1220' in ibid., pp. 74–5; G. Duby, *Warriors and Peasants*, p. 222; E.A. Kosminsky, 'Services and Money Rents in the Thirteenth Century', in Carus-Wilson (ed.), *Essays in Economic History*, vol. II, 1966 (first published 1962), pp. 39–42 where he suggests that villeinage remained a more important part of labour-supply on the larger estates while the smaller ones depended more on hired labour.

50 Among the lords were the seigneurs, or the banal lords, whose authority was derived from their exercise of the *ban*, theoretically the king's power to give orders, but actually usurped by lords from the eighth century onwards. Since it was by nature an arbitrary power, its flexibility as a source of income and authority was much prized by the seigneurs who had both land and men within their jurisdiction. Then there were the landlords whose control extended to the land. Besides, there were the non-territorial lords who derived their income from the right to collect taxes, tithes etc., a right they had either earned or had simply usurped; see Marc Bloch, *Feudal Society*, p. 251; J.S. Critchley, *Feudalism* (London, 1978), p. 67; G. Duby, *Warriors and Peasants*, pp. 174–7; Guy Forquin, pp. 133–6.

51 The power to administer justice was as stratified as the class of lords; see Critchley, p. 57; also Marc Bloch, *French Rural History*, pp. 78–80; Guy Fourquin, pp. 185–6; G. Duby, *Warriors and Peasants*, pp. 211–13, 227, 249–51.

52 The 'monopolies' comprised the mills for grinding corn, the oven for baking bread, the winepress for the grapes, and the bull and boar for replenishing the livestock of the village, etc. These monopolies were fiercely contested by the peasants; see Marc Bloch, *Land and Work in Medieval Europe*, pp. 135–68; Bloch, *Feudal Society*, p. 251; G. Duby, *Warriors and Peasants*, pp. 222–3, 227–9.

and selling the produce in the market[53] which was increasingly influencing the patterns of agricultural production. The agricultural progress of the eleventh, twelfth and thirteenth centuries had considerably increased the marketable surplus in the countryside and this in turn led to a noticeable growth in trade and urbanization in this period. On the other hand, trade and urban centres began, to an extent, to determine the patterns of production in the countryside. Of course, the demand for agricultural produce was growing in rural areas as well wherever the landless agricultural worker, being paid his wages in cash, had to buy his subsistence. Rural artisans were similarly placed.

The role played by trade as well as towns in the decline of feudalism in Europe has been examined by many historians and it is not necessary to go into the highly controversial theme here.[54] It does, however, appear on balance that the main direction of peasant migration in western Europe in the first five centuries after AD 1000 had been within the countryside itself. By and large, it was the land with lesser encumbrances that beckoned the peasants to uproot themselves from their old villages and resettle at long distances; the town played at best a marginal role in this movement. Indeed, when the west European peasantry broke into rebellion of literally continental dimensions during the fourteenth century, one of its chief demands was the right to free mobility, whereas most cities on the continent looked on passively whenever they did not help the lords suppress these uprisings.[55]

The changes in the west European countryside then, which had resulted from the interaction of the developing social structure and the given means of production in the first feudal age, undermined the very basis of feudal society. These changes had, above all, led to a process of differentiation in the countryside and the emergence of the complementary classes of the kulak and the landless agricultural worker together with—as a subordinate element and with great regional variations—the free peasant.[56]

[53] E.A. Kosminsky, 'Services and Money Rent', pp. 46–8.

[54] However, the paper on 'Maurice Dobb's Explanation' referred to earlier discusses this question in some detail on pp. 174–5.

[55] R.H. Hilton, *Bond Men Made Free*, pp. 128–9, 130, 132 and 206–7 where Hilton discusses the attitude of the urban bourgeoisie towards the Grand Jacquerie, the Catalan remensas, the Tuchin rebellion and other peasant movements respectively.

[56] L. Genicot and G. Duby have discussed this process of differentiation in considerable detail and with impressive clarity. See L. Genicot, 'Crisis', and Duby, *Rural Economy*, passim.

With the increased marketable surplus in the countryside, trade began to assume increasing importance in the west European economy from the eleventh century,[57] though it had never been absent earlier.[58] The use of the horseshoe-nail in this period greatly improved transport which in turn assisted in the promotion of trade.[59] There were, of course, considerable regional and local price variations and local price fluctuations. The short-term price fluctuations, however, occurred in the background of a long-term average price rise. The twelfth and thirteenth centuries were marked by a rise in production followed by a rise in prices.[60] Clearly, demand was growing faster than the supply.

Conditions were thus very favourable for production for the market. Both productivity and prices were rising. Labour could be hired. Wages would decline as the demand for foodgrains rose—both resulting from a growing population. It was also possible, of course, on some manors to combine production for the market with the use of the serf's unpaid labour.[61] These conditions began increasingly to drive agricultural production into patterns of commerce and this in turn lent strength to the process of differentiation.

There were many reasons for the rise of the class of kulaks, the most important amongst them being the bigger lords' agents or bailiffs, etc.[62]

57 G. Duby, *Rural Economy*, pp. 126–65.

58 For the existence of money and exchange in classical feudalism of earlier centuries, see Marc Bloch, 'Natural Economy or Money Economy: A Pseudo Dilemma', in his *Land and Work in Medieval Europe*, pp. 230–44. Witold Kula, constructing a 'model' of feudal economy, suggests the existence of 'monetary' and 'natural' sectors within every feudal 'enterprise' big or small, *An Economic Theory of the Feudal System*, tr. Lawrence Garner (London, 1976), p. 133.

59 R.S. Lopez, 'The Evolution of Land Transport in the Middle Ages', *Past and Present*, no. 9, April 1956, p. 24. Marc Bloch notes the construction of a large number of bridges all over Europe during the twelfth century, *Feudal Society*, pp. 69–70.

60 G. Duby, *Rural Economy*, pp. 302–5; Perry Anderson, *Passages*, p. 191. The rise in agricultural prices was especially steep in England between 1180 and 1220; see P.D.A. Harvey, 'The English Inflation of 1180–1220', in *Peasants, Knights and Heretics*, pp. 57–8.

61 G. Duby, *Rural Economy*, pp. 263–4; M.M. Postan, 'The Rise of a Money Economy', p. 7.

62 The large size of the noble or clerical domains within the range of 2000 to 4000 acres necessitated the recruitment of bailiffs to supervise production, storage, consumption, sale, etc. For the size of the estate, see Perry Anderson, *Passages*, p. 140; also Guy Fourquin, p. 172; G. Duby, *Warriors and Peasants*, pp. 46–7, 229; G. Duby, *Rural Economy*, pp. 228–31, passim. Duby's *Rural Economy* contains perhaps the best account

These agents, often originating at the lowest rungs of society,[63] were familiar with agricultural practices at first hand; they, however, considered touching the plough as beneath their dignity; they did not scruple to grab money at every opportunity whether from the peasants, the lords, the merchants or from God's own house, the Church.[64] Their power over the peasants corresponded to the lord's power.[65] But there was an incipient conflict between them and their masters. For as commercialization of agriculture proceeded, the agents took the lord's demesne on 'farm' or gradually purchased land. On this they employed their own and family labour supplemented by hired labour, with a view to selling its produce. They were thus emerging as alternative bases of economic power within the feudal society. This class of much-maligned *nouveaux riches*, of low social origins and moderate cultural tastes, the butt of the aristocracy's ridicule,[66] driven by the desire for profit, formed one of the chief dynamic elements in the later medieval economy of western Europe.

Besides the agents, the small lords, pushed by the need to sell in the market but constrained by the limits of their resources, found themselves alongside the bailiffs.[67] There were also the merchants, urban and rural, who entered the arena in search of profit.[68] They 'farmed' fragments of large estates which the lords were willing to hand over to them when feudal rents were declining.[69] They gradually purchased land on which they employed hired labour, the produce being sent to the market. They tried to expand the scale of production by reinvesting the returns.[70]

Some peasants were also able to rise. The number of such peasants was rather small and at any rate they were, in most cases, better off at the starting point than those from whose ranks they had risen. Some cases of peasants taking the lord's demesne on 'farm' have also been noted.[71]

---

of the transformation of the class of agents into rich farmers or kulaks.

63 Marc Bloch, *French Rural History*, pp. 191–2; G. Duby, *Warriors and Peasants*, p. 47; Henri Pirenne, pp. 60–1.

64 G. Duby, *Warriors and Peasants*, p. 229; Duby, *Rural Economy*, pp. 219, 245.

65 G. Duby, *Rural Economy*, pp. 244–5.

66 G. Duby, *Warriors and Peasants*, pp. 257–8.

67 E.A. Kosminsky, 'Services and Money Rents', pp. 46–8; Kosminsky, 'The Evolution of Feudal Rent', p. 35n; G. Duby, *Rural Economy*, p. 247; Duby, *Warriors and Peasants*, pp. 176–7.

68 Guy Fourquin, pp. 80–2; G. Duby, *Rural Economy*, p. 129.

69 L. Genicot, pp. 715–16.

70 Marc Bloch, *French Rural History*, p. 124.

71 G. Duby, *Rural Economy*, p. 236.

The small and marginal peasants, on the other hand, by and large, became landless agricultural workers. To use the new, capital-intensive technology, the small (and marginal) peasant had to depend upon loans. He had also to borrow money if he desired his franchise, or if he migrated elsewhere where he would need sustenance for the initial breathing period. He was thus subject to stiff borrowing conditions, either by the merchant-moneylender or the lord. The former would buy off a part or the whole of the peasant's surplus produce in advance repayment of the loan or the interest and thus deprive him of the advantage of a price rise. The lord, on the other hand, would impose stiff conditions, including, at times, labour services.[72] Real freedom came only to those peasants who had their own resources to buy it.[73] The lord also adjusted to the economic benefits of the age by replacing hereditary tenancies with fixed-time tenures and gradually even the latter with tenancies-at-will so that at each renewal of a tenure the advantage of any rise in productivity or prices could accrue to him.[74]

The small and the marginal peasants were thus subjected to many pressures. Deprived of the protection of the lord, the village community or even his own group of kinsmen, the slightest vagary of production or prices would compel this peasant to sell or forfeit his mortgaged land and implements and he would immediately go reeling into the ranks of the landless looking for work in the labour market. It is perhaps true that socially the small peasant suffered a depression in his status on losing his bit of land but economically, even as a landless agricultural wage-earner, he was better off than he was as a small peasant.[75] But this situation could last only so long as the society as a whole registered economic progress. With the slightest setback to the economy, those who were at its lower

[72] Ibid., pp. 252–9, 285. The intensification of labour services on the English estates towards the end of the thirteenth century has been sufficiently highlighted by Kosminsky, 'Services and Money Rents', pp. 46–7 and Hilton, 'Freedom and Villeinage in England', pp. 181, 184.

[73] G. Duby, *Rural Economy*, pp. 256–7.

[74] Ibid., pp. 257–8.

[75] L. Genicot suggests that during the fourteenth and the fifteenth centuries the small landowners suffered a depression and the landless agricultural workers and marginal farmers registered an improvement in their economic condition, so that 'at the end of the Middle Ages not the whole but the greater part of the rural population shared approximately the same economic standard of life', pp. 728–31. See also G. Duby, *Rural Economy*, pp. 152, 280, 305.

end had to pay the heaviest price. Famine would make its terrible appearance and wipe out large numbers of resourceless peasants.[76]

It was thus that feudal society was growing and, in the process, giving birth to two inter-related classes, and reviving an older one in greater strength, which were to destroy the parent structure through various stages and forms of struggle. The initial thrust for capitalist development originated in the countryside.

Agricultural progress in the twelfth and thirteenth centuries consisted primarily in the extension of the arable into the forest and pasture land; and it had also reduced the period of the fallow thereby utilizing the existing soil-fertility more intensively. This could, however, go on only up to a point, for a shrinking pasture would reduce the animal population which in turn would diminish the quantity of manure, scarce as it already was. The forest, on the other hand, also maintained a delicate ecological balance which would be disturbed by cutting down trees in large numbers. Besides, apart from wood, the demand for which was on the increase,[77] they provided supplementary food to both men and animals.

Historians are generally agreed that agricultural progress had begun to recede from the beginning of the fourteenth century all over western Europe, though the intensity of the recession varied regionally, for the land reclamation movement during the preceding two centuries had over-reached itself.[78] Given the unequal distribution of resources, the declining yields from the more marginal of the reclaimed lands, were beginning to weaken and sweep off a number of people from the poorer strata.[79] The availability of labour was itself, perhaps, inhibiting any further technical development.

The fourteenth century witnessed great social upheavals. There was also considerable ecological disturbance which was reflected in an appreciable fall in the temperature and continuous rainfall for long periods such

[76] G. Duby, *Rural Economy*, p. 286.

[77] Ibid., pp. 141–5.

[78] Ibid., pp. 317ff.; Perry Anderson, *Passages*, pp. 197–9; Marc Bloch, *French Rural History*, pp. 17, 112; M.M. Postan, *The Medieval Economy and Society*, pp. 63–79; R.H. Hilton, *Bond Men Made Free*, p. 16; E. Miller, 'The English Economy of the Thirteenth Century', p. 38. Guy Bois makes the point in the classic Marxist idiom: 'Above all, the system had exhausted its possibilities for expansion in a virtually complete conquest of the cultivable area', 'The Transition from Feudalism to Capitalism' (mimeo) presented to the Indo-French Seminar on the same theme at the University of Delhi, Jan. 1979, p. 21.

as in 1315–17. Famines resumed their dismal visitations and there was a series of epidemics. The famine of 1315–17 deprived western Europe of a tenth of its population.[80] The Black Death of 1348–50 was only one in a series of disasters, though the most catastrophic of them;[81] it wiped out anywhere between a quarter and a half of the population. Nor did the epidemics cease after this terrible toll. Thus, even assuming a lower death rate of 25 per cent in 1350, the west European population had lost 40 per cent of its strength during the course of the fourteenth century,[82] even if we assume that those who suffered acute malnutrition but still survived could be counted as full members of the work-force.[83]

The immediate consequence of these disasters was a price-scissors effect: the prices of foodgrains fell owing to a fall in demand, but wages and the prices of industrial goods were on the rise.[84] This was a direct challenge to the lords' standards of living, for their incomes from the land were declining but the cost of agricultural production and prices of luxury goods were rising. This should have reinforced the process of differentiation within the class of landlords, for the smaller ones, with no source of income other than land, were ruined more easily than the bigger ones who could still rely upon court-fines, monopolies etc.[85] Land was also available more freely now and in this way the free peasantry re-emerged in strength.[86]

80 For disturbed ecological balance, etc., see Perry Anderson, *Passages*, pp. 198–9; for famines and epidemics, see G. Duby, *Rural Economy*, p. 295. Also Ian Kershaw, 'The Great Famine and Agrarian Crisis in England 1315–22', in Hilton (ed.), *Peasants, Knights and Heretics*, pp. 85–132.

81 Philip Ziegler, *The Black Death* (London, 1970) (first published 1969); Perry Anderson, *Passages*, p. 201.

82 J.C. Russell, *Late Ancient and Medieval Populations*, p. 131.

83 Duby suggests that the middle-aged resisted epidemics with greater strength, *Rural Economy*, p. 308. This should reflect the decreasing resistance of the younger generation perhaps because of diminishing nourishment owing to the declining returns from the land. Slicher van Bath very sensitively discusses the physical and mental consequences of prolonged malnutrition, *Agrarian History of Western Europe, 500–1850*, tr. O. Ordish (London, 1963), pp. 11, 84.

84 Thus, for example, while between the thirteenth and the mid-fifteenth century agricultural prices fell by 10 per cent, wages rose by 250 per cent, R.H. Hilton, *Bond Men Made Free*, p. 154; Genicot, pp. 684, 692, 694; G. Duby, *Rural Economy*, pp. 307–8, 320; Guy Bois, 'Note on the Movement of Prices in Feudal Economic Systems' (mimeo), p. 2.

85 G. Duby, *Rural Economy*, p. 316.

86 Cristobal Kay, 'Comparative Development of the European Manorial System and

The aristocracy, on the other hand, took resort to war and plunder. Everywhere in western Europe this was a period of extensive wars—the Hundred Years' War in France, the Wars of the Roses in England; in Germany and Italy; in Spain and Flanders. Even the resurgence of the state during this period added its weight to the crisis by raising the level of its demand for taxes.[87]

But then it was not these developments which created the 'general crisis' of feudalism. Feudal society had, in the past, been familiar with over-population, wars, famines and deaths. The general crisis was, on the other hand, the result of the determination of men to get over the impasse according to their situation in society.[88] The class of feudal lords, faced with declining incomes and rising expenditures, still commanded the power of the state and took resort to an overt use of it. The state, which was reviving all over western Europe at this time, intervened on behalf of the lords by fixing wages at the pre-Black Death level, and by legally restricting peasant mobility—unlike in the first feudal age when peasant immobility was part of the production system. This was a challenge to the landless wage-earner, the small and marginal peasants who earned their living in part by selling their labour and the emerging class of kulaks who hired labour and therefore required a mobile peasantry. The 'feudal reaction' assumed similar forms everywhere.

The peasantry, on the other hand, was so situated as to be able to defend its gain much more forcefully than ever before, for demand for labour was much greater than the available supply. The desolate lands also provided opportunities to those peasants who had the other necessary means to emerge as free peasants. The peasantry thus responded to the 'feudal reaction' by bursting out in a string of rebellions everywhere in western Europe.[89]

The fourteenth century saw a series of minor peasant uprisings and some really massive rebellions, spread over the entire hundred years. A remarkable feature of these great rebellions was that most of them occurred in the most prosperous rural regions of western Europe and were

the Latin American Hacienda System', *Journal of Peasant Studies*, vol. II, no. 1, October 1974, p. 72.

87 L. Genicot, pp. 699–700; Guy Fourquin, p. 210.

88 Guy Bois, 'Transition', pp. 21–6; R.H. Hilton, 'A Crisis of Feudalism', *Past and Present*, no. 80, August 1978, pp. 11–18.

89 R.H. Hilton, *Bond Men Made Free*, pp. 85ff.

led by the most prosperous sections of the peasantry: the Flanders rebellion of 1323–27, the Grand Jacquerie of 1358, north of Paris; the Tuchin movement in central France from the 1360s to the end of the century, and, of course, the great peasant uprising of 1381 in the East Anglia region of England. The fifteenth century witnessed the massive outburst of the remensas of Catalonia.[90] Germany also had a series of peasant uprisings in the fourteenth and fifteenth centuries.[91]

It is also remarkable that in regions where poverty prevailed, the peasantry remained passive. In central Italy, rent-racking of the peasantry led to a decline in the rate of the growth of population, but, sadly, engendered no rebellion.[92] When the Grand Jacquerie was up in arms in the region north of Paris, one of the most prosperous regions in the European countryside, the area to the south-west of Paris, where poverty reigned, remained inert.[93]

The peasantry was thus rising to defend the gains it had made as a result of the emergence of a new mode of production in the countryside;[94] for rebellions occurred by and large in those areas where the emergence of the new mode of production was more pronounced, and where peasants were acquiring self-confidence, so essential to the act of rebellion, which, after all, is an act of great humanism.

By the end of the fourteenth century the failure of the feudal reaction had become apparent.[95] From the beginning of the fifteenth century western Europe began to recover its bases of strength. The ground for this recovery had been prepared by the preceding 'crisis' that had undermined much of the economic and social system which had become outmoded by its own tremendous onwards movement. The attainment of the abstraction of capitalism was yet a long way off.[96] But the movement had been set firmly in its direction.

[90] Ibid., G. Duby, *Rural Economy*, pp. 332–5.

[91] Peter Blickle, 'Peasant Revolts in the German Empire in the Late Middle Ages', *Social History*, vol. IV, no. 2, May 1979, pp. 223–39.

[92] Perry Anderson, *Passages*, p. 199 and n.

[93] R.H. Hilton appears to be astonished that 'the impoverished and badly harassed area to the south west of the city—precisely where one would expect an explosion of pure misery—was virtually untouched by the rebellion', *Bond Men Made Free*, p. 117.

[94] Ibid., pp. 82, 89–90, 94.

[95] Perry Anderson, *Passages*, p. 293.

[96] Maurice Dobb justly considers the fifteenth and the sixteenth centuries 'transitional' between feudalism and capitalism, *Studies*, p. 20.

II

Expressions of grave regret over the lack of adequate information on the social history of ancient and medieval India is perhaps the inevitable starting point of historical research on these periods. The paucity of information is felt more deeply when compared with the almost embarrassing amount of evidence available on medieval Europe. If, therefore, the contents of the following pages appear to be a string of conjectures and speculations, at least part of it could, perhaps, be blamed on the collective misfortune of historians that so little of the evidence from India's ancient and medieval centuries has survived.

If the meaning of the term 'feudalism' differs from one historian to another, as we noted earlier, it follows that the period of the history of a country—in this case India—characterized as feudal would also vary widely according to each historian's understanding of feudalism. Thus while some Soviet historians of India have found traces of feudalism in the *Arthasastra* of Kautilya,[97] for R.S. Sharma Indian feudalism originated in the fourth century AD reaching its peak during the eleventh and twelfth centuries.[98] With the establishment of the Delhi Sultanate, for political and economic reasons, feudalism, in B.N.S. Yadava's view, began to decline.[99] The distinguished Russian historian of the nineteenth century, M.M. Kovalevski, on the other hand, believed that the process of 'feudalization' in India started precisely with the 'Muslim conquests'.[100] For D.D. Kosambi, whose writings on Indian history enjoy a privileged status, the feudal system broke down around the middle of the seventeenth century, under Aurangzeb;[101] Col. James Tod, on the other hand, was witness to the functioning of what he believed was the classic form of feudalism in Rajasthan in the early nineteenth century.[102]

97 V.I. Kalyanov and I.P. Baikov cited in B.N.S. Yadava, 'Some Aspects of Changing Order in India During the Saka-Kusana Age', in G.R. Sharma (ed.), *Kusana Studies* (Allahabad, 1968), p. 80. For Baikov the exploitation of the two lower *varnas* or castes by the higher ones constituted feudalism.

98 R.S. Sharma, *Indian Feudalism*, pp. 1–76, 210–62.

99 B.N.S. Yadava, *Society and Culture*, pp. 172–3.

100 Daniel Thorner, 'Feudalism in India', in R. Coulborn (ed.), pp. 143–5.

101 D.D. Kosambi, *An Introduction to the Study of Indian History*, 2nd revised edn (Bombay, 1975) (first published 1956), pp. 391–2.

102 Col. James Tod, *Annals and Antiquities of Rajasthan*, W. Crooke (ed.), vol. I (London, 1920), pp. 155–6, 182–3, 190.

The point of comparison in the works of the historians mentioned above, and of many others who have considered the problem of Indian feudalism, invariably rests in medieval western Europe. This is understandable, for so long as we remain concerned with the question, 'Was there feudalism in India?', we must seek to answer it in the light of the most developed form of feudal social organization, which was west European. This comparison is quite independent of the answer to the question raised here. It is thus that Tod compared early nineteenth century Rajasthan with the west European feudal system as described in Hallam's *Middle Ages* (published 1824),[103] and found that four of the six elements which comprised feudalism were prevalent in Rajasthan.[104] D.D. Kosambi also drew upon Marion Gibb's *Feudal Order* and Maurice Dobb's *Studies*.[105] R.S. Sharma and B.N.S. Yadava have repeatedly referred to western Europe by way of comparison.[106] It is in relation to medieval Europe that Satish Chandra finds, 'in many respects', a similarity in the Indian concept of landownership.[107]

D.D. Kosambi provided a fresh outline for the study of Indian feudalism—his famous concept of feudalism from above and feudalism from below[108]—an outline that was unfortunately found inadequate by some other historians.[109] It was Professor R.S. Sharma who first made a systematic study of Indian feudalism in his book and in various articles.[110] Professor B.N.S. Yadava has added a great many details to Professor

[103] Tod, p. 154. Interestingly, Hallam's work still provides the reference point at least to D.C. Sircar, *Landlordism and Tenancy in Ancient and Medieval India as Revealed by Epigraphic Records* (Lucknow, 1969), p. 36.

[104] Tod, p. 190.

[105] D.D. Kosambi, *An Introduction &c.* pp. 353–5 and 403n. See also his *The Culture and Civilization of Ancient India in Historical Outline*, reprint (New Delhi, 1972) (first published 1970), pp. 23–4.

[106] R.S. Sharma, *Indian Feudalism*, pp. 1–2, 16, 34, 63–4, 84, 154, 208, etc.; B.N.S. Yadava, *Society and Culture*, pp. 171–2, 175–80, etc.

[107] Satish Chandra, 'Some Aspects of Indian Village Society in Northern India During the Eighteenth Century', *Indian Historical Review*, vol. 1, no. 1, March 1974, p. 51.

[108] D.D. Kosambi, *An Introduction &c.*, chs 9 and 10.

[109] For a critique of this concept, see Irfan Habib, 'Marxist Interpretation', *Seminar*, 39, Nov. 1962, pp. 36–7.

[110] R.S. Sharma, 'Problem of Transition', *Indian Feudalism*; 'Origins of Feudalism in India', *Journal of the Economic and Social History of the Orient*, vol. I, 1957–58, pp. 297–328; 'Indian Feudalism Retouched' (review article), *Indian Historical Review*, vol. 1, no. 2, Sept. 1974, pp. 320–30, etc.

Sharma's work by studying northern India in the early medieval period, particularly during the twelfth century.[111]

The main theme in the works of Professor Sharma and Professor Yadava is woven around the assumed antagonism between trade and urban life on the one hand and feudalism on the other,[112] and, particularly, the rise in importance of landed intermediaries owing to an increasing number of grants of land by the state to its officials and to the Brahmans in charity; this resulted in the subjection of the peasantry to the intermediaries and in the peasants' dependence on them. R.S. Sharma visualizes the development in India of almost all components of west European feudalism—serfdom,[113] manor,[114] self-sufficient economic units,[115] the process of feudalization of crafts and commerce,[116] apart, of course, from declining trade and urbanization. The elements which had allegedly undermined the European feudal structure, namely, the revival of trade and towns, the flight of the peasants to the towns to escape excessive impoverishment at the hands of the lord and the process of commutation of forced labour into monetary payments—all these, in Professor Sharma's view, developed in India also and similarly undermined Indian feudalism.[117] Indeed, the only important determinant of European feudalism which Professor Sharma could not trace in India was foreign invasions[118] —and B.N.S. Yadava

[111] B.N.S. Yadava, *Society and Culture*. Yadava's numerous articles rarely go beyond the arguments and evidence contained in his book.

[112] Thus the decline of trade—both internal and international—and, following it, the decline of urban centres is seen by R.S. Sharma as evidence of the rise of feudalism in post-Gupta times, and the revival of trade and city life, of feudalism's decline, *Indian Feudalism*, pp. 65–73 and 242–62. For a similar assumption of a trade-feudalism dichotomy in B.N.S. Yadava's work, see his *Society and Culture*, pp. 172–3 and 'Immobility and Subjection of Indian Peasantry in Early Medieval Complex', *Indian Historical Review*, vol. 1, no. 1, p. 27. Unfortunately, Yadava has misunderstood Moreland's phrase 'peasants' payments' in cash as 'the regular practice of payment *to* the peasants in cash', which contributed to the growth of economic mobility; Moreland was referring to the revenue paid *by* the peasants to the state or its agents; see W.H. Moreland, *Agrarian System of Moslem India* (Allahabad, 1929), p. 204 and Yadava, 'Immobility and Subjection', p. 27 (emphasis added).

[113] *Indian Feudalism*, pp. 53–9, 118, passim.

[114] Ibid., pp. 74, 271.

[115] Ibid., pp. 71, 242, 271.

[116] Ibid., pp. 238–41.

[117] For revival of trade and towns, ibid., pp. 242–62; flight of peasants to towns, p. 244; commutation, pp. 243–4, 262.

[118] Ibid., p. 74.

has made up even this deficiency by drawing attention to the barbarian, particularly the Hun, invasion of India which shattered the lame Gupta empire and contributed to the rise of feudalism. 'The Gurjara-Pratihara empire', says Yadava, 'arose in Northern India like the feudal Frankish Carolingian Empire'.[119] Of all these, the most critical element of Indian feudalism, in Professor Sharma's and Professor Yadava's view, consisted in the growing dependence of the peasantry on the landed intermediaries following the grant of more and more rights to them by the state. The dependence was manifested in terms of increasing restrictions on the peasant's mobility and his subjection to forced labour, which in turn was becoming increasingly intensive.[120]

It is not possible here to go into all the points made by Professor Sharma and Professor Yadava in establishing the similarity between Indian and European feudalism; at any rate, it is hard to disagree with the work of such eminent historians. I would confine my comments to some of the important arguments advanced in support of Indian feudalism.

The alleged antagonism between feudalism and the trade-urbanization complex has been a matter of great dispute between historians ever since Henri Pirenne's days; increasingly, however, the two are being seen as less incompatible than was the case in the 1930s and the 1940s—a point that we have noted earlier. At any rate, even in terms of historical evidence, D.C. Sircar and, more effectively, B.D. Chattopadhyaya have questioned the extent of the decline of trade and urbanization in the period concerned.[121]

More important, however, is the fact that while R.S. Sharma and B.N.S. Yadava have established considerable similarity in the features of Indian and European feudalism, the one basic difference appears to have been overlooked by them: in Europe feudalism arose as a result of a crisis in production relations based on slavery on the one hand and changes resulting from growing stratification among the Germanic tribes on the

119 B.N.S. Yadava, *Society and Culture*, pp. 137–9.

120 R.S. Sharma, *Indian Feudalism*, pp. 50–3, 121–2, 243, 283; R.S. Sharma, *Light on Early Indian Society and Economy* (Bombay, 1966), p. 73; B.N.S. Yadava, *Society and Culture*, pp. 163–73; Yadava, 'Immobility and Subjection', pp. 21–3.

121 D.C. Sircar, 'Landlordism Confused with Feudalism', in Sircar, ed., *Land System and Feudalism in Ancient India*, Calcutta, 1966, pp. 58–61; Chattopadhyaya, 'Trade and Urban Centres in Early Medieval North India', *Indian Historical Review*, vol. 1, no. 2, Sept. 1974, pp. 203–19, see also M.R. Tarafdar 'Trade and Society in Early Medieval Bengal', *Indian Historical Review*, vol. 4, no. 2, Jan. 1978, pp. 274–86.

other, the two coming into what Perry Anderson calls a 'catastrophic collision of two dissolving anterior modes of production—primitive and ancient'.[122] In other words, European feudalism developed essentially as changes at the base of society took place; in India, on the other hand, the establishment of feudalism is attributed by its protagonists primarily to state action in granting land in lieu of salary or in charity, and the action of the grantees in subjecting the peasantry by means of legal rights assigned to them by the state. It is, indeed, a moot point whether such complex social structures can be established through administrative and legal procedures.

Above all, however, it is the concept of the peasantry's 'dependence' that appears to be of uncertain value in the context in which it has been used. The evidence marshalled by Sharma and Yadava at best establishes the increasing *exploitation* of the peasantry; dependence, on the other hand, should consist of an extraneous control over the peasant's process of production, and this has yet to be proved in the Indian context. If one speaks of European peasants' 'dependence' on the lord, it is primarily because such dependence had become rooted in his very conditions of labour, as we have seen in section I above. The critical element in such dependence was the diversion of at least a part of the peasant's labour from his own process of production to that of the lord. It is doubtful whether this could be said of India. The nature of forced labour in India—of which there is considerable evidence throughout her history—is in its very essence different from that in Europe, for in India it is very rarely used for purposes of production.[123] There is, indeed, an objective

[122] Perry Anderson, *Passages*, p. 128.

[123] Forced labour rendered gratis appears to have been absent in the pre-Mauryan period, P.C. Jain, *Labour in Ancient India*, New Delhi, 1971, pp. 242–3; in the Mauryan period compulsory labour was used for purposes like the construction of state buildings, though it is not clear whether it was paid for or unpaid, ibid., and G.K. Rai, 'Forced Labour in Ancient and Early Medieval India', *Indian Historical Review*, vol. 3, no. 1, July 1976, pp. 26, 37. By the first century AD *visti* had acquired the characteristics of unpaid compulsory labour. Its scope began to expand even as a wider section of the people was subjected to the exactions under this heading; forced labour came to acquire a permanence in Indian society that is exceeded only by the caste-system, for we find continuing reference to it throughout the ancient and medieval periods; see R.S. Sharma, *Indian Feudalism*, pp. 48–53, 121–2, 242–3; Irfan Habib, *Agrarian System of Mughal India* (Bombay, 1963), pp. 150, 239, 248; H. Fukazawa, 'A Note on the Corvée System (Vethbegar) in Eighteenth Century Maratha Kingdom' in *Science and Human Progress* (Essays in Honour of the late Professor D.D. Kosambi) (Bombay, 1974); Harbans

reason for the absence of serfdom in Indian history, for conditions of production in India did not require serf-labour, as I shall try to argue later. Thus forced labour in India remained, by and large, an incidental manifestation of the political and administrative power of the ruling class rather than a part of the process of production.

Certain specific features of Indian agrarian history could perhaps be established clearly, even though only a small segment of it has been studied. The fertility of Indian soil in general appears to have been far higher than that of Europe until as late as the nineteenth century.[124]

Mukhia, 'Illegal Extortions from Peasants, Artisans and Menials in Eighteenth Century Eastern Rajasthan', *Indian Economic and Social History Review*, vol. XIV, no. 2, April–June, 1977, pp. 231–45; Henry Elliot, *Memoirs of the History, Folk-lore and Distribution of the Races of the North-Western Provinces of India*, John Beames (ed.), vol. II (London, 1859), p. 232. While forced labour was used for a variety of purposes like the construction of forts, repair of roads, carting of goods of the King's officials, etc., there is very meagre evidence of its use for agricultural production. R.S. Sharma cites only one source—the *Kamasutra*—where peasant women are required to work on the village headman's fields, apart from cleaning his house, carrying things from and into his house, etc., *Indian Feudalism*, pp. 51–2. But quite apart from the vagueness of the reference to peasant women working in the village headman's fields, one of a whole range of their tasks, even the interpretation that those women were rendering forced and unpaid labour has been questioned by G.K. Rai, 'Forced Labour', p. 30.

There is some primary evidence for the existence of forced labour for agricultural production such as in the *Bhagvata Purana* (not later than AD 800) cited in G.K. Rai, p. 33, and some village-level documents in Rajasthan cited in Harbans Mukhia, 'Illegal Extortions', p. 233. But on the whole its incidence is quite marginal and even Professor Sharma agrees that serfdom had not become 'a common trait of the Indian agrarian system in medieval times', 'Indian Feudalism Retouched', p. 328.

Curiously, it is the artisans who were continually subjected to forced labour from the post-Gupta period. In the *Arthasastra* they are treated as independent, Kautilya's *Arthasastra*, tr. R. Shamasastry (Mysore, 8th edn, 1967, first published 1915), bk IV, ch. I, pp. 229–32; but from the post-Gupta period, particularly from the sixth century, the artisans were attached to merchants and were liable to render forced labour, R.S. Sharma, *Indian Feudalism*, pp. 69–73. In the seventeenth century we still find them being subjected to forced labour, this time by the nobles: F. Bernier, *Travels in the Mogul Empire 1656–68*, tr. A. Constable (London, 1916), pp. 228–9 and Ali Muhammad Khan, *Mirat-Ahmadi*, vol. I, Nawab Ali (ed.) (Baroda, 1928), p. 260. The phenomenon is somewhat curious because there is little evidence of the scarcity of artisan labour. Of course, forced labour was not necessarily unpaid labour and there is a considerable amount of evidence of wages being paid to artisans. See, for example, F. Pelsaert, *Jahangir's India*, trs W.H. Moreland and Peter Geyl (Cambridge, 1925), p. 60 and *Waqai-Ajmer-wa-Ranthambor*, transcript, Andhra State Archives, Hyderabad, p. 227.

124 Elliot, for once championing the cause of India against a compatriot, argued in

Nature, on the other hand, permitted the Indian peasant to subsist at a much lower level of resources than his European counterpart. Secondly, and in part conditioned by the factors just mentioned, Indian agrarian history has been characterized by a predominantly free peasantry (in the economic rather than in the legal sense).

A number of indicators point to the high fertility of land in India, though, of course, there was considerable regional variation.[125] The cultivation of two crops, of one crop in each field, every year, which even the spread of the three-field rotation in Europe from the tenth or the eleventh century onwards could not ensure, was a feature of Indian agriculture from at least the Vedic period onwards.[126] Indeed, three crops are also mentioned in our sources which do not appear to treat the phenomenon as exceptional. It is quite difficult to establish whether every field yielded two or three crops a year; some of the references do clearly suggest that such indeed was the case, though it may be rash to accept their suggestion for all soils. Obviously, some lands did bear crops twice or thrice a year.[127]

1859 that the average produce of the Province of Allahabad was *double the average* of the scientific cultivators of England; he also noted the decline in soil-fertility in his own day, *Memoirs*, vol. II, p. 341 and n. (emphasis original).

125 Thus, while Abul Fazl speaks in glowing terms of the fertility of the *suba* of Lahore, he is far less enthusiastic about the provinces of Gujarat and Ajmer, *see Ain-i-Akbari*, Blochmann (ed.) (Calcutta, 1867–77), vol. I, pp. 538, 485 and 505 respectively.

126 The *Taittiriya Samhita* makes a clear reference to the harvesting of two crops of corn in a year from the same piece of land apart from beans and sesamum; this would naturally imply crop-rotation, see S.P. Raychaudhuri, L. Gopal and B.V. Subbarayappa, 'Agriculture', in D.M. Bose, S.N. Sen and B.V. Subbarayappa (eds), *A Concise History of Science in India*, New Delhi, 1971, p. 353, (hereafter *History of Science*); P.C. Jain, *Labour in Ancient India*, pp. 35–6. A.K. Ghosh and S.N. Sen accept the two crops but are less certain about rotation, 'Botany: Vedic and Post-Vedic period', *History of Science*, pp. 377–8. References to two crops can be found continually since the *Taittiriya Samhita*: in Megasthenes' account, Puspa Niyogi, *Contributions to the Economic History of Northern India*, Calcutta, 1962, p. 20; in Kautilya's *Arthasastra* pp. 131–2; in the *Brhatsamhita* of the Gupta period, S.P. Raychaudhuri, et. al., 'Agriculture', p. 361; in the *Ain*, vol. I, pp. 304–36 where all the revenue rates of Akbar's reign are mentioned for two crops—the winter and the spring.

127 Panini (*c.* 400 BC) refers to three annual crops, see P.C. Jain, p. 50; *Ain*, vol. I, p. 389 (*suba* Bengal where rice was harvested thrice), p. 473 (*suba* Khandesh where *jowar*—a millet—was similarly reaped thrice) and p. 513 (*suba* Delhi). The sources that leave one in no doubt regarding the cultivation of two or three crops in a year in the same field are: *Taittiriya Samhita* and *Ain*, vol. I, p. 389 (Bengal *suba*). The *Arthasastra*,

But even if we were to ignore this evidence, the outstanding fact still remains that no field remained uncultivated for more than a part of the year, something that even the three-field rotation was unable to achieve in late medieval Europe. Indeed, the negligible incidence, if not the complete absence, of the system of fallow in ancient and medieval India is a remarkable testimony to the high fertility of the Indian soil. Historians, while using the term 'fallow', have almost invariably referred in fact to either virgin or abandoned lands, or, at best, lands withdrawn from cultivation for brief periods, which corresponds to permitting the land a lea.[128] Fallow land, unlike the virgin or the abandoned land, is an integral

on the other hand, suggests the use of compulsion by the state to grow a second crop on the field if the state's interest so required, p. 273.

128 Thus in the law book of Narada (Gupta period) a tract of land that had not been cultivated for a year is defined as *ardhakhila*, Puspa Niyogi, *Contributions*, p. 21, and as *khila* if it had been uncultivated for three years, R.S. Sharma, *Indian Feudalism*, p. 35. khila is then rendered as 'fallow' by Professor Sharma, though Niyogi prefers 'half-waste' for her ardhakhila. Prof. Sharma also renders *bhumicchidra* as fallow, *Indian Feudalism*, p. 36, though the context clearly points to virgin land. R.P. Kangle in fact translates bhumicchidra as 'land which cannot be used for agriculture because it is unsuited for it', Kautilya's *Arthasastra*, part III (Bombay, 1965), p. 174. See also Niyogi, *Contributions*, p. 69. D.C. Sircar has a section entitled 'Reclamation of Fallow Land' which would appear curious but for the fact that 'fallow' denotes virgin or deserted land to most historians of ancient India. See Sircar, *Landlordism and Tenancy*, p. 4; P. Niyogi, *Contributions*, p. 1; B.P. Mazumdar, *The Socio-Economic History of Northern India* (1030–1194 AD) (Calcutta, 1960), p. 175. See also D.C. Sircar, *Indian Epigraphical Glossary* (Delhi, 1966), for *Khila* (rendered uncultivated land, fallow land), p. 157 and *khila-ksetra* (rendered fallow land), p. 157. To S.P. Raychaudhuri it appears that the system of fallowing was known in the age of the *Yajurveda*, though, unluckily, he says nothing more about it, in *Agriculture in Ancient India*, Raychaudhuri (ed.) (New Delhi, 1964), p. 81. However, even some of the later works dealing exclusively or partly with agricultural practices make no mention of the genuine fallow. See, for example, the *Arthasastra*, the *Krsi-Parasara*, G.P. Majumdar and S.C. Banerji (eds and trs) (Calcutta, 1960) and Sarngadhara, *Upavana-Vinoda*, G.P. Majumdar, (ed. and tr.) (Calcutta, 1936). The estimates of the date of *Krsi-Parasara* vary widely between 1300 BC, the post-Vedic but pre-Christian era, and between AD 100 and 600; see S.P. Raychaudhuri, 'Land Classification in Ancient India', *Indian Journal of the History of Science*, vol. I, no. 2, Nov. 1966, p. 107; A.K. Ghosh and S.N. Sen, 'Botany: Vedic and Post-Vedic Period', *History of Science*, p. 379 and G.P. Majumdar, 'Introduction', *Krsi-Parasara*, p. vi, respectively. Some of the recent secondary works also discuss the whole range of agricultural operations in ancient India but do not refer to fallow; see, for example, B.N.S. Yadava, *Society and Culture*, pp. 256–62. If modern historians have used the term 'fallow' for virgin or deserted lands, or for the lea, it is obviously because the genuine fallow hardly existed.

part of the cycle of cultivation. Indeed, it has to be ploughed more often than the land sown, for its soil must be repeatedly pulverized and weeds ploughed back or burnt down to be turned into green manure or potash. The practice of the fallow obviously suggests a soil that is quickly exhausted; the lea, or a brief withdrawal of the plough from the field, on the other hand, would be adequate for a soil relatively less prone to exhaustion. William Tennant, writing at the outset of the nineteenth century, noted that '. . . the Indian allows it (his field) a lea, but never a fallow', though he ascribes this to the general backwardness of Indian agricultural techniques.[129] Some other evidence also suggests the practice of the lea, but rarely of the fallow. The *Ain-i Akbari* describes the second of its four categories of land as one that '(the peasants) do not cultivate for a time and thereby increase its strength'.[130] The *Risala-i Ziraat* also mentions the prevailing practice, in the second half of the eighteenth century in Bengal, of the cultivation of fields in alternate years.[131] It is quite possible, of course, that instead of following the practice of the fallow, it would be simpler to abandon the exhausted fields and reclaim new ones, for, after all, there was no scarcity of land.[132] But there is very little evidence to suggest that it was widespread. Indeed, the reclamation of land is, after all, a costly process and would hardly be resorted to unless the cost of the restoration of soil-fertility through the use of manure outweighed the cost of reclamation. And manure, as Irfan Habib reasonably

[129] William Tennant, *Indian Recreations; Consisting Chiefly of Strictures on the Domestic and Rural Economy of the Mahomedans and Hindoos*, vol. II (Edinburgh, 1804), p. 16.

[130] *Ain*, vol. I, p. 297. This category is named *parauti*. However, the third category, *chachar*, is so classified when it falls out of cultivation 'owing to excessive rain or inundation', ibid., p. 301; and the last, *banjar*, when it loses its productive capacity through inundation, ibid. Thus, barring *parauti*, the forced exclusion from cultivation of the other categories of land is due to circumstances extraneous to the cycle of production. Indeed, the first class of land, *polaj*, is that which is never allowed to lie uncultivated, ibid., p. 297 and the other lands are to be slowly encouraged to develop into the polaj class by means of progressive taxation keeping pace with the diminishing period of their non-cultivation, ibid., pp. 301–2. I am grateful to Miss Shireen Moosvi for drawing my attention to the difference in the *Ain's* treatment of the parauti and the other lands.

[131] *Risala-i Ziraat*, Edinburgh University Library, Persian MS. no. 144, ff. 6b–7a.

[132] Irfan Habib, *Agrarian System*, p. 23 and n. Irfan Habib's informant speaks of the customary practice in Gorakhpur, eastern U.P., of reclamation of new land once the old soil had spent its fertility. The period is early nineteenth century. Mufti Ghulam Hazarat, the informant, however, makes it a point to highlight the low fertility of the region where the practice prevailed.

argues, should have been available in far greater quantity in the centuries before the beginning of the twentieth than after it.[133]

The system of manuring appears to have developed into a fine art if we go by the minute details of the methods and ingredients of preparing manures for different plants. It is far from certain whether Vedic Indians practised manuring.[134] But the *Arthasastra*,[135] the *Brhatsamhita*, the *Agni Purana*,[136] the *Krsi-Parasara*[137] and the *Upavana-Vinoda*,[138] among others, describe in very great detail the elements of which manures were made. The elements varied from cow-dung and goat's and sheep's droppings to the fat of pigs[139] and the flesh of cows;[140] green manure and a mixture of honey and clarified butter with some other elements have also been recommended. Some of these preparations were meant for the treatment of seeds before they were sown to ensure better germination.

Nor were the agricultural implements and practices too primitive for their age. Almost definitive evidence of the use of the plough has been uncovered at a pre-Harappan site, Kalibangan in Rajasthan, belonging broadly to the first half of the third millennium BC.[141] The Vedic age, of course, used the plough,[142] and it has naturally continued in use ever since. The size and weight of the plough varied from region to region

133 Irfan Habib suggests the following logic: Since in Mughal times between one-half and three-quarters of the land was cultivated compared to the area of such land at the beginning of the twentieth century, keeping in view regional variations, the medieval Indian peasant should have had at his disposal extensive wastelands and forests and therefore more cattle and draught animals. He could also have burnt firewood and used animal dung for manure. See Irfan Habib, *Agrarian System*, pp. 53–6. 116, and 'Potentialities of Capitalistic Development in the Economy of Mughal India', *Enquiry*, new series, vol. III, no. 3, Winter 1971, p. 4. If this were so of medieval India, it should have been truer of the earlier period.

134 A.K. Ghosh and S.N. Sen appear to be doubtful, 'Botany: Vedic and Post-Vedic Period', *History of Science*, p. 377.

135 p. 132.

136 B.N.S. Yadava, *Society and Culture*, p. 257.

137 pp. 74, 78.

138 pp. 81–3.

139 *Arthasastra*, p. 132.

140 P.C. Jain, pp. 60–1.

141 B.B. Lal, 'Perhaps the Earliest Ploughed Field So Far Excavated Anywhere in the World', *Purattatva*, no. 4, 1970–71, pp. 1–3. Professor Romila Thapar drew my attention to this evidence, for which I am extremely grateful.

142 P.C. Jain, pp. 32, 34; S.P. Raychaudhuri, et al., 'Agriculture', *History of Science*, p. 352, R.S. Sharma, *Light etc.*, pp. 55–6.

and, perhaps, from one stratum of the class of agriculturists to another.[143] It is true, as Elliot so derisively states, that the Indian plough—'simple... and wretched in construction'—merely scratched the topsoil,[144] but this appears to have been primarily due to the fact that the fertility of most soils in India lies at the surface.[145] Elliot himself noted that 'when anything like a mould-board is required, the people have sufficient ingenuity to frame one'.[146] Construction of a deep-penetrating plough should not have been beyond their capability, if it were required.

The literature of successive periods refers to many other implements used for agricultural production, besides the plough. The Vedic literature mentions the sickle and the sieve;[147] the *Ramayana* of Valmiki refers to the spade.[148] The *Amarkosa* speaks of the hoe and the harrow, besides mortar and pestle for separating the grain from the chaff, the winnowing fan, etc.[149] The *Krsi-Parasara* gives, with many details, the names and the dimensions of various parts of the plough.[150] From about 600 BC the use of iron in making agricultural implements appears to have been on the

143 The *Atharvaveda* refers to ploughs driven by six and twelve oxen, P.C. Jain, p. 35. There are references to the yoking of 6, 8, 12 and even 24 oxen to the plough, R.S. Sharma, *Light etc.*, p. 57. The *Krsi-Parasara* in a colourful verse suggests that 'a plough is said it have eight bulls, six for the ordinary use, four for the cruel and two for the cow-killers', p. 73. Abul Fazl implies that a peasant having four oxen for his plough was too poor to be taxed, *Ain*, vol. I, 287.

The regional variation in the shape of the plough as used today has been recorded by Jaya Datta Gupta and B.N. Saraswati, 'Ploughs and Husking Implements', in *Peasant Life in India*, Memoir No. 8, Anthropological Survey of India, Calcutta, 1961, pp. 25–9. The regional variation in the weight of the plough was noted by N.G. Mukherji, *Handbook of Indian Agriculture*, Calcutta, 1915, pp. 93 and 99 where the ploughs of Bengal and Bundelkhand are respectively estimated at 1.25 and 3.5 maunds. It is perhaps not unreasonable to assume that these variations are a legacy of the distant past.

Panini divides agriculturists into three classes according to the type of plough they used and whether the plough belonged to them or not, P.C. Jain, pp. 48–9.

144 Elliot, *Memoirs*, vol. II, pp. 340–1.

145 This was the conclusion reached by the Royal Commission on Agriculture in India, *Report*, London, 1928, pp. 110–12, cited in Irfan Habib, *Agrarian System*, p. 24n.

146 Elliot, *Memoirs*, p. 340n.

147 S.P. Raychaudhuri, et al., 'Agriculture', *History of Science*, p. 352.

148 D.R. Chanana, 'The Spread of Agriculture in the Ganges Valley', *Contributions to Indian Economic History*, no. 2, 1963, p. 115n. The Pali texts also refer to the spade, P.C. Jain, p. 43.

149 S.P. Raychaudhuri et al., 'Agriculture', *History of Science*, p. 360.

150 *Krsi-Parasara*, pp. 74–5.

increase.[151] It is, on the other hand, difficult to establish the origin of the seed-drill, but this important device which, in Elliot's words, 'has only within the last century been introduced into English field husbandry . . . has been in use in India from time immemorial'.[152]

Experts in agriculture recommended the ploughing of the field more than once, sometimes as many as five times.[153] It is not easy to say how far the recommendations were actually heeded, but Grierson did notice the ploughing of the field five times in modern Bihar,[154] although, of course, it might be a phenomenon of recent origin. Weeding was to take place twice.[155] Given the cycle of two or three crops in a year, crop rotation was 'practically a gift of nature and to know the combination which best suited particular soils would have been a matter of experience'.[156] The system of transplantation was also known;[157] and so was the treatment of diseased plants.[158]

It is in irrigation that the most important technological advance has been registered in ancient and medieval Indian agriculture. The *Rgveda* mentions some devices for lifting water (probably from a tank), but the technical details of these are as yet unknown.[159] The *Arthasastra* also refers to several methods of obtaining irrigation water from rivers, lakes, tanks and wells;[160] the Mauryan state apparently imposed a heavy irrigation cess—ranging from one-fifth to one-third of the produce[161]—even when the sources of water were privately owned.[162]

151 R.S. Sharma, *Light etc.*, pp. 57, 60–1.

152 Elliot, *Memoirs,* vol. II, pp. 341–2.

153 According to Panini, the field was at times ploughed twice and at other times thrice, P.C. Jain, p. 49; Kautilya suggested ploughing the field 'often', *Arthasastra,* p. 129; The *Krsi-Parasara* recommends five ploughings for abundant crops, p. 77.

154 Grierson, *Bihar Peasant Life,* 2nd edn, Patna, 1926, p. 172, cited in A.K. Chaudhuri, *Early Medieval Village in Northern-Eastern India AD 600–1200* (Calcutta, 1971), pp. 153–4.

155 *Krsi-Parasara,* p. 82.

156 Irfan Habib, *Agrarian System,* p. 26; also B.N.S. Yadava, *Society and Culture,* p. 257.

157 *Krsi-Parasara,* pp. 80, 81.

158 The *Vrksayurveda,* also attributed to Parasara, author of *Krsi-Parasara,* deals with the treatment of plants, as the title suggests, A.K. Ghosh and S.N. Sen, p. 379.

159 S.P. Raychaudhuri, et al., 'Agriculture', pp. 353–4.

160 p. 131.

161 Ibid.

162 R.P. Kangle, p. 174.

It was the spread of the noria from about the seventh century and of the Persian wheel from around the time the Delhi Sultanate was established in north India, that appears to have made a critical difference to the extension of agriculture at least in the Panjab,[163] the fertility of whose soil Abul Fazl considered unrivalled.[164] The canals, on the whole, appear to have been marginal to agricultural production. Firuz Shah Tughlaq[165] and Shah Jahan[166] did order the construction of canals, but for all practical purposes canal irrigation appears to be a more recent phenomenon.

If, owing to the natural richness of the soil and the relatively efficient tools and techniques, agricultural productivity in India was high, the subsistence level of the peasant was very low—thanks to climatic conditions, and, as we shall argue later, social organization. Consequently, the amount of land considered necessary for the subsistence of a peasant family in India was estimated at anywhere between nine and fourteen acres in the fifth century BC.[167] Unfortunately, there is little evidence to go by for the later periods of our history on this point, but unless we assume a significant decline in soil-fertility or rise in the subsistence level, this size of landholding was hardly likely to have changed drastically. Indeed, such a landholding, with traditional implements and practices, but with a reasonably assured supply of irrigation water, should even today earn the peasant family the pittance that it needs to survive and reproduce itself.

The relatively small size of holdings in India had the principal effect of averting wastage of labour in the process of production which occurred in Europe; consequently far less labour was required for agricultural operations here. Moreover, these operations could be spread over a much

163 Irfan Habib, 'Presidential Address', *Proceedings of Indian History Congress*, 31st Session (Varanasi, 1969), pp. 149–55.

164 *Ain*, vol. I, p. 538.

165 Zia-ud-din Barani, *Tarikh-i Firuz Shahi*, Saiyad Ahmad Khan (ed.) (Calcutta, 1862), pp. 367–71; Shams-i-Siraj Afif, *Tarikh-i Firuz Shahi*, M. Wilayat Hussain (ed.) (Calcutta, 1888–91), p. 127.

166 Sujan Rai Bhandari, *Khulasat al-Tawarikh*, Zafar Hasan (ed.) (Delhi, 1918), pp. 29–30, 36–7.

167 Baudhayana suggests a holding of six *nivartanas* for the purpose, R.S. Sharma, *Light etc.*, p. 62. A nivartana, according to Professor Sharma, comprised roughly an acre and a half, ibid., p. 73. Puspa Niyogi, on the other hand, suggests, on the basis of a longish discussion with many impressive details, that a nivartana was equal to 40,000 cubits, *Contributions*, p. 97, and n. That would bring it close to 2.3 acres.

longer period in the course of the year than in western Europe. Thus there does not appear to have been a highly concentrated demand for large amounts of labour during short periods. It is thus that the absence of serfdom in Indian history, except for some marginal incidence,[168] becomes intelligible. Indeed, even Sharma and Yadava are led by their evidence to conclude that serfdom was far from being the dominant feature in India.[169] For the process of production in India did not create an acute scarcity of labour; enserfment of the peasant therefore was hardly necessary. It is not as if the ruling class or the state in India was more compassionate to the primary producer than the feudal lords or the medieval state in Europe; it resorted even to enslavement of the peasants and the artisans[170] whenever it felt the need. But such need arose rarely and for short periods of time.

When historians, therefore, describe the Indian peasant as a serf[171] or a near-serf, they do so primarily on the basis of legal restrictions imposed on his mobility, the absence of the right to free alienation of land, and, of course, his subjection to the rendering of forced labour.[172]

It is true that the state in India, concerned as it primarily was with the collection of revenue from land, made it obligatory on the part of the cultivator to keep his field constantly under the plough. The *Arthasastra*

168 The Malabar Kannamkar, for example, tied to the land and working for the *janmi* landowners, could come near the category of serfs.

169 R.S. Sharma: 'On the whole while a great part of the time and energy of European peasants was consumed by their work on their master's fields the peasantry in India gave most of their time to their own fields, of the produce of which a considerable share went to the holders of the grants and other intermediaries; on the contrary, the number of free peasantry seems to have been far greater', *Indian Feudalism*, p. 75; also *Light etc.*, p. 83. B.N.S. Yadava: 'Thus the Sudra peasants cannot be equated with the unfree serf of Medieval Europe', in D.C. Sircar (ed.), *Land System and Feudalism*, p. 94; also *Society and Culture*, p. 171 and 'Immobility and Subjection', p. 25.

170 The state farms of the Mauryas were cultivated by slaves, amongst others, *Arthasastra*, p. 129; artisans were enslaved by the Sultanate of Delhi during the thirteenth and fourteenth centuries, Zia-ud-din Barani, *Tarikh-i Firuz Shahi*, pp. 313–14. See also Irfan Habib, 'Economic History of the Delhi Sultanate—An Essay in Interpretation', *Indian Historical Review*, vol. 4, no. 2, Jan. 1978, pp. 292–4, 297.

171 R.S. Sharma, *Indian Feudalism*, pp. 56, 118–24. In a recent article Prof. Sharma describes the Indian peasants as having been reduced to the position of 'semi-serfs as a result of numerous impositions made on them', 'Indian Feudalism Retouched', p. 327.

172 Irfan Habib, *Agrarian System*, pp. 115–16, 118; 'Economic History of the Delhi Sultanate', p. 298. Irfan Habib does not consider forced labour an important element in this situation.

recommends that the 'lands may be confiscated from those who do not cultivate them and given to others; or they may be cultivated by village labourers and traders, lest those who do not properly cultivate them might pay less (to the government)'.[173] The *Arthasastra* also places restrictions on the free alienation of land or the free mobility of peasants, once again with a view to preventing the loss of revenue: 'Tax-payers shall sell or mortgage their fields to tax-payers alone; Brahmans shall sell or mortgage their *brahmadeya* or gifted lands only to those who are endowed with such lands; otherwise they shall be punished with the first amercement. The same punishment shall be meted out to a tax-payer who settles in a village not inhabited by tax-payers'.[174] The state was advised even to compel the peasants to grow an additional crop on their fields if the king found himself in financial straits.[175] Manu prescribes the imposition of a fine on a cultivator who does not cultivate his field at the proper time or guard the crop against animals.[176] All this, however, did not violate the owner's title to the land even if it had been cultivated by another.[177] Indeed, the period for which the title remained legally valid went on increasing from 10 years at the time of Manu (*c.* second century AD) to 105 years in the thirteenth century, with limits fixed at 20 years, 60 years and 100 years between these dates.[178]

Thus, when Aurangzeb's *firman* to Muhammad Hashim[179] on the one hand recognized the peasant's ownership of land[180] (including the right to sell or mortgage it[181]) and on the other advised the use of persuasion and, if necessary, compulsion, to have the peasant till his land, it was really reiterating a very ancient Indian position.[182] If the state

[173] p. 46.
[174] p. 197.
[175] p. 273.
[176] Cited in B.P. Mazumdar, p. 171.
[177] *Arthasastra*, p. 197.
[178] R.S. Sharma, *Indian Feudalism*, pp. 149–50.
[179] Ali Muhammad Khan, *Mirat-i Ahmadi*, pp. 268–72.
[180] Ibid., article III.
[181] Ibid., articles XIII and XVI.
[182] Zafarul Islam reasonably questions Irfan Habib's suspicion of the testimony of the firman. While Irfan Habib thought the order had little relevance to the agrarian conditions in India for it was expressly drafted to set out the laws of the Shariat, *Agrarian System*, p. 113, Zafarul Islam, comparing its provisions with those of Islamic law, suggests its specific late seventeenth century relevance to India, 'Aurangzeb's Farman on Land Tax—An Analysis in the Light of the Fatawa-i Alamgiri', *Islamic Culture*, vol. 52, no. 2,

asserted its right to ensure uninterrupted cultivation of land, or to collect the revenue due to it even when the peasant neglected to cultivate his field,[183] or else to have the land tilled by another in case the owner had fled, the extent of its actual enforcement would vary from one situation to another. In the seventeenth century when the incidence of desertion of land had assumed serious dimensions, the state's insistence on its right became more emphatic.[184]

However, one aspect needs to be kept in view while discussing the problem of peasant immobility: we can hardly speak of a developed labour—or land—market in ancient and medieval India, though hired agricultural labour and instances of sale or mortgage of land have been mentioned in our sources.[185] Thus, it is primarily the economic, more than the legal, limitations on mobility which confined the peasant to his village,[186] though, of course, we must not visualize the ancient and medieval Indian peasant as completely immobile. Even if we were to accept state intervention in uniformly enforcing restriction on the peasant's movement or on his right freely to alienate his land, his mastery over the means and the process of production still remained intact, provided, of course, that he cultivated his field (in such manner as he

April 1978, pp. 117–26. It is possible to trace these provisions back to the *Arthasastra* and to later Hindu law books.

183 Aurangzeb's firman to Muhammad Hashim, article II.

184 Besides the firman to Muhammad Hashim, article II, B.R. Grover has brought to light pieces of evidence from Shah Jahan's reign wherein the Desais were charged with resettling in their original homes tenants who had migrated to some other villages, 'The Position of the Desai in the Pargana Administration of Subah Gujarat under the Mughals', *Proceedings of Indian History Congress*, 24th Session, Delhi, 1961, p. 152. Grover's evidence comes from some Persian documents located in Paris. The Desais, however, used persuasion and reassurance rather than coercion in carrying out their duties; but then the line between the two is very thin.

185 *Arthasastra*, p. 213; See P.C. Jain, pp. 236–9 for regulation of wage-payments by the law-giver of the Gupta age; Irfan Habib, *Agrarian System*, p. 120. For sale of land, see *Arthasastra*, p. 197; D.C. Sircar, *Land System and Feudalism*, p. 12; R.S. Sharma, *Indian Feudalism*, pp. 36, 149; B.R. Grover, 'Nature of Dehat-i-Taalluqa (Zamindari Villages) and the evolution of the Taaluqdari System During the Mughal Age', *IESHR*, vol. II, nos. 2 and 3, April and July 1965, p. 261.

186 R.S. Sharma, 'Indian Feudalism Retouched', p. 329: 'In fact even without compulsion peasants and artisans had no option but to stick to the village for the set up being the same everywhere, migration to another village could not materially change the situation'. B.N.S. Yadava stresses the role of ideology more than of law in enforcing immobility, *Society and Culture*, p. 166.

chose) and paid the revenue to the state or its assignees.[187] It is true, as many historians have pointed out, that the pre-modern Indian peasant did not enjoy modern or bourgeois proprietary rights over land, for he could not freely alienate, abandon or abuse his land;[188] obviously no historian expects the peasant to have enjoyed such a right. But then is it merely a legal problem? If, by some stretch of the imagination, these legal rights could be granted to the peasant of the ancient and medieval past, would they have made a material difference to his situation, other things remaining the same—when he could rarely find a buyer for his land or labour or when he could not easily give up cultivation for some other occupation? At any rate, the absence of these rights did not deprive him of control over his field or the plough or—above all—his labour.

And it is in this sense that we have earlier defined a free peasant, following Marx's insight. The question of the legal ownership of land, which has been discussed by a very large number of historians of ancient and medieval India,[189] and the other legal rights carries, at best, a moderate significance in the actual socio-economic context.

187 R.S. Sharma and B.N.S. Yadava have merely *inferred* that the state's grant of villages, enumerating a number of rights transferred to the intermediaries, should have led to the peasants' dependence on them. This is by no means certain. Villages, according to Professor Sharma's own evidence, were donated even by private individuals, *Indian Feudalism*, p. 61; these individuals were clearly in no position to change class relations in the countryside. As D.D. Kosambi remarks with characteristic perception, 'The recipients of a whole village gained at most the rights the state would normally claim. That is, they collected the taxes already fixed by usage. No portion of the tax was to be passed on to the state or any state official, but the donee had not the right to increase such taxes, nor any property rights over land and cattle', *An Introduction etc.*, p. 321. At any rate the creation of peasants' dependence implies changes in the processes and relations of production and these can hardly be brought about by administrative fiat.

188 D.D. Kosambi, *An Introduction etc.*, p. 323; Irfan Habib, *Agrarian System*, p. 115; S. Nurul Hasan, *Thoughts*, p. 3.

189 Historians, too numerous to be referred to here, have discussed the questions of landownership confining the options by and large to the state and the peasant. Communal ownership is definitively ruled out by all. Various combinations of the state's and the peasant's rights have also been suggested. Thus D.C. Sircar urges that it was the king who in theory owned the land and the cultivators were his tenants. However, they held permanent occupancy rights and the king was not expected to evict them, *Landlordism and Tenancy*, pp. 1–3. B.N.S. Yadava believes that royal ownership and private individual ownership of land were not mutually exclusive in the context of the land system of the twelfth century, *Society and Culture*, p. 254. For medieval India, B.R. Grover has strongly argued in favour of peasant-proprietorship of land, 'Nature of Land-Rights in Mughal

In this sense, free peasant production appears to have been consolidated in post-Maurya times. In Buddhist literature large farms are met with, sometimes with as many as five hundred ploughs, tilled by a gang of hired labourers.[190] The *Arthasastra* also speaks of state farms worked by 'slaves, labourers and prisoners'.[191] But in Gupta and post-Gupta times these large farms, whether owned by individuals or by the state, are no longer referred to; instead, there is the transformation of the sudras into petty producers. By the first half of the seventh century most, if not all, of the sudras had become peasants.[192] In part, at least, the spread of peasant production appears to have been due to the state policy of extending cultivation. The Maurya state undertook to settle new villages or resettle deserted ones 'either by inducing foreigners to immigrate' or by transferring excess population from the densely populated regions of the kingdom.[193] But individual reclamation of land may have become more common in post-Maurya times—a phenomenon reflected in the formulation of the *bhumicchidranyaya*: the field belongs to him who first removes the weed, as the deer to him who first shoots it.[194] It is reasonable to assume that with the spread of the noria and the Persian wheel, to which reference has been made earlier, considerable reclamation took place at the hands of those who could afford the price of the apparatus.[195] The medieval Indian state gives the impression of extreme keenness to extend cultivation if only because more evidence has survived from this period. Thus the grants made by the state in charity comprised two equal

India', *IESHR*, vol. I, no. 1, 1963, pp. 2–5; 'Dehat-i-Taaluqa', pp. 261–2. Irfan Habib, on the other hand, while accepting the notion of private property in land, qualifies it with the absence of the right to free alienation, etc., as we have noted above. Noman A. Siddiqi goes to the extent of denying to the peasants the right to sell or mortgage land, *Land Revenue Administration under the Mughals* (Bombay, 1970), pp. 11, 16.

190 P.C. Jain, pp. 44–5.

191 p. 129.

192 R.S. Sharma, *Indian Feudalism*, pp. 61–3. Elsewhere, Professor Sharma remarks of the post-Gupta period: 'Perhaps the major portion of land continued to be in the possession of free peasants, who paid revenue directly to the State', *Light etc.*, p. 83. Professor Sharma, of course, appears to derive his definition of free peasants from Fa-hsein who states that 'only those who till the king's land pay a land tax' and that they are free to go and stay as they please, ibid.

193 *Arthasastra*, p. 45.

194 Manu, cited in P.C. Jain, p. 51.

195 Irfan Habib, 'Jatts of Punjab and Sind', in Harbans Singh and N.G. Warrier (eds), *Essays in Honour of Dr Ganda Singh* (Patiala, 1976), pp. 92–103.

halves of cultivated and waste lands.[196] Among the duties of the revenue-collector of the Mughal state enumerated in the *Ain* is reclamation of wasteland for cultivation and prevention of arable land from falling waste.[197] Various other officials and semi-officials were similarly charged: the Karoris,[198] the Zamindars[199] and even the Jagirdars.[200] Thus when Aurangzeb's *firman* of Muhammad Hashim unambiguously recognizes the peasant's title to land reclaimed by him,[201] it merely establishes the continuity of a very old Indian practice of encouraging the extension of cultivation by individual peasants.

The primarily free peasant form of agricultural production gradually evolving from post-Maurya times characterized the agrarian economy of ancient and medieval India. This need not, however, blind us to the existence of other classes in the countryside, to the extreme poverty of the peasants and to the considerable changes within the agricultural economy of pre-modern times.

It is no longer necessary to try to prove the existence of stratification in the ancient and medieval Indian countryside, for there is now hardly any dispute about it. The caste system in particular appears to have maintained economic and social disparities, especially in making landless agricultural labour available for the cultivation of the lands of big land-owners.[202] When, therefore, we speak of free peasant production, it is by and large in terms of its primacy in the production system.[203]

If the Indian peasant's control over the process of production differentiated him from his medieval European counterpart, there is little reason to believe that he also enjoyed a higher standard of living. We have

196 *Ain*, vol. I, p. 199.

197 Ibid., pp. 285–6.

198 Abdul Qudir Badauni, *Muntakhab-ut-Tawarikh*, vol. II, Bib. Ind., p. 189.

199 B.R. Grover, 'Dehat-i-Taalluqa', p. 262.

200 See the 'Yad-dasht-i-izafa-i-dehat' (memorandum regarding newly settled villages) of Shah Jahan's time in Ziauddin Ahmed Shakeb (ed.), *Mughal Archives*, vol. I (Hyderabad, 1977), p. 295; also pp. 36–45. The fact that such memoranda were to be submitted enumerating the number and location of newly settled villages suggests that the official injunction to extend cultivation had to be taken seriously.

201 Article V: 'whoever turns (wasteland) into cultivable land should be recognised as its owner (malik) and should not be deprived (of land)'.

202 Irfan Habib, *Agriculture System*, pp. 121–2.

203 R.S. Sharma, *Indian Feudalism*, p. 75; R.S. Sharma, *Light etc.*, p. 83; B.N.S. Yadava, *Society and Culture*, p. 171; S. Nurul Hasan. *Thoughts*, p. 18.

noted earlier that nature in India allowed the peasant to subsist off very meagre resources; what nature permitted as the minimum level was made the maximum by social organization. There are continual references in our sources to the heavy demand of revenue and other taxes from the peasants and the consequent miserable level of their existence. The Pali texts draw a pitiful picture of the peasants' poverty.[204] Kautilya prescribes between one-fifth and one-third as irrigation cess, even when the source of irrigation is privately owned, as we have noted earlier.[205] As R.P. Kangle argues, with the *bhaga* or land revenue being fixed at one-sixth, the total would amount to one-half of the produce for peasants paying one-third as irrigation cess.[206] The law books had 'unalterably' laid down the rate of land revenue demand in the range of one-twelfth to one-sixth depending on the nature of the soil and its yields. Yet the actual collection varied between one-tenth and one-third according to the status of the ruler. Indeed, a specimen document in the *Lekhapaddhati* reveals that at times up to two-thirds of the produce was being collected in the eleventh and twelfth centuries.[207] In the *Sukranitisara*, different portions of which belong to a period after the eleventh century, the recommended land revenue rates vary between one-sixth and one-half of the produce.[208] King Lalitadiya of Kashmir (eighth century) gave advice to his heirs which Sultan Balban was to repeat in turn to his own heirs, five centuries later: Do not allow the villagers to accumulate more than they need for bare subsistence lest they revolt.[209] D.C. Sircar and B.N.S. Yadava have enumerated the formidable number of taxes and cesses collected from peasants and artisans[210] and if Professor Yadava reaches the conclusion that 'mostly the peasants appear to have been left with a bare margin for subsistence'[211] in the twelfth century, he is by no means overstating the case. It is in continuation of this tradition that the Sultans of Delhi and the Mughal Emperors collected anywhere between a quarter and a half of the produce

[204] P.C. Jain, p. 43.

[205] *Arthasastra*, p. 131.

[206] R.P. Kangle, p. 174.

[207] B.N.S. Yadava, *Society and Culture*, pp. 297–8.

[208] Puspa Niyogi, *Contributions*, p. 180.

[209] D.D. Kosambi, *An Introduction, etc.*, p. 365; D.C. Sircar, *Land System and Feudalism*, p. 21. For Balban's similar advice, see Zia ud-din Barani, pp. 100–01.

[210] Sircar, *Landlordism and Tenancy*, pp. 66–79; Yadava, *Society and Culture*, pp. 288–301.

[211] *Society and Culture*, p. 301.

as revenue from land.[212] It is possible, of course, that with technical progress such as the introduction of the noria and the Persian wheel and with great diversification of crops,[213] the value of produce from the land increased and the state raised its demand for revenue, but this is an aspect that needs to be carefully examined before a statement can be made with confidence.[214]

212 Irfan Habib, 'Potentialities etc' pp. 11–12, 27; *Agrarian System*, pp. 192–6. Irfan Habib suggests a major new argument that the Delhi Sultanate created 'an entirely new kind of agrarian taxation in India. Once implanted, the single massive land-tax was to last in India till practically the first half of this century. The State would henceforth regularly claim the bulk of the peasants' surplus . . . ', 'Economic History of the Delhi Sultanate', p. 297. The bulk of the surplus was, indeed, claimed by the Sultans, but in view of the evidence available for the pre-Sultanate period, particularly for the eleventh and twelfth centuries, we need really to be more certain whether they were doing anything unprecedented.

213 Even if we take only foodgrains into account, the increase in their number over the centuries has been very impressive. Thus, while barley, wheat and rice are referred to in the Vedic literature. R.S. Sharma, *Light etc.*, pp. 56, 58, the *Arthasastra* enumerates many crops, some of which remain unidentified, and the number of grains comes to about ten, p. 131. A twelfth century work refers to twenty-four kinds of food grains. P. Niyogi, *Contributions*, pp. 23–4. The *Ain* has revenue rates against twenty-nine varieties of grains and fourteen vegetables vol. I, pp. 298–301. Even of the same grain, a large number of varieties gradually began to be cultivated. We are informed that around the twelfth century fifty varieties of rice were grown in Bengal, B.N.S. Yadava, *Society and Culture*, p. 258. Abul Fazl makes nearly the same point when he remarks that if a single grain of each kind of Bengal rice were collected, a large vase would be filled up, *Ain*, vol. I, p. 389.

214 The water-wheel might have had a three—rather than a two—stage history which Irfan Habib has so painstakingly reconstructed. The arghatta (or the noria) had buckets attached to its rim and was thus functional only on surface water—in a pool or on the bank of a river. It also had to be manually operated. The fully developed Persian wheel, on the other hand, was an animal-powered, geared machine which collected water from a well in a bucket with a chain attached to its rim. A technologically intermediate stage appears to have consisted of the water-wheel with a bucket chain but without the gear. It was manually operated and drew water from wells. A three-stage history of the water-wheel, if valid, should suggest not only a longer period of development of this irrigation device but also a wider social participation in the process of its development, for a larger number of peasants could perhaps afford the wheel available in a wider range. The consequent rise in the productivity of land should also have had its impact on the process of state-formation between the seventh-eighth and the fourteenth century. The establishment of a highly centralized state-structure, collecting at times as much as half of the peasants' produce as revenue in the thirteenth and early fourteenth century, was perhaps not an act of conquest but the culmination of a process that started during the

The characteristics of agrarian history discussed above—high fertility of land, low subsistence level and free peasant production—also explain the relative stability in India's social and economic history. It is, after all, true that there has hardly been any concentrated social effort caused by acute tensions to change completely the means, the methods and the relations of production. Indeed, barring the *arghatta* (noria) and the Persian wheel, one can hardly speak of a major break in the means of agricultural production. It appears that the features we have discussed above have some relationship with the absence of these major breaks. In India, unlike Europe, there appears to have been no prolonged and acute scarcity either of labour or production; the routine increase in demand could perhaps have been met by the routine extension of agriculture.

Thus with a high quantum of agrarian surplus available in the form of land-revenue, cesses, etc. to the state—which formed the chief instrument of exploitation[215]—and because of the high fertility of land and the low subsistence level of the peasant,[216] a kind of equilibrium existed which facilitated the state's appropriation of the peasants' surplus in conditions of relative stability. Whenever the state tried from time to time to upset the equilibrium, the peasantry reacted by either abandoning cultivation

---

seventh century or thereabout. The first to notice the rise in productivity, owing to the spread of irrigation, were the village potentates and they might also have been the first to demand a greater amount of the peasants' produce in revenue. The state would take its own time to wake up to this new reality, but once it did, it introduced an element of systematization in the appropriation of the peasants' increased surplus through a relatively efficient and highly centralized, administrative apparatus. The establishment of this state can thus be seen as the culmination of a process that developed from the bottom upwards rather than from top downwards.

Clearly, this is still the very initial stage of a hypothesis and much research is called for to arrive at a conclusion.

215 Irfan Habib, *Agrarian System*, p. 257. Irfan Habib makes this remark in the context of medieval India, but this would as well be true of the earlier period irrespective of direct collection of revenue by the state-officials or on its behalf by assignees.

216 Bhimsen, a late seventeenth-century chronicler, grasped this point in his description of Tanjore: in the whole world nowhere else are there so many temples, he says. The cause of the building of these temples he assigns to the very high fertility of land—producing four crops a year—and the abysmal standard of peasants' subsistence which he describes in detail and 'without exaggeration'. Consequently, 'a large revenue is raised, the amount of which is known only to the Recording Angel', *Nuskha-i-Dilkusha*, Jadu Nath Sarkar (tr) (Bombay, 1972), pp. 193–4.

or even resorting to violence.[217] But it perhaps needs to be admitted that such cases of active resistance were rather rare, and, except for the peasant rebellions during Aurangzeb's reign, remained largely localized. For once the state's intrusion was rejected, the balance was again restored.

In combination with this factor, the peasant's independent control over his process of production eliminated the possibility of acute social tensions which may have necessitated significant changes in the entire system of production. The conflicts that characterized the economic history of pre-British India were conflicts over the distribution and redistribution of the surplus rather than over the redistribution of the means of production, which had changed the face of medieval European economy.[218] The conflicts over the redistribution of the surplus were resolved by and large within the existing social framework. It is thus that even when the Mughal empire was collapsing, one gets the impression that the class of zamindars at various levels was turning out to be the main beneficiary of this collapse. It was, in other words, an older form of property that was re-emerging in strength.[219] Medieval Indian society did not have enough tension in it to lead it to the bourgeois system of production.[220]

217 In the *Mahabharata*, Bhisma says, 'If the king disregards agriculturists, they become lost to him, and abandoning his dominions betake themselves to the woods', cited in P.C. Jain, p. 54; in the eleventh century Ksemendra bemoans the fact that the poor, with malice towards the property of the rich, were turning violent, B.N.S. Yadava, 'Problem of Interaction between Socio-economic Classes in the Early Medieval Complex', *Indian Historical Review*, vol. 3, no. 1, July 1976, p. 55; the Kaivarttas in east Bengal took to arms to resist the increasing state oppression in the last years of the eleventh century, R.S. Sharma, *Indian Feudalism*, p. 268; the peasantry of Doab revolted in the second quarter of the fourteenth century against the state's excessive exactions, Zia ud-din Barani, pp. 472–3; for the documentation of the widespread peasant rebellions of the second half of the seventeenth century, see Irfan Habib, *Agrarian System*, pp. 330–51.

218 It has been argued that Indian feudalism comes closest to European feudalism of the twelfth century, B.N.S. Yadava, *Society and Culture*, p. 171. Quite apart from the validity of this comparison in terms of historical evidence which is by no means conclusive, even if such evidence were conceded, a momentary convergence between two social systems following independent paths of historical development can hardly justify the conclusion that they were both marked by the same characteristics.

219 It is too early to be definitive about it, but some work on different regions of eighteenth century India is in progress at the Jawaharlal Nehru University to test this hypothesis.

220 For a persuasive argument regarding the absence of any potential for capitalist development in the Mughal economy, see Irfan Habib, 'Potentialities etc'.

To argue against the notion of an Indian feudalism need not lead one to the acceptance of the Asiatic mode of production.[221] Indeed, the concept of the Asiatic mode of production is based on the absence of private property in land,[222] which is far from the generally accepted view among Indian historians today. It is evident that a wide range of social formations have existed in the world prior to their subjection to the universality of capitalism, and this range cannot be exhausted with the concepts of feudalism and the Asiatic mode of production. Irfan Habib has questioned the validity of the concepts of feudalism and the Asiatic mode of production for Indian History[223] and has suggested a neutral term, namely, the Indian medieval economy.[224] I have perhaps been quite rash in emphasizing free peasant production as the characteristic feature of the Indian medieval economy. But a critique of the existing straitjackets of feudalism and the Asiatic mode of production may have this much to recommend it: it might clear the path for the search of a typology more

221 Irfan Habib vehemently questions the validity of the notion of the Asiatic mode of production; see his 'Problems of Marxist Historical Analysis', *Enquiry*, n.s. vol. VIII, no. 2, Monsoon 1969, pp. 52–67. For a recent re-statement of the rejection of this notion, see Bipan Chandra, 'Karl Marx, His Theories of Asian Societies and Colonial Rule' (mimeo). Unfortunately, in Bipan Chandra's discussion of ancient and medieval Indian history there is hardly a statement that can go uncontested. Marian Sawer has, in her *Marxism and the Question of the Asiatic Mode of Production*, referred to earlier, made a very interesting study of the history of this concept and the recent political context in which it has been discussed.

222 R.A.L.H. Gunawardana suggests that Marx had at some point abandoned the notion of the absence of private property in land in India, 'The Analysis of Pre-Colonial Social Formation in Asia in the Writings of Karl Marx', *Indian Historical Review*, vol. 2, no. 2, Jan. 1976, pp. 365–88. Gunawardana has in this connection drawn attention to evidence hitherto overlooked by historians. It remains true, however, that this evidence belongs to the period between 1853 and 1858; on the other hand in his writings of the latter phase of this period and afterwards Marx continued to insist on the absence of private property in land in that he spoke of its communal ownership: *Grundrisse*, Martin Nicolaus (tr) (London, 1973), pp. 472–3; *A Contribution to the Critique of Political Economy* (Moscow, 1970), p. 33n. (where Marx says that 'primitive communal property . . . is still in existence in India'); *Capital*, vol. I, pp. 357–8.

223 'Problems of Marxist Historical Analysis'.

224 'Economic History of the Delhi Sultanate', p. 298.

specific to pre-British India. Additionally, it might draw us away from Euro-centrism in the study of history.[225]

[225] Whenever we discuss the question of feudalism in any country and in any period, medieval western Europe inevitably provides the point of reference for such a discussion, whatever be our answer to this question. One can, of course, see the justice of comparing the history of other countries with that of western Europe in modern times for it was, after all, in western Europe that capitalism arose which was later to encompass the whole world; but it is difficult to see the logic of such a comparison in the ancient and medieval periods when it might only persuade us to ask questions which have so little relevance to our history.

It is possible, of course, to speak of regional variations of feudalism. One could thus argue in favour of an Indian feudalism, a Chinese feudalism, a West Asian feudalism, etc. apart from the west European and the Japanese one. However, I visualize two reservations with respect to this argument. First, the use of a common denominator for the whole range of regionally and temporally variant socio-economic systems could hardly be justified unless one could establish a fundamental similarity underlying these variations—a similarity that was precisely defined. Secondly, quite apart from the fact that feudalism as a category achieves universality only through the looseness of its definition, the very search for a universal category, equally applicable to different medieval regions, is based on the assumption that the medieval world was one world sharing a common socio-economic system. We thus attribute to the medieval world characteristics which more appropriately belong to the nineteenth and twentieth centuries.

Chapter Four

The Segmentary State: Interim Reflections*

BURTON STEIN

Aidan Southall formulated the segmentary state model for his study of the Alur in highland East Africa in 1956[1] for the same reason that I adapted his formulation for the Cholas of South India almost two decades later: in order to provide a conception of 'state' that satisfied empirical conditions in our respective researches as well as the desire to theorize political relationships in our different fields in new ways. Thirty years after his Alur formulation, when Southall addressed the matter once again, he confessed to being surprised, then astonished, that his African solution was taken up by Richard Fox to discuss Rajput polities in northern India and later by me. The reformulation that Southall produced in 1988[2] was, he says, partly to 'repay' my refinements of his earlier conception: similarly, this essay is in part my reply in the reciprocal exchange with Southall, but it is also something else.

First of all this discussion seeks to answer some of the accumulated criticisms of nearly a decade about my use of the segmentary state concept in several papers and in my books, *Peasant State and Society in Medieval South India* and *Vijayanagara*.[3] Secondly, the purpose is to clarify my present position on segmentary political relations in pre-modern India

* With minor variations, this paper was written for and will appear in a number of *Puruṣārtha* (v. 13, 1990), entitled 'De la royauté à l'Etat (les formes du politique dans le monde indien)', Editions de l'Ecole des Hautes Etudes en Sciences Sociales.

1 *Alur Society; A Study in Processes and Types of Domination* (Cambridge: Heffer).

2 'The Segmentary State in Africa and Asia', *Comparative Studies in Society and History*, 30 (January, 1988), pp. 52–82.

3 Published, respectively, by Oxford University Press, New Delhi, in 1980 and by Cambridge University Press as vol. 1.2 of The New Cambridge History of India, in 1989.

while remaining open about its final definition, and hence it is an interim report.

Easily the most difficult question confronting the historians of India has been how to characterize the state in pre-modern times, and the difficulty persists because it is only very recently that the question has been perceived as being problematic. Thirty years ago when I began my research on medieval South India, it became obvious to me that research on the Chola, Vijayanagara and other medieval kingdoms was flawed conceptually and empirically with respect to the treatment of the state. This was not a widely held conviction when I began my work, but I think it is fair to say that it is now widely accepted, though my proposed characterization of political relations in that earlier south Indian society as 'segmentary' is not. Older historical views insisted on seeing polities of the time as centralized and to a degree bureaucratized; lurking behind much of the writing of that time was a very modern, unitary state form. Indeed, this was the explicit formulation of the best of modern historians, K.A. Nilakantha Sastri,[4] and it was and remains an implicit understanding among many other historians still.

Given my discontent with that received wisdom, it became necessary to delineate another sort of state form, one that met the constraints of extant evidence on these early kingdoms and the underlying structure of material relations in the societies of each, and also one that could be theorized—provided with structure and content—in a way that made it a candidate form for other Indian societies and perhaps societies other than Indian as well.

At the time that I adopted the segmentary formulation I was insufficiently alert to a major discordant theoretical element which still remains a part of Southall's formulation. This is the relationship between what I was calling political segmentation or a 'segmentary state' and something called 'segmentary society'. For Richard Fox, a fellow debtor at Southall's African bank, this was less a problem because his ruling Rajputs were organized politically as segmentary lineages, but even for Fox there was a similar problem since these Rajput lineages did not extend from the bottom to the top of the political order, as the African Alur lineages do; moreover, the state regimes of Rajput houses have historically nested

[4] In his *The Colas* (Madras: University of Madras, 1935–37) and his *A History of South India* (Madras: Oxford University Press, 1955).

within larger political orders in which lineage principles were weak, or almost wholly absent—that of the Mughal state and its successors, the Marathas and the British.[5]

But mine was a more serious sort of difference at the level of theory, for I predicated segmentation of an altogether different sort from the segmentary lineages of Southall's Alur or Fox's Rajputs. Still, I did this within Southall's general formulation where he introduced the notion of pyramidal segmentation:

> Several levels of subordinate foci may be distinguishable, organized pyramidally in relation to the central authority. The central and peripheral authorities reflect the same model, the latter being reduced images of the former. Similar powers are repeated at each level with decreasing range.[6]

In *Peasant State and Society*, I took the hundreds of local societies called *nādu* in the inscriptions and literature of Chola times as the fundamental components, or pyramidally-organized segments, of the society; I saw these nadus as social and political communities and I also saw, and continue to see, the relationship between these hundreds of communities and the state, as crucial for an understanding of this Indian Society, or perhaps of other pre-industrial societies.

It is essential, however, to accept that *community* is understood according to the usual English signification of being simultaneously a people and a place, rather than in its limited and debased usage as sub-caste or religious group. Hence, community is to be understood as *janapada*, not *jāti*, and pertains to shared sentiments and values; however, community is also about shared rights or entitlements over human and material resources, and thus, in its particularities, pertains to smaller, local spatial entitles under conditions of pre-modern technology. It is because very localized affinities, sentiments and, especially, entitlements—*and the cultural, social, and political means for defending them*—continued to persist in India until well into contemporary times, that I have been encouraged to see segmentary political forms as extending well into the last century, thus giving the concept considerable historiographical reach.

5 R.G. Fox, *Kin, Clan, Raja and Rule* (Berkeley: University of California Press, 1971), pp. 56–7. Southall draws attention to these aspects of Fox's analysis in 'The Segmentary State in Africa and Asia', pp. 69 and 71.

6 Southall's definition is found in *Alur Society*, pp. 248–9; in Fox, *Kin, Clan, Raja and Rule*, p. 56; and in my *Peasant State and Society*, p. 265 and elaborated from pp. 265 to 285.

At the level of theory, the relationship between segmentation in the political order and a segmentary social base is as ambiguous in my previous formulations as it was in Southall's. Segmentary lineages do not figure in his first definition of the 'segmentary state'; it was only later that he examined this issue and concluded that political segmentation need not be based on segmentary lineage systems.[7] This view is reconfirmed in Southall's most recent formulation where he notes the contrastive treatments of Indian political segmentation by Fox and me, and appears to be untroubled by the differences. Nevertheless, the theoretical question remains. Its shadow is cast over some of what follows, and it must be readdressed below.

The South Indian Segmentary State and Its Critics

The concept I have used can be outlined in the following terms, though detailed understanding must depend on a reading of my *Peasant State and Society in Medieval South India*, 1980 and my volume on the Vijayanagara kingdom.[8]

The segmentary state refers to a political order which is distinguished from others. It is distinguished from the usual model of polities that lurks anachronistically in all of our heads—the unitary state with its fixed territory, its centralized administration and coercive power; it is also distinguished from the favoured alternative genus of the polity of historians, 'feudal', by which is meant a variety of political relationships, but most usually—as the Anglo-French species—a form of prebendalism based upon a high degree of political centredness. In positive terms, the segmentary state is a political order in which:

1. There are numerous centres or political domains;
2. Political power (in Indian classical reference, *kṣatra*) and sovereignty (or *rājādharma*) are differentiated in such a way as to permit appropriate power to be wielded by many, but full, royal sovereignty, only by an anointed king;

[7] 'A Critique of the Typology of States and Political Systems', in Michael Banton, *Political Systems and the Distribution of Power* (New York: F.F. Praeger, 1965), p. 126.

[8] Entitled *Vijayanagara*, to be published by Cambridge University Press as a volume in its series, The New Cambridge History of India.

3. All of the numerous centres, or domains, have autonomous administrative capabilities and coercive means;
4. There is *a* state in the recognition, by lesser political centres, often through ritual forms, of a single ritual centre, an anointed king.

An additional defining statement is required to complete the outline of the system which I have postulated. The political order of medieval South India to which I applied the concept of the 'segmentary state' is based upon a segmentary social order, which I called 'pyramidal', following Southall.[9] In the medieval south Indian segmentary state, the numerous political centres of the polity appeared to be based upon internally differentiated localized social structures, usually designated as nadu during the Chola period (9th to 13th century). These were stratified and ranked, occupationally diverse, and culturally varied territories which displayed what I took to be complementary oppositions. Hence, based upon the admittedly fragmentary evidence of that time, it could be argued that lineage and other kinship affinities were internally opposed and also balanced by occupational and sectarian principles of affiliation; the interests of peasant groups were opposed and, again, balanced, by the interests of herdsmen or artisanal producers; and among the latter, between those producing for markets and those whose products or services were locally consumed and mediated by the clientage relations usually designated by the term, *jajmānī*. Moreover, I argued that the enstructuration of localized, pyramidally-organized segments was obedient to and fundamentally shaped by varied social, political and cultural developments as well as by ecological or ecotypic conditions. This resulted in three different types of localities which I designated as 'central', 'intermediate', and 'peripheral' zones of the segmentary political system of Chola times.

Criticisms of this formulation have taken several different forms, and at times, what may have been intended as appreciation seems, paradoxically, to be the opposite. Take, for example, the banal appreciation of the

[9] Being insufficiently aware that Southall did not question whether a segmentary political order can exist without segmentary social forms, I simply proceeded on the basis that there must be a congruent relationship between political and social segmentation, and I saw no difficulty in attempting to specify this congruence, but in an Indian, rather than African idiom. Others have attempted to define similar differences in other ways, for example Sahlin's distinction between tribal orders and chiefdoms, in his 'The Segmentary Lineage and Predatory Expansion', *American Anthropologist*, 63, no. 2 (1963), pp. 32–45.

segmentary state concept as valuable in bringing to our notice the tendency in all political systems for central authority to weaken at their peripheries. Why this should be considered valuable, or even interesting, escapes me. A segmentary state, or political order, is *not* a centralized political or administrative order, hence to find the segmentary political concept valuable merely for noting the peripheral attenuation of central rule is to reduce a segmentary political system to an imperfect manifestation of centralized authority under paleotechnical conditions of transportation and communication.

More explicit critics of the segmentary state argument that I have made can be divided into the categories, strong and weak and intellectual and ideological.

Some of the weak, intellectual criticisms that have been lodged are the following. That in my formulation, I have denied any central features or forces at work in the kingdoms of the Cholas and Vijayanagara; that I am actually speaking, as B.D. Chattopadhyaya puts it, of a 'State *sans* politics'.[10] This, I submit, is a flawed reading of *Peasant State and Society*, where I drew attention to the highly centralized resource command of the Chola kings in the heartland of their kingdom, the wealthy Kaveri valley, and illustrated the point by reference to the massive mobilizations of Rajaraja I and Rajendra I for building their great royal shrines in Tanjavur and Gangaikondacholapuram. In *Peasant State and Society* I also spoke of the significant political sovereignty enjoyed by the numerous chiefs (*uḍaiyar*) of the Chola age as evidenced by their pooling and redistribution of resources, and I referred to the increased appropriative capacity and authority of post-Chola chiefs culminating in the Vijayanagara-age chiefs who, along with kings of the age, enjoyed a very high degree of coercive command over the varied institutions and ranked social groups within their domains.

The capacity of chiefs, *as well as kings*, to centralize resources is an important historical fact that is easily overlooked or trivialized because the simultaneity of enhanced power and authority by lesser and greater lords does indeed appear like a denial of centralization, as some critics charge. But that seems to me to essentialize central authority, forcing all historical kingdoms into the mould of the absolutist states that historians

[10] 'Political Processes and the Structure of Polity in Early Medieval India, Presidential Address, Ancient India Section, Indian History Congress, 44th Session, Burdwan, December, 1983.

see in sixteenth to eighteenth century Europe, as well as in parts of southern and western Asia, where increased central authority always appeared to come at the expense of lesser lordships.[11]

Another criticism is cultural as well as essentializing and racist: it is that no theoretical formulation that arises from sub-Saharan Africa can be given serious consideration in and for India, with its ancient reflective as well as normative texts and with its distinctive institution and ideology of caste and *varnāshramadharma.* Notice that this is not a xenophobic caveat when it comes from Indian critics, because most, like K.A. Nilakantha Sastri, have been quite pleased to find Fustel de Coulanges' city–state structures and even Byzantine bureaucracies in medieval South India, much as D.D. Kosambi, R.S. Sharma and others were pleased to find European feudal institutions and ideology. Comparisons with, and even borrowings from Europe have been acceptable, even eagerly sought, whereas merely a structural comparison of Indian and African forms gives offense to many Indians.[12]

Moreover, I have sought to demonstrate the ways in which a segmentary formulation of the sort that I have proposed is not only consistent with the medieval *dharma* and *niti* texts of India, but, arguably, may be the only political formulation that adequately captures the textual understandings of Indian kingship and the primary lines along which political affiliations can occur, according to these texts.[13]

Then there are criticisms from scholars with what I take to be programmatic objections to the segmentary state proposal. From the ideological right have come objections to this as to any proposal that even questions, much less repudiates, the substantialized conception of Indian society hyperthrophized as caste and varnashramadharma. I am referring

[11] Even here of course there is not perfect unanimity; Perry Anderson sees these 'absolutist states' as the highest stage of feudalism, the very antithesis of centralism! *Lineages of the Absolute State* (London: New Left Books, 1974).

[12] Some western scholars, with their own hegemonic notions about the concept of culture, have also criticized this African model on the basis of the literacy of India. This essentialization of cultural differences is then made to stand for a qualitatively different (i.e. lower) level of African culture, hence comparisons involving non-literate Africa and literate India are not like with like. That there are genuine differences between the historical societies of South Asia and those of sub-Saharan Africa is not denied, but that these differences are reducible to literacy and literate traditions can scarcely be credited when one considers the reach of Islam into Africa from the seventh century.

[13] *Peasant State and Society*, pp. 275–85.

here to scholars in India whose communalist views are known and whose historical understandings reflect these views. A similar programmatic bias comes from the left, from some Marxist scholars who ask of work on the Cholas what they ask of any other historical society: an analysis of classes, class conflict and relations between classes and the state and who also ask how the segmentary state formulation advances our understanding of the transition to capitalism at some very later time.

Such critics offer no research hypotheses, no historiographical formulations to be examined seriously and confronted with evidence; their views preserve certain formulations for their contemporary ideological utility only. To be sure, all of our histories are and must be framed by the interests and purposes of our time, but these must be expected to yield to the corrective of disciplined historical scholarship. In fact, however, almost no work has been done nor is being done on the state in pre-modern India by most ideologically committed scholars, and as a consequence, there is little scope for such formulations of ideological convenience to the right or the left to be challenged.

Of course, there is an obvious difference between naive marxist pronouncements, such as those of Kathleen Gough's proposals about a Chola 'slave economy',[14] and the sort of nuanced criticism I have been pleased to have from others, Marxists and non-Marxists, the cogency of whose comments on my segmentary state is related to their active studies of historical state systems.

I shall mention first among these strong criticisms of the segmentary state formulation those from S.J. Tambiah and Hermann Kulke with both of whom I have had rewarding and challenging discussions over the years. The former's 'galactic' state model, worked out for pre-modern Thailand, is, in its theoretical and descriptive specification, kinship generated—its sole filiational principle is blood.[15] That suggests an affinity with Southall's formulation, as the latter has recognized.[16] Whether or not Tambiah's formulation is satisfactory for Thai kingship and state I

[14] Gough in 'Modes of Production in Southern India', *Economic and Political Weekly* (Annual Number, February 1980), pp. 337–64; and her *Rural Society in Southeast India* (Cambridge: Cambridge University Press, 1981).

[15] *World Conqueror and World Renouncer* (Cambridge: Cambridge University Press, 1976).

[16] Southall, 'The Segmentary State in Africa and Asia', p. 53, where he also mentions Geertz's 'theatre state' as another 'idiosyncratic' ethnographical interpretation.

cannot say, but kinship—usually lineage affiliation—is only one of several principles that are seen to operate in the polities of early South India. I shall return to this question shortly, but for now it is also necessary to consider Kulke's criticisms of the segmentary state model. Like Tambiah who gives major importance to forms of ritual incorporation, Kulke has considered my formulation, but in the end rejected it for its lack of fit with the specific polity he was examining, that of medieval Orissa. There, he finds no intermediate forms resembling the nāḍu of Tamil country in Chola times that formed the basis, in my view, of the peripheral 'centres' of the segmentary polity. Kulke proposes something he calls an 'integrative polity' where the sole specified means of royal incorporation seems to be the symbolic capture of local, 'tribal' godlings by the royal cult of Vishnu as Jagannatha of whom the first worshipper was the Ganga or Gajapati ruler. How this incorporation was achieved and whether it was or can have been the sole political process at work is left unclear.[17]

In contrast to Tambiah and Kulke there are a set of critics of the segmentary state formulation whose reservations stem from their commitments to a modified, or 'Indian' feudalism. Adherents of the feudal formulation include not only many Indian scholars of medieval states, but also scholars of modern India who find in an 'Indian feudalism' a convenient foundation for their twin concerns with the rise of nationalism and the development of capitalism in modern India. Yet, notwithstanding its distinguished double paternity by D.D. Kosambi in the middle 1950s[18] and R.S. Sharma a decade later,[19] the feudal concept has never been seriously tested against the claims inherent in it nor has it been elaborated in any significant way.[20] Hence, the feudal conception remains either an article of left historiographical faith or a convenient residual position for those scholars who cannot accept that early Indian states were embryonic

[17] Kulke's paper entitled 'Fragmentation and Segmentation versus Integration? Reflections on the Concepts of Indian Feudalism and the Segmentary State in Indian History', a manuscript version of which the author sent me some years ago and since published in *Studies in History*, vol. IV, 2, 1982, pp. 237–64.

[18] D.D. Kosambi, 'The Basis of Ancient Indian History', *Journal of the American Oriental Society*, 1955.

[19] *Indian Feudalism: c. 300–1200* (Calcutta: University of Calcutta, 1965).

[20] Despite the recently edited work of D.N. Jha, *Feudal Social Formation in Early India* (Delhi: Chanakya Publications, 1987) containing essays by Sharma and Kosambi as well as several writers on South India: N. Karashima, Y. Subbarayalu, M.G.S. Narayanan and Veluthat Kesavan.

modern, unitary states. In either case, an Indian feudalism is flawed by the absence in any of the applications of the concept to what might have been the 'feudal state' which presumably expressed and preserved the interests of the host of what are called 'feudatories' allegedly found everywhere in pre-modern India. In other words, to alter a criticism of the segmentary state as 'a state without politics', in 'Indian feudalism' there is a highly variegated set of political forms, but no feudal state. Nor have any advocates of an Indian feudal polity given serious attention to the theoretical implications of the considerable evidence which exists on the processes of urbanization, trade and banking during the early and later medieval age in India.

The most incisive criticisms of the feudal conception of pre-modern Indian politics have been elucidated by Harbans Mukhia, who has attacked the feudal formulation from the point of view of its economic as well as political claims[21] and by B.D. Chattopadhyaya, who proposed an alternative model which he calls 'the samanta-feudatory system',[22] at least for the early medieval period of Indian history. From both of these scholars, too, have come the most probing queries about the segmentary state proposition: Mukhia asking for an analysis of the interests—class or other—represented in and protected by the segmentary states I posit; and Chattopadhyaya asking where lineage-based political entitles, the ancient and ubiquitous *sāmanta* of India—including the South—are to be found in my theory.

If the segmentary theory is to stand against the diffusely conceived feudal theory of political organization in pre-modern India, then these and other criticisms must be met. To Mukhia's question about the class character of the state, my response is that I see the medieval South, and perhaps other parts of the sub-continent, as a generalized polity of chiefdoms, that is as a system of enduring (but not necessarily permanent) political structures, based on strong hereditary regimes with extensive authority over wide areas and over varied and internally ranked local social segments; chieftains occupied the apex of pyramidal segments and derived their authority from local landholding groups or from conquest over such localities. However, chieftainship in medieval India cannot be taken as

21 'Was There Feudalism in Indian History?' and 'Peasant Production and Medieval Indian Society', in T.J. Byers and Harbans Mukhia (eds), *Feudalism and Non-European Societies* (London: Frank Cass, 1985).

22 'Political Processes and the Structure of Polity'.

either a complete system of authority nor as adequately theorized; for that the principle of monarchy is crucial. But, monarchy in its turn must be properly understood in its medieval Indian sense. For, ranked and ruling hereditary chiefs claimed to be kings (rājā or swāmī) and while they differentiated themselves from other, greater kings who held an exalted status through vedic anointment, these lesser or 'little' kings were deemed to share sovereignty with the greater ones.[23] The latter, far fewer in number, are *the* kings of those Indian polities which we designate as historical kingdoms, and a condition of being for these anointed kings was the preservation of the sub-stratum of chiefdoms, or 'little kingdoms', of which the great historic kingdoms consisted.

But, in answering Mukhia's question and objection about the interests protected and advanced in the segmentary state of my imagining, have I not conceded Chattopadhyaya's? For what is a *sāmanta* polity if not a polity of chiefdoms? Answering this hypothetical objection would be easier if we had a clearer idea of what the 'sāmanta-feudatory system' was and according to what principles it worked. Unfortunately we have had no greater specification of its workings than that afforded by Kulke, and Chattopadhyaya, in the end, falls back on Kulke's vague 'integrative polity', even though he deplores Kulke's failure to specify a 'political mechanism of integration'.[24]

That there have been historical political orders based on segmentary lineages in which the term 'sāmanta' and 'ruling lineages' figured importantly is not disputed. Among these are those whom Fox wrote about in the Gangetic plain and those of Rajasthan on which Chattopadhyaya, among many others, have worked and therefore about which a great deal has come to be known from James Tod's time, a century and a half ago. But even here, extensive regimes, 'kingdoms', have rarely emerged from the expansion of single lineages and in places other than Rajasthan, where there is the appearance of something like this occurring, it turns out to be something different, as Chattopadhyaya admits.[25]

[23] The term *dayada* is important here and is explored by Andre Wink in his *Land and Sovereignty in India: Agrarian Society and Politics under the Eighteenth-Century Maratha Svarajya* (Cambridge: Cambridge University Press, 1986); a translation of an important source dealing with the concept is found in V.D. Rao, 'Ajnyapatra Re-Examined', *Journal of Indian History*, 29, 1951, pp. 63–89.

[24] 'Political Processes and the Structure of Polity', 19 and note 116.

[25] Chattopadhyaya discusses this in an interesting if somewhat cryptic manner in 'Political Processes and the Structure of Polity', pp. 11–14.

Still, even where the sāmanta term is rarely encountered, as in South India, lineage political formations were important. From late Chola times in South India, lineages of powerful chiefs became so decisive as to bring the Chola regime to an end; and they continued to be important through the entire Vijayanagara period. Timing is important here, for such lineage-based regimes never displaced the control of high caste, corporate assemblies in the riverine valley cores of the Chola kingdom, but only in the dry, upland parts of the southern peninsula that were gradually opened then and later. Lineage polities arose from and were the political authority in societies of the moving agrarian frontier of the peninsula, those mixed pastoral and agricultural communities that converted jungle bush and pastures into arable land with the aid of tank irrigation and that retained martial characteristics which were available to greater lords, such as the Vijayanagara kings.[26]

Chattopadhyaya's concerns about the idea of 'feudal polity' and some of his criticisms of the feudal model reflect his laudable intention to launch upon or to participate in the construction of a generalized model of polity during India's medieval era. This intention is reflected in the seriousness of his judgements about specific elements of both the feudal and the segmentary state formulations. Notwithstanding his reservations however, he feels the major task for historians is to chart the evolution of state formations during the medieval era, and to 'plug the gap between polity and society' then.[27]

Before turning to an examination of changes in what I am calling a

[26] Several recent works elucidate this history: David Ludden's *Peasant History in South India* (Princeton: Princeton University Press, 1985) especially ch. 2; Pamela Price's '*Rajadharma* in 19th Century South India: Land, Litigation and Largess in Ramnad Zamindari', *Contributions to Indian Sociology (NS)*, 13 (1979), pp. 204–39; Nicholas Dirks' study of the Pudukkottai kings of South India, *The Hollow Crown; Ethnohistory of an Indian Kingdom* (Cambridge: Cambridge University Press, 1987), who achieved their differentiated status as 'king' in the late seventeenth century from the legitimate superior royal authority, the last ruler of the Vijayanagara kingdom

[27] 'Political Processes and the Structure of Polity', 4. Among his criticisms the latter pertains to the claim that samantas and other candidate 'feudatories' received 'feudal' assignments of land from greater lords. He doubts the existence of a contingently 'contractual' basis usually implied in feudal assignments, and he also denies that contract was an important element of political affiliation in early medieval India, though service assignments became important in later medieval times. This conforms with my own judgements in the analysis of the Chola kingdom and in marking the difference between the Chola and, as I continue to call it, the Vijayanagara segmentary state.

segmentary political order that must be made to meet the more serious criticisms against the formulation, I should say that I believe that a reconciliation of the views of Kulke and Chattopadhyaya with my own are possible as well as promising, and I do not mean by the usual compromise method of observing that we three are studying different places at somewhat different times, hence variations are to be expected. Of course, they are, but it is at the level of theory that I believe a convergence of views is both promising and likely, since I believe that each of us is actually dealing with evolving structures within a single broad form and in our own ways we are privileging certain elements and neglecting others.[28]

It may be useful therefore to briefly review how such a political evolution can be viewed in South India within a segmentary frame by considering the Chola and Vijayanagara kingdoms upon which I have worked.

The major core of Chola political authority from the late tenth to the thirteenth centuries was in the Kaveri basin, with secondary 'central zones' of the Chola segmentary state in other river valleys of the southern peninsula: the Ponnaiyar and Cheyyar in the northern Tamil plain, and the Vaigai and Tambraparni valleys in the south. The major core of the Vijayanagara kingdom, contrarily, was in the dry upland and watershed region of the peninsula, opened over several centuries by a process of agrarian expansion along a moving frontier. The corresponding state resource catchments thus varied in significant ways: in the Chola kingdom principal reliance was upon a share of the rich irrigated agriculture under corporate control in the collegial assemblies of Brahmans and Vellalas; in the Vijayanagara kingdom, principal reliance of all lordships was increasingly upon the wealth of trade within that broad region between and connecting the two trade coasts and less upon agrarian production from the largely dry cultivation of frontier zones under the control of the tough warrior chiefs of the upland. During the Vijayanagara period, also, the

[28] For instance, Chattopadhyaya is more attentive to urbanization in the evolution of early medieval polities than either I or Kulke are, and therefore provides a more balanced appreciation of the material basis of early polities than we do with our emphasis upon ritual forms of integration and incorporation in the evolving political structures of medieval Orissa and the far South. B.D. Chattopadhyaya, 'Urban Centres in Early Medieval India: An Overview', in S. Bhattacharya and R. Thapar (eds), *Situating Indian History* (Delhi: Oxford University Press, 1986).

former riverine zones of Chola dominance were reduced to subjugation to upland state regimes, a condition that was begun in the time of the Hoysala kingdom of Karnataka and brought to fulfilment by the Vijayanagara successors to the Hoysalas. Social organization and ideology of the riverine cores of the Chola kingdom nevertheless remained largely hierarchical in post-Chola times, while in 'intermediate zones' of the kingdom (including parts of the Tamil plain and its upland extensions) society and ideology tended to be pluralistic and less hieratic; it was here that the dual division of lower castes in those of the right and left (*valaṅgai* and *iḍangai*) were entrenched.

By Vijayanagara times, fundamental changes in society and economy, dating from the thirteenth century, had altered a great deal; forces of urbanization and commercialization generated by political and religious changes created opportunities for new groups to advance their standing against older elite groups, and widespread social conflict as a result of this and other factors can be documented. For example, more ambitiously centralizing chiefs of the lower Kaveri incited widespread local uprisings in 1429–30 as reported by N. Karashima and Y. Subbarayalu.[29]

There were also important changes in military organization. In Chola times there were local militias maintained by entrenched communally organized local societies with only a small standing force under royal control (*velaikkārar*) drawn from the heartland segments (*valanāḍu*) of the Kaveri basin. Vijayanagara military formations, under pressure to imitate the highly successful fourteenth century Muslim invaders into the southern peninsula, had adopted firearms and imported war-horses and came to maintain larger standing forces than ever before. Commanders of these enlarged and standing forces assumed increasing political roles, and a powerful generalissimo like Saluva Narasimha was able to seize royal authority in the late fifteenth century, founding a new Vijayanagara dynasty. Later, two of his commanders were to do the same during the sixteenth century.

To support such enhanced military capabilities required a greatly enlarged money revenue, and this was found in the expanding commerce

29 'Valangai Idangai, Kaniyalar and Irajagarattar: Social Conflict in Tamil Nadu in the 15th Century'. Originally published in N. Karashima (ed.), *Socio-Cultural Change in Villages in Tiruchirapalli District, Tamilnadu, India* (Tokyo: Institute for the Study of Languages and Cultures of Asia and Africa, 1983); reprinted in Jha, *Feudal Social Formation*, pp. 284–307.

of the age. Trade in the peninsula was stimulated by the dominating consumption centre of the Vijayanagara capital and by new chiefly and temple centres that proliferated as the royal style of Vijayanagara spread; another source of commercial stimulation was the expanding international trade around the coasts of the peninsula and the increasing number of commercial centres founded during the age. Commerce and temple developments went together to add to the forces of urbanization and monetization, and temples, which had a more modest political role during the Chola period (in contrast to the large Brahman settlement or brahmadēya), now became centres of political, administrative and commercial activities and were among the most important civil institutions of that later society.

This brief outline has the obvious purpose of showing that major structural changes in the southern peninsula between the Chola and Vijayanagara ages were accommodated within the framework of the segmentary state in South India. To be sure, the Vijayanagara state was a different kind of segmentary state from that of the Cholas, but it was segmentary nevertheless in the critical sense that its royal power never attained that degree of centralized control over the constituent chiefdoms of the kingdom as to enable the kingdom to transform itself into something other than a segmentary state.

There is considerable evidence of efforts made to achieve substantially greater centralization of royal authority in Vijayanagara times. The kings Devaraya I and II in the first half of the fifteenth century strove for this transformation by creating a more centralized military force based on mercenaries, including Muslim horsemen and gunners, under royal commanders and by seeking to mobilize part of the international trade wealth to provide the fiscal means of supporting these technological innovations. Military modernization along lines first presented by Muslims and later by Europeans is easily dismissed as having failed to attain the efficiency and impact of foreign armies and that handguns and cannons were more decorative than destructive of the foes of Vijayanagara. A close study of the reports that exist on the campaigns of Krishnadevaraya suggests otherwise, but even if this denigration is accepted, the measures taken to modernize their armies committed the Vijayanagara kings of the fifteenth and sixteenth centuries to new resource mobilizing strategies.

Paradoxically, however, a major effect of these measures was to simultaneously strengthen the chiefdoms of the realm. These became more centralized within their domains, and military chiefs regularly transformed prebendal service entitlements into hereditary entitlements. Military commanders of royal armies pursued separate, often anti-royal ends and local rulers along both coasts garnered the greatest part of the wealth from international trade. The most vigorous effort to centralize royal authority came under Krishnadevaraya who employed Brahman administrators and fortress commanders against the territorial chiefs of his realm. His efforts foundered soon after his death as a result of the dynastic machinations of his son-in-law, Aliya Rama Raja; the latter restored and strengthened the independent authority of chiefs in the Andhra tracts of Rayalseema and Telengana as a means of gaining their support for his own campaign for the Vijayanagara throne. Military commanders usually affecting the title of *nāyaka* have been converted by historians into royal servants in the so-called *nāyaṇkara* system. Actually, these commanders remained their own men, seeking advantage for themselves and their families in the tracts where they were appointed to serve royal interests. In these places they either pursued their own advantage by establishing independent lordships loosely linked to Vijayanagara kings, or these chiefs formed lethal coalitions against royal authority. Nor, apparently, was such independence from royal authority taken as illicit by the later rulers of Vijayanagara, for during the highly successful southern campaign during the 1550s of Vithala, the nephew of Rama Raja, no effort was made to limit the expansion of the emerging Madurai kingdom, or *samasthānam*, of Visvantha Nayaka. The Madurai nayakaship became a realm as large and as wealthy as the homeland of the Vijayanagara kings of the Aravidu dynasty of the late sixteenth century, and Madurai was only one of several such so-called 'nayaka kingdoms' that began its coalescence in the late days of the great Krishnadevaraya.

The failure to achieve that royal centralization sought by some rulers in imitation of the more centralized regimes of their Muslim enemies of the Deccani sultanates is one reason for adhering continuity in the segmentary state formed during the Chola era. Another reason for holding to a segmentary political conception was the vigour with which communal entitlements everywhere continued to be protected by all sorts of local groups in south Indian society. Not only were many ancient entitlements preserved, but new communal rights were granted by the more powerful, military rulers of local societies in the South, partly to fortify their local rule and partly, too, in order to attract migrant soldiers and artisans to their mini-realms to enhance their autarchic wealth. These extensive communal awards survived into the nineteenth century as *in'am* and were a legacy which such ambitious and powerful centralizers as Haidar Ali Khan, Tipu Sultan, and finally the East India Company sought unsucessfully but with great determination to abrogate.

This structure and ideology of communal or community entitlements together with the force to protect them grew during the eighteenth century and were largely intact during the early nineteenth century. They are the social, economic and moral side of the political question about the nature of the state in early and late medieval South India. And this structure of entitlements remains another reason for holding on to the conception of the segmentary state.

A Return to Theory and Revision of the Conception

As this is partly a colloquy with Aidan Southall, several points raised by his recent reformulation of the segmentary state concept require comment. One has to do with his invocation of a mode of production argument in order to close the conceptual gap opened by differences in the levels of economy of such diverse candidate 'segmentary states' as the Alur and Indian ones, and even Tambiah's Thailand and Geertz's Bali. His proposed solution is to postulate something called 'a kinship mode of production' and even a 'foraging mode of production'[30] for the Alur and possibly for other African societies, and, not surprisingly, an Asiatic mode for the others. But mode of production solutions merely confound political and economic processes, and there is the suspicion created that the former can be reduced to the latter. Given that Southall provides the barest outline of what he means by the 'Asiatic mode' and even less about what the 'kinship' or 'foraging' modes are, uncertainty is bound to exist, and this uncertainty is deepened by his suggestion that the kinship mode of production is an 'embryonic version' of the Asiatic mode.[31] Finally, he poses an empirical difficulty for me as well as I am sure for Noburu Karashima who has worked on the Cholas by adopting Kathleen Gough's

30 'The Segmentary State in Africa and Asia', pp. 53–4.
31 Ibid., p. 66.

characterization of the latter kingdom as an example of Asian despotism under the Asiatic mode of production.[32]

This leads to a second comment on Southall's reformulation. As I understand it, his position confuses conceptual levels. I cannot now understand whether he is saying that the 'segmentary state' concept is a formal system of political structure or whether it is a type of political organization entailed by particular modes of productive relations (say, 'kinship', 'foraging', 'Asiatic'), but not others. As my definition at the beginning of this paper confirms, I consider Southall's original proposal to have been formal in character, one that is free of any *necessary* relationship or conditionality arising from any particular social or economic configurations, except, as I have already said, a segmentary political structure has seemed to me to presume related forms of social segmentation. Nor am I certain about how important it is at the conceptual level that I, or another scholar, agree with Southall about what Marx might have meant by the Asiatic mode or whether Gough's application of the notion to the imperial Cholas is valid.

Some confusion is additionally engendered in Southall's reformulation with respect to which two somewhat different notions of social morpology guide his theoretical statements. Southall appears now to be more concerned about the origins and development of structures than their typological characteristics. Approving as I do of Southall's desire to bring into a single comparative frame the 'idiosyncratic interpretations' of Thambiah and Geertz, I do not see how this objective can be advanced by his evolutionary apperception that the 'kinship mode of production' of the Alur was an 'embryonic version' of the 'Asiatic mode of production' even as Alur shrines were 'embryonic versions' of temples in South India.[33] Morphological questions are certainly important, especially in our age when the zealots for a cultural-based social science hold such influence as they distressingly do in the US and increasingly in the UK. Only a serious comparative social science can check the drift into a nihilism of culturally hegemonic explanations. But a comparative analysis must be generated more along analogical lines than the homological lines that Southall seems to be advocating now.

Stemming from Southall, but also apart from his recent reformulation, are questions about segmentation and the very appropriateness of

32 *South Indian History and Society*, xxix.

33 'The Segmentary State in Africa and Asia', pp. 64–6.

deploying segmentary terminology at all. This is not an obvious problem for Fox, nor for that matter would it be for Chattopadhyaya, because Rajput ruling lineages and the ideal typical sāmanta are based upon segmentary lineages for them, much as they are for Henri Stern in his analyses of what he purports is the 'traditional' Indian polity of Rajasthan.[34] However, the segmentary conception based exclusively on patrilineage politics cannot be taken as a generalized political form in premodern India without first resolving certain questions. Southall drew attention to two of these questions by observing that Fox's Rajput lineages do not extend from the base to the summit of Rajput principalities, but pertain to ruling lineages alone and that these Rajput polities always exist within (and are probably not conceivable outside of) larger political formations—Mughal or British—where segmentary lineages were not important features.

These caveats to Fox's application of the segmentary state concept are not reasons for Southall's rejection of that application, nor should they be, though we may regret that Fox did not clarify the relationship between Rajput lineages and the societies that they ruled and did not consider the implications of Rajput politics being embedded in larger political formations. On these and other questions it is doubtful that Fox or anyone else who had not studied the histories of these particular Rajput-ruled societies could tell us how ruling patrilineages were related to the sub-structure of their political societies. This must depend on memories beyond the recall of the anthropological present of Fox and other anthropologists. Norman Ziegler has offered valuable understanding of the consequence for Rajput houses involved in the Mughal system, and this was important in shaping Rajput understanding of themselves as later discovered by Fox and Stern.[35] The other relationship—from the Rajput chief or king downward—is only now being uncovered in the work on the rich historical documentation of archives such as that of Jaipur. If, as a result of this research, the dominant political alignments of groups within these lineage polities are discovered not to have been segmentary, and these were not segmentary societies, then we must ask:

34 'Power in Traditional India: Territory, Caste and Kinship in Rajasthan', in R.G. Fox, *Realm and Region in Traditional India* (Durham, North Carolina: Duke University, Monograph and Occasional Papers Series, No. 14, 1977).

35 'Some Notes on Rajput Loyalties During the Mughal Period', in J.P. Richards, *Kingship and Authority in South Asia* (Madison: University of Wisconsin, 1978).

what was the social sub-structure, how were Rajputs beneath ruling lineages and non-Rajputs in these places linked to the ruling lineages there, and how, finally, was the pan-Indian ideology of hierarchy accommodated?

I am taking ideology to pertain to the reasoning of historical subjects about what values they considered of first importance and how such values were attained. In a long section of *Peasant State and Society*, I undertook to relate the theory of the segmentary state to moral as well as political conceptions that were current in normative texts of the age. On the strength of that examination in relationship to pre-modern, south Indian polity, I reassert my conviction that the segmentary state form was the only one that fits the evidence that we have of the broad pattern of political relations and of the ideology in pre-modern peninsular India.

I also realize that this stress upon ideology puts me at odds with Southall, who has revised the theoretical grounding of his segmentary state concept in accordance with material relations—modes of production. This opening to material factors may be dictated by, or at least responsive to, questions arising from African ethnology. However, this is not a movement forward in the Indian context for two reasons. The first is the confused status of the 'Asiatic mode' concept and its unacceptability to almost all scholars in India, including Marxists; Gough's application of the concept has, if anything, confirmed the irrelevance of that mode of production argument. Moreover, an extended debate a few years ago on modes of production in India concluded in such disarray that an opening in that direction, at least for the present, holds little promise.[36]

The opening from the present conception of the segmentary state and of state formations more generally in pre-modern India must be of another sort; it must be in the direction of culture and ideology. As never before, the scholarly resources for this line of inquiry into pre-modern states are adequate to the task. All bear critically upon the segmentary state concept and all, being the work of anthropologists, are centrally concerned with culture. Therefore, I conclude this discussion by assessing some of the recent scholarship and indicating some of the ways in which my earlier formulation must be modified.

36 See the percipient and succinct summary of that debate by John Harriss in his *Capitalism and Peasant Farming; Agrarian Structure and Ideology in Northern Tamil Nadu* (Bombay: Oxford University Press, 1982), pp. 10–16.

Brenda Beck's *Peasant Society in Konku* (modern Coimbatore in Tamilnadu)[37] sets groups of this region into a bifurcated frame of a dual division of castes for which there is conclusive historical evidence dating from late Chola times when Kongu was a frontier tract.[38] However, the terms and rhetoric of the dual divisions were not known to her informants when she did her research. Notwithstanding the remoteness and the implicate nature of the informing ideology of the Kongu social system, Kongu is treated as a segmentary order: 'a social whole . . . [consisting of] a set of Chinese boxes . . . or nesting tiers of social organization',[39] extending from the region as a whole (called a 'natu') through twenty-four ancient localities (also called nadus) to households. Its castes are divided by her into two general categories of which one—the right division or valaṅgai—was constituted of the dominant landholding caste of Coimbatore, Kavuntars, and their ramified dependent subcastes, and the second —the left division or iḍaṅgai—comprised artisans and traders linked to the nexus of the generalized commodity exchange of the peninsula. The behavioural norms of the right division was that of kings, while those independent of agrarian employment and clientage adopted the norms ('purity and self control') of the Brahmins of Kongu, who were also free of agrarian clientage. Brahmins as well as Tamil accountants were neutral, or stood aloof from, the broad caste divisions in Kongu as they do elsewhere.

According to Beck, contrastive attributes demarcate the right and left divisions of Kongu castes. These include the narrow territorial social and cultic affiliations of the right division as opposed to a general Tamil identity and universalist religious affiliations of the left division and the territorialized marriage systems and alliances of the former in contrast to the individualistic and advantage-seeking interests of left castes' marriage strategies. Notwithstanding these and other contrasts that she specifies, Beck emphasizes two features of Kongu culture that permeate all relationships: the ideology of hierarchy and chieftainship.

Hierarchy is an overdetermining factor as a result of religious activities that extend upwards from Kongu village shrines to a set of territorial

37 Published in 1972 at Vancouver, University of British Columbia.

38 Her evidence for this is both inscriptional as well as literary, especially 'The Story of the Brothers' referred to on page 33 for which a translation has since been published by her.

39 Beck, 1.

shrines devoted to Siva and Murugan and downward through lineage and family shrines; hierarchy also affects the clan organization of agrarian castes, for clan membership and ranking is not expressed in kinship terminology but in the display of seating and other orderings at the time of clan ceremonies as well as in an idiom of territoriality. However, the principle of hierarchy seems always to work through a screen of social and political segmentation. While this is very evident in Beck's detailed analysis of religious affiliations, the segmentary substructure is also to be observed with regard to political relations in Kongu.

In each of the twenty-four subregions of Kongu—its nadus—there were within the living memory of her informants powerful and prestigious offices filled by members of the dominant, landed Kavuntar subcaste called *nāṭṭamaikkārar* or simply *nāṭṭar* with revenue, judicial, police authority as well as the responsibility here, as in other places, of supervizing agricultural operations. In the villages of Kongu there were other, lesser-ranked Kavuntars of the locally dominant clan who, as headmen, carried out the same range of governing tasks, but over a more limited area. Kongu community-consciousness also rested on the authority held by four ancient chiefly houses to which all Kavuntar local magnates were linked, by marriage if possible, but by service and homage otherwise. These 'titled families' of Kongu or *pāṭṭakkārar* (from the Tamil *pāṭṭam,* meaning 'ruling title') were established during later Chola times, as inscriptions attest, and continued to influence as well to represent the unity of Kongu to most of the region. This sort of segmentary political organization was found in many other parts of the southern peninsula, especially the dry, upland portion that covers most of the peninsula.[40]

Kongu country (or Kongunadu) constitutes an historical metacommunity, one of five such major communities in Tamil country. Like many of the other Tamils, most of the Kongu groups have been segmented vertically into opposed right and left divisions of subcastes; they have been segmented horizontally into local communities or nadus within clans of the right division of landed castes had territorial bases and lineage and subcaste shrines. The right division of castes in most localities controlled the political structure but in Kongu as well as elsewhere in Tamil country,

[40] Noted by Beck, 69; also see T. Mizushima, *Nattar and the Socio-Economic Change in South India in the 18th and 19th Centuries* (Tokyo: Institute for the Study of Languages and Culture of Asia and Africa, Monograph No. 19, 1986).

cross-cutting features existed. Among these were the extra-territorial, universalistic and Brahminic claims of left castes along with cultic links to the world beyond Kongunadu, and these anti-segmental features, in their turn, were inflected by ranking considerations expressed in terms of the pan-Indian ideology of ritual purity, among other Hindu values.

Kingdom as a community, or as a territorial structure of relations and sentiment, is also the focus of Nicholas Dirks' study of the Tondaiman rajas of Pudukkottai. The Tondaiman kingdom came into being in the late seventeenth century by an enactment of the last king of Vijayanagara, Sriranga III (reign: 1642–72); this might have been the final royal installation by kings who for three centuries had exercised a powerful overlordship over the whole of the peninsula partly by ratifying the ruling credentials of subordinate chiefs of their realm in return for their military service. The ubiquitous chiefly stratum of 'poligars' (Tamil: *pāḷaiyakkārar*) of the southern peninsula trace their authority to such enactments by Vijayanagara kings of the sixteenth and seventeenth centuries.

Dirks' reconstruction of the pre-colonial, 'old regime' of the Pudukkottai realm makes explicit what is merely implied in Beck. He shows how, in texts and in social contexts, the territorially segmented system of authority and social organization of the Kallars was constituted as a unity by the royal enactments of gifting and privileging. Lesser Kallar lords were linked to their king by ties of service and kinship while Brahmans and other non-Kallars were bound by gifts.

In clearing a place for his ethnohistorical analysis, Dirks criticized Dumont's work on the Kallars as well as my segmentary state conception. Of the latter, he says, plausibly, that there is a lack of appreciation of 'cultural . . . mechanisms that were involved in the distribution and exercise of political authority throughout Indian society'.[41] However, until Dirks is prepared to offer a different general formulation of his pre-modern Pudukkottai kingdom, which he insists applies to other south Indian polities, I must suppose that he is also talking about a segmentary state but one in which the 'mechanisms' of what I called 'ritual sovereignty' are more clearly and better specified than in my work.

From the richness of Dirks' book, it is not difficult to support my last point. The Kallars of Pudukkottai are the dominant people of the tract, though not the most numerous, and their patrilineages are 'grouped

[41] Dirks, p. 404.

into territorially based exogamous subcastes called natus, a word which means social group in a marked sense but in an unmarked sense means territory or country . . . each of [the thirty four 'natus'] . . . represent discrete territorial groups . . .'[42] Kallar lineages, villages and nadus are, in their turn represented by headmen (*ampalam*) and by tutelary deities, and all are honoured in festivals, but as territorial, rather than lineage beings. Territoriality is a salient feature of Pudukkottai society, Dirks insists, but it is cross-cut as it is in Kongu by other elements of which the two most important are, again, kingship and Brahmins; both constitute a strong hierarchical force within Kallar society. Thus, while headmen of villages and nadus are seen as '*primus inter pares* in their social group',

> by virtue of their connection with the king, they do 'transcend', at some level, their own community. Most importantly, the king himself is at one level simply a Kallar, and not the highest one at that . . . Hierarchy in Pudukkottai concerns transcendence in the context of kingship, where the king is a member of a segmentary lineage system and the overlord of an entire kingdom.[43]

Brahmans are more ancient in Pudukkottai than Kallar Tondaiman kings; their well-endowed and autonomous settlements (brahmadeya) date from Chola times. Under Tondaiman royal patronage, Brahman settlements became larger, more numerous and wealthier; royal prestation signified that the Tondaimans were 'true Kshatriya kings' and the 'Brahmans themselves . . . emblems of the king's sovereignty and honor'.[44]

Other subjects of the Tondaiman kings included Maravars and the untouchable Pallars and Paraiyars. The dominance of the Kallars over the latter was manifested in the fact that the territoriality of the non-Kallars strictly followed that of their Kallar patrons. The Maravars were under a different form of domination from the Kallars, even though they enjoyed an equivalent status, and, along with the Akampitiyars, formed a cluster called the *mukkulattar* or 'three castes'. Concentrated in the southern part of the kingdom close to the Maravar kingdoms of Ramnad and Sivaganga, the Maravars of Pudukkottai were segmentary like the Kallars and Maravaras elsewhere, and they were brought under Tondaiman rule in precolonial times in two ways: by the settlement among their villages of agents with grants of income and police authority from the Tondaiman

[42] Ibid., p. 206.
[43] Ibid., p. 260.
[44] Ibid., p. 249.

kings and by the assertion of royal protection over and therefore superior powers in Maravar temples. Kallars appointed by the Tondaiman kings thereby displaced local Maravars as the chief worshippers and protectors of Maravar deities and as the receivers of the first divine honours (*prasadam*) from their gods.

We principally owe our understanding of the interposition of royal authority over temples as a form of conquest to Arjun Appadurai, and we now look to his work to gain some further understanding of segmentary polities.

Appadurai's monograph on the Srī Pārtasārati Svami temple in Madras city contributes to the concerns of this paper in two ways: it defines the temple in a way that permits us to better understand how temples served a set of ideological purposes in pre-modern South India and it provides an analysis of how temples were critical centres in the political processes of later medieval times.[45]

For Appadurai, the temple in South India is a space made sacred by the presence of a deity who is conceived of as a king; it is also a transactional process involving the god and the devotees who constitute a unified entity through sharing the god's honours; and it is a set of symbols concerning 'authority, exchange and worship' as well as being an arena where entitlements to these values were contested and confirmed. The notions of 'transactions', 'arena' and 'contestation' were first formulated by Carol Breckenridge, and they were applied by Appadurai to the situations of the temples of the fourteenth to the eighteenth centuries in order to elucidate and theorize a widespread political relationship among kings, sectarian leaders and temples. Using inscriptions from Tamil country and from Karnataka, he traced a process by which the kings and chiefs of the Vijayanagara period and somewhat later converted sectarian worship groups into political constituencies by collaborating with leaders of popular sectarian orders in the control of temple affairs. This collaboration was based on the understanding that in becoming the *yajamāna*, or the highest worshipper and protector of a god, a king or chief joined as a sharer, with other worshippers, in the grace of that god so as to become part of a community of worship just as other devotees became subjects

45 *Worship and Conflict under Colonial Rule; A South Indian Case* (Cambridge: Cambridge University Press, 1981); see especially his definitions on page 18 and his important historical reconstruction, 'Kings, Sects, and Temples: South Indian Srivaisnavism, 1350–700', ch. 2.

of the king. Beneath the conception of dharma was the conception of artha, one of royal ambition, of negotiations with and through sect leaders to gain followers, and of the pooling and redistribution of great wealth. But, more than that Appadurai showed the means by which disparate, localized communities of pre-modern South India were brought into an englobing hierarchical order of secular as well as sacred lordship without diminishing the autochthonous character of the communitarian parts of the whole. Rather, localized communities were validated and strengthened in certain ways, and among these was the manner in which they were represented at major centres of Vishnu worship in the South.

A similar phenomenon involving Siva temples in the South was examined by Marie Louis Reiniche some years ago.[46] Focussing on four Saivite centres in Tamil country, she outlined an hypothesis concerning the ways in which the precincts of each of these centres—and by extension, religious institutions generally among Tamils—were at once a representation of the particular totality of social relations and communities of the localities of which each centre was a part and a manifestation of the universal conceptions of Hindu ideology in which all particular forms are embedded. Her four communities differed substantially in socio-economic structure, traditions of authority and relations with larger social and political configurations; nevertheless, she was able to demonstrate how in spatial and social terms each centre encapsulated in its most general forms the social characteristics of its locality. But equally important for Reiniche was to indicate how the presence and interaction of the Brahman and the king—or the priest and ruler, however they might be designated—contributed to the total representation which each centre was. Hence, each of these centres could be seen as a reduced image of the larger political order of which it was a part, and how, correspondingly, each of these diverse centres represented the constituent elements of its particular locality—a quite powerful and complex segmentary conception.

I wish to conclude by briefly suggesting some of the ways I think my formulation on the segmentary state should be recast in light of all that I have said above.

First is the idea that a segmentary polity must depend upon a significant degree of social segmentation, though social segmentation is never

46 'Le temple dans la localité; Quatre exemples au Tamilnad', *Purusartha* 8, 1985, pp. 75–117.

a condition unmediated by ideas about authority and politics.[47] The particular sort of segmentation (i.e. whether it is the sort of pyramidal segmentation based on local, territorial assemblies of the Chola kingdom or segmentary lineages found everywhere in the dry upland of the peninsula after the Cholas) is not important, but the segmentation must be related to formal political processes as the nāḍu in Chola times was and as the systems of chieftainships in later times were, and there must be an ideological interface between dominant forms of segmentation and formal political processes and institutions.

Secondly, and accordingly, it is necessary to reject Southall's proposition that the 'spheres of ritual suzerainty and political sovereignty do not coincide'.[48] I am now convinced that in India the proposition is incorrect, that lordship for Hindus always and necessarily combined ritual and political authority. That is, the practice of political authority, or appropriate power, made it incumbent upon any lord to foster and to be involved with ritual actions and services, whether this was in relation to gods or to their subjects.[49] And this is true irrespective of whether we are speaking about great kings or minor chiefs, or whether we are speaking of the ritual of the *abhiṣekha* or that of receiving the first honours of a tutelary goddess. Insisting on the coincidental relationship of ritual and political authority has the additional clarifying advantage of reinforcing Southall's pyramidal principle. As restated at the beginning, this had to do with the authority of greater and lesser lords, it being posited that the nature of the authority of both was the same—that of the lesser being but a reduced version of the greater lord; hence it was the scope of authority, rather than its quality that was different.

Thirdly, there is need to be more clear about what is meant by 'pyramidality'. This remains an essential element in my thinking about

47 I am unable, however, to go as far as Raymond Jamous in stating that the segmentary order of the Moroccan Iqar'iyen is based upon the concept of honor, its representations and values, for this seems to me to privilege ideology and culture over structure and morphology unacceptably and to diminish the prospect of comparative analysis: *Honneur et Baraka; Les structures sociales traditionelles dans le Rif* (Paris: Cambridge University Press, editions de la Maison des Sciences de l'Homme, 1981), p. 184.

48 'The Segmentary State in Africa and Asia', p. 52.

49 The conceptions of A.M. Hocart on caste and kingship remain as persuasive and influential for me as for others like Dirks, *The Hollow Crown*, pp. 284 and 426 and Jamous, *Honneur et Baraka*, p. 10. Hocart: *Caste: a Comparative Study* (London: Methuen and Co., 1950) and *Kings and Councillors* (Chicago: University of Chicago Press, 1970).

the segmentary state. Indeed, the notion of pyramidality has taken on an enhanced import as a result of reviewing the work on South India by Beck, Dirks, Appadurai and Reiniche, and by considering the work and the criticisms of Chattopadhyaya and Kulke. Community in the sense outlined at the beginning inhabits the core of the notion of pyramidal segmentation, both socio-economic and political. Entitlements derived from as well as based in community structures do not merely reflect the nature of varied community structures in pre-modern South India but can be deemed constitutive of these structures. Shared social group rights were established by the political enactments of *mānya* and later of *in'am* grants from kings and chiefs, and these rights were confirmed, as well as contested, in temples. In *Peasant State and Society* as well as in my recent study of the Vijayanagara kingdom, I have sought to show how community-defining entitlements varied according to ecologically pre-figuring contexts in medieval South India. In being the socio-economic foundation of that medieval metasociety, these locality societies should not be thought of as isolated or complete in themselves; all were part-societies, linked to more extensive formations in ways dictated by historical contingencies in relation to their own attributes. Communities or localities were thus linked by political and cultic affiliations to the protection of great or small kings and gods and, increasingly, in later times, by commercial ties to even quite distant places in India and beyond. Still, as part-societies these communities of pre-modern South India retained historic identities and the capability to act with considerable independence regarding their internal constitutions and their external linkages.

This territorial imperative is admittedly a new and not easily assimilated emphasis for scholars of India as may be seen in Dirks' insistence, when reviewing and criticizing Dumont on the Kallars, that territoriality encompassed kinship and political allegiances inflected all relationships.[50] Pyramidality is a concept that permits us to engage the saliency of territory and community as the archetypal foundation (*urbild*) of pre-modern south Indian society and thereby confirms the validity of something like the segmentary state I continue to see there.

50 *The Hollow Crown*, pp. 258–61.

Chapter Five

State Formation in South India, 850–1280

JAMES HEITZMAN

The present study utilizes inscriptional records from the Chola period (AD 849–1279) in South India in order to address several major problems connected with Chola kingship in particular and with early Indian polities in general: (i) What were the mechanisms evolved by kings to exert their authority over relatively large areas and disparate human groups? (ii) To what extent did the authority of kings vary over distance and in relation to local conditions of geography and socio-economic organization? (iii) What was the relationship between royal political systems and local or intermediate powers?

I will describe the early state as a problem in intermediate authority, that is, an attempt to unite large numbers of localized social and economic units within varying ecological niches into overarching systems of political control through the creation or remodelling of mediating social institutions or communications. The goal of this description is to view kingship as an agency representing the dominating classes of an agrarian society but challenging, through its impact on political and economic organization, the positions of dominant groups. The methodology employed for this study utilizes descriptive statistics and strict controls over variables of time and space in order to relate changes in state institutions at the highest levels to changes in the productive and extractive modes operating in local environments.

The study addresses three models of state formation—bureaucratic, segmentary and feudal—that portray the state in pre-modern South Asia.

Acknowledgements: Many thanks to David Ludden and Carol Breckenridge, who read earlier drafts of this paper and made helpful comments.

These models focus on the relationship of state institutions with local and intermediate arenas of power, and their ultimate relationship with forms of production and control of resources in an agrarian world.[1] The models disagree on the nature of the relationship between royal administrative organs, however defined, and intermediate or local power-holders. Earlier scholars stressed central bureaucratic power,[2] students of feudalism have stressed independent, intermediate political offices,[3] and proponents of the segmentary state have stressed local authorities.[4] Each model takes its

[1] Hermann Kulke has discussed the three main models of pre-modern South Asian historiography in 'Fragmentation and Segmentation Versus Integration? Reflections on the Concepts of Indian Feudalism and the Segmentary State in Indian History', *Studies in History*, vol. 4, no. 2 (1982), pp. 237–54. See also James Heitzman, 'Socio-Economic Formations in Pre-modern South Asia: Case Studies and Methodology', *Peasant Studies*, vol. 13, no. 1 (Fall, 1985), pp. 47–60.

[2] R.C. Majumdar (ed.), *The History and Culture of the Indian People*, vol. 2 (Bombay, 1951), pp. 303–34; K.A. Nilakantha Sastri (ed.), *A Comprehensive History of India*, vol. 2 (Calcutta, 1957), pp. 50–66; Anant Sadashiv Altekar, *The Rāshṭrakūtas and Their Times* (Poona, 1934), pp. 174–6; Krishna Murari, *The Cāḷukyas of Kalyāṇi (from circa 973 AD to 1200 AD)* (Delhi, 1977), pp. 191–8; Romila Thapar, *Aśoka and the Decline of the Mauryas* (Delhi, 1961), pp. 98–123. Burton Stein has summarized South Indian versions of this historiography in 'The State and the Agrarian Order in Medieval South India: A Historiographical Critique', in Burton Stein (ed.), *Essays on South India* (New Delhi, 1975), pp. 65–9; *Peasant State and Society in Medieval South India* (Delhi, 1980), pp. 254–64.

[3] Ram Sharan Sharma, *Political Ideas and Institutions in Ancient India* (Delhi, 1959), pp. 199–230; *Indian Feudalism: c. 300–1200* (Calcutta, 1965); *Śudras in Ancient India: A Social History of the Lower Order Down to circa AD 600* (Delhi, 1980), pp. 171, 192–3, 243, 260–1; *Perspectives in Social and Economic History of Early India* (New Delhi, 1983), pp. 128–56; 'How Feudal was Indian Feudalism?' *Journal of Peasant Studies*, vol. 12, nos 2 and 3 (1985), pp. 33–6; D.D. Kosambi, *The Culture and Civilisation of Ancient India in Historical Outline* (New Delhi, 1981), pp. 192–8; Ganesh Prasad Sinha, *Post-Gupta Polity (AD 500–750): A Study of the Growth of Feudal Elements and Feudal Administration* (Calcutta, 1972), pp. 198–219, B.N.S. Yadava, 'Secular Land Grants of the Post-Gupta Period and Some Aspects of the Growth of Feudal Complex in Northern India', in D.C. Sircar (ed.), *Land System and Feudalism in Ancient India*, Centre of Advanced Study in Ancient Indian History and Culture, Lectures and Seminars no. 1-B (Calcutta, 1966), pp. 72–94.

[4] Burton Stein, 'The Segmentary State in South Indian History', in Richard G. Fox (ed.), *Realm and Region in Traditional India* (Durham, S.C., 1977); *Peasant State and Society in Medieval South India* (Delhi, 1980), pp. 101–9, 134–40, 173–82, 270–2; 'Politics, Peasants and the Deconstruction of Feudalism in Medieval India', *Journal of Peasant Studies*, vol. 12, nos 2 and 3, pp. 61–5; 'State Formation and Economy Reconsidered', *Modern Asian Studies*, vol. 19, part 3 (July 1985), pp. 393–400; Kenneth

position with different approaches to time and space. The bureaucratic approach is the most static, since it posits little structural change, or motivation for change, from the time of the Mauryas (fourth-third centuries BC) until the 'Muslim invasions' of the eleventh century and beyond. The segmentary state of Burton Stein contains explicit references to spatial variability, since it originates and flourishes in 'nuclear areas' of peasant farming communities within irrigated zones as distinct from non-irrigated, drier zones; ritual control becomes more tenuous with increasing distance from the nuclear zones, exhibiting central, intermediate and peripheral forms of political authority.[5] The dynamics for systemic change over time are not as clear as spatial dynamics in the segmentary model. Feudalism, on the other hand, offers a clear-cut chronological progression, from the crisis of an ancient socio-economic and political formation in the early Christian era through subsequent fragmentation of state rights. The feudal hypothesis remains weaker in its spatial aspects, since 'feudal' relations may be described almost anywhere in early South Asia, poorly articulated with local modes and relations of production.[6]

In the following discussion, I will address the central problem of historical models of pre-modern state formation—the articulation of central, intermediate and local authority—within parameters that explain spatial variability and temporal change. The Chola dynasty is the choice for this case study because the numerous records of the Chola period, amounting to over 10,000 inscriptions, provide data that allow statistical

---

Hall, 'Peasant State and Society in Chola Times: A View from the Tiruvidaimarudur Urban Complex', *IESHR*, vol. XVIII, nos 3 and 4 (1982), pp. 393–6; R. Champakalakshmi, 'Peasant State and Society in Medieval South India: A Review Article', *IESHR*, vol. XVIII, nos 3 and 4, pp. 411–26; Venkata Ragotham, 'Religious Networks and the Legitimations of Power in Fourteenth Century South India: A Study of Kumara Kampana's Politics of Intervention and Arbitration', in Madhu Sen (ed.), *Studies in Religion and Change* (New Delhi, 1983), pp. 150–66; David Ludden, *Peasant History in South India* (Princeton, 1985), pp. 26–40, 204.

[5] Stein describes nuclear areas as nadus, or agrarian zones clustered around common irrigation facilities and containing distinct social or kinship zones (*Peasant State and Society*, pp. 90–140). His interpretations rest on the work of Y. Subbarayalu, *Political Geography of the Chola Country*, Madras, 1973, pp. 19–55: 'The Cola State', *Studies in History*, vol. 4, no. 2 (July–Dec. 1982), p. 273.

[6] See suggestions of the 'proto-feudal' character of the Chola state in M.G.S. Narayanan's review of Noboru Karashima's *South Indian History and Society*, in *IESHR*, vol. XXII, no. 1 (Jan.–March 1985), pp. 95–101.

analyses impossible in most other areas of early South Asia for which data are scarcer and more fragmentary. The rich Chola-period data may produce insights that may then be extrapolated to other areas of South India or South-Asia as a whole, where historical sources are less plentiful for early times.

THE STUDY AREAS IN THE CHOLA HEARTLAND

The sources for the Chola-period history are inscriptions found almost entirely on the stone walls of temple structures in Tamil Nadu and surrounding states. These records describe gifts to Brahman communities and to temples in order to support ritual performances. Because almost all inscriptions contain brief or lengthy preambles mentioning the reigning king and his regnal year, approximately 90 per cent of the records engraved during the period of Chola hegemony may be dated with great accuracy.[7]

For purposes of statistical aggregation, the inscriptions fall into four sub-periods, each lasting about a century, and conforming to discernible changes in the political fortunes of the Chola dynasty and the formats of the records themselves. Sub-period one (849–985) saw the rise of the Chola dynasty within the central area of modern Tamil Nadu, with their capitals at Tañjāvūr and Paḻaiyāṟu within the Kaveri river delta. Most inscriptions during this time were short, concentrating on gifts of perpetual lamps to temples in memory of deceased relatives. Sub-period two (985–1070) began with the accession of the greatest of the Chola kings, Rājarāja I, who extended Chola military power throughout Tamil Nadu and over much of peninsular India. Under his immediate successors,

[7] We must note the peculiar nature of the inscriptional record, which is predominantly limited to records of donations for deities. On one hand, the inscriptions are a goldmine of information on contemporary social, political and economic organization, which emerges obliquely, and in a pristine form, from deeds that ostensibly record religious devotion. On the other hand, the necessity of concentrating historical inquiry on temple records constantly focuses attention on a forum that was certainly important, but probably only a single environment within a much larger universe of human activity. Even within the world of temple records, accidents of history have left us a limited view of the large number of social transactions occurring in the environs of religious institutions. In the present study, then, we analyse samples of samples that represent central historical processes but do not exhaust the potential for alternative social formations.

Chola military expeditions travelled as far as the Ganga river, Southeast Asia and Sri Lanka. Inscriptions during this time became more detailed and often included poetic preambles (*praśasti, meykkirti*) praising in chronological order the accomplishments of the kings. Sub-period three (1070–1178) began with the accession of Kulottunga I, who inherited the thrones of the Chola empire and the kingdom of the Eastern Chalukyas in modern Andhra Pradesh. Despite the union of two major royal lineages, Chola military power entered a period of slow decline. Inscriptions from this time contain increasing information on land transactions. During sub-period four (1178–1279) the Chola dynasty collapsed. The Pandya dynasty based in the southern town of Madurai, the Hoysala dynasty from modern Karnataka and local chiefs from northern Tamil Nadu divided up the Chola realm. Inscriptions record increasing land transactions and greater numbers of local leaders arrogating to themselves high titles and local powers.[8]

The present approach, building on the lead of Karashima and others,[9] concentrates on five discrete study areas, each containing large numbers of individual villages, each representing varying ecological, political and historical features characteristic of the Chola polity (see Map 1). The study areas lie within the traditional 'circle of the Cholas' (Cholamandalam), where we may expect the fullest possible record of political processes featuring the Chola kings. (i) Modern Kumbakonam taluk lies in the very centre of the Chola polity, near the capital of Palaiyaru, always controlled by the Chola dynasty. Its economy was, and is, oriented to the production of rice through artificial irrigation systems dependent on the Kaveri river and its effluents. (ii) Tiruchirappalli taluk lies on the southern bank of the Kaveri river, where lands benefiting from riverine irrigation have supported a rice economy and, in the Chola period, a number of important temples headed by the sacred Srirangam. This area was a

[8] The standard histories are K.A. Nilakantha Sastri, *The Cōḷas: A History of South India from Prehistoric Times to the Fall of Vijayanagar* (London, 1958), pp. 173–210; T.V. Sadasiva Pandarathar, *Piṟkalac cōḷar varalāṟu* (Annamalainagar, 1958–61). The four-part chronology used here appears first in B. Sitaraman, Noboru Karashima, and Y. Subbarayalu, 'A List of the Tamil Inscriptions of the Chola Dynasty', *Journal of Asian and African Studies* (Tokyo), no. 11, 1976, p. 89; Noboru Karashima, Y. Subbarayalu and Toru Matsui, *A Concordance of the Names in the Cōḷa Inscriptions* (Madurai, 1978), p. xiv.

[9] Noboru Karashima (ed.), *Socio-Cultural Change in Villages in Tiruchirappalli District, Tamilnadu, India*, part I, Pre-Modern Period (Tokyo, 1983); *South Indian History and Society: Studies from Inscriptions, AD 850–1800* (Delhi, 1984).

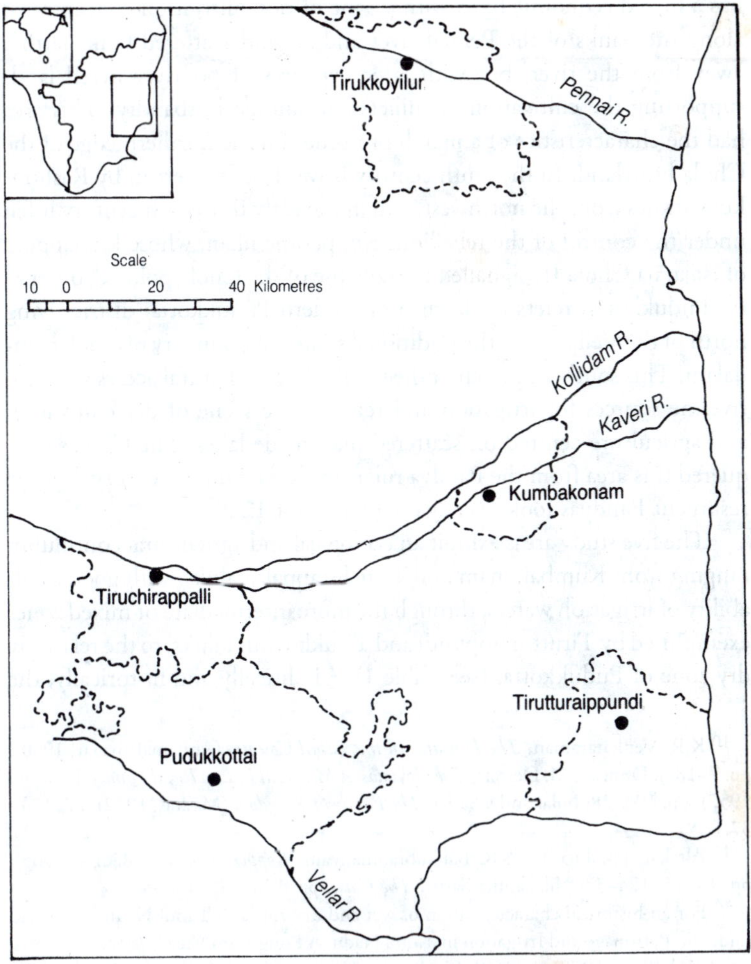

Map 1. The Five Study Areas in Cholamandalam.
The inset map shows the study areas in relation to the modern state of Tamil Nadu in India.

traditional part of the Chola homeland, but Pandya and Hoysala influence became more important as the Cholas collapsed after 1200.[10] (iii) Tirutturaippundi taluk lies near the ocean to the southeast, at the tail end of the irrigation channels carrying Kaveri river water. This area is a good example of a political backwater, always integrated within the Chola empire but having no impact on political affairs. (iv) Tirukkoyilur taluk has a mixed economic base, with a zone of rice cultivation concentrated along the banks of the Pennai river and around scattered tanks farther away from the river, but with large expanses of poorly-watered lands supporting the cultivation of millets and animal husbandry. This area had the characteristics of a march or border on the northern edge of the Chola heartland. In the tenth century it was briefly overrun by Rashtrakuta armies from the northwest, and in the early thirteenth century it fell under the control of the rebellious Kopperuñcinkaṉ, whose kidnapping of Rājarāja Chola III signalled the collapse of the Chola political order.[11] (v) Pudukkottai refers to the area of modern Pudukkottai district lying north of the Vellar river, the traditional southern boundary of Cholamandalam. This southern march of the Cholas had no natural access to major riverine sources for irrigation and remains the scene of dry cultivation and agriculture centred on scattered man-made lakes. The Cholas conquered this area from the Pandya rulers in the late ninth century, but the resurgent Pandyas took over again after about 1220.

The five study areas exhibit an ecological and agricultural continuum ranging from Kumbakonam and Tiruchirappalli taluks, with good availability of irrigation waters, through the more intermediate or mixed zones exemplified by Tirutturaippundi and Tirukkoyilur taluks, to the relatively dry zone of Pudukkottai (see Table 1).[12] Politically and historically, the

[10] K.R. Venkataraman, *The Hoysalas in the Tamil Country* (Annamalainagar, 1950), pp. 7–18; J. Duncan, M. Derrett, *The Hoysalas: A Medieval Indian Royal Family* (London, 1957), pp. 105–28; Nilakantha Sastri, *The Pāṇḍyan Kingdom* (Madras, 1972), pp. 124–37.

[11] Altekar, pp. 115–19; S.R. Balasubrahmanyam, *Kopperuñcinkaṉ* (Madras, 1965), pp. 14–15, 124–37; Nilakantha Sastri, *The Cōḻas*, pp. 128–34, 417–44.

[12] For an historical characterization of wet and dry zones in Tamil Nadu, see David Ludden, 'Patronage and Irrigation in Tamil Nadu: A Long-term View', *IESHR*, vol. XVI, no. 3 (July-Sept, 1979), pp. 349–65; *Peasant History in South India*, pp. 81–94; Christopher John Baker, *An Indian Rural Economy 1880–1955: The Tamilnadu Countryside* (Delhi, 1984), pp. 22–34; Hans-Georg Bohle, 'The Cauvery Delta: An Investigation into the History and Determinants of Agrarian Development and Rural Under-

five areas display a somewhat similar continuum from those zones closer to the centre of the Chola political system and controlled by the Chola kings for longer periods, to the outlying zones where political fortunes and distance from the centre contributed to shorter periods of control by the Chola kings.

TABLE 1

CHARACTERISTICS OF FIVE STUDY AREAS

Study Area	*Agrarian Ecology*	*Relationship to Political Centre*	*Period of Integration Within Chola Polity*
Kumbakonam taluk	wet	central	*c.* 850–1279
Tiruchirappalli taluk	wet	central	*c.* 850–1250
Tirutturaippundi taluk	wet/dry	intermediate	*c.* 850–1279
Tirukkoyilur taluk	dry/wet	peripheral	*c.* 880–950 975–1220
Pudukkottai	dry	peripheral	*c.* 880–1220

The methodology for this study involved the collection and reading of all extant Chola-period inscriptions from the five study areas, the compilation of references to key terms relating to state formation within the collected inscriptions and the breakdown of the distribution frequencies of those terms within the four sub-periods of the Chola period.[13] Changes in the distributions of the terms within the five study areas and over time suggest relative differences in political integration which may then be correlated with the ecological, political and historical characteristics of the different areas. The terms chosen for analysis refer to the king and the royal family, officials of the king, taxation and control over local property rights.

development', *Indian Geographical Journal*, vol. 58, no. 1 (1983), pp. 29–46; *Bewässerung und Gesellschaft im Cauvery-Delta (Südindien)* (Wiesbaden, 1981), pp. 10–38.

[13] 'Chola-period inscriptions' are all extant records from the five study areas containing references to Chola kings and/or regnal years that situate those records within the time period 849–1279. Also included within the data base are Rashtrakuta inscriptions and pre-1250 inscriptions of Kopperucinkan from Tirukkoyilur taluk and pre-1250 records of Pandyan or Hoysala kings from Tiruchirappalli taluk and Pudukkottai. The following discussions of the royal family and officials utilize only the records inscribed under the authority of the Chola kings. The later discussions of tax and property terms utilize the entire data base.

THE KING AND THE ROYAL FAMILY

The kings personally appear very rarely in the Chola-period inscriptions. In a few records pious donors instituted rituals for the well-being or success of the king, indicating that some localities were officially concerned with the ruler's illnesses or military adventures.[14] In one case the great Rājarāja I appeared on a tour of inspection through the Tiruchirappalli area, and in several cases the kings personally intervened in the arbitration of local disputes.[15] But if we expand the concept of royal presence to include members of the Chola lineage, and especially the wives of the kings and princes, we obtain a larger population of records describing the activities of the royal house as a whole.[16] The policies of the Chola house fall into the two main categories of donations and royal orders.

Donations include a number of gifts to temples by the king or other members of his family in order to institute and support Brahminical sacrifices and/or the worship of the god Śiva. Most of these donations were large gifts such as ornate shrines, images and ornaments of precious stones and metals to adorn images, and funds for the expensive and elaborate consecration ceremonies initiating temple worship. Even in this sphere the kings themselves appeared relatively infrequently, since queens or princesses usually performed the honours. The royal family appears to have been the major contributors of large-scale donations, when ostentatious public support of the moral universe, in the name of personal piety, was the explicit message.[17]

[14] *SII* 23: 252; *IPS* 169; KK 128; ARE 1917: 280. Following are the compendia of published inscriptions used in this study, with their abbreviations: *Annual Reports on Epigraphy (ARE); Epigraphia Indica (EI); Inscriptions of the Pudukkottai State (IPS) Kuṭantai Kalveṭṭukkaḷ (KK); South Indian Inscriptions (SII); Tirutturaippūṇṭi kalveṭṭukkaḷ (TK).* All *ARE* references indicate unpublished records viewed in transcript or estampage form in the Epigraphy Office in Mysore. My thanks to Dr K.V. Ramesh, Chief Epigraphist, and his staff for their assistance in reading unpublished inscriptions.

[15] *SII* 23: 310; *ARE* 1908: 468; 1914: 109; 1918: 1; 1927: 229, 231, 1931–32: 70, 71.

[16] George W. Spencer, 'When Queens Bore Gifts: Women as Temple Donors in the Chola Period', in K.V. Raman (ed.), *Śrīnidhiḥ*: *Perspectives on Indian Archaeology: Art and Culture* (Madras, 1983), pp. 361–73.

[17] Examples of the kings' donations include *SII* 3: 276; 6: 28, 33; 23: 52, 307; *KK* 18, 43. Important examples of donations by female members of the royal family include *SII* 3: 96; 4: 542; 8: 237; 13: 197; 23: 42; *KK* 144, 147, 154; *ARE* 1908: 459. Donations

Royal orders occur in altered contexts featuring direct royal interference into local temple affairs. A standard scenario for the issuance of a royal order begun with the presentation of an official request (*viṇṇappam*) by a person bearing high honorific titles, typically asking permission for the deferment of taxes on agricultural land and their transfer for the funding of rituals at a specific temple. The king, hearing the request, granted permission for tax deferment and ordered that the official transfer of taxes to the temple be entered in the public records. Some inscriptions appear to be word-for-word transcriptions of these interchanges, indicating that the king was personally involved.[18] The royal order was called the *tirumukam* or 'sacred face' of the king; when the written form of a royal order reached local villages for implementation, village leaders greeted and revered it as if it were the king himself.[19] Descriptions of court procedures show that, in keeping with the quasi-sacred character of the royal order, careful transcription and checking of the written forms was the standard procedure.[20] It seems certain that even those inscriptions beginning with the simple phrase 'according to the royal order' (*tirumukattup paṭi*) reflect the final, locally inscribed versions of a decision-making process revolving around the king personally. It is doubtful whether the ceremonial issuance of the royal order indicated in all cases royal control over local resources, since in many instances the official request by local leaders may have marked local initiatives with the simple acquiescence of the king.[21] Nevertheless, the centrality of the ruler in these transactions demonstrates a marked interest in, and ultimate control over, the resource allocations associated with temples at the local level. In

---

by members of the royal family outnumber donations by the kings 67 to 11 in the five study areas.

18 *SII* 5: 723; 7: 1012; *IPS* 141, 153; *TK* 39. Related phenomena are inscriptions describing the exact location of the king or queen during the issuing of a royal order: *SII* 5: 706; 8: 223; 23: 48, 272, 351; *ARE* 1921: 533; 1934–35: 184; 1937–38: 3, 21; 1961–62; 429.

19 Village leaders, along with the person requesting the royal order, met the order when it arrived, placed it on their heads to show obeisance, and then circumambulated donated lands with the royal order, mounted on a female elephant (*SII* 3: 72; 23: 264; *ARE* 1931–32: 74).

20 *SII* 8: 222, 223; *ARE* 1931–32: 74.

21 Burton Stein, 'All the King's Mana: Perspectives on Kingship in Medieval South India', in J.F. Richards (ed.), *Kingship and Authority in South Asia* (Madison, 1978), pp. 136, 144–6.

distinction to royal donations, usually involving one-time gifts within a cash nexus, royal orders reflect penetration into local agrarian economy.

TABLE 2

DISTRIBUTIONS OF REFERENCES TO DONATIONS AND ROYAL ORDERS OF THE CHOLAS IN FIVE STUDY AREAS

Key to Columns: A = *Royal orders*
B = *Donations*

	Sub-period 1 (849–985)		*Sub-period 2 (985–1070)*		*Sub-period 3 (1070–1178)*		*Sub-period 4 (1178–1279)*	
	A	*B*	*A*	*B*	*A*	*B*	*A*	*B*
Kumbakonam taluk	3	14	6	28	14	5	21	2
	.01*	.05	.04	.20	.08	.03	.17	.02
Tiruchirappalli taluk	5	6	3	5	3	4	20	5
	.03	.07	.03	.05	.02	.03	.19	.05
Tirukkoyilur taluk	0	5	5	1	4	0	3	1
	.00	.03	.04	.01	.03	.00	.03	.01
Tirutturaippundi taluk	1	1	1	0	1	0	1	0
	.01	.01	.05	.00	.05	.00	.01	.00
Pudukkottai	0	1	0	0	1	0	5	0
	.00	.01	.00	.00	.02	.00	.06	.00
Totals	9	27	17	24	23	9	50	8
	.01	.04	.04	.06	.04	.02	.09	.01

* Ratios refer to the number of occurrences in each sub-period to the total of all inscriptions in that sub-period.

Table 2 portrays the number and relative frequency of inscriptions containing references to either donations of the Cholas or royal orders of the kings. The spatial distributions reveal a clear concentration of the activities of the kings and their family members within the two central areas of Kumbakonam and Tiruchirappalli taluks, for these two areas yield 134 out of 167 total records, or 80 per cent of all references. The other more distant study areas yield very few references, especially in the category of donations (9 out of 68 records, of 13 per cent), suggesting that the kings and other members of their families rarely went outside the central areas around the Kaveri river. Changes in distributions over time reveal a consistent decline in the references to donations and a consistent increase in the references to royal orders, a trend visible in all study areas. In Kumbakonam taluk, for example, royal orders increased from only three in the tenth century to twenty-one in the thirteenth, while donations declined from a high of twenty-eight in the eleventh century to only two in the thirteenth.

The original dominance of donations in the early period of the Cholas may mirror an emphasis on displays of ritual primacy in the construction or consecration of temples and the patronage of brahmanical rituals, a policy that peaked during the period of greatest Chola power in the eleventh century. But the eleventh century also witnessed a shift toward greater penetration of the royal will into local arenas of power through the issuing of royal orders, an activity still surrounded by an ideology of ritual primacy but entailing an active royal role in the allocation of resources at the local level. This policy of local involvement continued to grow even as the Chola state contracted in the thirteenth century.

The Officials of the Chola Kings

The identification of 'officials' working for the Chola kings is a continuing problem that revolves around the interpretation of personal names in the inscriptions. As they appear in the surviving records, personal names follow a typical south Indian format: first comes a place intimately associated with the person, perhaps his/her native place or a village where property is owned, then comes the father's/husband's name and then the personal name. Additional names and terms usually follow the personal name as aliases, including a variety of honorific terms denoting high status (*arāyan*) or modelled after the epithets of the Chola overlords (e.g. *Rājarāja coḻa muventaveḷān*), and a separate series of titles that seem to denote functions. Historical scholarship has tended to concentrate on all these additional terms as markers of participation in state structures. Older studies assumed that all honorific titles indicated a role within the administrative system of the bureaucratic state, an approach that has continued with modifications until today.[22] Burton Stein's segmentary state model has suggested that all additional terms were pure honorifics perhaps bestowed by the kings but empty of administrative functions outside those already performed by locality leaders.[23] In the present study I will avoid these two extreme viewpoints and concentrate instead on the more limited group of terms that more obviously point to supervisory functions.[24] These functional terms are divisible into two general categories.

The first group of terms appears at first sight to denote persons whose roles may well include participation within an articulated administrative framework. A category of men performing the 'settlement of the nadu' (*nāṭu vakai ceykiṉṟa*) in inscriptions of the tenth and eleventh centuries is reminiscent of the more recent officials who compiled 'settlements' of land revenue in British India. In a typical example, the 'chief superintendant' (*kaṇkāṇi nāyakaṉ*) called together temple officials at Tirunamanallur to determine the amounts due annually from several villages and assemblies, and the requisite allocations for temple deities.[25] There are also 'administrators' (adhikāri) appearing at court and also in more outlying areas, taking care of a variety of supervisory tasks, along with 'leaders of the army' (*senāpati*). For example, a record from Tiruvidaimarudur describes the intervention of adhikāri Ciṟṟinkaṉ uṭaiyāṉ, the performer of 'sacred work' (*srī kāryam*) at the temple. He heard various arguments concerning the revenue obligations of the local community, ordered leaders to produce relevant documents, and on the basis of these records adjusted the scale of allocations for worship.[26] Then there are a number of persons associated with the retinue (*parivāram*) of the king and the royal family (e.g. *paṇi makaṉ*, or 'work son'), concentrated near the

22 Krishnaswami Aiyangar, pp. 264–72, 376–7; Nilakantha Sastri, *The Cōḷas*, pp. 462–74; Sadasiva Pandarathar, pp. 477–86; R. Champakalakshmi, pp. 415–17.

23 Burton Stein, *Peasant State and Society*, pp. 257–8; 270–3.

24 Earlier studies in this vein are Karashima, et al., *A Concordance of the Names in the Cōḷa Inscriptions*, vol. 1, pp. xlv-lvi; Y. Subbarayalu, 'The State in Medieval South India 600–1350' (Ph.D. dissertation, Madurai Kamaraj University, 1976), pp. 134–63, 192; 'The Cōḷa State', pp. 281–85; 288–91.

25 *ARE* 1939–40: 228. See also *SII* 7: 988; 8: 580 (*a*); *IPS* 90; *Transactions of the Archaeological Society of South India*, 1958–59, pp. 84–110.

26 *SII* 3: 202, 203; *SII* 5: 718. See also *SII* 7: 1000; 23: 225; *IPS* 234; *TK* 95; *ARE* 1914: 6. M.T. Rajakumar has stressed the importance of these types of interventions in local decision-making for political unification under a sacred kingship: 'Kōyil poruḷātārattil aracin panku', *Cenkai māvaṭṭavaralāṟṟuk karuttaranku*, R. Nagaswamy (ed.) (Madras, 1978), pp. 124–9.

palaces but also appearing as donors in other areas of the Chola heartland.[27]

A close inspection of the circumstances in which all these 'officials' appear provides a composite picture of their functions. When the officials did not act simply as donors in their own right, they acted as arbitrators of local disputes, perhaps resolving problems concerning amounts due to the god from particular plots of land. Typically, an official came into a village, investigated (*ārāy*) relevant documents and heard relevant testimony, and in the presence of local assemblies delivered a judgement that had the force of law. With very few exceptions, all persons bearing functional titles who performed such investigations—nadu settlement performers, *adhikāris*, *senāpatis*—seemed to act either on their own initiative or with a generalized fiat from the Chola king, and had no apparent relationship with royal administrative machinery or with standardized procedures. There was a body of persons bearing these titles congregated at the royal court, and it appears that as local disputes arose and came to the court's attention someone from this floating body of loyal, honourable men would receive the commission to handle the problem.[28] The various performers of tasks for the royal family fit the pattern of a household staff rather than a ramified administrative organization. Investigation of these 'official' terminologies reveals, then, little indication of a ramified bureaucratic system for ruling the Chola state, but rather an 'extended court' peopled by high-ranking associates of the king, including the creatures of the king, scions of other noble families allied to the Chola dynasty and close relatives of the royal family. Despite the rather ad hoc basis for the interventions of these royal representatives, they did function as arms for royal penetration into local affairs and therefore performed crucial roles for the extension of royal influence outside the framework of a centralized bureaucracy.

27 Most often these persons are part of the 'entourage' (*parivāram*) of the king or other members of the royal family (*SII* 5: 706, 723; 8: 234). Many of these persons appear as donors of memorial lamps after the death of prince Rājāditya in battle in 949 (*SII* 7: 954–66). Other palace servants worked as dancers, waiting women or accountants in one of the palaces (*veḷam*) in a capital of the Cholas. Some of the associates of the rulers appear as 'intimates' (*aṇukkaṉ*) or 'friends' (*saciva*) of the kings; these latter persons often claim ranks higher than those of other palace servants, including titles of lordship (*araiyaṉ, nāyakaṉ, uḍaiyāṉ*) (*SII* 23: 243, 286, 339: *ARE* 1927: 336).

28 These courtiers are the 'overlords who have joined together' (*uṭaṉ Kūṭṭattu atikārikaḷ*).

Later inscriptions include references in a quite different group of royal representatives described as members of the 'land revenue department' (*puravu vari tiṇaik kaḷam*). While the agents of the extended court performed wide ranging actions, members of the land revenue department focussed on one objective: the recording of land measurements and the amounts of taxes due from lands for the royal government or its chosen beneficiaries. Often the department appeared in records featuring royal orders, and several long inscriptions portray the role of the department in effecting the king's will and its articulation with other political structures. When the king issued an order, it was transcribed and then witnessed by several high-ranking persons in the royal presence, and often by a host of adhikāris who happened to be present. Only then did the royal writ come to members of the land revenue department, who in contrast to the rather undifferentiated mass of *adhikāris* appeared as holders of specific, hierarchically organized offices associated with the processing of the royal order and its transmission to the locality it affected. Their tasks included the overseeing of the department, copying of the record and affixing of the royal seal, and in several cases were linked with local agents or with the activities of other accounting departments in the palace.[29] The rationality of procedures and recruitment in the land revenue department must not be carried too far; some of the stages in document processing seem quite generalized and even redundant, and a majority of members in the department appear as 'possessors' (*uḍaiyār*) of landed wealth in their own right and were thus members of the class and status group that produced the *adhikāris*.[30] Nevertheless, the land revenue department exhibits systematic, centralized features—a specific topic of activity, a chain of command with differentiated, hierarchized roles and subordination to the orders of the king—that mark this as a bureaucratic state organ.

Table 3 portrays the relative frequencies of inscriptions from the five study areas yielding references to either extended-court or bureaucratic

[29] *SII* 6: 34; 8: 222, 223; 23: 288, 389, 292; 24: 46, 142; *ARE* 1931–32: 74, 115; 1978–79: 291.

[30] Y. Subbarayalu, 'The State in Medieval South India', pp. 151–2. For discussions on 'possessors', see Noboru Karashima, *South Indian History and Society*, pp. 15–23, 26–30, 57–8. The concept of 'bureaucracy' used here conforms to Max Weber's idea of rationality under legal authority in *The Theory of Social and Economic Organisation*, Talcott Parsons (ed.) (New York, 1964), pp. 328–45.

TABLE 3

DISTRIBUTIONS OF REFERENCES TO THE EXTENDED COURT AND THE LAND REVENUE DEPARTMENT IN FIVE STUDY AREAS

Key to Columns: A = Agents of the extended court
B = Agents of the land revenue department

	Sub-period 1 (849–985)		*Sub-period 2 (985–1070)*		*Sub-period 3 (1070–1178)*		*Sub-period 4 (1178–1279)*	
	A	*B*	*A*	*B*	*A*	*B*	*A*	*B*
Kumbakonam taluk	26	0	21	3	11	10	3	21
	.10*	.00	.15	.02	.06	.06	.02	.17
Tiruchirappalli taluk	1	1	8	4	18	4	14	14
	.01	.01	.09	.04	.12	.03	.13	.13
Tirukkoyilur taluk	26	0	14	0	4	6	2	1
	.18	.00	.10	.00	.03	.04	.02	.01
Tirutturaippundi taluk	6	0	1	0	0	1	0	2
	.09	.00	.05	.00	.00	.05	.00	.02
Pudukkottai	2	0	9	1	0	1	2	2
	.03	.00	.36	.04	.00	.02	.02	.02
Totals	61	1	53	8	33	22	21	40
	.08	.001	.13	.02	.06	.04	.04	.07

* Ratios refer to the number of occurrences in each sub-period to the total of all inscriptions in that sub-period.

agents of the Chola kings. The spatial pattern displayed here is familiar from the discussion of the royal family above; the central study areas of Kumbakonam and Tiruchirappalli generally provide larger numbers of references to officials than do the outlying taluks. The two former areas alone yield 159 out of 239 total records, or 67 per cent of all references. The general pattern over time again resembles the changing patterns in the activities of the royal family; agents of the extended court formed the largest category in the early Chola period, but tended to decline subsequently, while the bureaucratic agents of the land revenue department appeared more frequently after the beginning of the eleventh century. In

Kumbakonam taluk, for example, twenty-six records of the extended court in the tenth century declined to three records in the thirteenth, while references to the land revenue department simultaneously increased from none to twenty-one.

The data in Table 3 portray the progressive replacement of more arbitrary, occasional administrative policies by those involving direct penetration into local economy and the precise determination of royal rights and their allocations through royal orders. During the early stages of Chola rule, the more decentralized policies were in order, as the polity rested on the ritual supremacy of a generally distant king. After about 1000, with the triumphs of Rajaraja I, royal policies continued to stress ritual leadership but began to subtly change the rules of the game by introducing the land revenue department and royal orders more frequently into local arenas. Ritual, arbitrational forms were thus the hallmark of early political integration, more centralized forms were the result of later and more formalized central control. The data from Tiruchirappalli taluk provide the exception that proves the rule. Unlike the other study areas, where manifestations of the extended court were decreasing by 1070, in this area they increased dramatically. This phenomenon may be traced to dislocations connected with the accession of Kulottunga I and the concomitant incursions of the Hoysalas and Western Chalukyas into the Tiruchirappalli area at that time.[31] The renewed instability of the west resulted in an increase in displays of ritual sovereignty around Srirangam, followed later in the twelfth century by the increased presence of the land revenue department. The segmentary state and the ritual polity thus appear as stages in the political development which the Chola dynasty took steps to abolish as far as they were able to, once their military control was firmly established. The extent of the changes they were able to effect depended, however, on the distance from the centre of the polity and on the military strength of opposing monarchs.

Taxes and Tax Collectors

Terms generally described as taxes (*vari*) usually appear in lists at the end of inscriptions which record the transfer of rights to the produce from

[31] Nilakantha Sastri, *The Cōḷas*, pp. 305–10.

land. The purpose of such donations was to endow tax-free land for religious institutions, and the tax lists provide the names of various cesses defrayed for the purposes of religious sacrifice and worship.[32] The following discussion pursues the analysis of tax terminology—important for an understanding of any state's finances—by defining major categories of taxes, tracing changes in the distribution of major tax terms over time, and finally studying the agencies most likely to collect these cesses in different study areas.

Two main divisions of land cesses existed during the Chola period in relation to the processes of production and distribution of agrarian produce.[33] (i) At the local level, a variety of duties were incumbent on the controllers of lands to pay for the annual expenses associated with the maintenance of irrigation facilities and local processes of self-government within the villages. (ii) Beyond the local level there were demands from superior agencies for proportions of agrarian produce, in turn entailing several kinds of exactions. Land taxes called *kadamai* were generally paid in kind, according to schedules that were, at least in the central area of the Chola heartland, determinable by the land revenue department. Additional payments in cash or kind were necessary to defray the expenses arising from the collection of land taxes, especially for the temporary maintenance of collection agents. The two main divisions of agricultural

32 These lists of terms only rarely provide hints concerning the meaning of individual terms, and much of the work done on these terms has concentrated on glossaries or, more recently, large scale studies of their distributions: T.V. Mahalingam, *South Indian Polity* (Madras, 1954), pp. 421–8; T.N. Subrahmaniam, *South Indian Temple Inscriptions*, vol. 3 (Madras, 1953–57), part 2, Annexure; D.C. Sircar, *Indian Epigraphical Glossary* (Delhi, 1966); Noboru Karashima and B. Sitaraman, 'Revenue Terms in Chola Inscriptions', *Journal of Asian and African Studies*, no. 5 (1972), pp. 87–117. See also Nilakantha Sastri, *The Cōḻas*, pp. 520–45; P. Shanmugam, 'Revenue System under the Cholas (850–1279 AD)' (Ph.D. dissertation, University of Madras, 1977); R. Tirumalai, *Studies in the History of Ancient Townships of Pudukkottai* (Madras, 1981), pp. 199–268; 357–8.

33 This discussion passes over a variety of commercial cesses—significant transactions in the dynamic economy of south India during the Chola period—levied on or collected by mercantile groups. In the five study areas, such commercial cesses appear rather rarely, concentrated mostly in Tirukkoyilur taluk. See James Heitzman, 'Gifts of Power: Temples, Politics and Economy in Medieval South India', (Ph.D. dissertation, University of Pennsylvania, 1985), pp. 388–92. This concentration may relate to an extended commercial network focused on Kanchipuram to the north. See Kenneth Hall, *Trade and Statecraft in the Age of the Cōḻas* (New Delhi, 1980), pp. 83–97, 123–30; Kenneth Hall and George W. Spencer, 'The Economy of Kāñchipuram. A Sacred Center in Early South India', *Journal of Urban History*, vol. 6, no. 2 (Feb. 1980), pp. 128–33.

cesses found expression in the categories of the 'upper share' (*melvāram*) due to the superior agents, comprising land taxes in kind and collection expenses, and the 'lower share' (*kīḻvāram*) retained by the controllers of the land and used to pay all cultivating expenses.[34]

Aside from isolated and random references to fees for various forms of village government,[35] the largest number of local cesses concerned expenses for the annual or occasional upkeep of irrigation facilities, so crucial for an economy dependent on water for rice cultivation. Terms relating to irrigation dues carried with them connotations of local collection and expenditure, at times in cash but mostly in personal labour; the frequency of these terms peaks in the records of the early twelfth century but declines thereafter.[36] A separate term for 'dues of cultivators' (*kuḍimai*) refers to similar types of local personal labour, but occurs more often in contexts suggesting collection by superior agencies outside the village; this term is rare in the early Chola period but becomes steadily more frequent in later times.[37] The use of the more generalized term *viniyogam* similarly increases which contextually includes the cesses for

[34] These terms are rarely mentioned in the Chola-period inscriptions of the five study areas, but the existence of the broad divisions between upper and lower shares is well-known (and debated) in a number of studies and in modern parlance: A. Appadurai, *Economic Conditions in Southern India (1000–1500 AD)*, Madras, 1936, pp. 171–8; Nilakantha Sastri, *The Cōḻas*, pp. 522–7; Leonid Alayev, 'The System of Land-Rights in Southern India (900–1300 AD)', in *Proceedings of the Fifth International Conference-Seminar of Tamil Studies*, vol. 2, part 14 (Madras, International Association of Tamil Research, 1981), pp. 17–22; R. Tirumalai, pp. 204–6; Kathleen Gough, *Rural Society in Southeast India* (Cambridge, 1981), pp. 110–11, 152.

[35] These terms range from cesses for village government (*ūr ācci, ūr iṭu vari, ūr kaḷancu*) or nadu government (*nāṭacci*) to fees for plough teams (*erp pon*), marriage (*kaṇṇālak kāṇam*) or legal expenses (*vivastai*). The terms are scattered randomly through time and space, and there are not more than six references to any individual term. We may assume that such local cesses were ubiquitous, but rarely crop up in inscriptions because they were rarely defrayed in donation arrangements.

[36] Terms for irrigation dues include several kinds of *veṭṭi* and *vetiṉai* (often glossed as 'forced labour'), *kulai* and *kurampu* (terms for embankments), *nīr* (water) or *āḷ* (manual) *amañci, muṭṭaiyāl* and *cuṭṭi*.

[37] Most occurrences of the term kuḍimai refer to labour services for local agencies, especially temples or other public buildings (e.g. *SII* 24: 58, 94; *ARE* 1927: 211, 355; 1931–32; 89). One instance records kuḍimai levied by the nadu (*IPS* 327). A number of references describe kuḍimai going for 'the sacred victorious gate' (*tiruk koṟṟa vācal*), meaning either the temple or the king's palace but probably the latter (*SII* 24: 64; *ARE* 1917: 276). How or when labour services for the king were enforced remains nuclear, although periodic military or construction labour seems plausible.

local personal labour with an element of supra-village control (see Table 4).[38] The data on labour dues suggest a twelfth-century decline in local responsibilities in relation to an increase in the involvement of supra-village agencies.

TABLE 4

DISTRIBUTION OF MAJOR TAX TERMS IN FIVE STUDY AREAS

Tax terms	*Sub-period 1 (849–985)*	*Sub-period 2 (985–1070)*	*Sub-period 3 (1070–1178)*	*Sub-period 4 (1178–1279)*
Eccoru	25 .08*	11 .03	8 .01	3 .001
Antarayam	2 .002	5 .01	35 .06	38 .07
Kadamai	26 .04	26 .06	39 .07	79 .15
General tax terms	1 .001	5 .01	32 .06	32 .06
Irrigation dues	38 .05	45 .11	57 .11	17 .03
Kudimai	1 .001	12 .03	33 .06	39 .07

* The ratios refer to the tax term to total inscriptions from each sub-period.

The single greatest demand for agrarian produce was the land tax, *kaḍamai* or more rarely *iṟai.*[39] It is currently impossible to determine the percentage of the yield demanded as kaḍamai, but there was an attempt during the eleventh century to standardize the evaluation and measurement of rice land and to impose standard land tax rates in the areas around

[38] There are viniyogams for the village, the Brahmin assembly and agricultural castes (*TK* 132, 190), and viniyogam including a variety of local labour cesses (*TK* 212; *ARE* 1927–28: 205). See also *irāja niyogam* (*SII* 17: 540) and viniyogam including kuḍimai and kaḍamai (*TK* 163).

[39] The term kaḍamai rarely appears in a generic sense as a 'duty' to pay all kinds of taxes (e.g. *SII* 24: 53). Iṟai takes the place of kaḍamai at times in Kumbakonam taluk (e.g. *SII* 8: 611; *ARE* 1917: 227) and often in Pudukkottai (e.g. *IPS* 135, 151, 158, 190).

the Kaveri river.[40] During the later centuries the growing land revenue department was concerned primarily with the determination of kaḍamai rates on agricultural land of various sorts. Occurrences of the term kaḍamai increase constantly in the inscriptions of the Chola period (see Table 4). Paralleling this increase was a rise in the occurrence of a general term for the 'large tax' (*peruvari*) which apparently applies to the cesses of the upper share or kaḍamai.[41]

Expenses for the collection of superior taxation fell into the early concept of *eccoṟu*, a term referring to various supplies of cooked rice provided for officials.[42] This term was prevalent during the early Chola period but steadily declined over time (see Table 4). Simultaneously another term referring to 'intermediate income' (*antarāyam*) steadily increased in frequency, contextually connected with several other words suggesting expenses of the threshing floor and ratios of produce. The intermediate income was a tax in cash coupled consistently with the land tax in kind, and determined by the land revenue department as part of the share for the Chola kings.[43] The decline of eccoṟu, a term connoting occasional provisions tendered in the village, relates to the rise of antarāyam, a cess linked to a more standardized and centrally managed tax structure.

Table 4 portrays the frequencies of important tax terminology during the four temporal divisions of the Chola period. The central changes in taxation during that time are visible by treating the six major terms as three separate pairs. Eccoṟu and antarāyam, referring to the expenses of superior tax collection, show an obvious inverse relationship, with a steady decrease in the frequency of the more nebulous and perhaps occasional eccoṟu cess and a steady increase in the frequency of antarāyam, a cess determined by the revenue department of the Chola kings. A similar relationship exists between the aggregated terminology connected with local irrigation cesses and the term kudimai which was more closely

40 Noboru Karashima, *South Indian History and Society*, pp. 94–105.

41 Whereas the term peruvari does not occur in the data base in contexts that explain its meaning, references to the paired term for 'small tax' (*cilvari*) often include descriptions of other, local cesses comprised within it. The term 'lower tax' (*kīḻ iṟai*) reinforces a parallel between large taxes as part of the upper share and small taxes as part of the lower share (*IPS* 90; *KK* 72, 73, 74; *ARE* 1931–32; 93).

42 P. Shanmugam, pp. 39–40.

43 Heitzman, pp. 395–7. For explicit references to the royal collection of antarāyam, see *SII* 6: 33; 23: 49; *ARE* 1911: 211.

associated with collection by superior state agencies. As the term kuḍimai came into more general use, increasing from one occurrence in the tenth century to thirty-nine in the thirteenth century, the local terms declined after the late twelfth century. Meanwhile, relative frequencies of the land tax (kaḍamai) and other general tax terms (peruvari and viniyogam), officially the prerogatives of the Chola kings, continually increased over time, occurring by the thirteenth century in 15 per cent of all inscriptions.

A consistent pattern emerges from the study of major tax terms during the Chola period, pointing toward a greater concentration of tax-collecting power in the hands of superior agencies and a decline in the importance of cesses collected and officially controlled by village administrations. These findings suggest an increasing penetration of the village environment by outside agencies officially subordinate to the Chola kings. A comparison of tax developments with the changes in the actions of the Cholas themselves and the duties of their official representatives supports the view of increasing royal authority and control of local agricultural environments after about AD 1000.

Kumbakonam, Tiruchirappalli and Tirutturaippundi taluks, all participating in various degrees in the irrigation economy connected with the Kaveri river water, provide no indications that agencies other than those of the Chola kings (especially the land revenue department) were in charge of the collection of taxes. Central royal control was tied to the presence of the kings themselves and the concentration of their officials within the geographical area of the Kaveri river basin. This centrality of state control is less visible in the more outlying study areas.

The Tirukkoyilur area was the centre of operations for subordinate families even at the dawn of written records, when Malaiyamāṉ chiefs ruled there at the beginning of the Christian era and defied the ancient Chola, Pandya and Chera kings. During the late tenth century, as Rājarāja I consolidated the empire, a family of Milāḍu chiefs came to power in Tirukkoyilur and retained local prerogatives in return for service to their Chola overlords. After 1070, the leaders of the Tirukkoyilur area called themselves Malaiyamāṉ, hearkening back to the glories of their more ancient predecessors, and supported the Chola cause to the bitter end around 1250.[44] These latter Malaiyamāṉ chiefs appear in numerous

44 S. Srinivasan, 'A Study of the History of Tirukkoyilur down to AD 1600' (Ph.D. dissertation, Karnatak University, Dharwad, 1980), pp. 117–19, 147ff.

instances as collectors of special 'protection' taxes (*pāḍikāval*), cesses almost unknown from the other four study areas during the Chola period.[45] In addition, several cases suggest that the Malaiyamāṉ family at times collected land taxes (kaḍamai) and other cesses associated elsewhere with the superior rights supposedly due to the kings.[46] It appears that the Chola kings made arrangements with locally powerful families in the Tirukkoyilur area, allowing a certain amount of local autonomy in finances in return for military support and the handling of local administration.

In dry Pudukkottai to the south, some of the administrative and tax-collecting activities elsewhere associated with the agents of the king remained the responsibility of the *nāṭṭār*, or assembly of nadu leaders. A large percentage of references to the nāṭṭār within the five study areas comes from Pudukkottai alone, despite the fact that this area has yielded relatively few inscriptions.[47] When the nāṭṭār met together in Pudukkottai, they sometimes performed the arbitrational activities of adhikāris or allocated taxes in the manner of the land revenue department.[48] But within Pudukkottai they did not always act in this way. Larger percentages of inscriptions refer to their activities in the tenth and thirteenth centuries, with a distinct fall in references during the eleventh and twelfth centuries.[49] It is surely no coincidence that the periods of their decline correspond to the times of greatest Chola power, while the periods of their greatest visibility were times when royal authority was most tentative. The Chola kings and their officials extinguished the primacy of local assemblies when they consolidated power in the south, but as the Chola kings and their administrative organs retreated the local assemblies bounced back to establish their own local dominance.

45 Y. Subbarayalu, 'The State in Medieval South India', pp. 53–4; P. Shanmugam, pp. 60–1; Karashima and Sitaraman, p. 91. Within the inscriptions of the five study areas, references to pāḍikāval number 54, with 47 occurrences from the post-1070 Tirukkoyilur taluk.

46 *ARE* 1906: 158; 1934–35: 135, 186, 190.

47 Total numbers of Chola-period inscriptions from the five study areas are as follows: Kumbakonam taluk—743; Tiruchirappalli taluk—541; Tirukkoyilur taluk—631; Tiruttturaippundi taluk—231; Pudukkottai—245. References to the nāṭṭār in the data base total 43; references to the nāṭṭār from Pudukkottai alone number 21, or 49 per cent.

48 *SII* 17: 462, 540; *IPS* 125, 285.

49 Thirteen total references to nāṭṭār occur in records pre-dating 985, seventeen references occur in records post-dating 1178. The time of greatest royal power (985–1070) yields only five references to nāṭṭār.

It is possible now to discern three types of supra-local political authority competing with varying success for tax revenues extracted from the village economies. At times of imperial weakness, dry and tank-irrigated zones, with their discrete and fragile economic bases, supported nāṭṭār assemblies which balanced local political tensions and performed arbitrational functions. The limited zones of riverine irrigation around the Pennai river supported the lineages which acted as little dynasties, complete with ancient legends and the poetic praises surrounding royal families.[50] The big irrigation systems within the Kaveri river basin supported the imperial Cholas, the biggest kings. The Cholas were so big that their military power and ritual pre-eminence overshadowed the outlying areas of central Tamil Nadu. They destroyed for some time the effectiveness of discrete nāṭṭār assemblies and reduced to subordination the smaller 'kings' of the smaller river systems. The boundaries of these three types of political institutions were never fixed; the outlying parts of the Chola country experienced different mixes of centralized, chiefly or nāṭṭār administration, depending on the energy of the centre and the resistance of the localities. In this way the Chola agents and the nāṭṭār acted side-by-side in Pudukkottai, or Chola agents, nāṭṭār and Malaiyamāṉ chiefs acted side-by-side in Tirukkoyilur taluk. The general tendency seen in the variables of royal activity, official presence and important taxation favours a period of increasing central dominance from at least 1000 to 1150, as more 'segmentary' or 'feudal' political organizations succumbed to royal dominance. After 1150, the political forms typical of local ecology and economy re-emerged as significant arbiters of revenue allocation and political power.

Changing Property Relations in the Chola Heartland

The main causes of the Chola collapse were invasions by external enemies (the Hoysalas and Pandyas) and rebellions by chiefs in the northern parts of the Tamil country. But were these sufficient causes for the decline of the Chola state? Evidence indicates that as time went on the Cholas were getting more effectively involved in local economic spheres and in the

[50] R. Nagaswamy, *Tirukkōyilūrppāṭṭu* (Madras) discusses the extended praises of the land and rulers of Tirukkoyilur in *SII* 7: 863.

manipulation of tax revenues. Royal orders and central taxation generally increased in all study areas until the thirteenth century, although concentrated as usual in the central areas of the empire. If the dominance of the Chola polity rested on the ability of the kings to direct or mediate the allocation of local resources, then the very moment of its collapse was paradoxically the time of its greatest central authority. The power base that had allowed the Cholas to dominate their neighbours for so long failed them against those same enemies. Some weaknesses in that power base may have underlain this failure.

Evidence from the inscriptions concerning property relations holds the key to an understanding of the changing local power during the Chola period and the infrastructural developments that actually weakened royal control as it expanded. The evidence concerns the frequent use of a crucial term for control over property—*kāṇi.*

The term kāṇi, related to the verb 'to see' (*kaṇ*), has immediate connotations of overseeing some right or thing, and in later times referred to 'possession, right of possession, hereditary right'.[51] Within the five study areas, the term occurs within three main contexts: (i) Occupational kāṇi describes a situation in which property or possession entailed performance of a specified duty within a village or a temple. The relatively few extant references to this type of right point to a general custom of granting village lands as the property of occupational specialists—accountants, security personnel, musicians, doctors—conditional upon the performance of their duties.[52] (ii) Kāṇi in temples refers to the enjoyment of properties or prerogatives as a member of the temple staff. The performance of rituals or administrative tasks in a temple depended on the support of personnel through grants of temple land which remained the personal property of the holders as long as they performed

51 *Tamil Lexicon,* p. 859; Noboru Karashima, *South Indian History and Society,* p. 18. Other recent discussions of the term kāṇi are contained in Peter A. Granda, 'The "Gift after Purchase" in Vijayanagara Inscriptions', *Journal of the Epigraphical Society of India,* vol. 6 (1979), pp. 25–31; 'Property Rights and Land Control in Tamil Nadu: 1350–1600' (Ph.D. dissertation, University of Michigan, 1984), pp. 89–110, 142–4, 221–2, 409; Dharma Kumar, 'Private Property in Asia? The Case of Medieval South India', *Comparative Studies in Society and History,* vol. 27, no. 2 (April 1985), pp. 340–66; David Ludden, *Peasant History,* pp. 38–9, 85–8.

52 In the five study areas, there are twenty-five total instances of this type of kāṇi holding. For more extended discussions of all types of kāṇi, see Heitzman, 'Gifts of Power', pp. 123–47.

their stipulated temple functions.[53] (iii) Kāṇi in land appears in three forms: (*a*) Donors possessed their own kāṇi land, inherited it or purchased it from third parties, or alienated it to religious institutions with all rights to cultivation.[54] (*b*) The land tax in kind is called *kāṇi kaḍan̠*, or the 'dues from kāṇi', indicating that royal cesses were due from land that was officially possessed by persons or corporate bodies.[55] (*c*) Temple lands were 'property of the holy name' (*tirunāmattuk kāṇi*), obtained at times through alienation of the rights of the donors described above.[56]

Several aspects of the term kāṇi indicate that it refers to the private property of individuals. Donors had the right to inherit, bequeath, alienate or subdivide their kāṇi land. Possessors of kāṇi in temples, typically Brahmins, at times seem to have manipulated the land as their private property.[57] Taxation depended on payment by the official possessor of kāṇi land. Temples possessed kāṇi lands in their own right as corporate owners. On the other hand, other contextual aspects of kāṇi imbued the individual rights it conferred within a variety of social duties. Occupational kāṇi and kāṇi in temples were contingent upon the performance of public services, while kāṇi in land necessitated the payment of taxes. Official title to land also masked a variety of social limitations on individual initiative. Privately possessed holdings were shares (*pangu*) within village communities dominated by assemblies of village notables who often made collective decisions over land use, including at times the essential questions of irrigation waters, agricultural labour or cropping.[58] Inheritance customs put forward a single person as the official possessor

53 Possessors of these rights are typically called the 'Siva Brahmans possessing kāṇi' (*kāṇi uṭaiya civapirāmmaṇar*) in Chola-period inscriptions. There are fifty-six total instances of these terms in the data base.

54 In a typical transfer of kāṇi, a Brahmin assembly sold waste land (*pāḻ*) in their village to a certain Taṇṭtoṭṭam uḍaiyān̠, who enjoyed the land as his kāṇi, with crops of his choice, paying kaḍamai and kuḍimai taxes (*SII* 23: 303).

55 There are fifteen total references to kāṇi kaḍan̠ in the data base, fourteen from Kumbakonam and Tiruchirappalli taluks alone.

56 *SII* 23: 187; *TK* 131, 213, 223; *ARE* 1939–40: 242, 389; 1978–79: *B* 293.

57 *ARE* 1906: 130, 146, 147. See also 'days' in the temple as transferable rights of Brahmans (*ARE* 1911: 267; 1914: 46; 1931–32: 115).

58 Ludden, *Peasant History*, pp. 86–9. Kathleen Gough has interpreted the system of shares as a type of village communal property, with the king as landowner, in 'Modes of Production in Southern India', *Economic and Political Weekly*, vol. 15, no. 1 (Jan.–Mar. 1980), pp. 343–6. Lately Burton Stein has stressed 'communal' ownership in 'Politics, Peasants', pp. 75, 82.

of property, but there were limits to the ability of that person to alienate or alter property without considering family dependents.[59] Embedded within ramified systems of social claims, and perhaps existing in the absence of a land market, kāṇi nonetheless referred to an indigenous structure of ownership that was invoked for officially private purposes in a number of Chola-period records.

TABLE 5

TOTAL NUMBERS AND PERCENTAGES OF RECORDS REFERRING TO KĀNI IN FIVE STUDY AREAS

Study area	*Sub-period 2 (985–1070)**	*Sub-period 3 (1070–1178)*	*Sub-period 4 (1178–1279)*
Kumbakonam taluk	12 / .08+	61 / .35	94 / .75
Tiruchirappalli taluk	2 / .02	11 / .08	61 / .57
Tirukkoyilur taluk	2 / .01	9 / .06	14 / .13
Tirutturaippundi taluk	5 / .26	9 / .40	98 / .87
Pudukkottai	2 / .08	10 / .22	5 / .06
Totals	23 / .05	100 / .19	272 / .51

* Note that there are no references to kāṇi from the inscriptions of sub-period 1 (849–985).

+ The ratio refers to the number of records from each sub-period containing references to kāṇi divided by the total number of records from that sub-period.

Table 5 displays the changes in the relative frequency of references to kāṇi in the inscriptions from the five study areas. The lack of references before 985, and the relatively few occurrences until about 1070 are notable. The relative and absolute number of references continue to increase dramatically thereafter, especially in those areas more closely

[59] J. Duncan M. Derrett, *Essays in Classical and Modern Law*, vol. 2 (Leiden, 1977), pp. 21–5, 86–91; Günther-Dietz Sontheimer and J. Duncan M. Derrett, 'Der Begriff des Eigentums im Hindurecht', in J. Duncan M. Derrett, Günther-Dietz Sontheimer and Graham Smith, Beiträge zu *Indischem Rechtsdenken* (Wiesbaden, 1979), pp. 90–3, 103; Yvonne Bongert, 'La notion de Propriété dans l'Inde, *Travaux et Recherches de l'Institut de Droit comparé de l'Université de Paris*, 23, Etudes des Droit Contemporain, 1962, pp. 156–9, 162.

connected to riverine irrigation. For example, in Tiruchirappalli taluk two references in the eleventh century increased to sixty-one references in the thirteenth century. The percentages of records containing references to kāṇi eventually outstrip those records mentioning the king, his officials and even centrally-oriented taxation. Compare the most frequent occurrence of the land revenue department in Kumbakonam taluk (in 17 per cent of the records) with the much higher figure for kāṇi (75 per cent) in the thirteenth century (Tables 3 and 5).

The interpretation of this terminological shift depends on the connections between word usage and local property control. Karashima has seen the growth of kāṇi in Tiruchirappalli as part of the consolidation of larger, private domains in the hands of 'possessors' (*uḍaiyār*) during the later Chola period, as influxes of plundered wealth and religious donations disrupted earlier communal properties within villages.[60] Transfers of kāṇi land to temples within the five study areas do reveal a predominance of 'possessors' among secular donors.[61] Although the phenomenon of property differentiation may indeed have been important in the twelfth and thirteenth centuries the more generalized increases in kāṇi references may reflect a greater specification of individual rights rather than the origination of a completely new system of property rights.

A key may lie in parallel although rarer increases in terms specifying cultivators' rights (*kuḍi kāṇi*), the official recognition of the right to cultivate land even without a title to that land as a private possession. Records especially from Pudukkottai describe donation arrangements with provisos that the cultivators of donated land may not be excluded (*kuḍi nīnkā*) from tenancy under the new temple owners. At times it seems as if those permanent cultivators were the donors themselves.[62] These provisos may provide a clue to procedures underlying many other land donations featuring kāṇi transfers. Official changes in ownership of property could entail the retention by previous owners or their previous tenants of considerable rights to agrarian produce. Increasing specification

60 Noboru Karashima, *South Indian History and Society*, pp. 21–35.

61 Out of 65 recorded transfers of kāṇi land in the data base, 48 instances (74 per cent) involved persons whose names included the honorific titles for 'possessor' (uḍaiyār), 'elder' (*kiḻavaṉ*), or 'lord' (*araiyaṉ*).

62 A total of 26 references to the term kuḍi nīngā in the data base includes 16 references from post-1070 Pudukkottai. See donor-cultivators in *SII* 23: 257; *Transactions of the Archaeological Society of South India*, 1958–59, pp. 84–110, plate 13.

of kāṇi rights was thus part of a larger movement toward greater specification of all kinds of property rights, in order to insure the preservation of local privileges within the framework of religious endowments.

A major cause of class differentiation and terminological change may lie in the activities of the Chola state that we have traced in this paper. The kings gradually and inexorably altered the rules of the political game by moving into local arenas such as Pudukkottai, traditionally dominated by local leaders or nāṭṭār. The main weapon for this penetration was increasingly a taxation system attempting to effectively control allocations of large proportions of agrarian produce. The kings simultaneously continued their support of ritual integration by building and endowing temples, a policy that in earlier stages of political consolidation was crucial for the political integration of local allies. The nāṭṭār, appearing less frequently as arbiters of local administration, were increasingly threatened in their own backyards. Paradoxically, a way out was provided by the kings themselves, and lay in religious donations. A local possessor could on one hand establish his own position as a protector of the moral universe and supporter of the Chola kings, and ensure continued control over the distribution of local agrarian produce, by alienating lands to temples. On the other hand he could create provisos entailing continued rights to cultivation for himself or his client cultivators, or retain unofficial rights to the appointment of ritual specialists or allocation of sacral food connected with the ritual enactments supported by donated lands.[63] Most donated lands were made tax-free by royal orders after local requests, or were made tax-free through lump sums given by donors to defray all future taxes; it may have been worth an initial expense to eliminate later royal taxation in an environment where those taxes showed signs of rising further. Alienation of titles to temples in these ways did not entail a decrease in the burden of the upper share extracted from the producers, but signified a redirection of control over its uses that ultimately favoured local authorities.

The donation of lands to temples and the verification in inscriptions of the particular rights enjoyed by all participating parties, were thus the signs of an increasing flight from royal control and the creation of tax

[63] Arjun Appadurai, 'Kings, Sects and Temples in South India', *IESHR*, vol. XIV, no. 1 (Jan.–Mar. 1977), pp. 47–73; Arjun Appadurai and Carol Breckenridge, 'The South Indian Temple: Authority, Honour and Redistribution', *Contributions to Indian Sociology*, vol. X, no. 2 (July–Dec. 1976), pp. 187–211.

shelters in religious institutions. The greater implementation of a centralized Chola state thus led to ever greater alienation of officially granted individual rights to temples, and the progressive starvation of the central state at the time of its greatest need. From this view the local leaders were major actors in the growth of religious institutions, especially temples, and their need for differentiated and specified property rights spurred on a widespread terminological change that mirrored renewed political localism. But as the central state fell apart, temple endowments expanded until the temples themselves became the greatest institutions in South India, major landlords and political forces in themselves.

Conclusion

The study of the Chola period has revealed two main policies of royal political unification. The first and earliest policy displays the characteristics of the ritual segmentary state through which the Chola kings attempted to unite disparate and fairly autonomous local leaders under a single, mediating agency through ritual means. The key to this mediating royal role was (i) the manifestation of royal protection over religious institutions (Brahmin settlements and temples) through the establishment of tax-free revenue grants and construction of shrines and (ii) periodic arbitration of local disputes, typically involving religious institutions, either in person or more often through representatives who were drawn from allied local elite groups. A second and later policy involved a tightening of royal control over local resources through the recruitment of elites into a more bureaucratic tax collection agency, and the implementation of tax collection or reallocation within the rich agricultural zones that supported religious institutions. This second policy reveals a drive toward increased revenue extraction and greater centralized control within the core area of the empire. The Chola kings remained ritual leaders but aspired to be managers in the *Arthaśāstra* style.

The success of royal integrative policies depended on local variables of geography. The most striking feature of the data presented here is the rapid decrease in the penetration of all aspects of royal influence with increasing distance from the centre of the polity. Even within the outer reaches of Cholamandalam, the core area of an extended polity, the kings were more likely to strike deals with local leadership than to implement a centralized administrative apparatus. The nature of local leadership in turn varied according to ecological characteristics that underlay varying productive regimes. Smaller riverine tracts, with their relatively greater and assured agricultural surpluses, supported dominant lineages that appropriated some of the ritual or administrative characteristics of kings. When the Cholas overran peripheral riverine tracts, they reinstalled or created dominant lineages which supported their overlords in return for continuing local autonomy, in a process that resembles more closely 'feudal' political subordination. In drier zones, with discrete and more insecure productive regimes based on rain-fed fields or small artificial lakes, the kings encountered collective assemblies of many local powerholders. The local assemblies became insignificant as the waxing royal system absorbed leadership into the roles of nadu settlement officials, adhikāris, and eventually tax department members. But as royal power waned, the assemblies of local leaders again came into view as forums for articulating and adjusting the disputes of the dry zones.

The three configurations of political dominance—royal centralization, 'feudal' subordination, or nāṭṭār assembly—thus rested ultimately on the ecology and modes of production that underlay them in different areas. The determinative impact of ecological features intersected with the historical processes whereby the Chola kings, through their military successes, consolidated enough power to enable their own agents to penetrate into the peripheral zones during the eleventh and twelfth centuries.

Despite the importance of the varying interactions of these superior political organizations or alliances for the historical development of the Chola state, the underlying dynamics of state formation rested on the ability of those superior agencies to co-ordinate the aspirations of elites emerging directly from the village level. Political and economic leadership within the predominantly agrarian economy rested on the possession of land and/or rights to the produce from land. The contexts of the term kāṇi in the Chola inscriptions suggest that power over land and its produce was not communal (despite a variety of collective controls), but was instead divisible into a number of officially determinable legal rights or ownerships. Differential access to these rights brought to the fore locally-dominant kinship groups and individuals representing their interests—individuals who entered nāṭṭar assemblies, who called themselves 'possessors', and who ultimately interacted with superior state agents. The policies of these local leaders included the preservation or extension of their authority over agricultural resources. When superior state organizations encouraged these local prerogatives, local leaders offered support; thus the early policies of the Chola kings, who rarely entered into local affairs but offered avenues for local legitimation and opportunities for booty, enlisted support for imperial policies. But when a superior state attempted to manipulate the village economy more directly, the arbiters of village affairs were naturally willing to abolish that state; thus policies of royal centralization called forth the creation of tax shelters and ultimately open rebellion by the thirteenth century. In these ways the behaviour of local elites within fertile agricultural tracts was crucial to the political fortunes of pre-modern dynasties in South India.

The results of the present study exemplify the qualitative differences between 'nuclear areas'—zones of rich alluvial soil and abundant water—and zones where stable agriculture was less rewarding or more insecure. The emergence of the Kaveri river delta as a dynamic agricultural tract was the salient feature underlying the hegemony of the Chola kings, who in turn initiated projects designed to stimulate further agrarian expansion. The dynamism of the Kaveri delta fuelled an imperialism that further stimulated investment in land reclamation and irrigation expansion within other lesser riverine tracts and in peripheral areas. The impact of the Chola state was, then, to provide formats for the expansion of leaders within the agrarian society of Tamil Nadu. Several levels of leadership represented the upper level of a hierarchically organized production process that exploited advantages of land and water to create fertile agricultural tracts. The Chola period was thus a time when the riverine zones were being filled up, when complex, unequal social management brought techniques of land and water exploitation toward the limits of the riverine zones. The political figures in this drama were the several layers of nobles and landowners, resting on the fruits of peasant cultivation, who interacted with the kings and constituted state institutions. The Chola polity was an 'early state'[64] in the sense that its agrarian base and the political power of its elites were at an early stage of expansion.

64 See discussions of the features of the early state in H.J.M. Claessen and Peter Skalnik, *The Early State*, The Hague, 1976. The authors conclude that political organization was a relatively closed system standing outside and exploiting large number of local communities, a feature corresponding to Marx's ideas of the Asiatic mode (pp. 546–54, 604–6, 642–3). The emphasis of the present study on intermediate authorities suggests that a variety of elite groups emerging from village-level production relations could

What were the legacies of the Chola polity as an early state? Perhaps the most striking images of secular change were the numerous and beautiful temples that dotted the landscape of fertile agricultural zones in south India—the legacy of an imperial policy that encouraged ritual manifestations of temporal authority. Behind the temples was an expanded agrarian and commercial base that found its expression in the urbanized environment that grew up around the holy sites and in larger areas of green fields at harvest time tilled by peasant cultivators. Four centuries of relative peace and encouragement of local initiatives had spurred on the medieval expansion, but the Chola kings had also instituted a new level of governmental involvement in the fertile nadus, including periodic overseeing of economic activities, the mediation of centrally-sanctioned officials and the collection of taxes. The accomplishments of the Chola period—expansion, urbanization and central involvement in local affairs—were not lost during the succeeding Pandyan and Vijayanagara periods but were exploited by later dynasties to build larger and more impressive state structures.

---

interact with the central state apparatus and wield effective power in their own right in the early state.

Chapter Six

Political Processes and the Structure of Polity in Early Medieval India*

BRAJADULAL CHATTOPADHYAYA

Colleagues,

I am grateful to the Executive Committee of the Indian History Congress for the honour they have done me by inviting me to preside over the Ancient India section at the session this year. I confess that I am as surprised as I am overwhelmed at this honour, not only because my association with the Congress has so far been only minimal but also because my own assessment of my meagre research output, mainly of an exploratory nature, falls far short of the value the Committee have so kindly chosen to attach to it. I suppose being in the profession commits one to the responsibility of presenting one's credentials publicly to fellow-practitioners at some stage or the other; in me the responsibility has evoked a sense of awe, and all that I can do to get over this is to try and turn it to my advantage by bringing to you a problem which, for me, is beginning to take the shape of a major academic concern. Unable to present the results of a sustained empirical research, I am here instead with my uncertainties, but as I see it there can be no better forum for bringing one's problems to than this annual meet of historians, which

* Presidential Address, Ancient India Section, Indian History Congress, 44th Session (Burdwan, 1983).

(Due to constraints of space, I have tried to limit the references to recent writings and to use earlier publications mostly for the purpose of comparison. My thanks are due to Sri Asok V. Settar and especially to Sri P.K. Basant, research students at the Centre for Historical Studies, Jawaharlal Nehru University, for the help that I have received from them in the preparation of this Address.)

accommodates various shades of thinking and encourages exchange of ideas beyond narrow barriers.

The problem I refer to concerns the study of polity in early medieval India. There is hardly any need to underline that this erstwhile 'dark period' of Indian history (a characterization deriving incidentally from the 'absence' of vast territorial empires in the period) is fast emerging as one in which significant changes were taking place[1]—a useful reminder that historical assessments never remain static and need to go through a process of constant revaluation. As one interested in the study of early medieval India, my feeling has been that the problem of the political formation of this period is in an urgent need of revaluation, and while it is presumptuous to think in terms of a single empirical work which will cover the problem at the level of the entire subcontinent, one can at least pose the problem, constant reminders regarding regional variations notwithstanding, at the subcontinental level, from the perspective of the possible processes in operation. My own interest in the study of the early medieval polity derives not so much from the recent spate of publications on the early state and the possibility of analysing early Indian political systems in the light of new ideas[2] but from more pragmatic considerations. The foremost among these is the resurrection, through the study of polity, of an interest in the study of the political history of the period. I apprehend that this sentiment is likely to raise a murmur of protest and I am also

[1] The stereotype of the 'dark period', however, seems to persist; see Simon Digby in T. Raychaudhuri and Irfan Habib, eds, *The Cambridge Economic History of India*, vol. I: *c.* 1200–*c.* 1750 (Cambridge University Press, 1982), pp. 45–7.

[2] Evidence of recent interest in the study of the early state will be found in the range of contributions and bibliographies in two recent publications: H.J.M. Claessen and Peter Skalnik, eds, *The Early State* (Mouton Publishers, 1978); and *The Study of the State* (Mouton Publishers, 1981). The focus of most of the contributions in such publications is on the emergence of the early state which is often distinguished only from the modern industrial state and is therefore of little value in understanding processes of change. Relevant ideas on the emergence of the state have been used for the study of the pre-state polity and origin of the state society in India by Romila Thapar, 'State Formation in Early India', *International Social Science Journal*, 32.4 (1980), pp. 655–69 and *From Lineage to State: Social Formation in the Mid-first Millennium* BC *in the Ganga Valley* (Bombay, 1984), and by R.S. Sharma, *Material Culture and Social Formations in Ancient India* (Delhi, 1983); 'Taxation and State Formation in Northern India in Pre-Maurya Times (*c.* 600–300 BC)', reprinted in R.S. Sharma, *Aspects of Political Ideas and Institutions in Ancient India*, third revised edition (Delhi, 1991), ch. 15; Idem, 'From Gopati to Bhupati (a review of the changing position of the king)', *Studies in History*, 2.2 (1980), pp. 1–10.

likely to be reminded that we have had enough of political history which may be sanctioned well-earned rest for some time to come. I wonder if this is really so, since I feel that historical revaluation of the nature of change in a period implies revaluation of its sources in their entirety. As a teacher of ancient Indian history I notice a growing trend among students to be interested only in 'social and economic history' since political history with its endless dates, genealogical charts and catalogues of battles involves senseless cramming and serves no intellectual purpose at all.[3] Given the nature of ancient Indian political historiography,[4] the distaste is understandable, but if in sheer frustration we turn away from a serious study of political history, we shall, perhaps unwittingly, be leaving out a substantial chunk of Indian history. After all, the study of polity essentially involves an analysis of the nature, organization and distribution of power, and in a state society in which the contours of inequality are sharp, relations of power encompass relations at other levels in some form or the other.[5] Even the seemingly bewildering variety of details of the political history of early medieval India—the absurdly long

[3] It is necessary to keep it in mind that a study of social and economic history by itself is not a sufficient guarantee of the quality of history. Most available monographs on social and economic history of the period, including my own, are no more interesting readings than dynastic accounts.

[4] The dominant trend in the writing of the political history of early medieval India is towards the reconstruction of dynastic accounts, and the trend carried to an extreme has yielded more than one monograph for a single 'dynasty'. We have thus at least three monographs on the Yādavas and the same number of works on the Candellas. For a very useful critique of dynastic reconstruction, through 'concatenation' of distinct segments of the same ruling lineage, see David P. Henige, 'Some Phantom Dynasties of Early and Medieval India: Epigraphic Evidence and the Abhorrence of a Vacuum', *Bulletin of the School of Oriental and African Studies*, 38.3 (1975).

[5] I have only to refer here to the statement made by Perry Anderson in the Foreword to his *Lineages of the Absolutist State* (Verso edition, London, 1979, p. 11): 'Today, when "history from below" has become a watch-word in both Marxist and non-Marxist circles, and has produced major gains in our understanding of the past, it is nevertheless necessary to recall one of the basic axioms of historical materialism: that secular struggle between classes is ultimately resolved at the *political*—not at the economic or cultural level of society. In other words, it is the construction and destruction of State which seal the basic shifts in the relations of production . . . A "history from above" . . . is thus no less necessary than a "history from below".' Elsewhere (p. 404) he writes: ' . . . pre-capitalist modes of production cannot be defined *except* via their political, legal and ideological superstructures, since these are what determine the extra-economic coercion that specifies them'.

genealogies, the inflated records of achievements of microscopic kingdoms, the rapidity of the rise and fall of centres of power—are ultimately manifestations of the way in which the polity evolved in the period and hence is worthy, not so much of cataloguing, but of serious analysis. I make an additional point in justification of my plea for the study of political history by saying that an occasional comparison of notes with the historiography of medieval India would help, because medieval historians have continued to enrich our knowledge of political history and its study is essential for our understanding of that period.[6]

I

The relevant approaches to the study of the early medieval polity will be discussed later; I will begin with a brief reference to the basic opposition between the two broad strands of assumptions that bear upon a study of the Indian polity. In one assumption, polity in pre-modern India is variously characterized as 'traditional'[7] or 'Oriental Despotic';[8] in fact, it

[6] A few works which illustrate this interest in what may be called the post-J.N. Sarkar phase may be cited: Satish Chandra, *Parties and Politics at the Mughal Court, 1707–1740*, 3rd edn (Delhi, 1979); M. Athar Ali, *The Mughal Nobility Under Aurangzeb* (Asia Publishing House, 1968); Iqtidar Alam Khan, *The Political Biography of a Mughal Noble Munim Khan Khan-i-Khanan: 1497–1575* (Orient Longman, 1973); and J.F. Richards, *Mughal Administration in Golconda* (Clarendon Press, Oxford, 1975).

[7] 'Traditional polity' is implied in the statements and titles of writings on disparate periods of Indian history, in which a long-term perspective is absent and in most of which the accent is on Kingship and rituals associated with Kingship; see, for example, the following collections, Richard G. Fox, ed., *Realm and Region in Traditional India* (Delhi, 1977); R.J. Moore, ed., *Tradition and Politics in South Asia* (Delhi, 1979); J.F. Richards (ed), *Kingship and Authority in South Asia* (South Asian Studies, University of Wisconsin, Madison Publication Series, Publication No. 3, 1978). S.N. Eisenstadt's typologies of 'centralized historical bureaucratic empires or States' in which he curiously clubs together Gupta, Maurya and the Mughal empires as 'several ancient Hindu States' also essentially correspond to the notion of 'traditional polity', *The Political System of Empires* (New York, 1969).

[8] That 'Oriental Despotism' characterizes changeless polity and society will be clear from the following statement of K.A. Wittfogel, '. . . varying forms of semicomplex hydraulic property and society prevailed in India almost from the dawn of written history to the 19th Century', *Oriental Despotism: A Comparative Study of Total Power*, 7th Printing (Yale University Press, 1970), p. 260. For the genesis of the concept of Oriental Despotism, its incorporation into Marx's notion of 'Asiatic mode' and its relevance in the Indian context, see Perry Anderson; Irfan Habib, 'An Examination of Wittfogel's

has been considered possible by different individual authors—all apparently subscribing to the assumption of 'traditional polity'—to view political ideas and structures of disparate periods of Indian history in terms of a model of pre-State polity.[9] It would of course be too simplistic to lump a wide variety of writings on traditional pre-modern polity together because both in their empirical and theoretical contents such contributions vary substantially, but basically the broad assumption underlying most of them remains that traditional polity was essentially changeless: 'a continual kaleidoscopic reorientation of a given political and social content'.[10] Opposed to this view of 'traditional' polity, within which 'early medieval' is not clearly demarcated, is the other assumption

---

Theory of Oriental Despotism', *Enquiry*, 6, pp. 53–73; 'Problems of Marxist Historical Analysis', in *Science and Human Progress*, Essays in honour of Prof. D.D. Kosambi (Bombay, 1974), pp. 34–47; Romila Thapar, *The Past and Prejudice* (Delhi, 1975); H.J.M. Claessen and P. Skalnik, 'The Early State: Theories and Hypotheses' in *The Early State*, pp. 7–8. Recently D. Lorenzen has argued ('Imperialism and Ancient Indian Historiography' in S.N. Mukherjee (ed.), *India: History and Thought*, Essays in honour of A.L. Basham (Calcutta, 1982), pp. 84–102) that Oriental Despotism was a key concept in the pro-Imperialist interpretations of the ancient Indian polity and society and that the concept is present in the writings of nationalist historians in its inverted version.

9 I refer here to the model of the 'segmentary state', constructed by A. Southall on the basis of his study of a pre-state polity in East Africa, *Alur Society: A Study of Processes and Types of Domination* (Cambridge, 1953); for further discussion, idem, 'A Critique of the Typology of States and Political Systems', in M. Banton (ed.), *Political Systems and the Distribution of Power* (ASA Monographs 2, Tavistock Publications, 1968), pp. 113-40. The model is found applicable in the Indian context in relation to the *maṇḍala* theory by J.C. Heesterman, 'Power and Authority in Indian Tradition', in R.J. Moore, pp. 77–8; by Burton Stein in relation to south Indian polity from the Cola period onward: 'The Segmentary State in South Indian History', in R.G. Fox (ed.), pp. 1–51 and *Peasant State and Society in Medieval South India* (Oxford University Press, 1980); and by R.G. Fox in the context of the organization of the Rajput clans in Uttar Pradesh in the late Mughal period (without, however, much reference to the Mughals), *Kin, Clan, Raja and Rule: State-Hinterland Relations in Pre-industrial India* (Berkeley, The University of California Press, 1971). For recent vindications of the model in the context of Africa and India in terms of its empirical validity, see A. Southall, 'The Segmentary State in Asia and Africa', *Comparative Studies in Society and History*, vol. 30 (1988), pp. 52–82; B. Stein, 'The Segmentary State: Interim Reflections', in J. Pouchepadass and H. Stern (eds), *From Kingship to State: The Political in the Anthropology and History of the Indian World* (Paris, 1991), pp. 217–37.

10 Frank Perlin, 'The Pre-colonial Indian State in History and Epistemology: A Reconstruction of Societal Formation in the Western Deccan from the Fifteenth to the Early Nineteenth Century', in H.J.M. Claessen and Peter Skalnik (eds), *The Study of the State*, p. 276.

which envisages possibilities of change and, curiously, it is within this purview that most empirical studies on early medieval India can be located. Here too views on change or on mechanisms of change are not identical; the majority of works on early medieval political history and institutions in fact contain generalizations which are mutually contradictory. The king in all the monarchical states is the source of absolute power and wields control through bureaucracy; there is thus nothing much to distinguish him from the 'absolute despot' despite his benevolent disposition; and yet, the malaise of polity is generated by feudal tendencies.[11] Change, expressed mostly in terms of dynastic shifts, becomes, in the early medieval context, a concern over the size of the emperor's territory; imperial rulers down to the time of Harṣa endeavoured to stem the tide of disintegration and fragmentation, which is seen as a disastrous change from the ideal imperial pattern and which is invariably assessed against the ultimate failure to retain what used to be called—and I fear many of our much used text books continue to call—the Hindu political order.[12] Concern with the failure of the early medieval political order—a concern not only noticeable in works on political history[13] but a starting point in serious monographs on social and economic history[14] as well—has logically led to value-judgements on the structure of polity; a single quote from a widely read text book on polity, out of many such available, will

11 See, for example, A.S. Altekar, *State and Government in Ancient India*, reprint of 3rd edn (Delhi, 1972), chs 16–17. In the context of south India, while T.V. Mahalingam (*South Indian Polity*, University of Madras, 2nd edn, 1967, ch. 1, sec. 2) talks of checks on royal absolutism and the presence of *sāmantas* or *maṇḍaleśvaras*, K.A. Nilakantha Sastri (*The Colas*, reprint of 2nd edn, University of Madras, 1975, pp. 447–8) characterizes Cola polity as indicating change from 'somewhat tribal chieftaincy of the earlier time' to 'the almost Byzantine royalty of Rājarāja and his successors'. For a relevant discussion, see Lorenzen.

12 R.C. Majumdar, for example, writes in his preface to *The Struggle for Empire* (vol. 5 of the History and Culture of the Indian people, Bombay, 1957, xliii): 'This volume deals with the transition period that marks the end of independent Hindu rule'. See also K.M. Panikkar's Foreword to Dasarath Sharma's *Early Cauhan Dynasties* (Delhi, 1959). R.C.P. Singh (*Kingship in Northern India, Cir. 600 AD–1200 AD*, Delhi, 1968, ch. 8) analyses this failure in terms of the nature of Hindu kingship. Most works on the political history of the period dealing with changes in the loci of power are charged with communal overtones, completely ignoring the fact that such shifts were constantly taking place in Indian history.

13 D. Sharma, ch. 27.

14 B.P. Mazumdar, *Socio-economic History of Northern India (1030–1194 AD)* (Calcutta, 1960), preface.

serve to illustrate the sentiment common to most historians of early medieval India: '[the] ideal of federal-feudal empire, with full liberty to each constituent state to strive for the imperial status but without permission to forge a unitary empire after the conquest, thus produced a state of continuous instability in ancient India'.[15] I have chosen this quote to underline the kind of ambivalence which permeates the writings even of those who tend to think in terms of change: there is dichotomy between 'constituent state' and 'unitary empire', the dichotomy deriving in the present case from adherence to the model provided by ancient political thinkers; the dichotomy is not timeless because its emergence is located in the fourth century AD and yet it 'produced a state of continuous instability in ancient India', instability being change from the norm, i.e. the centralized, unitary state.

Irrespective of the merit of the terminologies used in these writings, historiographically the interesting correlation is between change in polity and feudalism. 'Feudalism' is thus not a new historiographical convention; its use, limited to the political plane, has been as a synonym for political fragmentation and the term has in fact been shuttled back and forth in Indian history to suit any period in which no 'unitary empire' could be located on the political horizon.[16]

We know that a major breakthrough in the application of this term to the Indian context came in the form of a new genre of empirical works from the fifties;[17] here for the first time 'feudal polity' is not an entity-

[15] Altekar, p. 388.

[16] H.C. Raychaudhuri (*Political History of Ancient India*, 6th edn, University of Calcutta, 1953, p. 208) speaks of *māṇḍalika-rājas* in the period of Bimbisāra as 'corresponding perhaps to the Earls and Counts of medieval European polity'. A.L. Basham speaks of quasi-feudal order in the pre-Mauryan age, and when 'that empire broke up . . . Mauryan bureaucracy gave way to quasi-feudalism once more', *Studies in Indian History and Culture* (Calcutta, 1964), p. 5.

[17] Serious analytical work of this genre starts with D.D. Kosambi, *An Introduction to the Study of Indian History*, Bombay, 1956, and R.S. Sharma's *Indian Feudalism, c. 300–1200*, University of Calcutta, 1965, is the first thoroughly researched monograph on the subject. In terms of documentation another important work is by B.N.S. Yadava, *Society and Culture in Northern India in the Twelfth Century* (Allahabad, 1973). The literature on 'Indian feudalism' is of course growing and useful bibliographical references will be found in R.S. Sharma and D.N. Jha, 'The Economic History of India upto AD 1200: Trends and Prospects', *Journal of the Economic and Social History of the Orient*, 17.1, pp. 48–80; D.N. Jha, 'Early Indian Feudalism: A Historiographical Critique', Presidential Address, Indian History Congress, Ancient India Section, 40th Session (Waltair,

in-itself; through a reasoned argument—irrespective of whether we accept the argument or not—'feudal polity' is shown to be a stage which represents a structural change in the Indian social and economic order; it envisages the emergence of a hierarchical structure of society in place of the binarily opposed entities of the state and the peasantry, and it is basically this hierarchical structure with its different tiers of intermediaries which explains the mechanism of exploitation and coercion of the early medieval state. The distinctive contribution of the study of 'Indian feudalism', from the perspective of the problem I have in view, consists in the attempt to bridge the gap between polity and society.

In concluding this brief review of various strands of opinions on early Indian polity, which tend to be organized into two opposite sets, I feel that the opposition cannot be pushed to any extreme limits. If the feeling represents a curious contradiction, the contradiction is embedded in available historiography. For, even those who work within the framework of traditional polity do not all necessarily work with such ahistorical models as 'Oriental Despotism';[18] similarly, the current construct of 'feudal polity' carries over elements from past historiography, which in a way hinder the formulation of a long-term perspective of change. The opposition perhaps ultimately lies in the realm of ideologies and perspectives than in the realization of the necessity of study of change. We turn now to the specificity of the problem which this historiographical situation has created for a study of early medieval polity.

II

The structure of the construct of Indian feudalism, which is spoken of as a variant form, rests, so far as the study of polity is concerned, on two

1979); H. Mukhia, 'Was there Feudalism in Indian History?', Presidential Address, Medieval India Section, Indian History Congress, 40th Session (Waltair, 1979); B.N.S. Yadava, 'The Problem of the Emergence of Feudal Relations in Early India', Presidential Address, Ancient India Section, 41st Session (Bombay, 1980).

[18] Compare, for example, two articles by Nicholas B. Dirks written on two different periods of south Indian history: (i) 'Political Authority and Structural Change in Early South Indian History', *The Indian Economic and Social History Review*, 13.2 (1976), pp. 125–58; (ii) 'The Structure and Meaning of Political Relations in a South Indian Little Kingdom', *Contributions to Indian Sociology*, 13.2 (1979), pp. 169–206. B. Stein too (*Peasant State and Society . . .*) attempts to see change from the Cola to the Vijayanagar period. Their perception of change is, of course, not in terms of feudal polity.

interrelated arguments. Since detailed studies of early medieval political formation within the framework of the feudalism hypothesis are still a desideratum,[19] they therefore need to be stated: (i) feudal polity emerged from the gradual breakdown of a centralized bureaucratic state system, empirically represented by the Mauryan state, the implication of the argument being that the emergence of diverse centres of power of the later periods would correspond to a process of displacement of bureaucratic units. Feudal polity, however, crystallized eight centuries after the disintegration of the Mauryan state, although elements of feudal polity—suggested by a two-tier or three-tier structure of the administrative system—are identified in the Kuṣāṇa polity of north India and the Sātavāhana polity of the Deccan;[20] (ii) the system of assignment of land, apparently absent in the Mauryan state because of the practice of remuneration in cash, became widespread and intermixed with the transfer of the rights of administration, corroding the authority of the state and leading to the 'parcellization' of its sovereignty.[21] It may be interesting to

[19] Detailed documentation is found only in R.S. Sharma, *Indian Feudalism*, ch. 2, which analyses 'feudal polity' in three kingdoms; B.P. Mazumdar, chs 1–2, and B.N.S. Yadava, *Society and Culture*, chs 3–4; for a regional pattern, see D.D. Kosambi, 'Origins of Feudalism in Kashmir', *Journal of the Bombay Branch of the Royal Asiatic Society*, 1956–57, pp. 108–20 and Krishna Mohan, *Early Medieval History of Kashmir (with special reference to the Loharas,* AD *1003–1171)* (Delhi, 1981), ch. 4. An earlier work, not usually cited but deserving attention for its wealth of material, is N.C. Bandyopadhyaya, *Development of Hindu Polity and Political Theories* (ed.) N.N. Bhattacharyya (Delhi, 1980). For recent contributions to the study of the early medieval state, see Y. Subbarayalu, 'The Cola State', *Studies in History*, vol. 4, No. 2 (1982), pp. 265–306; R.N. Nandi, 'Feudalization of the State in Medieval South India', *Social Science Probings* (March, 1984), pp. 33–59.

[20] R.S. Sharma, *Aspects of Political Ideas and Institutions in Ancient India*, 2nd edn (Delhi, 1968), ch. 15; Kosambi, *An Introduction*, ch. 9; B.N.S. Yadava, 'Some Aspects of the Changing Order in India During the Śaka-Kuṣāṇa Age', in G.R. Sharma (ed.), *Kuṣāṇa Studies* (University of Allahabad, 1968), pp. 75–90.

[21] This supposition is based on two sets of evidence: (i) reference in the *Arthaśāstra* (5.3) to payment of state officials in coined money; and (ii) actual circulation of coined money in the Mauryan period. However, there seems to be a contradiction in the *Arthaśāstra* itself; cf. 5.3 with 2.1.7. Even 5.3, which deals with the payments to state officials, states: ' . . . He should fix (wages for) the work of servants at one quarter of the revenue, or by payment to servants . . . ' (R.P. Kangle's translation, 2nd edn, Bombay, 1972, p. 302). More importantly, there is no necessary correlation between the circulation of coined money and payment in cash. This will hold true not only for the post-Mauryan period to the fifth century at least but for the medieval period as well, although in the medieval period the remuneration was computed in cash.

dilate on this characterization of the Mauryan state and its choice as a starting point for the study of feudal polity because at one level it carries over from past historiography the equation: feudal polity=political fragmentation =dismemberment of a centralized state; at another, it represents an unstated search for a prototype of the state system of the Classical West, the breakdown of which provides a starting point for the study of western feudalism. However, for our purpose, the validity of the arguments stated above can be subjected to a single test: do they sufficiently explain the total political configuration of what is called the feudal formation? The explanation has to relate not to the structures of individual monarchies alone but also to the political geography of the subcontinent at any given point of time—a requirement suggested by frequent shifts in the centres of power and the ongoing process of the formation of new polities as a result of transition from pre-state to state societies. It is considerations such as these which have led to considerable rethinking regarding the Mauryan state itself,[22] which—the focal point in the concentration area of the earlier *mahājanapadas* of the upper and middle Ganges basin—represents basically a relationship between the nucleus which is the metropolitan state and a range of differentiated polities. The disappearance of the metropolitan Mauryan state did not create a political or economic crisis either in areas where state polity had been in existence or in areas of pre-state polity incorporated within the Mauryan empire. In fact, Mauryan territorial expansion and similar expansions at later times seem to have created a fresh spurt in the emergence of local states in areas of pre-state polity—a phenomenon certainly not to be confused with the process of the decentralization of a centralized administration.[23]

Two further points regarding the current historiography on the

[22] Interestingly, Beni Prasad, as early as in 1928, held the 'unitary' character of the Mauryan State as suspect, *The State in Ancient India* (Allahabad, 1928), p. 192; Romila Thapar has considerably changed her views on the character of the Mauryan State: compare *Aśoka and the Decline of the Mauryas*, 2nd edn (Oxford University Press, 1973), ch. 4 with her 'The State as Empire' in H.J.M. Claessen and P. Skalnik, *The Study of the State*, pp. 409–26 and *From Lineage to State*, ch. 3. For other discussions, I.W. Mabbett, *Truth, Myth and Politics in Ancient India* (Delhi, 1972), chs 5–6; S.J. Tambiah, *World Conqueror and World Renouncer* (Cambridge University Press, 1976), pt. I, ch. 5; Heesterman, 'Power and Authority . . . ', p. 66.

[23] S. Seneviratne, 'Kalinga and Andhra: The Process of Secondary State Formation in Early India', in H.J.M. Claessen and P. Skalnik (eds), *The Study of the State*, pp. 317–37.

genesis of feudal polity need to be made. First, not all criticisms levelled against the use of landgrant evidence for explaining the genesis of feudal polity can be brushed aside lightly. The fact remains that the major bulk of epigraphic evidence relates to *brahmadeyas* and *devadānas*, grants to brāhmaṇas and religious establishments, and the element of contract is largely absent in the system of early and early-medieval landgrants. The presence of a contractual element cannot be altogether denied;[24] it would also be difficult to disagree with the view that the system of assignments brought in important changes in agrarian relations in areas where such assignments were made[25]—but how does it all help us to understand the genesis of feudal polity? Let me clarify. The *sāmanta*-feudatory system has been considered to be the hallmark of the structure of polity in early medieval India[26]—and there is no reason to dispute the empirical validity of this point—but it has not been seriously examined as to how even the system of secular or service assignments to officials led to the emergence of a *sāmanta*-feudatory network. It has been conceded that the general chronology of the epigraphic evidence for service-assignments postdates the genesis of feudal polity.[27] The conclusion which ought to follow from

[24] See N.C. Bandyopadhyaya; see the important paper of B.N.S. Yadava, 'Secular Landgrants of the Post-Gupta Period and Some Aspects of the Growth of Feudal Complex in North India', in D.C. Sircar (ed.), *Land System and Feudalism in Ancient India* (University of Calcutta, 1966), pp. 72–94. The general absence of a contractual element in the vast corpus of epigraphic material seems to be irrefutable; for contents of grants in general, cf. the writings of D.C. Sircar, *Indian Epigraphy* (Delhi, 1965), ch. 5; *Political and Administrative System of Ancient and Medieval India* (Delhi, 1973); *Landlordism and Tenancy in Ancient and Medieval India as Revealed by Epigraphical Records* (Lucknow, 1969) and *The Emperor and the Subordinate Rulers* (Santiniketan, 1982). Sircar's critique of 'feudal polity' is curious since he freely uses such terms as 'fiefs' and 'vassals' in the Indian context; see R.S. Sharma's criticism of Sircar's approach to the problem: 'Indian Feudalism Retouched', *The Indian Historical Review*, 1.2 (1974), pp. 320–30. For me, however, the 'contractual' element remains important as otherwise the logic of service assignments does not appear intelligible. See also fn. 26.

[25] See fn. 17 for references. A restatement of this will be available in R.S. Sharma, 'How Feudal was Indian Feudalism?', *The Journal of Peasant Studies*, vol. 12, nos. 2–3, pp. 19–43.

[26] Yadava, *Society and Culture . . .*, ch. 3.

[27] R.S. Sharma, 'Landgrants to Vassals and Officials in Northern India *c.* AD 1000–1200', *Journal of the Economic and Social History of the Orient*, 4 (1961), pp. 70–1; idem, 'Rajasasana: Meaning, Scope and Application', *Proceedings of the Indian History Congress*, 37th Session (Calicut, 1976), pp. 76–87. For other details of such grants known variously as *prasāda-likhita*, *prasāda-pattalā*, *jīvita*, *rakta-koḍagi* and so on, see N.C. Bandyopadhyaya; Yadava, 'Secular Landgrants . . .'; *Society and Culture . . .*, ch. 3; K.K. Gopal,

it is that service grants present a facet and not the precondition for the emergence of the overall pattern of political dominance. Secondly, irrespective of whether administrative measures can bring in changes in societal formations or not,[28] there is the larger question: what generates administrative measures? Land assignments as administrative measures are, we have seen, presented as deliberate acts which corrode the authority of the state; the state not only parts with its sources of revenue but also with its coercive and administrative prerogatives. Thus feudal polity arises because pre-feudal polity decides, to use an all-too-familiar expression, to preside over the liquidation of its own power. This is a curious position to take, which could be understandable only in terms of a crisis of structural significance in pre-feudal political and economic order. We have argued earlier that the breakdown of the Mauryan State does not appear to have generated such a crisis;[29] in fact, in a situation in which the state polity was expanding horizontally and the final annihilation of the *gaṇa-saṃgha* system of polity was taking place,[30] it would be a difficult exercise indeed to construct a reasoned theory of crisis in state power.

One must then look for an alternative explanation. In presenting the above critique of the historiography of the genesis of early medieval polity, the differential distribution of power represented by the *sāmanta*-feudatory structure is not disputed; what is questioned is the rather

---

'Assignment to Officials and Royal Kinsmen in Early Medieval India (*c.* 700–1200 AD)', *University of Allahabad Studies* (Ancient History Section) (1963–64), pp. 75–103. Three points may, however, be noted: (i) the generally late chronology of such grants in some of which only the 'contract' element is explicitly stated; (ii) they are, including *grāsas* and *aṅgabhogas*, more an evidence of the sharing of lineage patrimonial holdings than of service grants; (iii) in terms of total area controlled by dominant sections in a polity such grants may be found to constitute a relatively insignificant proportion.

28 This point has been raised by H. Mukhia.

29 Recent attempts to 'construct' a crisis lean heavily on the Brāhmaṇical perception of the evils of Kaliyuga and on the correlation of the evils with actual changes in terms of shifts in the positions of *varṇas* and producing classes, decline of urbanism, decentralization of polity and so on; see B.N.S. Yadava, 'The Accounts of the Kali Age and the Social Transition from Antiquity to the Middle Ages', *The Indian Historical Review*, 5, pp. 1–2 (1979), pp. 31–64; R.S. Sharma, 'The Kali Age: A Period of Social Crisis', in S.N. Mukherjee (ed.), pp. 186–203. The 'crisis', of course, is chronologically located several centuries after the Maurya period, but in any case, the historical roots of the 'crisis' are not clear.

30 See note 22; also the Allahabad Pillar Inscription of Samudragupta in D.C. Sircar, *Select Inscriptions Bearing on Indian History and Civilization*, vol. I, 2nd edn (Calcutta University, 1965), pp. 262–8.

one-track argument, wholly centred around a particular value attached to the evidence of the landgrants, for the emergence of the structure in pre-Gupta and Gupta times. In fact, in no state system, however centralized, can there be a single focus or level of power, and the specificity of the differential distribution of power in early medieval polity may be an issue more complex than has hitherto been assumed. And perhaps a revaluation of the evidence of the majority of landgrants may be called for within this complexity.

III

At one level this complexity derives from the presence of trans-political ideology in all state systems, even though in the context of early medieval India one may not perceive such an ideology from the perspective of anthropologists or anthropology-oriented historians. One dimension of this was the need for constant validation of power not only in areas where a community was passing from the pre-state to the state-society stage but even in established state societies. The root of this need which, in the early medieval context, may be understood by broadly labelling it as the 'legitimation' process, lay in the separation between the temporal and the sacred domain.[31] The domains, if one goes beyond theory and

[31] The literature on the 'legitimatization' process in early medieval India is growing; relevant discussions will be found in Romila Thapar, 'Social Mobility in Ancient India with Special Reference to Elite Groups' in her *Ancient Indian Social History: Some Interpretations* (Delhi, 1978); B.D. Chattopadhyaya, 'Origin of the Rajputs: Political, Economic and Social Processes in Early Medieval Rajasthan', *The Indian Historical Review*, 3.1 (1976), pp. 59–82; H. Kulke, 'Early State Formation and Royal Legitimation in Tribal Areas of Eastern India', *Studia Ethnologica Bernensia*, R. Moser & M.K. Gautam (eds), 1 (1978), pp. 29–37; idem, 'Legitimation and Town Planning in the Feudatory States of Central Orissa', in *Kings and Cults. State Formation and Legitimation in India and Southeast Asia*, (Delhi, 1993), pp. 93–113; 'Royal Temple Policy and the Structure of Medieval Hindu Kingdoms' in A. Eschmann, et al. (eds), *The Cult of Jagannath and the Regional Tradition of Orissa* (Delhi, 1978), pp. 125–138; N. Dirks, 'Political Authority . . . '; G.W. Spencer, 'Religious Networks and Royal Influence in Eleventh Century South India', *Journal of the Economic and Social History of the Orient*, 12 (1969), pp. 32–56; S. Jaiswal, 'Caste in the Socio-Economic Framework of Early India', Presidential Address, Ancient India Section, Indian History Congress, 38th Session (Bhubaneswar, 1977), pp. 16ff; idem, 'Studies in Early Indian Social History: Trends and Possibilities', *The Indian Historical Review*, 6.1–2 (1979–80), pp. 1–63; J.G. De Casparis, 'Inscriptions and South Asian Dynastic Tradition' in R.J. Moore (ed.), pp. 103–27. The

tries to grasp their relationship in concrete existential terms, must be seen as interdependent; if temporal power needed 'legitimatization' from 'spiritual' authority, so did the human agents of 'spiritual' authority require sustenance from temporal power. Viewed from this perspective, it should not be surprising that priestly validation of temporal power continued beyond the period of 'Hindu' dynasties; the brāhmaṇa, in a situation of reciprocal relationship, could continue to prepare the *praśastis* of the rule of a Sultan and Sanskritize his title to *Suratrāṇa*.[32] Emphasis on legitimation alone obfuscates crucial aspects of the exercise of force and of the secular compulsions of state power, but as a part of the overall political process it nevertheless offers us a convenient vantage point from which to view the ideological dimension of the state. Temporal power, in early as well as in later theoretical writings, was required to guarantee protection; it would be too narrow a view of 'protection' to take it simply to mean the physical protection of subjects. Protection related to the ideal social order as defined by the guardians of the sacred

---

discussions show that 'legitimatization' could take various forms: performance of rituals, including sacrificial rituals, genealogical sanctity and the construction of temple networks. The relationship between temporal authority and the sacred domain of which the 'legitimatization' process is a manifestation is explored in A.K. Coomaraswamy, *Spiritual Authority and Temporal Power in the Indian Theory of Government* (American Oriental Society, 1942); also, L. Dumont, 'The Conception of Kingship in Ancient India', *Religion, Politics and History in India* (Mouton Publishers, 1970), ch. 4. The following statement of Dumont is important: 'While spiritually, absolutely, the priest is superior, he is at the same time, from a temporal or material point of view, subject and dependent' (p. 65). J.F. Richards (*Kingship and Authority in South Asia*, Introduction) claims that a recent perspective '. . . has revealed that too facile usage of only half recognized Western terms and concepts such as legitimation, and the Church-State dichotomy have obscured the complexity and true significance of Kingship in India', and Heesterman in his contribution ('The Conundrum of King's Authority', ibid., pp. 1–27) initially agrees with this claim but finally concedes that the 'King and brahmin were definitely separated and made into two mutually exclusive categories. The greater the King's power, the more he needs the brahmin'. Cf. also C.R. Lingat, *The Classical Law of India* (Berkeley, University of California Press, 1973), p. 216.

32 See the Cambay Stambhana Parsvanath temple inscription of AD 1308 referring to Alauddin as *suratrāṇa*, Appendix to *Epigraphia Indica*, 19–23, Nos. 664. An interesting record from Kotihar in Kashmir, dated AD 1369, refers to Shihab-u-din as Shāhabhadana and traces his descent from the Pāṇḍava lineage, B.K. Kaul Deambi, *Corpus of Śāradā Inscriptions Of Kashmir* (Delhi, 1982), pp. 113–18; the Veraval record of 1263 from Junagadh equates the Prophet with Viśvanātha—viśvarūpa—and begins with his *praśasti* and refers to the Hijri era as *Śrīviśvanātha-pratibaddha-nau-janānām-bodhaka-rasula-Muhammada saṃvat*, D.C. Sircar, *Sel. Inscr.*, vol. 2 (Delhi, 1983), p. 303.

domain. *Daṇḍa* or force which may have had both secular and non-secular connotations was intended by the guardians of the sacred domain primarily not as a political expedient but for the preservation of the social order.[33] Curiously, the ideal social order was defined, but *dharma*, nevertheless, was not uniform, and although the king was required to preserve social order, he was at the same time enjoined to allow the disparate *dharmas* of regions, guilds and associations and of social groups to continue.[34] If there is an anomaly here, the anomaly may help us to understand the massive support which the ruling elites extended to the representatives of the sacred domain in the early medieval period. The territorial spread of the state society required cutting through the tangle of disparate *dharmas* by ensuring the territorial spread of the brāhmaṇas and of institutions representing a uniform norm in some form or the other; they did not necessarily eliminate the disparate norms but they could provide a central focus to such disparate norms by their physical presence, their style of functioning and their control over what could be projected as the 'transcendental' norm.[35]

Another dimension of this central focus becomes noticeable with the crystallization of the Purāṇic order, implying the ascendancy of the Bhakti ideology. In sectarian terms, Bhakti could lead to the growth of conflicts in society,[36] but from the standpoint of the state, Bhakti could, perhaps much more effectively than *Dharmaśāstra*-oriented norms, be an instrument of integration.[37] If there was opposition between *Dharmaśāstra*-

33 See Beni Prasad, *Theory of Government in Ancient India*, 2nd edition (Allahabad, 1968), pp. 333–5; Mabbett, ch. 8.

34 For details, see P.V. Kane, *History of Dharmaśāstra* (Ancient and Medieval Religious and Civil Law), vol. III, 2nd edn (Poona, 1973), ch. 33; also Heesterman, 'The Conundrum . . . '.

35 Heesterman, 'Power and Authority . . . '.

36 R.N. Nandi, 'Origin and Nature of Saivite Monasticism: The Case of Kālāmukhas' in R.S. Sharma and V. Jha (eds), *Indian Society: Historical Probings* (In memory of D.D. Kosambi) (Delhi, 1974), pp. 190–201; R. Champakalakshmi, 'Religious Conflict in the Tamil Country: A Re-appraisal of Epigraphic Evidence', *Journal of the Epigraphical Society of India*, 5 (1978).

37 Bhakti could provide the allusion of equality among the lower orders which in reality remained a delusion even in the ritual area; R.N. Nandi convincingly points to the shift in the ideology of the Bhakti movement as also to the change brought about by its temple base and Sanskrit-educated priesthood, supported by members of ruling families, 'Some Social Aspects of the Nalayira Prabandham', *Proceedings of the Indian History Congress*, 37th Session (Calicut, 1976), pp. 118–23; Kesavan Veluthat, 'The

oriented norms and community norms, Bhakti, at least ideally, provided no incompatibility: local cults and sacred centres could be brought within the expansive Purāṇic fold through the process of identification. Though originating in an earlier period, the temple grew to be the major institutional locus of Bhakti in the early medieval period,[38] and for temporal power, the temple, as a symbol in material space of the sacred domain, could provide a direct link with that domain in two ways: (i) The king could seek to approximate the sacred domain through a process of identification with the divinity enshrined in the temple. The practice initiated by the Pallavas and augmented by the Colas, taken to be similar to the Devarāja cult of south-east Asia, is an example of such a process;[39] (ii) the second way was to surrender temporal power to the divinity, the cult of which was raised to the status of the central cult and to act as its agent. This process is illustrated by the stages through which the cult of Jagannātha emerged as the central cult in Orissa and the ritual surrender of temporal power to the divinity by King Anaṅgabhīma.[40] The centrality of the cult in relation to others in this process implied the centrality of its agents as well.[41] The Cola and Coḍagaṅga practices are perhaps facets of the same concern—to have direct links with the sacred domain.

The process of legitimatization thus cannot be viewed simply in terms of a newly emerged local polity seeking validation through linkage with a respectable Kṣatriya ancestry or by underlining its local roots; the constant validation of temporal authority really relates to the complex of ideological apparatus through which temporal power was reaching out to its temporal domain. '[If] the State [is] a special apparatus, exhibiting a peculiar material framework that cannot be reduced to the given relations

---

Temple Base of the Bhakti Movement in South India', ibid., 40th Session (Waltair, 1979), pp. 185–94.

[38] Nandi; idem, *Religious Institutions and Cults in the Deccan* (Delhi, 1973), pp. 10ff; Veluthat.

[39] K. Veluthat, 'Royalty and Divinity: Legitimisation of Monarchical Power in the South', *Proceedings of the Indian History Congress,* 39th Session (Hyderabad, 1979), pp. 241–39; see also B. Stein, *Peasant State,* pp. 334ff.

[40] H. Kulke, 'Royal Temple Policy . . .'; idem, 'King Anaṅgabhīma III, the Veritable Founder of the Gajapati Kingship and of the Jagannatha Trinity at Puri', *Journal of the Royal Asiatic Society of Great Britain and Ireland,* 1 (1981), pp. 26–39.

[41] For an interesting analysis of this process, H. Kulke, 'Legitimation and Town-planning in the Feudatory States of Central Orissa', in *Kings and Cults. State Formation and Legitimation in India and Southeast Asia,* (Delhi, 1993), pp. 93–113.

of political domination',[42] then it becomes imperative to study the pattern of use of the available ideological apparatus which constituted an integral part of the overall political order.[43] From the perspective of the interdependence between temporal power and sacred authority, it becomes understandable that assignments such as *brahmadeyas* and *devadānas* were not an administrative but a socio-religious necessity for the temporal power; the earthly agents of the sacred domain—and such agents were ultimately defined by the changing contexts of both the temporal and the sacred order—generated a pattern of dominance in their areas of preserve, but it would not be compatible with the argument presented here to generalize either that temporal power in early medieval India was a tool in the hands of the brāhmaṇas and the temple managers,[44] or that massive support to the representatives of the sacred domain meant parcellization of temporal power, an assumption which in any case will have to presuppose that temporal power emanated from a single source. It needs also to be underlined that the duality of the temporal and sacred domains does not necessarily imply that the relationships between the domains remained unchanged from the Vedic times to eternity.[45] From the standpoint of temporal power, Vedism, Purāṇism, Tantrism and other forms of heterodoxism could simultaneously acquire the connotation of the sacred domain.[46] What is required is to analyse the regional and group perception

42 N. Poulantzas, *State, Power, Socialism* (London, 1980), p. 12.

43 Poulantzas further explains (ibid., p. 37): '. . . ideological power is never exhausted by the State and its ideological apparatuses. For just as they do not create the dominant ideology, they are not the only, or even primary factors in the reproductions of the relations of ideological domination/subordination. The ideological apparatuses simply elaborate and inculcate the dominant ideology'.

44 This view seems to be projected by both K. Veluthat, 'Royalty and Divinity . . .' and P.M. Rajan Gurukkal who considers the Kulaśekhara state of Kerala to be 'in a way the creation' of a dominant landed group among the brāhmaṇas, 'Medieval Landrights: Structure and Pattern of Distribution', ibid., pp. 279–84.

45 See footnotes 31 and 90.

46 This requires to be underlined in view of the changing patterns of patronage in different periods. For the early medieval period, the relative neglect of the implications of the deep penetration of Tantrism into religion and polity will bear out the point I am trying to make. Devangana Desai argues that the patronage of Tantrism is reflective of feudal degeneration, as it served the two dominant interests of the kings and feudal chiefs of early medieval India: War and Sex, 'Art under Feudalism in India', *The Indian Historical Review*, 1.1 (1974), p. 12; also idem, *Erotic Sculpture of India* (Delhi, 1975). This seems to be too narrow a view to take of the profound impact of Tantrism in early medieval society. If Tantrism represented esoteric knowledge, then the remark of

of the sacred domain. This will help us understand the curious contradiction between general support and cases of persecution; the overwhelming domination of the brāhmaṇa groups and temples in south India juxtaposed with the incorporation of Jaina tenets in the religious policies of individual rulers of western India[47] or the appointment of a *devotpāṭananāyaka*, an official in charge of uprooting images of gods from temples and of confiscation of temple property, by an early medieval ruler of Kashmir.[48] Taking even the uncommon cases as aberrations would be to bypass the issue; the point is how in the early medieval context the relevance of the sacred domain was defined by temporal power.

Another aspect of the complexity we have talked about concerns the territorial limits of the temporal domain. Temporal domain was defined by the extent of royal power but Kingdom was not defined in concrete territorial terms; even the *janapada* or *rāṣṭra*, one of the constituent limbs of the state in the *Saptāṅga* formulation, was not 'internally coherent and closed towards the outside'.[49] The state was thus not a static unit but one that was naturally dynamic.[50] Even the territory of the Mauryas, which for the period of Aśoka alone can be clearly defined by the distribution of his edicts, was designated as *vijita* or *rājaviṣaya*[51]—an area over which the rule of the emperor extended. The territorial composition of the Mauryan empire in Aśoka's period can be characterized as a combination of several nodes such as Pāṭaliputra, Ujjayinī, Takṣaśilā, Tosali and

F. Edgerton, made in relation to the Upaniṣads, seems relevant here: 'Knowledge, true esoteric knowledge, is the magic key to Omnipotence, absolute power. By it one becomes autonomous . . . ', 'Upanisads: What Do They Seek and Why', in D.P. Chattopadhyaya (ed), *Studies in the History of Indian Philosophy*, vol. I (Calcutta, 1978), p. 136. For Tantric impact on Purāṇic as well as heterodox religious orders and its close association with temporal power, R.N. Nandi, *Religious Institutions . . .*', David N. Lorenzen, *The Kāpālikas and Kālāmukhas: Two Lost Saivite Sects* (New Delhi, 1972); R.B.P. Singh, *Jainism in Early Medieval Karnataka, (c. AD 500–1200)* (Delhi, 1975); B.D. Chattopadhyaya, 'Religion in a Royal Household: A Study of Some Aspects of the *Karpūramañjarī*', (1994).

47 A.K. Majumdar, *Chaulukyas of Gujarat* (A survey of the history and culture of Gujarat from the middle of the tenth to the end of the thirteenth century) (Bombay, 1956), pp. 310, 315.

48 *Rājataraṅgiṇī*, vol. VII, 1091.

49 Heesterman, 'Power and Authority . . .'.

50 De Casparis, 'Inscriptions and South Asian Dynastic Tradition'.

51 Major Rock Edicts, II, XIII; see D.C. Sircar, *Sel. Inscr.*, 1, pp. 17, 35–6.

Suvarṇagiri as well as areas of such peoples as Bhojas, Raṭhikas, Pulindas, Nābhakas and that of the *āṭavikas* or forest people.[52] Such fluid situations—for there is no guarantee that this territorial composition remained static throughout the Mauryan period—are schematized in the *maṇḍala* concept of the political theorists who locate the *vijigīṣu* at the core of the *maṇḍala*,[53] and the 'royal mystique',[54] represented by the *Cakravartin* model of kingship, is a logical follow-up of this formulation. It has been the bane of writings on the political history of early and early-medieval India to search for approximations of the *Cakravartī* among the kings of big-sized states;[55] the ideal is only a recognition of the existence of disparate polities and of military success as a precondition of the *Cakravartī* status which was superior to the status represented by the heads of other polities.

IV

Within the parameters of the interdependence of temporal and sacred domains, and more precisely the essentially dynamic contours of these domains, the political processes of early medieval India may be sought to be identified. I would venture to begin by suggesting that political processes may be seen in terms of parallels with contemporary economic, social and religious processes. The essence of the economic process lay in the horizontal spread of rural agrarian settlements, and this remains true even for the early historical period, despite the accent on urban economy or

52 Ibid.

53 The concept is found in such texts as *Arthaśāstra*, 6.2; *Kāmandakīya Nītisāra*, 8.45 and so on. See Beni Prasad, *Theory of Government* . . . , pp. 143ff; Altekar, pp. 293ff; for recent comments, Heesterman, 'Power and Authority . . . ', pp. 77–8.

54 T.R. Trautmann, 'Tradition of Statecraft in Ancient India', in R.J. Moore (ed.), pp. 86–102. Trautmann defines 'royal mystique' as 'a network of interrelated symbols' its vehicles being 'works of art such as courtly epics, royal biographies and ornate ideologies found in inscriptions'; he takes Rājendra Cola's expedition to the north and north-east as an expression of this 'mystique'.

55 Even R. Inden, who by no means suffers from the limitations of traditional political historiography, cannot seem to resist the search for a 'paramount king of all India', 'Hierarchies of Kings in Early Medieval India', *Contributions to Indian Sociology*, N.S. 15, 1–2 (1981), p. 99.

money economy of the period.[56] The process of caste formation, the chief mechanism of which was the horizontal spread of the dominant ideology of social order based on the *varṇa*-division—despite, again, the ascendancy of heterodoxism in the early historical period[57]—remained the essence of the social process which drew widely dispersed and originally outlying groups into a structure which allowed them in large measure to retain their original character except that this character was now defined with reference to the structure.[58] In the related religious process too the major trend was the integration of local cults, rituals and sacred centres into a pantheistic supra-local structure; the mechanism of integration was by seeking affiliation with a deity or a sacred centre which had come to acquire supra-local significance.[59] Applied to the study of the political

56 R.S. Sharma, *Perspectives in Social and Economic History of Early India* (Delhi, 1983), ch. 10.

57 For example, despite the substantial support extended to the Buddhist sects by both the Sātavāhanas and the Western Kṣatrapas, the dominance of *Varṇa* ideology is evident in their records; cf. the expression *vinivatitacātuvaṇasaṃkarasa* applied to Gautamīputra Sātakarṇi in a *praśasti* written in his memory, and the expression *sarvva-varṇairabhigamya-raksaṇārtham patitve vṛteṇa* applied to Śaka Rudradāman I in the Junagadh inscription of AD 150; Sircar, *Sel. Inscr.*, 1, pp. 177–204.

58 Despite their differences in many respects, N.K. Bose's model of 'tribal absorption' and M.N. Srinivas's model of 'Sanskritization' are being drawn upon to make this generalization. A useful review of the contributions of these two authors, with complete bibliographical references, will be found in S. Munshi, 'Tribal Absorption and Sanskritization in Hindu Society', *Contributions to Indian Sociology*, N.S., 13.2 (1979), pp. 293–317. It must be made clear that 'tribal absorption' is merely a broadly defined process and not the only process, and that the continuity of internal organization in a large measure does not imply status of equality within the social order; a misreading of the caste formation process would totally miss the hierarchical ordering in the caste structure down to the level of the untouchables. Secondly, the ethnic group as a whole, in view of the complex operation of the social mobility process, does not retain its pre-caste character; otherwise, we would not have had brāhmaṇas, Kṣatriyas, Śūdras and so on emerging from the same stock. For a useful discussion, see Jaiswal, 'Studies in Early Indian Social History . . .'.

59 Synoptic studies on processes of cult formation in early medieval India are not known to me, but the excellent study on the cult of Jagannātha may help illuminate the process, A. Eschmann et al (eds), *The Cult of Jagannath and the Regional Tradition of Orissa*, particularly, pt. 1, chs 3, 5; pt. 2, chs 13–14. In the case of Tamilnadu in the Cola period, note the remark of R. Champakalakshmi, 'The early Chola temples . . . systematically used the *liṅga* mainly due to its assimilative character as the only aniconic form which could incorporate in canonical temples, local and popular cult practices centring round the *Kangu* or pillar and tree, thus providing a constantly widening orbit for bringing in divergent socio-economic and ethnic groups into Śaiva worship', 'Peasant

process, these parallels would suggest consideration at three levels: the presence of established norms and nuclei of the state society, the horizontal spread of state society implying the transformation of pre-state polities into state polities, and the integration of local polities into structures that transcended the bounds of local polities. In other words, in trying to understand the political processes and structures in early medieval India it may be more profitable to start by juxtaposing the processes of the formation of local state polities and supra-local polities than by assessing the structures in terms of a perennial oscillation between forces of centralization and decentralization.

The parallelism drawn here is in a sense misleading since in polity, as in society or religion, no given structures could be immutable in view of the underlying dynamism I have already drawn attention to, but the point about the process essentially being a range of interactions still remains valid. The specific complexities of early medieval political formation have, therefore, to be stated in clear empirical terms. The first major point which may be put forward with regard to the post-Gupta polity is that the state society, represented by the emergence of ruling lineages, had covered all nuclear regions and had progressed well into peripheral areas by the end of the Gupta period. I assume details of political geography need not be cited to substantiate this generalization. And yet, it is significant that inscriptions from the seventh century alone, from different regions of India, begin to produce elaborate genealogies, either aligning the alleged local roots of ruling lineages with a mythical tradition or by tracing their descent from mythical heroic lineages.[60] The emergence of genealogy has been taken as a shift from 'yajña to vaṃśa',[61] indicating a change in the nature of kingship, but in the totality of its geographical distribution, the genealogical evidence has a more significant implication: the proliferation of actual ruling lineages defining the domain of political power. The state society even in nuclear areas did not have a stable locus; the mobilization of military strength could not only displace a ruling lineage but could create a new locus and a new network of political relations. The shift from the Badami Cālukyas to the Rāṣṭrakūṭas and then again to the Cālukyas of Kalyāṇa, or from the Pallavas and the

State and Society in Medieval South India: A Review Article', *The Indian Economic and Social History Review*, 18, 3–4 (1982), p. 420.

60 De Casparis.

61 Dirks, 'Political Authority and Structural Change . . .'.

Pāṇḍyas to the Colas was not simply a change from one lineage to another; each change redefined the locus of the state in a geographical context which had nevertheless experienced a long and uninterrupted history of the state society. In such contexts, the use of the term 'state formation', primary, secondary or even tertiary, would be highly inappropriate and would obscure the distinction with areas which were indeed experiencing the passage from the pre-state to the state society on a significant scale. The distinction remains valid throughout Indian history due to the uneven pace of change, and transitions from the pre-state to the state society have been documented through medieval to modern times.[62]

I have been using expressions such as 'lineage domain'[63] and 'state society'[64] without a clear reference to the state in the early medieval context. This is because of some definitional problems which could be clearly stated by working out the geography of the loci of political power over a few centuries. I can however make a very brief reference to a selected span of time—the eleventh century—the two reasons for considering the span as significant being: (i) evidence for this period—particularly from south India—has recently resulted in the urge for a revaluation of

62 A. Guha, 'Tribalism to Feudalism in Assam: 1600–1750', *The Indian Historical Review*, 1.1 (1974), pp. 65–76; Surajit Sinha, 'State Formation and Rajput Myth in Tribal Central India', *Man in India*, 42.1 (1962), pp. 35–80; K. Suresh Singh, 'A Study in State-formation among Tribal Communities', in R.S. Sharma and V. Jha (eds), *Indian Society: Historical Probings*, pp. 317–36; H.R. Sanyal, 'Malla-bhum', in Surajit Sinha, ed., *Tribal Politics and State Systems in Pre-Colonial Eastern and North-Eastern India* (Calcutta, 1987), pp. 73–142.

63 'Lineage' is simply used here to translate such terms as *kula*, *vaṃśa* or *anvaya* which were suffixed to the names of the ruling families. 'Lineage' in this sense does not denote a pre-state stage of polity as it may have done in the nascent stage of the emergence of the state in early India (Romila Thapar, *From Lineage* . . .).

64 The range of definitions of the state is enormous, and to view the state as opposed to chiefdom in terms of the former's capacity to arrest fission in society and in terms of a 'centralized and hierarchically organized political system' (R. Cohen, 'State Origins: A Reappraisal' in *The Early State*, pp. 35–6) will not be compatible with long-term histories of state societies. Morton Fried's definition (*The Evolution of Political Society*, New York, 1967, p. 229) of the state 'as a complex of institutions by means of which the power of the society is organized on a basis superior to kinship' also does not seem sufficient. The real question is the context of power. Since the basis of the state lies in separation between producing and non-producing groups, there is no incompatibility between state society and the organization of political power along lineage ties or/and in other terms. State society, however, only points to the existence of this separation and does not suggest the historical specificity of the total complex of a State structure.

commonly used concepts on the state; (ii) the eleventh century, in relation to the centuries preceding and following it, does not present any major fluctuations in the list and geography of the distribution of ruling lineages. At a rough estimate the number of ruling lineages of this century could be put around forty;[65] the number is reconstructed on the basis of specific references to lineage names and excludes cases where, despite the use of a regal title or a title approximating it, descent is not clearly indicated. In a sense the reconstruction of such numbers would be futile since I am not sure that I can convert these numbers into the number of states and say that forty states existed in India in the eleventh century. Terms such as the Cola State, Cālukya State or Pāla State in place of 'kingdoms' or 'empires' may not raise serious objections, but I am doubtful if I would be equally justified in going ahead with the use of this terminology in relation to, say, the Kadambas of Vanavāsī, Hangal and Goa;[66] the Cāhamānas of Śākambharī, Broach, Dholpur, Pratabgarh, Nadol and Ranthambhor;[67] the Paramāras of Malwa, Lāṭa, Candrāvatī, Arbuda and Suvarṇagiri;[68] and similarly, Noḷamba State, Bāṇa State or Raṭṭa State,[69] signifying the domains of these respective lineages, may be found to be equally inappropriate. The reason is not simply the status of a lineage; the point really is whether there is always a necessary correspondence between a lineage and a static territorial limit. Early medieval evidence suggests that this is not so. I have cited the cases of the Kadambas and the Cāhamānas; many more are readily available. The Kalacuris, an ancient lineage, are found in western Deccan in a comparatively early

[65] This estimate is based on: H.C. Ray, *The Dynastic History of Northern India (Early Medieval Period)*, 2 vols, reprint (Delhi, 1973); F. Kielhorn, 'A List of Inscriptions of Northern India', Appendix to *Epigraphia Indica*, 5, pp. 1–96; D.R. Bhandarkar, 'A List of the Inscriptions of Northern India in Brāhmī and its Derivative Scripts, from about 200 A.C.', Appendix to *Epigraphia Indica*, pp. 19–23; F. Kielhorn, 'Synchronistic Tables for Southern India, AD 400–1400', *Epigraphia Indica*, 8.

[66] G.M. Moraes, *The Kadamba-Kula. A History of Ancient and Medieval Karnataka* (Bombay, 1931).

[67] Dasarath Sharma; also 2nd edn (Delhi, 1975).

[68] P. Bhatia, *The Paramāras* (Delhi, 1968); also, H.V. Trivedi, *Inscriptions of the Paramāras* (*Corpus Inscriptionum Indicarum*, vol. 7.2) (New Delhi, n.d.).

[69] See M.S. Krishnamurthy, *Nolambas: A Political and Cultural Study* (Mysore, 1980); D. Desai, *The Mahāmaṇḍaleśvaras Under the Cālukyas of Kālyaṇī* (Bombay, 1951); M.S. Govindaswamy, *The Role of Feudatories in Pallava History* (Annamalai University, 1965); Idem, 'The Role of Feudatories in Cola History', Ph.D. thesis (Annamalai University, 1973); V. Balambal, *Feudatories of South India* (Allahabad, 1978).

period, but they established several nuclei of power, as in Tripurī and Ratanpur, in the upper Narmada basin in the early medieval period, whereas one of its segments ventured into such a remote area of north-eastern India that it came to be designated as Sarayūpāra.[70] The movements of the Karṇāṭas outside Karnataka, although the particular lineages involved are not always specified, led to the establishment of new ruling families in Bengal and Bihar,[71] and possibly also to the formation of such Rajput clans as the Solankis and Rathods.[72] The ruling lineage in its entirety is the point of reference in the case of major lineages in many records, as suggested by expressions like *Pallavānām* or *Kadambānām.*[73] What I am, therefore, arguing is that since the changing distribution patterns of ruling lineages do not necessarily correspond to static territorial limits, an initial study of polity has to start with an analysis of the formation of lineages and of the pattern of the network they represent, both territorially and in inter-lineage combinations, at *different levels in the organization of political power.* Such an analysis may ultimately clarify relations in the structures of supra-local polities, which alone seem to be issues in historiographical debates on the polity of early medieval India. The focus then will have to shift from extremities like 'virtual absence of' or 'construction and collapse of' the administrative apparatus. In fact, as the empirical evidence from regions like Rajasthan suggests, the distribution of political authority could be organized by a network of lineages within the framework of the monarchical form of polity, retaining at the same time areas of bureaucratic functioning.[74] A remark, made with reference to medieval Deccan, seems pertinent here: 'The development of State bureaucracy and private lordly organization was neither mutually exclusive nor confined to two different stages of a process. In this agrarian

70 For the records of different Kalacuri lines, see V.V. Mirashi, *Inscriptions of the Kalachuri-Chedi Era* (*Corpus Inscriptionum Indicarum,* vol. 4, pp. 1–2) (Ootacamund, 1955).

71 For a recent discussion, see D.C. Sircar, *Pāla-Sena Yuger Vaṃśānucarita* (in Bengali) (Calcutta, 1982).

72 The common origin of the Cālukyas of Karnataka and the Calukyas or Solankis of Gujarat has been doubted by many, including A.K. Majumdar, but Majumdar himself points to the existence of common traditions among them, 5; Rathod is derived from Rāṣṭrakūṭa, the name being in existenee at Dhalop and Hathundi in Rajasthan in the early medieval period, D. Sharma (ed.), *Rajasthan Through the Ages,* I (Bikaner, 1966), p. 287; also Chattopadhyaya, 'The Origin of the Rajputs . . .'.

73 De Casparis.

74 Chattopadhyaya, 'Origin of the Rajputs . . .'.

society private and State interests developed simultaneously and in terms of one another'.[75]

The formation and mobilization of lineage power did not, of course, develop along a single channel; it could involve the colonization of areas of pre-state polity and change of the economic pattern of the region by expansive lineages;[76] in particular contexts, the emergence of ruling lineages would correspond to 'primary state formation' and the introduction of the monarchical ideology of rule; it could even be the simple replacement of one lineage by another. All these processes could and did operate simultaneously, but—and this needs to be underlined if we are to take an all-India perspective—not in isolation from one another. Polities were interactive and interlocking—if nothing else, inventories of battles fought in the early medieval period would be a sure index of this—and this often resulted in the formation of new blocks and networks of power in which the original identity of a lineage was obliterated.[77]

Two further points about lineages as bases for the study of political power may be made. First, the Kalacuri or Cāhamāna evidence has shown that lineages could be amazingly expansive but there are other levels at which the relationships between lineages and territories can be examined. Pre-tenth century evidence from Tamilnadu has been cited to show that the nucleus of the power of a lineage could be an area comprised of two or three districts. The relationship between the lineage and its territory was expressed in the form of the name of the area in which the lineage was dominant; examples of this are common in the south and in the Deccan: Cola-nāḍu, Cera-nāḍu, Toṇḍai-nāḍu, Oyma-nāḍu, Iruṅgola-pāḍi, Gaṅga-pāḍi, Nuḷamba-pāḍi, to mention a few, bear out this relationship. The growth of a lineage into a supra local or supra-regional power would result in the reorganization of the *nāḍus* or *pāḍis* into administrative units, as suggested by the emergence of the *vaḷa-naḍus* and *maṇḍalams* in the Cola State,[78] but, from our point of view, what is important is that

[75] Perlin, p. 279.

[76] Yadava, *Society and Culture*, p. 103, fn. 623; Chattopadhyaya, 'Origin of the Rajputs . . . ', pp. 63–4; an example of this is provided by the Ajayagadh rock inscription in which Ānanda, the brother of Candella Trailokyavarman, is said to have reduced to submission the 'wild tribes of Bhillas, Śabaras and Pulindas', *Epigraphia Indica*, 1, p. 337.

[77] Apart from the cases of the Solankis and the Rathods, those of the Coḍagaṅgas and Veṅgi Cālukyas may be cited to illustrate this process.

[78] Y. Subbarayalu, 'Mandalam as a Politico-Geographical Unit in South India', *Proceedings of the Indian History Congress*, 39th Session (Hyderabad, 1978), pp. 84–6.

such administrative units emerged by integrating pre-existing lineage areas. It must be conceded that the pattern available for the south and the Deccan cannot be applied to all regions; in Bengal, for example, such details of lineage geography are simply not available. Elsewhere, as in early medieval Rajasthan and Gujarat, the trend seems to have been towards the parcellization of the area variously called Gurjara-bhūmi, Gurjaratrā, Gurjara-dharitrī and Gurjaradharā—all obviously derived from the ethnic term Gurjara[79]—into strongholds of several lineages, only some of which traced their descent from the Gurjara stock.[80]

Secondly, the formation of ruling lineages can be seen also from the perspective of the social mobility process in early medieval India. In a situation of open-ended polity and of a congenial climate for 'Kṣatriyization',[81] any lineage or segment of a larger ethnic group, with a coherent organization of force, could successfully make a bid for political power and lay the foundation of a large state structure. The origin of the Hoysaḷa State, which lasted for about three centuries and a half, goes back to the *mālepas* or the hill chiefs of the Soseyūr forests and the hill forces that the chiefs could command at that stage.[82] Here too the pattern of the formation of a lineage and the level of power a lineage would reach would not be identical in all areas. Generally, the mobility upward was from a base which could be broadly characterized as agrarian, and political changes from the seventh century, again in western India, provide an idea of the sequences in the political mobility process. We have noted that Gurjaratrā or Gurjarabhūmi was the base from which several lineages tracing descent from the Gurjaras emerged; the separation of the ruling lineages from the common stock is suggested by the general name Gurjara-Pratihāra used by the lineages, and while the base of one such lineage

---

For details of the political geography of the Cola country, see idem, *Political Geography of the Chola Country* (Madras, 1973). Subbarayalu convincingly argues to show that *nāḍus* were basically agrarian regions and not 'artificial administrative divisions' (*Political Geography*, pp. 32–3), but from the point of view of polity the important point is the correlation in many cases between 'chieftaincies' and *nāḍus* and *pāḍis* (*Political Geography* . . . , ch. 7); see also Stein, *Peasant State* . . . , ch. 3.

79 A.K. Majumdar, pp. 17–22.

80 Chattopadhyaya.

81 See references in note 31.

82 J.D.M. Derrett, *The Hoysaḷas* (A Medieval Indian Royal Family) (Oxford University Press, 1957), pp. 7–8; S. Settar, *Hoysala Sculptures in the National Museum, Copenhagen* (Copenhagen, 1975), p. 16.

in the Jodhpur area seems to have been established by displacing pre-existing groups, in the Alwar area in eastern Rajasthan there is clear indication of a sharp distinction which had developed between Gurjara cultivators and the Gurjara-Pratihāra ruling lineage.[83] It is on this base that the Gurjara-Pratihāra supra-regional power, which began with the expansion of one of the lineages and extended at one stage possibly as far east as Bengal, was built up. Elsewhere, for example, the presence of Vellāla generals and warrior elements and of feudatories in the Pallava and Cola polities in south India[84] or the formation of the Ḍāmaras into a major political group in the Lohara period (*c.* AD 1000–1170) in Kashmir[85] would suggest a similar process of the emergence of potentially dominant elements from within local agrarian bases.

V

The structure of supra-local or supra-regional polities has then to become understandable in a large measure with reference to its substratum components, and it is in the characterization of this reference that the perspectives of historians substantially differ. Before the debate is taken up for review, the geographical loci of large polities need to be briefly touched upon. The large polities tended to emerge, throughout Indian history, in what geographers call 'nuclear' regions,[86] providing such polities with a

83 Rajorgadh Inscription of Mathanadeva, *Epigraphia Indica*, vol. 3, pp. 263–7.

84 Dirks, 'Political Authority and Structural Change . . . ', p. 130; Stein, *Peasant State* . . . , p. 188; for reference to Velirs of Kodumbalur as feudatories of the Pallavas, see Govindaswamy, *The Role of Feudatories in Pallava History*, pp. 70ff.

85 Kosambi writes, 'The essential question is: Were the Ḍāmaras feudal lords? Did they hold land as feudal property? The answer is fairly clear, in the affirmative', 'Origins of Feudalism in Kashmir'; Yadava, 'Secular Landgrants . . . ', p. 90 too refers to a merchant called Jayyaka who amassed wealth and became a Ḍāmara chief. These assertions seem to result from a misreading of the *Rājataraṅgiṇī* evidence. The reference relating to Jayyaka (VII. 93–95) seems to show him to be from a peasant family, who traded in foodgrains with foreign countries and achieved the status of a Ḍāmara (see also IV. 347–48). The possible tribal background of the Ḍāmaras, their transformation into peasantry and emergence into a dominant section may have striking parallels with the Vellālas and other dominant peasant sections elsewhere; see the Appendix on Ḍāmaras in Krishna Mohan.

86 The concept of 'nuclear' regions or even 'sub-nuclear' regions has been used by historians working on this period: Kulke, 'Royal Temple Policy . . . '; B. Stein, 'Integration

resource base potentially much richer and easier to integrate administratively than relatively isolated pockets where 'state formation', a chronologically phased phenomenon, would reveal less integrative patterns of polity. The Ganges basin, Kaveri basin, Krishna-Godavari *doab* and Raichur *doab* are cited as examples of 'nuclear' regions, and indeed the large state structures of the early medieval period all thrived in these regions. Two qualifications are, however, necessary. First, a 'nuclear' region is finally a historical-chronological and not purely a geographical region; the nuclearity of a region is related to the way historical factors converge on it and not merely to its resource potential. Warangal, away from the nuclear Krishna-Godavari *doab*, remained a base of the large structure of the Kākatīya State;[87] the Caulukya State of Gujarat, with its base at Aṇahilapāṭaka, emerged in a region which, from the point of view of its basic agrarian resource potential, was not sufficiently 'nuclear'.[88] Secondly, larger polities did not necessarily originate in nuclear areas; military mobilization could generate a movement towards nuclear areas and result in major transformations in polity. The movement of the Pratihāras from Rajasthan to Kanauj, of the Pālas from southeast Bengal to the middle and the lower Ganges basin,[89] the descent of the Hoysaḷas from the hilly region of the Soseyūr forests into the areas of south Karnataka held by the Gaṅgas for centuries, produced a steady growth of political structures of substantial dimensions in these regions.

I have already noted in the beginning that recognition of the dispersed foci of political power was present even in traditional historiography in the form of the formulation of 'feudal tendencies', although the formulation was applied generally to a pattern of polity which was considered

---

of the Agrarian System in South India', in R.E. Frykenberg (ed.), *Land Control and Social Structure in Indian History* (Madison, 1969), pp. 175–216. Theoretical discussions will be found in R.I. Crane (ed.), *Regions and Regionalism in South Asian Studies* (Duke University, 1966); J.E. Schwartzberg, 'The Evolution of Regional Power Configurations in the Indian Subcontinent', in R.G. Fox (ed.), pp. 197–233. I have, however, mainly followed the idea of the relative order of regions outlined in O.H.K. Spate and A.T.A. Learmonth, *India and Pakistan* (University Paperback, Delhi, 1972), chs 6, 13.

[87] G. Yazdani (ed.), *Early History of the Deccan* (Oxford University Press, 1960), vol. II.

[88] However, for irrigation and development of the agrarian base of the Caulukyan state structure, see V.K. Jain, *Trade and Traders in Western India (AD 1000–1300)* (Delhi, 1990), ch. 2; for Rajasthan, B.D. Chattopadhyaya, 'Irrigation in Early Medieval Rajasthan' (1994).

[89] D.C. Sircar, *Pāla-Sena Yuger* . . . .

not sufficiently large in terms of its approximation to an all-India empire and which could not, therefore, be considered centralized. Recent perspectives specifically related to only early medieval India have shifted from acceptance of 'centralization' and 'bureaucracy' as essential characteristics of a large state structure to detailed analyses of dispersed foci of power within such structures. This concern appears to be common both to those who characterize these structures in terms of 'feudal polity' and their critics to whom the 'feudal' model is either 'outworn' or is an exclusively European formation which hinders a proper understanding of the uniqueness of the Indian political system.[90] Where then does the difference lie? Reducing the discussion to the level of political relations alone, the fundamental difference seems to lie, as I understand it, between their respective notions of 'parcellized sovereignty' and 'shared sovereignty'. Opposition to the 'feudal' model[91] is best articulated in the model of the 'segmentary state' which is currently bandied about, at least in the circle of Western Indologists, as a major breakthrough in our understanding of the traditional Indian political system. The model which is directly lifted from the analysis of a pre-state polity in East Africa but, in the Indian

[90] This particular brand of criticism in respect of Indian polity has emanated, curiously, from American academic institutions, and in the context of early medieval polity been initiated by B. Stein, 'The State and Agrarian Order in Medieval South India: A Historiographical Critique', in B. Stein (ed.), *Essays on South India* (Delhi, 1976), pp. 64–91. Stein proposed the alternative model of a 'segmentary state' ('The Segmentary State . . . ') which has proved a rallying point for South Asia experts from these institutions and even for initial detractors. For example, Dirks ('Political Authority and Structural Change', p. 126) in 1976 declared: 'The segmentary state model is neither well calibrated to index changes in political or social relations, nor is it culturally sensitive enough to identify the differences between East Africa and India, or *even more particularly between north and south India* (emphasis added; the implication perhaps is that the differences between north India and south India are greater than those between East Africa and India); by 1979 his criticism of the model had mellowed down considerably ('Structure and Meaning of Political Relations'). R. Inden considers the model a 'real break with previous approaches', 'Ritual, Authority, and Cyclic Time in Hindu Kingship', in J.F. Richards (ed.), pp. 28–73; see also B. Stein, 'All the King's Mana: Perspectives on Kingship in Medieval South India', ibid., pp. 115–67; idem, 'Mahanavami: Medieval and Modern Kingly Ritual in South India', in B.L. Smith (ed.), *Essays on Gupta Culture* (Delhi, 1983), pp. 67–92. The real point of convergence in these writings is that they view the Indian State system, whatever be the period, as a ritual system.

[91] The discussion here is restricted only to the construct of 'feudal polity' and to the particular brand of criticism it has recently been subjected to. It does not take into account the total range of the critique of the feudal formation.

context, is mixed up with concepts of kingship derived from literature, presents the following characteristics of the 'segmentary state': (i) limited territorial sovereignty which further weakens gradually as one moves from the core to the periphery, and often 'shades off into ritual hegemony'; (ii) the existence of a centralized core with quasi-autonomous foci of administration; (iii) the pyramidal repetition of the administrative structure and functions in the peripheral foci; (iv) the absence of absolute monopoly of legitimate force at the centre; and (v) shifting allegiances of the periphery of the system.[92] In the schema of the segmentary state, as it has been variously worked out in the Indian context, the major integrative factor is 'ritual sovereignty' rather than 'political sovereignty', and attempts at explications of the concept of 'ritual sovereignty' locate the king as the principal ritualist. The 'new modality of relations between the chiefs and the King', one writer argues in the context of the later phase of Pallava polity [which] 'represents the expansion of a regional system into a

[92] See note 9 for references to Southall's writings in which the 'segmentary state' model has been constructed. The applicability of the model has been debated in the volume edited by R.G. Fox; various points regarding the empirical validity of its application to the Cola State by Stein have been raised by R. Champakalakshmi, 'Peasant State and Society . . .', and in greater detail by D.N. Jha, 'Relevance of Peasant State and Society to Pallava and Cola times', *The Indian Historical Review*, vol. 8, nos. 1–2 (1981–82), pp. 74–94. I do not wish to re-examine the question of empirical validity here, but will briefly touch upon the internal consistency or the validity of the model itself. Southall constructs his model by drawing a distinction between the 'segmentary state' and the 'unitary state', which is, for a historian, as irrelevant as the dichotomy between the 'early state' and the 'industrial state'. If pre-state polity has a varied range (and according to Southall's own characterization, his East African Alur polity would approximate the 'chiefdom' category), so too has State polity, and to equate the State with a 'unitary state' is to totally ignore historical experience. Curiously, Southall's 'segmentary state' and 'unitary state' are not ultimately distinctly separate categories either; they are two extreme points in the same structure, which change positions, depending on the degree of centralization or decentralization in existence in the structure at any given point of time (p. 260). Secondly, Southall posits the 'segmentary state' as a counterpoint to 'feudal polity' but ends up by suggesting its applicability to a series of historical political structures ranging from feudal France to 'traditional states of India, China and inner Asia' (pp. 252–4). There is no dearth of models one can draw upon (for example, the model of a 'galactic' state constructed by Tambiah on the basis of evidence from Thailand), and Stein is certainly not unaware of the curious position taken by Southall (Stein, 'Segmentary State . . .'), but the point remains that the model is projected as a key to our understanding of polity in 'traditional' India. Is it that it is being used to fill the vacuum created by the decline of 'Oriental Despotism' or of the venerated tradition of East-West dichotomy?

trans-regional system' is nothing more than a shift from an earlier ritual system, and the different foci of power nothing more than ritual accessories.[93] It is the kingship which is 'incorporative' and, one may say by extending this logic, whatever be the territorial spread of the state, it is ritual space.

All this is a fine example of the study of the state *sans* politics. While the analytic inseparability of 'State structure from State ritual'[94] is understandable, particularly in south India where material for the study of such a relationship is plentiful, the subordination of the political and economic dimensions of the state structure to its ritual dimension has led to the inevitable neglect of two imperatives under which a state is expected to operate: (i) stability in its power structure; (ii) resource mobilization[95] which, logically, cannot be separated from the process of the redistribution of resources to integrative elements within the state structure. To briefly illustrate the implications of these omissions, too narrow a definition of the 'core' of the Cola territory would leave unanswered why the Cola territorial reorganizations included apparently peripheral areas like Gaṅga-vāḍi and Nolamba-vāḍi[96] or why territorial conquests of strategic areas and areas of resource potential sought to eliminate existing power-holders and to convert them, in some cases at least, into extensions of patrimonial holdings.[97] The concept of a 'core' area as remaining permanently limited to the lineage area in the context of a supra-local polity is untenable; its definition too has to be seen more as functional than geographical.[98] The second omission has resulted in the postulate of the

93 Dirks, 'Political Authority and Structural Change . . . '.

94 Dirks, 'Structure and Meaning of Political Relations . . . '.

95 See Eisenstadt, xv–xvi, pp. 7–8.

96 Subbarayalu, 'Mandalam as a Politico-Geographical Unit . . . '.

97 The emergence of Cola power had its basis in the elimination of Muttaraiyar power in the Kaveri basin and then its penetration into *Toṇḍaimaṇḍalam*. Koṅgudeśa, Pāṇḍya country, Gaṅgavāḍi and Veṅgi, to mention only a few regions, lay inside the orbit of the Cola political interests, irrespective of the duration and fluctuations in actual control, whereas on the fringes of the Cola region proper local lineages could continue, although Subbarayalu thinks that the families of the 'Chiefs' were enlisted for the 'Chola army and administrative staff' (*Political Geography*, p. 80). For an attempt to determine the core of the Cola dominion through a study of the distribution pattern of Cola records, see G.W. Spencer and K.R. Hall, 'Toward an Analysis of Dynastic Hinterlands: The Imperial Cholas of 11th Century South India', *Asian Profile*, 2.1 (1974), pp. 51–62.

98 I have already referred to the dispersed nodes of the Mauryan State (note 52); in the case of the Kuṣāṇas too Gandhāra in the north-west was a 'core' region and Mathura

'politics of plunder' as the major mechanism of resource acquisition and redistribution[99]—in fact, a mechanism which is essentially identical with the one present in the polity of the 'chiefdoms' of the Sangam age.[100] It is indeed curious that the postulate of the 'politics of plunder' has been put forward in relation to the Cola State in which a vast agrarian surplus sustained integrative elements in society and in which the state penetration into growing networks of trade and exchange could diversify and expand its resource bases enormously.[101]

The 'segmentary state' model or the concept of 'ritual sovereignty' cannot in fact resolve the problem of the political basis of integration since a rigid use of the 'segmentary state' concept relegates the different

---

in the upper Ganga-Yamuna basin was another such region (B.D. Chattopadhyaya, 'Mathurā from Śuṅga to Kuṣāṇa Times: An Historical Outline', in Doris M. Srinivasan (ed), *Mathurā: The Cultural Heritage* (Delhi, 1989), pp. 19–30). 'Core', in the context of supra-local polities, has thus to acquire a flexible connotation.

99 Stein, 'The State and Agrarian Order . . . '; the idea has been elaborated by G.W. Spencer, 'The Politics of Plunder: The Cholas in Eleventh Century Ceylon', *Journal of Asian Studies*, 33.3 (1976), pp. 405–19. (Since I have not been able to consult Spencer's publication, *Politics of Expansion: The Chola Conquest of Sri Lanka and Sri Vijaya* [Madras, 1983], I can only state his formulations in the article cited here.) Spencer's own evidence contradicts his conclusion since it shows that Cola expansion was motivated more by strategic-commercial considerations, particularly considerations relating to the Pāṇḍya country, than by resource acquisition through raids. One may suggest that despite the revenue survey evidence of the time of the Colas and the actual occurrence of revenue terms (N. Karashima & B. Sitaraman, 'Revenue Terms in Chola Inscriptions', *Journal of Asian and African Studies*, 5 (1972), pp. 88–117; N. Karashima, 'Land Revenue Assessment in Cola Times as Seen in the Inscriptions of the Thanjavur and Gangaikonda-colapuram Temples', cyclostyled copy) the revenue yield may have been limited, but the real issue is whether it was 'plunder' or agricultural surplus which sustained the ruling and non-ruling elites of society in eleventh century India. The answer is, of course, obvious, and studies on both the north and the south suggest that revenue demand in the early medieval period was on the increase.

100 R.S. Kennedy, 'The King in Early South India, as Chieftain and Emperor', *The Indian Historical Review*, 3, 1 (1976), pp. 1–15.

101 A recent detailed study on this is K.R. Hall, *Trade and Statecraft in the Age of the Colas* (Delhi, 1980); idem, 'International Trade and Foreign Diplomacy in Early Medieval South India', *Journal of the Economic and Social History of the Orient*, 21 (1978), pp. 75–98. In fact, the phenomenon of the emergence of networks of exchange from the ninth–tenth centuries, which, in littoral regions, converged with those of international trade of that period was widespread; for Gujarat, see V.K. Jain; for local centres of exchange coinciding with centres of ruling lineages in various parts of India, see B.D. Chattopadhyaya, 'Urban Centres in Early Medieval India: An Overview' in S. Bhattacharya and Romila Thapar (eds), *Situating Indian History* (Delhi, 1986), pp. 8–33.

foci of power to the 'periphery' and does not really see them as components of the state structure. The phenomenon of different foci of power was not peculiarly south Indian but cut across all major political structures of the early medieval period, and there is thus a need for a common perspective, irrespective of the quality or the volume of material available from different regions. These diffused foci of 'quasi-autonomous' power are represented by what is broadly labelled as the *sāmanta* system which, although present in some form or the other in all major polities, has not been taken proper cognizance of by the protagonists of the 'segmentary state' model.[102] *Sāmanta* is of course a broad-spectrum category and encompasses a proliferating range of designations in use in the early medieval period. Not all the designations emerge simultaneously, but by the twelfth-thirteenth centuries such terms as *mahāsāmanta, sāmanta, mahāmaṇḍaleśvara, maṇḍaleśvara, rāṇaka, rāuta, ṭhakkura* and so on came to indicate a political order which was non-bureaucratic and in the context of which, in the overall structure of polity, the *rājapuruṣas* constituting the bureaucracy had only a limited part to play.[103] The order assumed the characteristics of a hierarchical formation, and this is clear not only in the binary hierarchy of *mahāsāmanta* and *sāmanta* or *mahāmaṇḍaleśvara* and *maṇḍaleśvara* but in the attempted schematization of the order in early medieval texts like the *Aparājitapṛcchā* as well.[104] The *sāmanta* in its trans-political connotation corresponded to the 'landed aristocracy' of the period; in addition, the spate of land assignments and other forms of prestation to various categories of donees, including those rendering military service to the state,[105] were factors which, apart from the presence of the *sāmanta* landed aristocracy, weakened, it is believed, the hold of

[102] Stein (*Peasant State* . . . , ch. 3) talks of local, autonomous chiefs in connection with the *nāḍu*, but his study of the Cola State has virtually no reference to the actual political linkage between them and the organization of Cola power. The report presented by N. Karashima and Y. Subbarayalu ('Statistical Study of Personal Names in Tamil Inscriptions: Interim Report II', *Computational Analysis of Asian and African Languages*, No. 3, 1976, pp. 9–20), on records from seven districts, lists more than 28 titles as 'feudatory', refers to their association with the administration and to distinctions between these titles; for details of different patterns of political and kin linkages, see Balambal; also Govindaswamy, 'The Role of Feudatories in Chola History'.

[103] For details for north India, see Yadava, *Society and Culture* . . . , ch. 3.

[104] Ibid.; also R.S. Sharma, *Social Changes in Early Medieval India (circa AD 500–1200)* (Delhi, 1969); a detailed study of the evidence has recently been made by R. Inden, 'Hierarchies of Kings . . . '.

[105] See note 24.

the state over both the polity and the revenue potential of its constituent territorial units.

The composition of the elites in any given state structure may have varied, but my argument requires that we begin with an explanation of the formation of a political structure rather than with a statement of its decentralized character. In other words, if the *sāmanta* system was, as has been suggested, the keynote of early medieval polity, then it needs to be recognized that from a pattern of relations characterized by *grahaṇa-mokṣa* (i.e. capture and release) in the early Gupta phase,[106] there was a shift towards a pattern in which the *sāmantas* were integrated into the structure of polity and in which the overlord-subordinate relation came to be dominant over other levels of relations in the structure. The political exigency of this integration from the Gupta period specially—and I posit *political* integration as a counterpoint to the decentralized polity of the feudal model—lay in the interrelatedness of polities caused by what I have called the horizontal spread of the state society and represented, geographically, by the lineages at their varied local bases. The exigency is expressed with some clarity in the following quote: 'The larger the unit the greater the King's power, and hence the greater his chances of being efficient within his geographical scope. Hence the constant urge to conquer . . . '.[107] The structure of polities was only partly based on the elimination of existing bases of power, by the expansion of the kin network of the lineage that emerged as dominant or by the organization of a bureaucracy that could connect different nodes in the structure, but the fact that political relations were regularly expressed as those between the overlord and his feudatories suggests that the dominant mode in the formation of the structure was by encapsulation of the existing bases of power, the spearhead in the structure being the overlord.

The current state of research on the political history of the period makes it impossible to advance any generalization, from the vast corpus of early medieval material, regarding the composition of the feudatories,

106 Allahabad Pillar inscription of Samudragupta, Sircar, *Sel. Inscr.*, 1, p. 265. The expression means the same as *gṛhīta-pratimuktasya* which occurs in Kālidāsa's *Raghuvaṃśam*, IV. 33. And yet, it is from the fifth–sixth century that the term *sāmanta* comes to denote a subordinate position in relation to an overlord, L. Gopal, 'Samanta—its Varying Significance in Ancient India', *Journal of the Royal Asiatic Society of Great Britain and Ireland*, 1963, pp. 21–37.

107 Derrett, p. 177.

but two suggestions may be made: (i) since the emergence of the overlord himself had its basis mostly in local lineage power, the expansion of a lineage into a supra-local power was through pooling military resources and perhaps other forms of support of other lineages;[108] (ii) more importantly, pooling not only required a circulation or redistribution of resources[109] acquired in the process of expansion but required a system of ranking as well. These suggestions are in consonance with integrative polity and the transformation of the *sāmanta* into a vital component of the political structure is itself an evidence of ranking and in turn clarifies the political basis of integration. Ranking was associated with roles and services, and it may be postulated that a correlation was worked out between such roles as those of the *dūtaka*, *sāndhivigrahika*, *daṇḍanāyaka* and so on and ranking in the *sāmanta* hierarchy.[110] The gradual crystallization of ranking permeated the early medieval society to such an extent that the status of members within individual ruling lineages came to be expressed in terms of ranks[111] and that ranks extended to even

108 A detailed examination of this will prove that the basic mechanism of the growth of the overlord–feudatory axis was not through the assignment of land and the transfer of state power. The Pratīhāras, for example, in the process of their emergence as a supra-regional power received support from the Cālukyas of Gujarat, Cāhamānas and other minor Pratihāra lineages; see *Epigraphia Indica*, 9, pp. 107–9; ibid., vol. 18, pp. 87–99; the reference to the *samastāṭavikasāmantacakra* in the *Rāmacarita* will also hardly fit the suggestion that the *sāmantas* were basically created, K.K. Gopal, 'The assembly of the sāmantas in early medieval India', *Journal of Indian History*, 42 (1964), pp. 231–50. For similar evidence regarding Pallava and Cola polities, see Dirks, 'Political Authority . . . '; Stein, 'All the King's Mana . . . '; Govindaswamy and Balambal (works cited above).

109 Cf. references in the records of Rāṣṭrakūṭa Kṛṣṇa III to the distribution of conquered dominions among his subordinates, *Epigraphia Indica*, 4, p. 285; ibid., 5, p. 35; for reference to the award, in the Cola period, of chieftainship for the suppression of *raja-drohis*, *Annual Report on South Indian Epigraphy*, 1913, p. 40.

110 Sharma (*Social Changes . . .*) too uses the term 'feudal ranks' but not in the sense of a system which emerges in the context of interdependent polities. Ranking is suggested by the pairing or other forms of combination of *sāmanta/mahāsāmanta* with designations which are basically administrative in connotation. For details, see Yadava, *Society and Culture . . .* , ch. 3, although Yadava does not view the evidence from the position that I would like to take; also L. Gopal; for the south, see Karashima and Subbarayalu 'Statistical Study . . . '; D. Desai, *Mahāmaṇḍaleśvaras . . .* , Balambal; and Govindaswamy.

111 Cf. the interesting case of the great queen Bammaladevī being addressed as *Mahāmaṇḍaleśvarī* in a record of 1179, *Epigraphia Carnatica*, 12, Tm. 35; for evidence from Rajasthan, see Chattopadhyaya, 'Origin of the Rajputs . . . '.

non-ruling groups and individuals.[112] And in terms of the social process, the transformation of political ranking could in the long run take the form of caste ranking.[113]

Rank as the basis of political organization implies differential access to the centre as also shifts within the system of ranking. The description in the *Aparājitapṛcchā*, although built up around an overlord of the ideal *cakravartī* model, nevertheless points to the relative positioning of different categories of ruling elites including *daṇḍanāyakas*, *maṇḍaleśas*, *māṇḍalikas*, *mahāsāmantas*, *sāmantas*, *laghusāmantas*, *caturaśikas*, *rājaputras* and so on. The system of ranking in relation to the overlord as offered in the text which was composed at the Caulukyan court in Gujarat may be reflective more of the text's perception of *Cakravartī* power than an actual order, but significantly, a correlation between territorial political hold and rank can be detected in its description.[114] Since the basis of territorial and political hold was not static, rank was not static either. In fact, even inadequate studies available so far would suggest that ranks held by individual families underwent changes,[115] that ranks varied from one generation to the next[116] and that aspirations for higher ranks were operative within individual political structures.[117] If the idea of ranking as the political basis of the organization of both local and supra-local structures be accepted, then it may be followed up for locating the potential sources of tension on the political plane: between the rank-holders as also between them and the overlord. Channels open for the diffusion of such tensions would not have been many; expansion of the kinship network, itself encompassed by the system of ranking, assignments

112 Śūlapāṇi who was the head of the *Varendraka-śilpī-goṣṭhī* (guild of *sūtradharas* of north Bengal) is mentioned as a *rāṇaka* in the Deopara *praśasti* of the twelfth century, Sircar, *Sel. Inscr.*, 2, p. 121; a record of 1263 from Jalor refers to the 'head worshipper' of a Mahāvīra temple as *Bhaṭṭāraka Rāvala*, Appendix to *Epigraphia Indica*, 19–23, No. 563.

113 K.P. Ammakutty, 'Origin of the Samanta Caste in Kerala', *Proceedings of the Indian History Congress*, 41st Session (Bombay, 1980), pp. 86–92. In Bengal and Orissa, *sāmanta*, *mahāpātra*, *paṭṭanāyaka* and so on are related to caste position.

114 R. Inden, 'Hierarchies of Kings . . .'.

115 For example, a record of 1151 from Tumkur district, *Epigraphia Carnatica*, 12, Tm. 9: the range is between *Pañcamahāśabda mahāsāmanta* and *nāyaka*.

116 Cf. the article by D. Shukla, 'The Trend of Demotion of Feudal Families in the Early Medieval Indian Complex', *Proceedings of the Indian History Congress*, 41st Session (Bombay, 1980), pp. 177–83.

117 Derrett, p. 179.

in return for services as a means of displacing locally entrenched lineage power or diversification of the composition of ruling elites by drawing in non-ruling groups in the system of ranking[118] could only create new loci of power. Crisis was thus built into the process of the formation of the structures; a concrete statement of the crisis as it manifested itself in individual cases is a detail which has still to be satisfactorily worked out.

VI

Before concluding, I wish to reiterate what I said in the beginning: what has been presented is essentially a statement of my groping for a framework for the study of early medieval polity. I have said that the genesis of the specific features of early medieval polity cannot be satisfactorily comprehended either by isolating a single unit and analysing the relationship of its segments in ritual terms or by the notion of decentralized polity in which bases of power are created from above through individual or institutional agents. If we take an all-India perspective, the shifting political geography of the lineages of the period seems, on the other hand, to suggest that the structure of early medieval polity was a logical development from the territorially limited state society of the early historical period to a gradual but far greater penetration of the state society into local agrarian and peripheral levels, generating continuous fissions at such levels. The feudatory and other intermediary strata in the early medieval structures of polity, in the absence of a definite correlation between service assignments and the formation of these strata, may thus be seen in terms of an 'integrative polity',[119] with potential sources of tension built into the structures. The early medieval phase of polity was perhaps in a way an intermediate phase—a prelude to the exercise of greater control by the medieval state through its nobility and its regulated system of service assignments, but then if the broad-spectrum *sāmanta* category was a

[118] For examples of big merchants and merchant families being elevated to the ranks of *daṇḍa-pati, daṇḍādhipati* and even *nṛpati* with appropriate insignias, see V.K. Jain, pp. 323ff.

[119] H. Kulke ('Fragmentation and Segmentation Versus Integration? Reflections on the Concepts of Indian Feudalism and the Segmentary State in Indian History', *Studies in History*, vol. 4, no. 2 (1982), pp. 236–7), also speaks of integration at the regional level but generally avoids discussing the political mechanism of integration.

dominant element in early medieval polity, so did the broad-spectrum category of 'zamindars' continue as an 'irritant' in the medieval state structure.[120]

All this, at the moment, is essentially a hypothesis, but I venture to place the hypothesis before you because of my conviction that historical studies progress through sharing, though not necessarily through consensus, and that history is not only a continuous dialogue between historians and their material from the past but is also an equally continuous dialogue between historians themselves.

120 I. Habib, *The Agrarian System of Mughal India* (Asia Publishing House, 1963), ch. 5; idem, 'The Peasant in Indian History', General President's Address, Indian History Congress, 43rd Session (Kurukshetra, 1982); S. Nurul Hasan, 'Zamindars Under the Mughals' in R.E. Frykenberg (ed.), pp. 17–32; also A.R. Khan, *Chieftains in the Mughal Empire During the Reign of Akbar* (Simla, 1977), Introduction.

Chapter Seven

The Early and the Imperial Kingdom: A Processural Model of Integrative State Formation in Early Medieval India*

HERMANN KULKE

I

After the decline of the Gupta Empire and of the 'transient' successor state under King Harṣa in the early seventh century, the overwhelming majority of the early medieval states of India emerged from a process of continuous agrarian expansion and political integration. Since the middle of the first millennium AD this development took place mainly in those areas of the South Asian subcontinent which had lain at the periphery or even outside the core areas of ancient state formation. This process started from local nuclei of early socio-economic and political development and increasingly came to include their hinterlands.

Generally speaking this process of integrative state formation in early medieval India pertained to three concentrically connected geographical areas and accordingly went through three chronologically distinct stages of state development. These geographical zones were (i) the local nuclear area from which the political development issued, (ii) its surrounding peripheral zones and (iii) beyond these peripheral zones the nuclear areas of (originally) independent 'neighbours' (*sāmanta*). These three spatial

* I am indebted to Dr Pamela Price for her considerable help to improve the English translation of my paper originally written in German. I am particularly grateful for her valuable comments and for suggesting 'processural model' as a subtitle of this paper. The original German version began with a lengthy introduction into existing theories of state formation in early medieval India. This portion has been partly incorporated into the above Introduction which therefore, in a way , has to be regardrd as a companion paper of the present one.

zones found their chronological dimension in three successive stages of state formation which may be termed as chiefdom, early kingdom and imperial kingdom.[1] In Sanskrit terminology this process would somewhat correspond with the evolution from 'king' (*rājā*) to 'great king' (*mahārāja*) and 'supreme king of great kings' (*mahārāja-adhirāja*). Four factors will receive special attention: (i) the foundation and extension of chiefly power within a nuclear area, (ii) the emergence of the early kingdom through a stepwise penetration into, and integration of, the peripheral zones and, to a lesser extent, of the neighbouring nuclear areas respectively, (iii) the emergence of the imperial kingdom with a considerably enlarged core region, consisting of the original dynastic nuclear area and its conquered and integrated hinterland and (iv) processes of integration during these three stages of state formation with particular references to aspects of 'ritual policy'.

The following delineations emphasize aspects of a continuous and multifarious process of state formation rather than static structural features of the state and its society. The conceptual model of integrative state formation which emerges from an analysis of the dynamics of these interdependent socio-economic, political and cultural processes is a model which may be called processural. It stresses diachromic development and change rather than synchronic structures and their static nature. For analytical purposes, however, it operates with the heuristical tool of three successive stages of *state formation*. This combined method of historical and structural analysis may give a wrong impression of the existence of three successive stages of distinct *states* or even social formations. This however apparently was not the case although distinct traits of structural changes *within* the early medieval state are clearly discernible.

II

For centuries, the local nuclear areas of future early medieval kingdoms had been under Hindu and, at least right into the Gupta period, at times also under Buddhist influence, or had indirect contact (e.g. through trade) with remote centres of higher state and cultural development. In the first

[1] See also H. Kulke, 'The Early and the Imperial Kingdom in Southeast Asian History', in idem, *Kings and Cults. State Formation and Legitimation in India and Southeast Asia* (New Delhi, 1993), pp. 262–93.

centuries of the first millennium AD the Śātavāhana kingdom played for Central India as significant a role as the tribal principalities and early kingdoms of the Sangam period in South India during periods of marked Hinduization. For the further development of the whole of India, then, the Gupta empire was of immense significance: although its political influence extended only temporarily beyond the Vindhya mountains, its culture radiated perceptibly into the distant South India as well as into South East Asia. But it was characteristic of the further early medieval development of the post-Gupta period that the vast majority of the early medieval kingdoms did not arise from the centres of the Gupta empire or from its provincial capitals. They arose rather in their autonomous peripheral hinterland and in intermediate regions which had not yet been conquered, but which had already come under a wide range of influences of the Gupta empire. These were therefore regions in which local princes had the chance to establish their local rule under the influence (or better, on the model) of more advanced forms of economic and political development and to consolidate it undisturbed over many generations. Initially, wandering Brahmins might have offered their 'higher' knowledge to the chiefs of these local nuclear areas in the hinterland of the earlier kingdoms. However, it may have been the local chiefs themselves who far more frequently invited the Brahmins 'deliberately' as the most highly qualified 'development specialists' at that time.

It is of the greatest importance for the process of early medieval state formation that these developments usually originated from inside local nuclear areas and evolved further from here in concentric radiation. This development was only seldom thrust forcibly from outside, as for example through conquest by neighbouring kingdoms. However, even in the few cases in which an emigration or conquest is assumed (e.g. Pallavas), usually several generations elapsed before these new dynasties had consolidated their rule within a conquered nuclear area to such an extent that they could make their influence prevail beyond their peripheral regions or into external regions.

Let us have a look at the local nuclear regions which form the nuclei of incipient state formation. So far, scarcely any systematic investigation of the origin and early history of these nuclear areas exists.[2] Their

[2] For South India, see C. Maloney, 'Archaeology in South India: Accomplishments and Prospects', in B. Stein, *Essays on South India* (Honolulu, 1975), pp. 1–40; N. Dirks,

topography and their early history, however, make it clear that they lay mostly in the ecologically favourable riverine landscapes, for example those of the entire east coast with its numerous rivers, which enabled agrarian extension through paddy cultivation and, thereby, led to an increase in population.[3] Another factor of their early development was the occasional participation in early inter-regional trade. This appears to apply in particular to the early local nuclear areas in the western highland of the Deccan, of which some lay strung like pearls in a chain on the 'southern path' (*dakṣiṇāpatha*) which formed a north-south axis since Mauryan times. The upsurge of nuclear areas lying near the eastern coast of the lower courses of the rivers of South India, too, seems to have been influenced by international sea trade.[4] All these variables indicate that the economic factor played a considerable if not a decisive role in the early development of the local nuclear areas. This development may have led to a professional differentiation and—strengthened by Hindu influence—to a nascent social stratification. However, this process of social differentiation might have been considerably slower than is often presumed. Even when in inscriptions of this period the adherence to the *varṇa* system is mentioned, there is no justification in most of the cases for inferring the existence of all four varna castes. The terms Śūdras and Vaiśyas and names of the real *jāti* castes appeared in epigraphical documents only centuries later.

For early medieval India it is not yet possible to answer the question,

'Political Authority and Change in Early South Indian History', in *IESHR*, XIII, 1976, pp. 125–57; S.D.S. Senaviratne, 'Kalinga and Andhra: The Process of Secondary State Formation in Early India', in *Indian Historical Review*, 7, 1980, pp. 54–69; B. Stein, *Peasant State and Society in Medieval South India* (Delhi, 1980), pp. 90ff; G. Berkemer, *Little Kingdoms in Kalinga. Ideologie, Legitimation und Politik regionaler Eliten* (Stuttgart, 1993), pp. 83–152.

3 An almost ideally typical description of the expansion of such a 'nuclear area' is contained, for example, in the Prithu legend in the Viṣṇupurāna: 'Prithu accordingly uprooted the mountains. Before his time there were no defined boundaries of villages or towns, upon the irregular surface of the earth there was no cultivation, no highway for merchants: all these originated in the reign of Prithu. Where the ground was made level, the king induced his subjects to take up their abode. Before his time, also the fruits and roots which constituted the food of the people were procured with great difficulty . . . Thence proceeded all kinds of corn and vegetables upon which people subsist now and perpetually.' *The Vishnupurana*, translated by H.H. Wilson (London, 1840), pp. 86ff. (I, 13, 81ff).

4 C. Maloney, p.19.

heatedly discussed by sociologists and anthropologists, as to whether these economic and social factors led to new political formations in order to protect class privileges,[5] or whether classes represent only sequels of preceding political developments.[6] So far scarcely any separate investigation in these matters exists. But what matters more is that the first inscriptions from these nuclear areas originate in a period in which these developments had already progressed considerably and therefore permit only very limited *a posteriori* conclusions for earlier periods. In spite of this uncertainty, many things point to the fact that the founding of local rule was far more frequently the result of a physical coercion, e.g. of the eldest tribal prince of a clan or—in exceptional cases—of a conqueror, rather than the result of a voluntary agreement of the people (or more likely, the elite) as is traditionally maintained by Hindu *śāstra* texts and the Buddhist theory of the origin of the state.[7] Furthermore it can be inferred from the epigraphical evidence that in most cases this decisive political change in the early history of the local nuclear areas coincided with the migration of the Brahmins settled in the immediate neighbourhood of the new seat of power who were invited to do so. They were not only highly qualified ritual specialists, but also, by virtue of their monopolistic access to the *śāstra* texts, had a command of a considerable body of knowledge on state administration and political economy.

Most important appears to have been the legitimizing function of the Brahmins during this early phase of local political development. For, the material reproduction of this new form of political authority demanded—as is widely agreed—a continuously increased appropriation of socially produced surplus which required new forms of religio-political legitimation. Creating such legitimation was pre-eminently the task incumbent on an invited Brahmin.[8] Raising the status of the new rulers was a most

[5] M.H. Fried, *Evolution of Political Society* (New York, 1967).

[6] E.R. Service, *Origins of the State and Civilization: The Process of Cultural Evolution* (New York, 1975).

[7] On Gopāla, the founder of the Pāla dynasty, it is reported in the Khalimpur inscription of his son Dharmapāla that he had been elected by the 'people' (*prakṛti*) in order to put an end to 'the law of the fishes' (*matsya-nyāya*). R.C. Majumdar, *The History of Bengal*, 1971, p. 97, presumes quite probably with justification that this election was made by the 'leading chiefs'. However, whether it is possible then to speak of a 'bloodless revolution which both in its spirit and subsequent results reminds us of what happened in Japan about 1870 AD' (ibid.) is questionable.

[8] Probably Max Weber was the first to emphasize this important legitimizing role of

urgent necessity in order to legitimize the claim to a regular system of imposts and, later, revenues. This happened in different ways. One way was for the Brahmins to create genealogies which traced the origin of the new local ruling 'dynasty' (*vaṃśa*) back to a mythical progenitor of remote epic antiquity or even directly to a god.[9] Further, Brahmins vested the new rulers with the paraphernalia of Hindu royalty. To these belonged, for example, the obligatory royal umbrella (*chattra*) and the construction of the first Hindu temples. Even if these temples or shrines were initially insignificant edifices, inside of them the Brahmins held sway over a cult which differed impressively from local village and tribal cults.[10] This new Hindu cult comprised, on the one hand, a *regular* sequence of daily rites and was directed, on the other hand, to a permanently 'present' god who was worshipped either in the form of an *anthropomorphic* divine idol or as a Śaivite liṅgam.[11] This god, who was always present and visible, required also regular offerings. In contrast, the local tribal deities manifested themselves just now and then in their non-iconic symbols or in a priestly medium and received offerings only on these definite occasions. This comparison between the Hindu temple cults and the cults of the autochthonous local deities of the nuclear areas might have induced the people of the early nuclear areas to also draw comparisons between the status of their earlier tribal chiefs and that of a new Hindu rājā. In the basically egalitarian tribal societies the chiefs could assume a more elevated position only temporarily and in certain functions (as for example while waging war). Only in this functional position could they expect some regular presentations and services from people outside their own clan (villages?). The Hindu rājā claimed an altogether different position. In

---

the Brahmins: See H. Kulke, 'Max Weber's Contribution to the Study of "Hinduization" in India and "Indianization" in Southeast Asia', in H. Kulke, 1993, pp. 240–61.

9 See R. Thapar, 'Origin, Myths and the Early Indian Historical Tradition', in idem, *Ancient Indian Social History. Some Interpretations* (New Delhi, 1978), pp. 294–325; N. Dirks, 'The Past of a Pālaiyakārar: The Ethnohistory of a South Indian Little King', in *JAS*, 41, 1982, pp. 655–83; S. Sinha 'State Formation and Rajput Myth in Tribal Central India', in the present volume.

10 A. Eschmann, 'Hinduization of Tribal Deities in Orissa', in *The Cult of Jagannath and the Regional Tradition of Orissa*, ed. by A. Eschmann, H. Kulke, G.C. Tripathi (Delhi, 1978), pp. 79–97.

11 Often an anthropomorphic image is put in front of the original aniconic idol. For further details, see H. Kulke, 'Tribal Deities at Princely Courts: The Feudatory Rājās of Central Orissa and their Tutelary Deities (iṣṭadevatās)', in H. Kulke, 1993, pp. 114–36.

the Brahminical theory of society he occupied an elevated rank which towered above that of his former tribal brethren. In this new 'representation' he demanded regular tributes—as the ever present 'new' Hindu god in the temple nearby demanded worship continuously. This kind of legitimation was successful not only in India for transforming voluntary offerings into the demand for regular levies!

However, with all these new forms of legitimization of Hindu royalty, in no way was only the status of the rājā and his 'dynasty' elevated. An exclusive elevation of the ruling family might have led to the reverse of the stabilization of rule and could have instigated rebellions leading to the fall of the 'newly rich' parvenu. Therefore the inhabitants of the nuclear area or at least the privileged groups participated in the 'elevation' of their new ruler. Thus the origin of a clan as a whole was directly associated with the mythical 'history' of a rājā, by, for example, claiming that the entire clan was one of the 'lost tribes' of the epic times of the Mahābhārata. Still more important and effective in the long run was the 'royal' promotion of autochthonous local and tribal cults, since such a promotion involved concrete social advantages for those concerned. Of particular importance in this connection was the Great Goddess who was equally feared and venerated for her power (*śakti*) by the local population. Usually no temples were set up to these tribal gods in the early phase of the local evolution of power. But their tribal priests were invited on certain occasions to the court where their deity then manifested itself through the medium of one of its priests. Or the deity would be carried along to the royal court by the tribal priests in a holy object into which the deity had already 'entered' at its place of origin, as for example in Orissa in a long bamboo stick (*khila muṇḍa*).[12] During their presence at court, the tribal priests and their deity were hosted by the king and rewarded with gifts. The king and his *rājaguru* also made a visit to the deity in its place of origin on the occasion of religious festivals. An important characteristic of the courtly cults of these early local nuclear areas was thus the incorporation of mighty local cults and the (temporary) integration of their non-Brahmin priests into the courtly circle.

The major aim of this integration of local cults into the courtly cult was to create a 'vertical legitimization' in order to legitimize the new rule

[12] See H. Kulke, 'Legitimation and Townplanning in the Feudatory States of Orissa', in H. Kulke, 1993, pp. 93–113 and B. Schnepel, 1995.

within the nuclear area and its people. The Hindu temple at the court, the creation of Kṣatriya genealogy, and other symbols of Hindu kingship also served, on the other hand, the purpose of 'horizontal legitimization'. It aimed at equating the status of the 'new' rājā and his dynasty (*rāja-vaṃśa*, which originally implied 'lineage of the rājā') with that of the neighbouring princes and Hindu rājās. The task of the court Brahmins consisted mainly in uniting these different areas and functions of the courtly cult into a system which would be comprehensible even to the non-Brahmin inhabitants of the nuclear area. This task brought about integration in two respects: on the one hand, the integration of local cults, in the manner described, into the courtly cult and on the other hand the integration of this courtly cult into the sacral Hindu topography of the near and far precincts of the nuclear area.[13]

As mentioned above, we have little evidence about socio-economic causes and the impact of this early political development on the local population. It appears to be doubtful that the Brahmins and their privileged position as landowners and court officials had already at this early stage a significant influence on the social structure of the local population, as postulated by the concept of Indian feudalism. However, it is very likely that their settlement had a direct impact on the agrarian extension. As these Brahmins depended solely on the agrarian surplus produced by their 'villages', at least some of them would have tried to increase this surplus through an improvement in agricultural methods, particularly through irrigation and rice production. But the rulers of these chiefdoms and early kingdoms, too, are known to have improved the irrigation system of their nuclear areas. The Cōḷa ruler Karikala of the Śaṅgam age was praised for his irrigation work in the Kaveri valley and the inscriptions of the early eastern Gaṅgas of Kalinga provide ample evidence of 'royal' initiative in local irrigation works.[14] Another important consequence of

[13] J. Rösel, 'Sakralstädte als Kristallisatoren regionaler Tradition—das Beispiel der indischen Tempel-und Pilgerstadt Puri', in *Regionale Tradition in Südasien*, H. Kulke and D. Rothermund (eds), (Wiesbaden, 1985), pp. 149–70.

[14] Thus the inscriptions of Indravarman of Kalinganagara of the late sixth century mention a *rājataṭāka* and a *kṣatriyataṭāka* (tank) and interesting details about sluices (*taṭāka-udara-bandha*), water regulations, etc. (*Inscriptions of Orissa*, vol. II, S.N. Rajaguru (ed.), [Bhubaneswar, 1960], pp. 24ff). For Rajasthan see B.D. Chattopadhyaya, 'Irrigation in Early Medieval Rajasthan', in idem, *The Making of Early Medieval India* (New Delhi, OUP, 1994), pp. 57–88.

the increasing number of settled Brahmins in the newly developing nuclear areas must have been the opening up of new channels of translocal communication and trade. All these factors may have had a stronger influence on the social differentiation and incipient social stratification of the rural population than the mere settlement of Brahmins.

The most important characteristic of the early development of the state was thus the founding as well as the consolidation and legitimization of political authority *within* the local nuclear area. In contrast to this, the relations with the peripheral zones and the still remoter neighbouring areas played only a subordinate role. What was certainly of importance in this respect was the increase in the barter and trade relations with the peripheral zone of the nuclear area. This barter trade may have taken place in those times in the same way in which it can still be observed in the weekly markets, for example, in Orissa at the outskirts of tribal areas. Further, it is also probable that even in this early period, tribal warriors were occasionally recruited in the peripheral zones for the troops of the local nuclear area. In those cases in which the local rājā himself came from one of the tribes of the area, his rule was based to a large extent on institutionalized relations with this tribe.[15] Common campaigns and division of the booty may then likewise have been normal, as the already mentioned integration of the tribal cults in the courtly cult of the nuclear area. Of particular relevance in these cases were the ritual privileges of these tribes during the coronation of the rājās and during the annual festivities as, for instance, in later centuries during Durgāpūjā. But everything points to the fact that even if a tribal chief rose to the status of a Hindu rājā of a local nuclear area, the tribes of the peripheral zones endeavoured to preserve their independence.

The relations with the nuclear areas of neighbouring princes, often separated by extensive forests, created no problems in this early phase. They were mainly limited to marriage relations and sporadic campaigns, which however remained in this early period without any significant long-term consequences. Permanent subjugation and annexation after a military victory were still scarcely conceivable. Considering the power potential at the disposal of the early local principalities, the neighbouring seats of the rulers were still far beyond their sphere of permanent political control.

15 A good example is provided by Keonjhar in North Orissa and its relations with the tribe of the Hill Bhuiyas; see S.C. Roy, *The Hill Bhuiyas of Orissa* (Ranchi, 1935). For south Orissa, see B. Schnepel 1992.

III

This situation was to change appreciably only in the second phase of state formation in early medieval India—with the emergence of the early kingdoms. The important characteristics of this second phase of the development of the state are: (i) intensification of political control through hierarchization in the nuclear area, (ii) its (at least partial) extension to peripheral zones and (iii) the attempted enforcement of conditions of tributary dependence on the neighbouring chiefs and rājās.

With the emergence of the early kingdoms there began the fight—proverbial in India—following the 'law of the fishes' (*matsya-nyāya*): the big fish swallows the small one. The question of which local nuclear area would attain success in this fight, when the risky 'war of elimination' for 'trans-local' hegemony began, depended in this incipient phase of development certainly to a large extent on the charisma of the rājā and the abilities of his advisers. However, sustaining for several generations a hegemony—and thereby the founding of a dynasty—came to be based then entirely on the powers and economic resources of the original nuclear area. The latter continued to remain the major, if not the sole, basis for the new regional power.

Since in the preceding period of local rule the entire nuclear area had in no way been under direct control in its full geographical extent, it must have been the urgent concern of the ruler who had been able to upgrade his position to that of a 'great king' (*mahārāja*) to subjugate his original nuclear area as far as possible to his central and direct rule. Here, at least, the claim of the monopoly of legitimate and uncontested physical power and more or less direct revenue collection had to be established and—even though mostly in a protracted process—successfully implemented. The inscriptions of this period show that the 'great kings' of these early kingdoms were obviously zealously engaged in creating hierarchically graded administrative levels from a 'provincial' administration of districts down to the village and in associating these levels with a hierarchy of administrative powers and officials. Even if the ideal prescribed in the *śāstra* texts and repeated in the inscriptions was only rarely realized even within the nuclear area, there can be no doubt that the efforts to translate this ideal into reality contributed considerably to the extension of royal authority within the extended nuclear areas.

The astonishingly large number of land gifts to Brahmins was another striking characteristic of these early kingdoms. While in the early phase of the development of the nuclear area mostly individual Brahmins were settled in the immediate neighbourhood of the seat of the ruler, mahārājas now bequeathed entire villages (*agrahāra* or *brahmadeya*) in the whole nuclear area to increasingly larger groups of Brahmins.[16] However, the lavish conferment of immunities and privileges did not necessarily lead to a loss of these privileges by the king, as presumed by the adherents of the 'school of Indian feudalism'. Rather the exact opposite may have happened—at least at the period of the endowment. The copper-plate inscriptions mention in great detail and in a standardized manner the future rights of the Brahmins. What is perhaps most important in this context: the levies devolving on them were, probably for the first time, by means of these gift deeds unified norms of royal dominion proclaimed for the whole nuclear area. In fact the king may have transferred privileges which he himself was not yet in a position to enjoy fully in the areas where the endowments were made. Most significant in this connection is that every donation of land to Brahmins and the public proclamation of its legal conditions and implications for the villagers can be equated with the setting up of legal norms for the whole environs of the Brahmin villages. By enmeshing the entire nuclear area in a net of such privileged Brahmin settlements with standardized rights with regard to the taxes and services on the part of the local inhabitants, obligatory standards were—most likely for the first time—created also for those 'royal' areas which were not under the levying power and administration of the Brahmins. Moreover, the kings unequivocally handed over the power to implement these 'manorial' claims in these Brahmin villages to the Brahmin donees, for in all endowment inscriptions entry into the donated land was forbidden for royal administrative officials. Thus, it devolved upon the Brahmins the difficult task not only to create validity for the 'royal' rights transferred to them, but also to develop a village-level administration necessary for the implementation of these demands. Further, the judicial power to punish dilatoriness on the part of the village population was conferred upon the Brahmins. In a pre-modern state, police or even military means could have been scarcely more effective than this form of intensification of royal authority by means of a group of loyal Brahmins

16 It was mainly R.S. Sharma's contribution (*Indian Feudalism*, 1965) which has explained this change in the land policy of Indian kingdoms.

whose existence depended on their implementation of the *rājadharma*. In the long run of course, these Brahmin villages deprived (in the sense of 'Indian feudalism') the state of the administrative hold on the land and people and certainly became (in the sense of the 'segmentary state') part of the constellation of local power. However, persistence in exercising their own 'royal' privileges, existentially necessary for the Brahmins, continued to strengthen those of the king, too. Brahmin settlements were and remained, therefore, in this sense foremost pillars of the normative order of Hindu kingdoms and, one should add, inexpensive and efficient ones.[17]

The extension of royal authority in the extended nuclear area was accompanied by an intensification of the royal presence within the nuclear area itself, so that one can speak for the first time of the capitals of these kingdoms. This development was promoted as much by the extension of the residential area of the expanding court as by the intensification of craft and trade within the nuclear area. As a basically new element of town-planning, there appears in this period the building of new, bigger temples which were erected throughout Central and South India, for the first time built of stone. In certain cases—as for example, with the Pallavas of Kanchipuram, the Cālukyas of Aihole/Badami and in Orissa—a definite synchronism can be ascertained between the emergence of the early kingdoms in the late sixth century AD and the first appearance of free-standing sacral Hindu stone architecture. Quite a number of early capitals may have increasingly become sacral centres too with the settlement of new groups of temple priests and the celebration of temple festivals. The latter were 'public' in contrast to the early royal Vedic sacrifices and their influence on the hinterland also increased correspondingly. This over-all temple development was further strengthened by the fact that, with the central power's penetration of the nuclear area and its peripheral zones, autochthonous cults met with growing royal patronage. Some of these cults of mighty local gods were elevated in the course of the development to the status of dynastic family divinities (*kuladevatā*). Thus, in the phase of the early medieval kingdoms too the integration of local autochthonous cults formed an important characteristic of the courtly cults. This trend received a strong impetus from the bhakti cults which were spreading

17 For a more detailed study see H. Kulke, 'Some Observations on the Political Functions of the Copper-Plate Grants in Early Medieval India' in B. Kölver (ed.), *The State, the Law, and Administration in Classical India* (Munich, 1977), pp. 237–43.

from South India in these centuries and by means of which the local gods acquired the dignity of being manifestations of the great Hindu divinities. This process was repeated in various respects by the rise of local princes as manifestations of great Hindu rājās.

IV

In addition to the systematic extension of royal power within the entire nuclear area, there emerged in the second phase closer relations between the 'centre' and the peripheral zones and neighbouring areas. The relations of the central nuclear area with its peripheral zones were determined by their geographical conditions and their inhabitants. These regions were often covered by the thick jungles and chains of hills which surrounded the riverine landscape of the nuclear area. These were usually occupied by tribes who were frequently feared for militancy.[18] Thus, these areas, which often barrier-like encircled the early local nuclear areas, remained 'excluded' for centuries from the development of the nuclear areas in the river valleys. In the thirteenth rock edict Aśoka referred to the 'forest dwellers' (*aṭavī*) who allegedly lived within his empire, and Samudragupta too in his famous Allahabad inscription proudly claimed that he 'had made all kings of the forest kingdoms [his] vassals' (*paricārakīkṛta-sarva-āṭavika-rājasya*).[19] However, both inscriptions indicate that the 'forest dwellers' of these two mighty empires of Indian antiquity had preserved their nearly unlimited autonomy. In the sixth century AD several kings in Central India and Orissa also identified 'forest kingdoms' (*āṭavi-rājya*) as a part of their kingdoms[20] which lay obviously in the peripheral zones of their nuclear areas. Even in these cases, however, we may legitimately doubt whether these 'forest kingdoms' were subjected to the actual control of the respective early kingdoms. But it is significant that the

[18] For the theory of the five landscapes (*tiṇai*) in early Tamil Literature and their socio-economic and cultural relevance; see G.D. Sontheimer, *Pastoral Deities in Western India* (New York, 1989).

[19] Allahabad inscription of Samudragupta, line 21, in D.C. Sircar, *Select Inscriptions*, vol. I (Calcutta, 1965) p. 265.

[20] Koh inscription of Saṁkshobha from the year AD 529, verse 8, in ibid., p. 395 and Kanas inscription of Lokavigraha's from the year AD 599, in E.I., vol. 28, p. 329.

references to tribal principalities emerged around 600 AD just in that period when the evolution of states in these areas entered the second phase and the expanding royal power of the nuclear areas advanced for the first time to the peripheral zones.

There may have been mainly two causes for expansion into the peripheral zones. Firstly, these zones formed the hinterland for the expanding population of the nuclear area which required arable land for the increase of area under cultivation. Secondly, it was through these peripheral zones that the lines of communication with the outside world passed, particularly with the *sāmantas,* the 'neighbours' and future tributary princes. Gaining new areas for agrarian extension and securing lines of communication[21] might therefore have been important objectives for the population and the rājās of the nuclear areas. However, the penetration of the peripheral zones was quite a laborious process. At first it took place mainly in the immediate neighbouring regions of the nuclear areas and in 'outposts' which lay inside the peripheral zones in the valleys of tributary rivers and on transit roads. The extension of cultivable area was certainly not always peaceful and was carried out mainly by the peasants of the adjacent neighbourhood who were concerned with the extension of their economic basis. This effort was promoted by means of *temporary* tax concessions which, as we know from many *śāstra* texts, new settlers obtained. The settlers were followed by Brahmins. The privileges granted to them on a *long term* basis played a similar role in the establishing of administrative institutions as has been described above for the nuclear areas.

While an expansion of the nuclear area took place by stages in the regions which lay in the immediate neighbourhood of the riverine landscapes, development in the 'outposts' may have proceeded differently. Here winning new land for cultivation through settlers from the nuclear area was not as important as gaining settlements of traders in the area around already existing seats of power of the tribal leaders. Sooner or later Brahmins certainly followed them, too. But at least in the early period of this development they may have been invited by these tribal chiefs themselves, rather than having been sent out by the kings of the nuclear area. Even when the king of the nuclear area was mentioned in the documents

[21] e.g. an inscription of Indravarman of the Gaṅga dynasty of Kaliṅga mentions in the late sixth century a 'royal road' (*rājamārga*), E.I., vol. XXV, pp. 194–8.

of land grants, they may have represented in this case the subsequent sanctioning of local *fait accompli* rather than an act of direct royal control.[22] However, it would be wrong even in these cases to belittle the long-term results of such land grants to Brahmins. In the tribal area as well they led to the formation of administrative institutions previously unknown to the tribes. The spreading of these administrative forms was of use to the tribal chief in equal measure as it was to the king of the nuclear area. It may have been the gradual development of these seats of local tribal chiefs, under the influence of the nuclear areas, which was entered as *āṭavika-rājya* in the inscriptions around 600 AD. Some of these tribal princes found themselves similarly involved in the process of Hinduization and rose to become tributary princes (*sāmanta*) in the course of further development, while others in their turn could preserve their autonomy for centuries right up to the threshold of the third, the imperial phase.

V

Beyond the peripheral zones the 'neighbours' (*sāmanta*) ruled over their own nuclear areas. The expression *sāmanta* (from *samanta* 'all around', 'adjacent') referred at first to the *independent* neighbours, as for example in Asoka's second rock edict to the Cōḷas, Pāṇḍyas, Satiyaputras and Keralaputras in the distant, unconquered South. However, a significant change of meaning took place in the course of the following centuries, when, in the seventh century at the latest, the expression *sāmanta* had become generally prevalent as the title for 'neighbouring tributary princes'.[23] The institution of tributary princes were certainly as old in India as the known history of the sub-continent. But it was new that *neighbours* were simply identified with *tributary princes* in the period of the early medieval kingdoms. This semantic change implied that for the rulers of a nuclear area, at least theoretically, there were no longer independent neighbours—only

[22] This interpretation follows B. Stein's concept of 'ritual sovereignty' of the central king. (B. Stein, 'The Segmentary State in South Indian History', in R.G. Fox (ed.), *Realm and Region in Traditional India* (Durham, 1977), pp. 3–51.

[23] L. Gopal, 'Sāmanta—Its Varying Significance in Ancient India', in *Journal of the Royal Asiatic Society*, 5, 1963, 21–37. For further studies on the role of the *sāmantas* in early medieval India see the above Introduction.

independent nuclear areas could exist beyond these subjugated neighbours. Thus the rājās of the nuclear areas were confronted with the choice of either conquering their immediate neighbours or themselves becoming a *sāmanta* tributary prince of a mighty neighbour. Exactly this development set in in the second phase of early medieval state formation. Such a politico-military struggle of subjugation is certainly nothing unusual. But it is characteristic for India that this development led to a new political institution, the *sāmantacakra.* The 'circle of tributary princes' who surrounded the kingdom became an established part of the early medieval kingdoms and their ideology. No true kingdom could exist without a circle of illustrious tributary princes, for only the brilliant ornaments on their heads let the Mahārāja shine in his entire greatness—a favourite theme in the *praśasti* panegyrics of the inscriptions. The Sāmantas were once again installed in their allodial rule after their subjugation, but they had to pledge themselves to the payment of a (rather nominal) tribute (*kara-dā*), to a participation in the royal assemblies and to the donation of damsels (*kanyā-dāna*) to the royal harem.[24]

These sāmantas were a product of the genesis of the medieval kingdoms of India as their institution influenced permanently the structure of these kingdoms. For, the early kings of the nuclear areas were, in spite of increased revenues from their now extended nuclear areas, seldom capable of controlling directly their militarily overthrown 'neighbours' nor of replacing them by followers of their own court. An important reason for this weakness was the fact already mentioned that the opening up of the peripheral zones proceeded only very hesitantly and therefore a permanent control of all sāmantas beyond these peripheral zones often failed as a result of spatial-logistic problems. Thus the sāmantas continued to remain at first autonomous rājās in their own nuclear areas, they had their own centre of power and some of them also independently made land donations to Brahmins. However, they had to mention always in their inscriptions their mahārāja and 'overlord' and as the date of donation mostly his year of reign. If such a reference to the king of the central nuclear area is missing in an inscription and instead the sāmanta assumes royal titles (e.g. mahārāja), it always points to a weakening of the central power and frequently also to the attempt of the sāmanta to attain unrestricted independence or even to wrest for himself the supremacy over

24 These duties of the 'frontier kings' (*pratyantanṛpati*) are best depicted in Samudragupta's Allahabad inscription.

the *sāmantacakra.* In this period of early kingdoms Stein's assertion is certainly valid: that with increasing distance from the centre the chances of tributary princes entering into alliances with hostile neighbours also increased.[25]

The period of early kingdoms marked at the same time the peak of the power of the sāmantas. Their almost unbroken power in their own principalities was enhanced in this period still further by their increasing influence in the central royal court. Loyal princes of the *sāmantacakra* were appointed *mahāsāmantas* by the kings, they sent daughters to the royal harem and took over high offices at court. This power and high status enjoyed by the sāmantas could not remain without affecting the structure of the royal nuclear area. For, in the face of the rise of the sāmantas in the royal union, the status of the officials of the central administrative apparatus, as for example that of the provincial governors (*upārika*), declined increasingly. It could therefore be only a question of time till they also strove for the sāmanta title and looked upon their provinces more and more as their 'fief'.[26] Thus a 'sāmantaization' of the early kingdoms took place, which could be termed an 'Indian variant' of feudalism so far as the political structure is concerned. The origin of this development, however, is to be sought less in the decline of earlier empires than in a development 'from below' as once pointed out by D.D. Kosambi in a different context.[27]

The 'sāmantaizing' of the early medieval kingdoms certainly also led to a strengthening—and in many cases even to the founding—of new local centres of power. This structural development in the peripheral zones and in the sāmantacakra resulted also, in a very few cases, in a fragmentation of the central political power. But this development of new local centres was rather the consequence of a general growth of governmental institutions which was not restricted to the royal nuclear area. And it was this process of extension of the local basis of governmental institutions which created the political and also economic conditions for the rise of future regional empires. These future empires were built on the basis of already existing local centres of power, which—to a certain extent, if not

[25] B. Stein, 1977, p. 10.

[26] R.S. Sharma, p. 159.

[27] D.D. Kosambi, *An Introduction to the Study of Indian History* (Bombay, 1956), pp. 353ff.

even in their overwhelming majority—originated in the period of local autonomy from the sāmantacakras of the various early kingdoms.

It should further be mentioned that in the period of these early kingdoms there began for the first time in large parts of India a process which slowly led to the integration of 'scattered' local centres into considerably enlarged regional core regions, as far as various economic, cultural-religious, social and political matters were concerned. The centripetal forces which slowly emerged and which became more strongly effective in the future regional kingdom, created the basis for regional developments, the precursor of the present-day regional cultures and regionalism.

VI

The imperial kingdoms represent the third and final stage in the development of Hindu statehood before the founding of Islamic states in India and the rise of 'patrimonial-bureaucratic' states in late medieval India.[28] Among these imperial kingdoms of early medieval India the kingdoms of the Cōḷas, Rāṣṭrakūṭas, Cāḷukyas of Kalyāṇī and Pālas have to be mentioned, as well as Eastern Gaṅgas and later the Sūryavaṃśa Gajapatis in Orissa. An important characteristic of these states is that the establishment of their regional hegemony was often closely associated with significant ruler personalities. As examples could be mentioned King Dharmapāla of the Pālas, King Rājarāja and Rājendra of the Cōḷas and King Anantavarman Coḍagaṅga of the Gaṅgas of Orissa. All of them expanded, sometimes by several times, their original realms by means of successful campaigns. Nevertheless, even these empires were no new creations of warlords. They too emerged from a continuous process of integrative state formation which had its origin in the development of local centres of power. As earlier in the development from local chieftaincies to early kingdoms, the development to the imperial level was also characterized by a strong continuity of structural traits. Nevertheless, new factors and characteristics made their appearance, a few of which turned into distinct structural features in the course of the development.

28 See S.P. Blake, 'The Patrimonial-Bureaucratic Empire of the Mughals', in the present volume and the relevant portions of the above Introduction.

Among these structural features, which varied in their appearance in the imperial kingdoms, were:

1. A considerable extension of the directly controlled area by the union of two or several earlier nuclear areas or even early kingdoms and their intervening zones to a new 'core region'.
2. Shifting of the capital to the centre of this core region.
3. Expansion of the central administration within this enlarged core region.
4. Systematic enlargement of an apparatus of legitimation directed towards the imperial centre.
5. Increasing integration of the whole system.

A decisive new characteristic of the imperial kingdom was the considerable extension of the directly controlled area far beyond the 'natural' frontiers of the original nuclear areas of the early kingdoms. Since all the imperial kingdoms emerged from a violent dynastic change, certain similarities can be identified in the course of these imperial state formations.[29] In most of the cases, the dynasty of the old nuclear area (weakened by preceding battles) was overthrown by a powerful tributary prince who had already come to occupy a strong place in the central court. Examples of this are the overthrow of the Pallavas by the Cōḷas or that of the Cāḷukyas of Badami by the Rāṣṭrakūṭas and in turn their overthrow by the Cāḷukyas of Kalyāṇī. As opposed to this, the cases in which independent neighbouring princes conquered the weakened kingdoms 'from outside' are rare, occurring, for example, in Orissa in the overthrow of the Bhauma-Karas of central Orissa by the Somavaṃśīs of Dakṣina Kośala and later of the Somavaṃśīs by the Eastern Gaṅgas from southern Kaliṅga. Whether the dynasty was overthrown by a tributary prince or by a neighbouring king, in both cases this conquest, associated with dynastic change, usually led to the unification of at least two nuclear areas: one of the conqueror and the other of the conquered. The conqueror thus contributed his own

[29] Here also the Pālas appear to be an exception. The long list of the sāmantas who are mentioned in the Rāmacaritam and whose support King Rāmapāla could 'buy' in his fight against the Kaivartas only by giving huge presents, shows their unbroken power. The power of the Pālas in Bengal rested obviously not on a strong central area, but on a power balance within or above the allodial local princes, a balance which had to be constituted anew time and again. On the structure of the Pāla empire, see S. Bhattacharya, *Landschenkungen und politische Entwicklungen im frühmittelalterlichen Bengalen* (Wiesbaden, 1986).

nuclear area towards the founding of the new kingdom. While in the phase of the early kingdom the conquered 'neighbours' were mostly reconfirmed as sāmanta tributary princes in their largely autonomous rule, the conquered ruler of a neighbouring nuclear area met with an entirely different fate in the phase of imperial kingdoms.[30] For, in order to merge a conquered nuclear area permanently with that of the victor, the removal of the conquered dynasty from power was unavoidable. No doubt the descendants of overthrown dynasties sometimes succeeded after generations in temporarily reviving the ruling power of their ancestors.[31] However, from the fact that in most cases we hear nothing more about the overthrown dynasties, we may draw the conclusion that the loss of power would usually have been radical and complete.

A similar fate overtook most of the little autonomous principalities which had existed between these unified nuclear areas. Confronted now by imperial dynasties that had been considerably strengthened, their autonomy had a chance of survival only if the principalities lay in remote, rather inaccessible areas. But in contrast to the annexation of neighbouring kingdoms, the 'union' of these intermediary zones was not always accompanied by violence. Instead, the earlier peripheral zones and the large areas of the early sāmantacakra of the victorious dynasty usually underwent processes of intense integration. Important means of integration were further agrarian extension, inclusion into translocal trade networks and the spread of the 'state society'[32] of the dynastic core region. Tribals from the forests and mountain regions were increasingly recruited

[30] Thus the late Cāḷukyas of Kalyāni traced their lineage to the early Cāḷukyas of Badami. In contrast to the Pāndyas who continued to exist in their capital of Madurai even at the height of the Cōḷa power, the Pallavas appeared at first to have been completely destroyed by the Cōḷas and their capital Kanchipuram became the second capital of the Cōḷas. Nevertheless, Kopperuñjinga, who claimed to be a descendant of the Pallavas, succeeded temporarily in the early thirteenth century in taking prisoner the Cōḷa king, Rājarāja III, and conquering extensive parts of the Cōḷa empire, K.A.N. Sastri, *The Cōḷas*, 1955, pp. 422ff.

[31] Relations between the regional kingdoms and the tribes of the mountainous hinterland were not always smooth. There are several examples of the violent insurrections of tribes against Hindu mahārājas. It appears, for example, that at the end of the thirteenth century there was a regular invasion of Kaliṅga by the Śabara tribes living in the hills (vide *E.I.*, vol. VI, p. 260).

[32] This important term was introduced by B.D. Chattopadhyaya, 'Political Processes and the Structure of Polity in Early Medieval India' in the present volume; see also the above Introduction.

as troops of the empires. The means of communication through these former peripheral zones were further improved and sometimes secured by means of fortified garrisons. Beyond these peripheral zones, in the earlier sāmantacakrās, the process of the increasing erosion of allodial rule continued. It often started with marriage alliances with the central royal family and the rise of sāmantas to mahāsāmantas and generals at the court. But in contrast to similar developments in the preceding phase, this time the process often led to the replacement of the allodial rulers by members of the central dynasties or their courts. Thus from earlier tributary principalities of the sāmantacakra there gradually evolved provinces or districts of the extended core region of the imperial kingdom. A good example of this 'provincialization' is offered by the semantic change of the term *maṇḍala.* During the period of the early kingdoms in Orissa maṇḍala was always a term for an autonomous principality or the area of an allodial sāmanta prince. But in the period of the imperial kingdom of the Gaṅgas it came to indicate unequivocally a province of the imperial kingdom under a governor appointed by the central power.[33]

VII

After the setting up of an imperial kingdom by conquest, the annexation of neighbouring kingdoms and the initiation of the process of integration of intermediary zones, the new 'imperial dynasty' was soon confronted with the question of enlarging, shifting or re-establishing its capital. There were basically three alternatives: maintaining one's own old capital, taking over and expanding the conquered one, or founding a new capital. Examples of all three possibilities are known to us from medieval history. But in this respect too a clear difference is evident between the early kingdoms and their 'imperial' successors. The early kingdoms usually preserved their original capitals around which they then established their sāmantacakra. It was different in the case of the imperial kingdoms. With

[33] For Orissa, see S.K. Panda, *Herrschaft und Verwaltung im östlichen Indien unter den späten Gaṅgas (c. 1038–1434)* (Wiesbaden, 1986), pp. 60–86 and more recent idem, 'From Kingdom to Empire. A Study of the Medieval State of Orissa under the Later Eastern Gaṅgas, AD 1038–1434', in: *IHR*, 17, 1993, 149–60; for the Cōḷas, see Y. Subbarayalu, 'The Cōḷa State', in *Studies in History*. 4, 1982, 269–306 and J. Heitzman in the present volume.

the conquest and annexation of neighbouring kingdoms, the original ancestral land and its capital often lost its central position in the framework of the extended imperial kingdom. It was necessary to overcome this marginality by the founding of a new, more centrally situated capital. The Rāṣṭrakūṭas offer a good example. About a hundred years after their victory over the Cāḷukyas of Badami, in the middle of the eighth century, they founded a new capital in the centre of their new empire in Mānyakheta. It lay almost equidistant from Badami, the capital of the conquered Cāḷukyas in the south, and their own ancestral land in the north. The Eastern Gaṅgas also shifted their capital from Kalinganagara in southern Kalinga to the central deltaic region of Orissa in Cuttack after their victory over the Somavaṃśa dynasty of central Orissa in the early twelfth century. From the beginning of the thirteenth century they proudly called their new capital 'New Benares' (*Abhinava Vārāṇasī*).

The shifting of the capitals aimed, however, not only at the acquisition of a geometrically exact central location. Some cases show that this shifting of the capital was accompanied by the successive development of the state. The capitals of the Cōḷas offer a good example of this. During their early history up to the time of the Pallava hegemony (seventh and eighth centuries), when the Cōḷas were tributary princes, Uraiyur in the upper 'head' of the Kaveri delta was their capital. King Vijayālaya, the founder of the 'Imperial Cōḷas', shifted the capital in the late eighth century to Tanjore (Tanjāvūr) in the centre of the Kaveri delta area. This became the nuclear area of the Cōḷa empire in subsequent centuries. In the beginning of the eleventh century, King Rājendra however went even a step further and founded Gaṅgaikoṇḍacōḷapuram down the river as the new capital, as if, at the height of the policy of overseas expansion by the Cōḷas, he was striving to also bring the coastal area under the direct control of the capital. The shifting of the capital of the Gaṅgas after their conquest of central Orissa appears to have also aimed mainly at exchanging their small ancestral nuclear area at the lower course of the Vamsadhara river with the considerably larger deltaic area of the Mahanadi river, which became the centre of the new core region of the 'Imperial Gaṅgas'. The major intention of shifting the capital of a regional kingdom was the penetration into a larger, potentially richer nuclear area, bringing it under the direct control of the new 'imperial' dynasty, thus gaining a considerably larger hinterland of the new capital. The shifting or founding anew of the capitals of the imperial kingdoms was thus often directly connected with the creation of an extended core region and the attempt to control it directly.

VIII

These central areas of the imperial kingdoms were not, however, unified state territories, subjected exclusively to a central administration which was equally effective everywhere. Autonomous local administrative areas, which were only loosely connected with the central administration, continued to exist. Allodial principalities and tribal chiefdoms in remote forests and mountainous regions lay 'interspersed' in the extended core regions of the imperial kingdoms. Thus, in the final analysis, the concentric model of the processural state with its political authority decreasing in its outer 'rings' continued to apply also to the core region of the imperial kingdoms.[34] However, there were considerable differences here from the early kingdoms. First, it seems as if the court and its officers in all these states lived mainly on their own landed property and on benefices which might have been limited in time or heredity. This decentralized system of extracting socially-produced surplus had already existed in the nuclear areas of the early kingdoms. But the major difference between the early and the imperial kingdoms in this regard was the fact that the imperial court was able to extend this system into the annexed provinces of the enlarged core area. According to the growth of this core area and the centre's power of disposal, the number of courtiers and officers grew without changing the decentralized system as such. But the mere increase in the number of courtiers who obtained a living from 'their' villages in the countryside increased—directly or indirectly—the impact of the centre on its hinterland. There may indeed have been only little 'resource transfers of a political nature' from the more distant places of the core area to the centre. However, what was new was the dense network of mutual dependency which linked the centre and its enlarged core area to an hitherto unknown degree. Whereas the court of the early kingdom depended mainly on the resources of its direct hinterland, the whole enlarged core area of the imperial kingdom was linked with the centre by

[34] For the important issue of spatial differentiation of agrarian and political processes within the core region of south Indian kingdoms which was first raised by Y. Subbarayalu (1973) and B. Stein (1969, 1977), see the above Introduction.

a system of decentralized collection of duties and their redistribution. Second, the radius of these 'imperial power rings' had widened considerably, whereby the power potential of the inner circle, particularly at the capital seat of the ruler and its immediate surroundings, also increased correspondingly. Third, the degree of the decrease of central power could be reduced considerably in the outer regions of the central area. Or, in other words and expressed less 'theoretically': At the height of political authority of imperial kingdoms there existed in the rather far-extended core regions, in spite of still existing local autonomy, no potential putsch-leader and also no centrifugal tendencies with the goal of entering into alliances with a neighbouring kingdom. The unity of the imperial kingdom was not challenged any more for long periods.[35] Even a dynastic change (as for example that of the Rāṣṭrakūṭas to the Cāḷukyas of Kalyāṇī in the tenth century) implied only a geographical displacement or just an enlargement of the central core region through the inclusion of the homeland of the new dynasty.

The core regions were often surrounded by a quite amorphous conglomerate of autonomous polities (often 'successors' of the earlier sāmantas), allies and independent kingdoms which lay in the intermediary zone separating the next imperial kingdom. The differences in definition between tributary states and allies and independent kingdoms fluctuated continuously. The partial instability of the political system of the imperial kingdoms had its origin mainly in these geographical intermediate and peripheral zones. Incursions which could also have an effect on the stability of the central core region took place here through a change in alliances and through the striving for independence of dependent kingdoms. Most of the fights between imperial kingdoms therefore aimed at the control of these 'forefields'.

More extensive and detailed studies would be needed in order to arrive at comparative and sufficiently accurate conclusions about the function and effectiveness of the central administrative apparatus of the regional empires. For we are aware that questions about the structure of the central administration and revenue collection within the core region,

[35] Cf. on this also what O.W. Wolters says on the founding of the empire of Angkor in the year 802: 'Local independence was no longer the acceptable objection as it had been in the eighth century. The integrity of the Angkorian kingdom was no longer in question', O.W. Wolters, 'Jayavarman II's Military Power: The Territorial Foundation of the Angkorian Empire', in *Journal of the Royal Asiatic Society*, 1973, p. 30.

or the extent of the subordination of the conquered areas to this administration and questions as to whether and under which circumstances autonomous forces could maintain or even strengthen their autonomy, are some of the most vehemently discussed controversies of the various schools of Indian historians. As has been pointed out in the Introduction, the concepts of Indian feudalism and of the segmentary state succeeded in effectively destroying the 'conventional' picture of the medieval regional kingdoms as centrally governed unitary states for North as well as South India. Nevertheless, recent investigations show that some rulers of the larger imperial kingdoms were at least temporarily successful in their attempt to overcome the 'structural weaknesses' of the kingdoms by systematically improving the central administrative apparatus and also by appointing more local officers and leaders who could be controlled from the centre. An example for these centralizing measures for Orissa is the introduction of the ministerial *pātra* and *parīkṣā* systems in the twelfth and thirteenth centuries.[36] The success of these endeavours of the centre was repeatedly challenged by local forces or even nullified by them. But this power struggle not only demonstrates the weakness of the central rulers, but quite often also gives evidence of the occasional triumph of their attempts which, however, soon evoked corresponding counter-forces. But the lack of long-term success of these measures of the central dynasties justifies the designation of the imperial kingdoms of medieval India as exclusively segmentary states as little as the occasional success of these measures of the centre does not prove these states to be strong 'unitary states'. We will be doing justice to the structure of these regional kingdoms only if we are willing to analyse them as historical processes of various structural historical developments. Certainly it is as much legitimate to interpret these regional kingdoms 'from below', viewing them from the perspective of the local segments and their continuity, as it is permissible to explain them 'from above', from the point of view of the centre and its successes. Both these 'one-sided' approaches will do only partial justice to the overall structure of these states and their societies. The structural history of the imperial kingdoms—as that of nearly all pre-modern states—was as much the expression of the continuance of local power groupings as of a stage by stage extension of the organs of the central power.

36 S.K. Panda, 1986, p. 175. For similar centralizing tendencies in the Coḷa state Heitzman's paper in the present volume and Subbarayalu 1982.

IX

The elevation of the Hindu 'great kings' (mahārāja) to 'imperial lords' (*mahārājādhirāja*) was accompanied also by a change in the ideology of the Hindu kingship. It is true that even the kings of the early kingdoms were praised in the *praśasti* eulogies of their inscriptions for their divine-like qualities. But this was done in an allegorical way for the most part. The kings of the large kingdoms rose, on the other hand, more and more to the status of earthly representatives of the tutelary deity (*rāṣṭradevatā*) of the kingdom who was mostly Śiva, and since the twelfth century, Viṣṇu. Under the influence of the Bhakti cult these deities had also been elevated to the status of great gods (*mahādeva*) in the preceding centuries. In the way that the Mahārājas underwent some sort of 'deification' as their earthly representatives, the mahādevas went through a process of 'royalization'. They were increasingly transformed into imperial lords by fitting them out with all the symbols of an earthly mahārāja and by assimilating their temple rites increasingly to the palace rites. For, the greater the ostentation of the mahādeva and his divine court, the more legitimate was the splendour and power of his earthly representatives and his royal court. This development contributed decisively to the legitimation of the mahārāja who, while not really deified, was brought, nevertheless, nearer to divinity.[37]

This new royal ideology is abundantly evident in the new temple architecture.[38] In the period between *c.* AD 1000 and 1250 when the large regional kingdoms were at the height of their power, there arose a series of monumental imperial temples ('Reichstempel') which exceeded in their dimensions several times over the temples of the earlier medieval kings of the respective regions. Among them are the Kaṇḍarīya Mahādeva temple of Khajuraho (about 1002), the Rājarājeśvara temple in Tanjore (about 1012), the Udayeśvara temple in Udaipur and the Liṅgarāja temple

[37] In their recent study on the political culture of Nāyaka Tamil Nadu, V.N. Rao, D. Shulman and S. Subrahmanyam agree that in early medieval South India there existed a 'culturally given distinction between the king and the god'. However, this distinction has been transformed since the seventeenth century when the Nāyaka kings 'assumed the identity of the god in his shrine'. (V.N. Rao, D. Shulman, S. Subrahmanyam, *Symbols of Substance. Court and State in Nāyaka Period of Tamil Nadu*, New Delhi: OUP, 1992), p. 187.

[38] H. Kulke, 'Royal Temple Policy and the Structure of Medieval Hindu Kingdoms', in Eschmann (see note 10), pp. 125–38.

in Bhubaneswar (both about 1060/70), the Jagannātha temple in Puri (after 1135) and the Sūrya temple in Konarak (about 1250). Their cults developed into imposing state cults which were increasingly oriented towards the rulers, as is evident from the central liṅgas in the temples of Tanjore and Udaipur which were named after their respective donors, Rājarāja and Udayāditya. Tanjore is moreover a good example of the extent to which an entire kingdom could be drawn into this cult. Hundreds of priests, temple guards, dancers, musicians, book-keepers and craftsmen, mentioned in the large inscriptions of Tanjore by name and place of birth were brought to Tanjore from various parts of the kingdom. While most of the craftsmen and temple guards had to be further provided for with food by their native villages, King Rājarāja instituted for the maintenance of the priests and dancing girls tax revenue villages which were distributed over the extended core area of the kingdom. Thus the kingdom was covered by an additional network of relationships directed towards the royal-sacral imperial centre—relationships which were as much economically as politically legitimate. Surplus revenues and profits from the temple were loaned to the surrounding villages and districts, which utilized this finance for agricultural developmental projects as well as for other purposes, leading to a further economic strengthening of the Cōḷas' own hereditary lands.[39] Rājarāja's successors also built further monumental temples in the proper ancestral land of the Cōḷas in the lower course of the Kaveri river: his son Rājendra in Gaṅgaikoṇḍa-cōḷapuram, Rājarāja II (1146–1173) in Darasuram and Kulottuṅga III (1178–1216) in Tribhuvanam. As a result of the establishment of these large temples in the extended dynastic hereditary land they came to increasingly assume the character of sacral zones of the empire within the larger core region.

Since the late eleventh and the beginning of the twelfth century, however, more important than the building of new monumental temples was the systematic enlargement and embellishment of already existing

[39] K.A.N. Sastri, 'The Economy of a South Indian Temple in the Cōḷa Period', in *Malaviya Commemoration Volume*, 1932, pp. 305–10; see also G.W. Spencer, 'Temple, Money Lending and Livestock Redistribution in Early Tanjore', in *IESHR*, v, 1968, pp. 279–93 and idem 'Religious Networks and Royal Influence in Eleventh Century South India', in *JESHO*, 12, 1969, pp. 279–93; J. Heitzman, 'Ritual Polity and Economy: The Transactional Network of an Imperial Temple in Medieval South India', in *JESHO*, 34, 1991, pp. 23–54.

holy places (*tīrtha*) which had turned into centres of pilgrimage of regional importance under the influence of the Bhakti cult in the preceding centuries. By the continuous extension of the temple lay-out, construction of numerous new subsidiary temples and halls, corridors for promenade and (in South India) tall temple gateways (*gopuram*), these centres grew into substantial temple cities. Cidambaram, the centre of the cult of the dancing Śiva-Naṭarāja, and Puri, the seat of Viṣṇu as 'Lord of the World' (Jagannātha), are particularly good examples of the systematic royal expansion of local cult centres by generous royal patronage since the early twelfth century.[40] Therefore, it need not surprise us that these temple towns became in ever greater measure also centres of royal influence and thus assumed in some respects the function of the imperial palatine of German Middle Ages. This political function of the temple towns became particularly evident at places where huge 'thousand pillar halls' were constructed which occasionally (as for e.g. in Cidambaram) bore the name 'royal hall' (*rājasabhā*). By means of this systematic enlargement and the promotion of numerous temple cities which were distributed over the entire core area of the empire, the kings covered this vast area with an 'additional' network of direct royal, political and ritual influence.

But the political significance of the temple towns was in no way limited to their being occasionally also 'royal towns'. Far more important was their role as cosmic centres and the source of the highest legitimation of the royal authority.[41] Very soon the founder kings were included in the temple legends in which they were elevated to mythical heroes of the hoary past. In a temple māhātmya of the temple of Puri it is mentioned still more clearly that only by the construction of the (first) Jagannatha temple by the mythical king Indradyumna, famines and mass deaths came to an end in Orissa and therefore mankind had happily submitted itself to his rule. On the other hand, it is expressly stated in the same text about the other kings that they were interested only in the collection of unjust

[40] J.C. Harle, *Temple Gateways in South India: Architecture and Iconography of the Chidambaram Gopuras* (Oxford, 1963), pp. 31ff.

[41] H. Kulke, *Cidambaramāhātmya. Eine Untersuchung der religionsgeschichtlichen und historischen Hintergründe für die Entstehung der Tradition einer südindischen Tempelstadt* (Wiesbaden, 1970), pp. 126ff; see also D. Shulman, *Tamil Temple Myths: Sacrifice and Divine Marriage in South Indian Śaiva Tradition* (Princeton, 1980), pp. 40–55 and Friedhelm Hardy, 'Ideology and Cultural Contexts of the Śrīvaiṣṇava Temple', in B. Stein (ed.), *South Indian Temples* (New Delhi, 1978), pp. 119–52.

taxes but not in the welfare of the people.[42] Which greater legitimation could the dominion of the kings of the Gaṅga dynasty of Orissa have enjoyed in the period around 1300 when this māhātmya was written down? The priests and pilgrims did look upon the kings of the Gaṅga dynasty as direct successors of the mythical king Indradyumna. And many of them still knew that Anantavarman Cōḍagaṅga, a member of this dynasty, had got constructed 'anew' only a few generations earlier the great temple admired by them. The message of these temple legends, which the priests propagated to the pilgrims during their visits to the temple cities, were carried by them to villages even in the remotest areas of the kingdom.

A further, perhaps even more important aspect of the temples (and also of the kings' 'temple policy') was their integrating function within the regional kingdoms. The great temples were associated 'vertically' in an often closely meshed network of ritual and legendary relations with 'sub-regional' and local cults of their hinterland, as well as 'horizontally' with other temples of the region. Thus, for example, in South India the liṅgas of five great Śaivite temples were assigned to the five elements: Kancipuram to the earth, Jambukesvara to the water, Tiruvannamalai to the fire, Kalahasti to the wind and Cidambaram to the spirit-ether (*akāśa*). Again in Orissa, the biggest temples of the five important cults were brought together into a system of the 'five gods' (*pañcadevatā*): Viṣṇu/Jagannātha in Puri, Śiva/Liṅgarāja in Bhubaneswar, Durgā/ Virajā in Jaipur, Sūrya in Konarak and Gaṇeśa (here vicarious for the tribal cults) in Mahavinayaka. What is of significance is that all these 'regional' temples lay inside the extended core areas of the respective regional kingdoms. The effect of this 'temple policy' was to link local loyalties of the earlier nuclear areas and their peripheral zones with the cults of the central temples and then, at the level of 'horizontally interlinked systems', to integrate them into a new regional cult as a basis of a new regional loyalty.

This regional integration similarly took place in numerous other spheres, through the development of regional kinship and caste systems ('sanskritization'), by the codification of regional norms (*deśa dharma*),[43]

[42] *Puruṣottamamāhātmya of the Skanda Purāṇa*, XI, pp. 125ff, Venkatesvar Press, VS, 1966; see also R. Geib, *Indradyumna-Legende: Ein Beitrag zur Geschichte des Jagannātha-Kultes* (Wiesbaden, 1975), pp. 97ff.

[43] A. Wezler, 'Dharma und Deśadharma', in *Regionale Tradition in Südasien*, H. Kulke and D. Rothermund (eds), (Wiesbaden, 1985), pp. 1–22.

by the social and economic integration of the tribes ('kṣatriyaization') and by the inclusion of tribal deities and rituals ('Hinduization') into Hindu cults. The medium in which the new 'regional loyalty' was propagated was no more the Brahminic-court Sanskrit, but the regional languages. Non-Brahminic itinerant preachers, sectarian leaders and holy men emerged more and more as the propagators of the new 'mission'. The growth and history of the medieval imperial or regional kingdoms were thus accompanied—and in some cases even accomplished—by the emergence of a new regional identity. It was the forerunner of today's regional cultures of India and thus perhaps the most important heritage of medieval India.

X

Summarizing these delineations on a processural model of integrative state formation in early medieval India, the three successive stages of spatial and socio-political development may be characterized by three key-terms, i.e. rājavaṃśa, sāmantacakra and maṇḍala. Rājavaṃśa pertains to the chiefdom and the establishment of local rule under a 'royal' lineage (*vaṃśa*) in a nuclear area. Sāmantacakra refers to the early kingdom and the process of extending political authority within the nuclear area and the establishment of tributary relations with the circle (cakra) of formerly independent neighbours (sāmanta), without however annexing them. The term maṇḍala stands for the imperial kingdom and the process of annexation of the sāmantacakra and its, partly, administrative transformation into maṇḍala provinces. This political development is as well based on, as accompanied by, continuous processes—emanating from the central nuclear area—of agrarian extension, social stratification (*'jatification'*), political hierarchization and cultural integration.[44] In its final stage of an imperial kingdom the early medieval state in India was therefore based on an impressively enlarged and centrally dominated core region with its own 'state society' and a highly developed integrative cultural identity, a stage, however, which only few historical kingdoms were able to reach.

[44] The most recent and comprehensive evaluation of the whole range of parameters of structural change and continuity in early medieval India is B.D. Chattopadhyaya's 'Introduction: The Making of Early Medieval India', in idem (1994), pp. 1–37.

Chapter Eight

Towards an Interpretation of the Mughal Empire[1]

M. ATHAR ALI

It is common for current Indian history textbooks to treat the various 'empires' that successively occupied the stage of Indian history, with their respective 'administrations', as so many successive repetitions with merely different names for offices and institutions that in substance remained the same: namely, the king, ministers, provinces, governors, taxes, land-grants and so on. But D.D. Kosambi, in his *Introduction to the Study of Indian History* (Bombay, 1975), rightly observed that this repetitive succession cannot be assumed, and that each regime, when subjected to critical study, displays distinct elements that call for its analysis in the context of 'relations of production' (as he put it) existing at that time.

Of all the 'empires' prior to the British, we know most, of course, about the Mughal Empire. And this empire displays so many striking features that it should in fact attract an historical analyst of today as much as it did Bernier. In its large extent and long duration, it had only one precedent, the Mauryan Empire, some 1900 years earlier. Well might Havell[2] regard it as the fulfilment of the political ambitions embodied in Indian polity for three millennia. And yet there is also a temptation to see in the Mughal Empire a primitive version of the modern state. Its existence belongs to a period corresponding to the dawn of modern technology in Europe—and some of the rays of that dawn had also fallen

[1] This is a revised version of my presidential address presented to the Indian History Congress, Muzaffarpur Session, 1972, Section on Medieval India. This essay first appeared in *Journal of the Royal Asiatic Society*, 1978.

[2] E.B. Havell, *A History of Aryan Rule in India* (London, n.d.), pp. 520—1.

on Asia. Can it then be said, as Barthold[3] implied, that the foundations of the Mughal Empire lay in artillery—the most brilliant and dreadful representative of modern technology, as much as did those of the modern absolute monarchies of Europe? Can we say, further, that the Mughal Empire, far from being the climax of traditional Indian political endeavour, represented one of the several unsuccessful experiments of history towards that titration which has at last given us the distinct modern civilization of our times?

These questions are unlikely to be answered easily, or perhaps ever, with a simple yes or no. The factors to be considered are too numerous, and often too remote, to be evaluated or assessed with any reasonable assurance of comprehensiveness and accuracy. But is there any student of the period who does not, in his private thoughts, have a predilection for one or the other setting for the Mughal Empire, i.e. for regarding it either as the most successful of the traditional Indian states or as an abortive quasi-modern polity?

My attempt here is to discuss certain matters which may be of interest to a contingent debate on the theme which I have briefly outlined. Most of my conclusions are naturally tentative; and I can hope for no more than that the aspects touched upon may be found to be deserving of close scrutiny.

A question that comes to mind as we are on the theme of a general characterization of the Mughal Empire is, what was new—or if not new, then, at any rate, exotic—in the polity of the Mughal Empire?

In the view of a number of historians, including Professor Rushbrook Williams[4] and Professor R.P. Tripathi,[5] the institutions and mutual relations of kingship and nobility in the Mughal Empire essentially derive from Turko-Mongol traditions, contrasted with the 'Afghān'. The former

[3] V.V. Barthold, 'Irān', G.K. Nariman, tr., in *Posthumous Works of G.K. Nariman*, S.H. Jhabvala (ed.) (Bombay, 1935), pp. 142–3.

[4] 'It will thus be seen that Babur had not merely to conquer a kingdom; he had to create a theory of kingship. He was determined to be no sultan, hampered by all limitations which had beset the Lodi dynasty; but a *pādshāh*, looking down upon even his highest *amīrs* from the towering eminence upon which the divine right of Timur's blood had placed him', *An Empire Builder of the Sixteenth Century* (London, 1918), p. 161.

[5] 'The Chaghatai conqueror Bābar came to India with ideas (of Sovereignty) that were not quite similar to those of either the early Turkish rulers of Delhi or the Afghans', *Some Aspects of Muslim Administration* (Allahabad, 1936), p. 105, et seq.

conferred on the emperor absolute powers over his nobles and subjects, whereas the latter, particularly in the circumstances of the fifteenth century, tended to place the king in no higher a position than of the first among equals. This view has been criticized, first through an analysis of the surviving Turkish and Mongol traditions (for both were not only distinct, but historically different) in the Central Asia of Bābur's time, it being shown that these by no means prescribed an absolute despotism.[6] The other criticism is that it is possibly inaccurate to describe the Indo-Afghān or Lodi polity as a mere tribal confederation; for this would underestimate the underlying powers of the monarch that certain tribal forms only barely concealed.[7]

There is still a third factor to which, perhaps, sufficient attention has not been paid. This is the continuing survival of the framework of the administration of the Delhi Sultanate, established under the Khaljīs and Tughlaqs, especially the land-revenue system. Abū'l-Faẓl's statement that Sher Shāh sought to copy the administrative measures of 'Alā'al-Dīn Khaljī which he had read about in Baranī's *Tārīkh-i Fīroz-Shāhī* would have been effective as a gibe had Sher Shāh not proved himself a realist by his success in carrying out these measures. This success testified to the similarity, if not identity, of the administrative system of the early sixteenth century with that of the fourteenth.

The contribution too of the Sūr regime to the structure of Mughal polity needs to be borne in mind. Sher Shāh and Islām Shāh created the *ẕabṭ* system of land-revenue assessment, the corner stone of Akbar's land-revenue administration. They imposed the *dāgh*, or horse branding, an equally basic device for controlling the army. If 'Abbās Sarwānī is to be believed, Sher Shāh attempted a conscious centralized despotism; and Islām Shāh certainly gave shape to it by bringing the whole of his empire under direct control (*khāliṣa*), thus anticipating Akbar's measures of 1574.

These achievements were acclaimed by the Afghān historians of the late sixteenth and seventeenth centuries; but they also won wider recognition. There are guarded admissions in Abū'l-Faẓl; and a paean of praise for Sher Shāh is found in a letter written in 1611 by Mirzā 'Azīz Koka,

[6] Iqtidar Alam Khan, 'The Turko-Mongol Theory of Kingship', in *Medieval India: A Miscellany*, II, 1972, pp. 8–18.

[7] Iqtidar Husain Siddiqi, *Some Aspects of Afghan Despotism in India* (Aligarh, 1971), pp. 1–60.

himself one of 'the old wolves' of the Mughal state.[8] What more could be required as a testimony of the popular admiration of Sher Shāh, than that Dāwar Bakhsh, a claimant to the Mughal throne in 1627, should assume for himself the very same title of Sher Shāh?[9]

But, quite obviously, Mughal polity could not have been a simple continuation of the Sultanate and Sūr polity. Had it been such, its comparatively greater success would be impossible to explain. What, then, were the new elements of political chemistry out of which Akbar compounded such a large, stable, long-lasting political structure?

At the risk of over-simplification, I would say that these were an extreme systematization of administration, a new theoretical basis for sovereignty and a balanced and stable composition of the ruling class.

I venture to think that in spite of the work done on Akbar's administration, notably by Moreland, Saran and Ibn Ḥasan, there has not been an adequate appreciation of Akbar's achievement in his systematization of administration. We see such systematization in his creation of *manṣab*, classifying all individual officers into definite categories. Whereas before Akbar each appointment, promotion, fixation of pay and obligation was in the case of higher officers a separate ad hoc arrangement, under Akbar every such action was reduced to a change in the manṣab (the number assigned to a man). Increase or diminution of pay and obligation followed a change in the manṣab as a matter of course, under set regulations. Much research has gone towards discovering the 'decimal system' of the military organization under the Delhi Sultans and the Mongols. But manṣab has really little kinship with any such system. It has been shown, I think quite persuasively, that there was no manṣab or number-rank in existence before 1574.[10] I would add that no analogous system of numbered ranks can be found in any Central Asian or Middle Eastern state—and certainly not in the Tīmūrid, the Uzbek, the Ṣafavid

[8] 'Sher Shāh Afghān was not a king (*malik*) but an angel (*malak*). In six years he gave such stability to the structure that the foundations still survive' (B.M. MS Add. 16859, f. 19a).

[9] This curious fact is not mentioned in the Indian chronicles. But it is the title Dāwar Bakhsh assumes in his *farmān* of 1627 to Rāja Jai Singh (Bikaner, old serial no. 176, new S. 021). This is corroborated by the *Tārīkh-i 'ālam ārā-i 'Abbāsī*, Tehran (ed.), A.H. 1314, 750.

[10] A.J. Qaisar, *Proceedings of the Indian History Congress,* Delhi Session, 1961, pp. 155–7.

and the Ottoman Empires. The manṣab system was a unique and, as far as centralization went, an unrivalled device for organizing the ruling class.

We get the same sense of systematization in the development of *jāgīr* as the pure form of land-revenue assignment. It is possible to argue that the jāgīr fits the definition of *iqṭā*ʿ given in the *Siyāsatnāma* of Niẓām al-Mulk Tūsī (twelfth century).[11] But whereas in all earlier states the iqṭāʿ in practice always became confounded with general administrative charges, the jāgīr in actual practice exactly fitted the standard definition of iqṭāʿ. The maintenance of *jamaʿdāmī* (estimated revenue) figures and the assignment of jāgīr to a manṣab holder, rigidly on the basis of the approved jāmaʿdāmī equalling the *ṭalab*, or his sanctioned pay, the constant transfers of jāgīrs, and the restricting of *jāgīrdars*' powers to revenue collection alone,[12] are again measures for which precedents and parallels in the Islamic world are not easy to find.

Akbar's division of his empire into *ṣūbas*, *sarkars* and *maḥalls* and his largely successful attempts to make the entire administrative structure of one ṣūba into the exact replica of the other, with a chain of officers at various levels ultimately controlled by the ministers at the centre, gave identity to Mughal administrative institutions irrespective of the regions where they functioned.

The systematization continued under Akbar's successors. When new administrative categories were created, whether *duaspa-sihaspa* ranks under Jahāngīr or the month scale under Shāh Jahān, they too appear, in the ultimate analysis, to substitute general categories for individual exceptions.[13] Even in the sphere of land-revenue administration, where regional differences were inevitable, the ẓabt system—the characteristic institution of the Mughal revenue administration—was extended to the Deccan by Murshid Qulī Khān.

Side by side with this immense work of centralization and systematization, we see a new stress on the absoluteness of sovereignty. The accepted Mughal doctrine of sovereignty was derived from several distinct sources which could by no means be logically inter-related. It partly consisted of

11 *Siyāsatnāma*, C. Scheffer (ed.) (Paris, 1891–3), p. 28.

12 Cf. Irfan Habib, *Agrarian System of Mughal India, 1556–1707* (London, 1963), pp. 256ff.

13 Cf. W.H. Moreland, 'Rank (Mansab) in the Mughal State Service', *JRAS*, 1936, pp. 641–65; Irfan Habib, 'The Mansab System, 1595–1637', *Proceedings of the Indian History Congress*, Patiala Session, 1968, pp. 221ff.

an exaltation of the blue blood of the Mughal dynasty. The long history of the Mughals as a ruling dynasty, going back to Tīmur and Chengiz Khan, rulers not of obscure states but of world empires, was an asset which the Mughals put to skilful use. Abū 'l-Fazḷ's *Akbarnāma* offers a superb example of the propaganda carried on for the dynasty on the basis of its past. The Mughals accentuated the consciousness of their exalted status by abstaining from marrying princesses of the dynasty to anyone except a member of the imperial family. On the other hand the privilege of marrying a daughter to a prince or emperor came to be zealously guarded by a few Irānian, Tūrānian and Rājpūt families of high status. The historic halo around the dynasty justified the submission of the chiefs of the proudest clans to its suzerainty.

A second element derived from the earlier Muslim political thinkers. In the chapter, *Rawāi-i rozī*, in the *Ā'īn-i Akbarī*, Abū 'l-Fazḷ repeats the well-known theory of social contract to justify the sovereign's absolute claims over the individual subject. The strength of this theory lies in its secular character and its foundation in alleged social needs. It has the further merit of being rational.

But rationality was probably not deemed a sufficient incentive to the total obedience that the Mughal sovereign sought. A third element then entered, and that was religious. Ever since the Ṣafavids had successfully utilized their past as religious leaders and based their sovereignty on their spiritual authority, the attractions of a similar position for *sunnī* sovereigns were irresistible. The Ottomans ultimately purchased from existing claimants the authority of the 'Abbāsid caliphate; but they were anticipated by Akbar, who, through the *maḥzar* of 1579, attempted to assume the position of an interpreter of Islamic law and, in spheres where the existing corpus was silent, of a legislator.[14]

For reasons into which we cannot go here, Akbar's attempt to establish such a position within the framework of Islam proved abortive.[15] Moreover, it did not solve the problem of spiritual authority in his relations with non-Muslim subjects. It therefore gave way to a new attempt in which it was claimed that the emperor enjoyed the position of a spiritual guide and that this position derived not from any particular religion but directly from God. 'Sovereignty is a ray of light from the Divine Sun',

[14] Cf. S. Nurul Hasan, 'The Mahzar of Akbar's Reign', *Journal of U.P. Hist. Soc.*, XVI, 1968, p. 126.

[15] Cf. Iqtidar Alam Khan in *JRAS*, 1968, pp. 34–5.

claims Abū 'l-Faẓl.[16] As such men of all faiths were beneficiaries of the Divine Light. Thus Aurangzeb would write to Rānā Rāj Singh when seeking the throne:

Because the persons of the great kings are shadows of God, the attention of this elevated class (of kings), who are the pillars of the great court, is devoted to this, that men belonging to various communities and different religions should live in the vale of peace and pass their days in prosperity, and no one should interfere in the affairs of another. Any one of this sky-glorious group (of kings) who resorted to intolerance, became the cause of dispute and conflict and of harm to the people at large, who are indeed a trust received from God: in reality (such a king) thereby endeavoured to devastate the prosperous creations of God and destroy the foundations of the God-created fabric, which is a habit deserving to be rejected and cast off. God willing, when the true cause (i.e. Aurangzeb's own cause) is successful, and the wishes of the sincerely loyal ones are fulfilled, the benefits of the revered practices and established regulations of my great ancestors, who are so much esteemed by the worshipful ones, will cast lustre on the four-cornered inhabited world.[17]

Akbar initiated the practice of *jharoka darshan*, a striking innovation which nevertheless seemed in accordance with Hindu tradition. To a more select circle of disciples, styled the *irādat-gazīnān* by Abū 'l-Faẓl, Akbar was the spiritual guide. Akbar's successors enlarged this circle to include practically all their nobles; and it became a convention for every high noble, whether Muslim or Hindu, to address the Emperor as *Pir-ō murshid* and designate himself as his *murīd.*

It can be seen that, combined with the tolerant religious policy of which Akbar was the author, the basing of political authority on spiritual sanctity was an intelligent device to strengthen the sovereign position. Its logical implications lay, however, not in secularism, but in an as yet dormant and unelaborated concept of religious equality. Abū 'l-Faẓl's claims for his master could only be justified by the theories of Dārā Shukoh.

The third important element which Akbar introduced into imperial polity was, as I have mentioned, the establishment of certain principles governing the relations between the king and the nobles. That Akbar created a composite nobility has been well recognized since the seventeenth century when the author of the *Dabistān-i mazāhib* ascribed the

16 *Ā'īn-i Akbarī*, 3.

17 For the text of the *nīshān*, see Kaviraj Shyamaldas, *Vir Vinod*, 11, 419–20 note.

prosperity of the Mughal dynasty to the fact that Akbar had succeeded in removing the dependence of the sovereign on the Muslim nobility alone.[18] Though the attribution of the creation of a composite nobility to Akbar is now a part of the established historical dogma, it can be accepted only with much qualification. A composite nobility, in terms of race, existed already under the Khaljīs (1290–1320); and a composite nobility, in terms of religion, under Muḥammad Tughlaq.[19] The latter sultan too linked his policy towards the nobility with innovations in his religious policy, such as a repressive attitude towards the Muslim orthodoxy, public discourses with *yogīs* (Hindu mendicants) and personal participation in the *holī* festival.[20] And yet the effort to give stability to the political structure of the sultanate by this means had not been successful.

It may be that there are also autonomous causes for the greater success of Akbar in creating a loyal nobility. For instance, the gradual progress of Islamic-Persian court culture among the higher classes of non-Muslims, including the Rājpūts, might have generated a common cultural groundwork for the political alliance between sections of Muslim and non-Muslim aristocracies.

There is also another factor to consider. The rural aristocracy, descendants of the ruling class of the twelfth century, had not only fresh memories in the thirteenth and fourteenth centuries of their past glories, but probably then objected to the imposition of the exotic fiscal system, whereby the bulk of the agricultural surplus was claimed by the sultan as *kharāj* (land-tax) to be distributed among his nobles, the *muqti's* or iqtā'-holders. By the sixteenth century, the kharāj system could no longer be seen as an innovation, and the rural aristocracy, having been reduced to the status of *zamīndārs*, must have largely accommodated themselves to it.[21] It was thus possible to introduce into the Mughal nobility certain zamīndār elements (e.g. the Rājpūt chiefs, Ghakkars, etc.) without endangering its foundations.[22]

18 *Dabistān-i mazāhib*, Nazar Ashraf (ed.) (Calcutta, 1809), p. 432.

19 See my article, 'Foundations of Akbar's Organization of the Nobility: An Interpretation', *Medieval India Quarterly*, III, nos. 3 and 4, 1958, pp. 80–7.

20 Iṣāmī, *Futūḥ al-salāṭīn*, Usha (ed.), p. 515.

21 Cf. Irfan Habib, 'Social Distribution of Landed Property in Pre-British India', *Enquiry*, old series no. 12, pp. 54–6.

22 Dr Ahsan Raza Khan in his unpublished thesis on the chiefs under Akbar has

Both these factors are easily admitted. But one significant contribution of Akbar that continued to be honoured by his four immediate successors must be given due recognition. This was the enunciation of an essentially humane approach to the individuals constituting the nobility. In this respect, the Mughal Empire stood apart from the Sultanate; and it also stood apart from the Safavid and other polities of the contemporary Islamic world.

The official chronicler of Shāh Jahān tells us:

> In matters of punishments, His Majesty does not regard the nobles as different from ordinary human beings. If perchance mention is made in His Majesty's presence of the cruelty of the Emperors of Constantinople, Irān, and Uzbeks, and of their ferocity in awarding punishments, His Majesty gets so perturbed that the signs of sadness are apparent from his illustrious forehead. His Majesty has often been heard to say that God has given the kings authority and made all men their subjects for the sole purpose that the entire attention of kings be directed towards the maintenance of justice, which is the basis of the functioning of the world and the races of men. Therefore, the king should so award punishments that the cruel cannot oppress their victims, and (the nobles) may treat the poor mildly, and the garden of the world flourish owing to the removal of the thorns of cruelty. Not that in the name of awarding punishments the king should slaughter large numbers of men for a small fault, and on a small suspicion injure fellow beings, who are a trust from God.[23]

The boast for the Mughal Empire implicit in this passage was not an empty one. The Mughal emperors really shine by contrast with their despotic contemporaries. Taking the *Tārīkh-i 'ālam ārā-i 'Abbāsī*,[24] I compiled a list of the leading nobles executed by Shāh 'Abbās I (1587–1629), the great Ṣafavid emperor. I found that during thirty-one years, he executed no less than forty-eight prominent officers of his, generally upon the slightest suspicions. Some of the executions were on religious grounds.[25] When we turn from this gory record to the annals of the Mughal Empire, we find that even dismissals, let alone executions, are very rare. When high officers were dismissed for major faults, they were usually pensioned off with land grants. Confiscation of individual nobles'

---

collected interesting data about the chiefs (high *zamīndārs*) who were granted *manṣabs* under Akbar.

[23] Lāhorī, *Bādshāhnāma*, I, pp. 139–40.

[24] Tehran (ed.), AH 1214.

[25] e.g. in his seventeenth regnal year.

property, as punishment, was unknown. So also the humiliation of the family of a noble no longer in favour. It was only in the rare cases of rebellions or wars of succession that the nobles met violent ends. Even here an unwritten custom provided that only under exceptional circumstances were nobles of the defeated side to be executed after the battle. In an overwhelmingly large number of cases, nobles who escaped death on the battlefield could be sure of escaping it at their captor's hands. In the wars of succession, it remained indeed usual, until 1713, to offer appointments to the supporters of the defeated claimants. During the war of 1658–9, for example, neither Aurangzeb nor Dārā Shukoh executed any noble. It was only the princes of royal blood whose lives remained insecure, ever since Shāh Jahān in 1628 established the practice of executing possible rivals.

It is this approach to the nobility, in which loyalty to the throne was assumed from everyone, that was perhaps a major factor that enabled the Mughals to avoid a crisis in their relations with the nobles after the aristocratic rebellion of 1580. This approach had a corollary to it. While the Mughal emperor undertook no obligation to maintain a hereditary nobility, and in theory could appoint anyone to any manṣab, in actual fact recruitment to the nobility was confined to certain foreign racial elements and indigenous clans which, in spite of their diverse backgrounds, were bound to the Mughal dynasty in grateful obedience. If one collects data about the manṣab-holders under the different emperors, one is surprised at the unvarying nature of the proportions shared by the various elements.

In the following table I give the composition of (*i*) the 98 manṣabdārs alive in 1595 and enjoying the manṣab of 500 and above; (*ii*) the 100 highest manṣabdārs in service in 1620; (*iii*) the 100 highest manṣabdārs in 1656; (*iv*) the 202 manṣabdārs appointed/promoted to the manṣabs of 2000/1500 and above during the period 1658–78; and (*v*) 277 manṣabdārs of the same ranks serving during 1679–1707.[26]

[26] These data are based (*i*) on the *Ā'īn-i Akbarī*'s list of *manṣabdārs*; (*ii*) on Irfan Habib's list (unpublished) of *manṣabdārs* under Jahāngīr, mainly based on the *Tuzuk-i Jahāngīrī*, and (*iii*) on Wāris, *Bādshāhnāma*, Ethe, 329, for the list of *manṣabdārs* in 1656. The racial composition has been established by detailed checking with the biographical information in the chronicles (e.g. Lāhorī) as well as the *Zakhirat al-khawānīn* and the *Ma'āṣir al-'umarā'*. (*iv*) and (*v*) are based on the list of *manṣabdārs* of Aurangzeb's reign given in my book, *The Mughal Nobility Under Aurangzeb* (London, 1966).

	Turani	*Iranis*	*Afghans*	*Indian Muslims*	*Other Muslims*	*Rajputs*	*Marathas*	*Other Hindus*	*Total*
(*i*) 1595	33	23	2	14	4	21	0	1	98
(*ii*) 1620	22	33	8	11	4	21	1	0	100
(*iii*) 1656	22	33	5	10	3	21	5	1	100
(*iv*) 1658–1678	37	67	15	26	14	27	14	2	202
	18.5%	33.5%	7.5%	13%	7%	13.5%	7%	1%	
(*v*) 1679–1707	42	65	18	35	34	28	47	8	277
	15.5%	24%	6.6%	12.5%	12%	10%	17%	3%	

It will be seen from this table that the main disturbance in the proportionate strength of the various elements in the Mughal nobility was caused by the entrance of the Marāthās and other Dakhinis (the real strength of the latter is concealed in the break-up of the table we have given), who appear in increasing numbers from 1656 onwards. This intrusion is, of course, explained by the increasing involvement of the Mughal Empire in the Deccan, especially during the reign of Aurangzeb (1659–1707).

Thus we see two opposites reconciled successfully in Mughal polity, namely the absolute despotic power of the emperor, bolstered by immense centralization and a theory of semi-divine sovereignty; and a structure heavily systematized with such conventions governing the relations between the king and his nobles as to deserve even the appellation of 'constitution', with a small if not a capital 'c'. We have seen, further, that in the formation of this policy both the development of institutions, already in existence under the previous regimes, and a deliberate policy on the part of the Mughal emperors, had distinct roles to play. These two causal factors did not have a directly 'modern' origin, even taking that imprecise term in the widest possible sense.

And yet it is possible that some of the changes that took place at the dawn of the modern era did exercise certain influences on the last stage, but crucial, development of medieval institutions that we have just considered, and on the ideas and intellectual atmosphere in which what was new in the Mughal imperial polity was formulated.

I would begin by taking up a small point: the system of coinage. The Mughal system of coinage was tri-metallic, with coins made in three metals, gold, silver, and copper, with the highest degree of purity achieved anywhere in the world. Such coinage too had its predecessor in the sultanate coinage of the fourteenth century. But during the fifteenth century coinage had been heavily debased, the main coin being a copper *tanka* with a progressively declining silver alloy. Sher Shāh sought to eliminate the debased coinage, and he minted the first rupee, a coin of 178 grains of practically pure silver. By the end of the sixteenth century the attempt that had continued under the later Sūrs and yet more vigorously under Akbar, succeeded in making the rupee the basic unit of currency actually in use.[27] It is useless to dilate upon the importance of this achievement for successful functioning of commerce and credit, and the importance of the latter, in turn, for the functioning of a highly centralized administration. Yet it is not to be forgotten that the coming of the rupee was linked to the Spanish discovery of the New World, because that led to a heavy influx of silver, plundered and minted in the newly discovered continents, into the 'Old World', thereby ending the silver famine that had prevailed there since the fourteenth century. Thus what would have been otherwise exceptionally difficult, if not impossible—namely, the institution of a pure silver currency, previously limited by conditions of very high silver prices—became possible as an economic by-product of the Age of Discovery.

There is also the role of the artillery to be considered. It is true that the Mughal army, like the Ṣafavid and Uzbek, and even the Ottoman army, was mainly a cavalry force. It was characteristic that the manṣab indicating the size of the military contingent its possessor was obliged to maintain, was styled *suwār* or 'horseman'. But it would be wrong to think that artillery had no more than a marginal role to play in the Mughal army, especially when we remember that we ought not to be thinking of cannons only, but also, and even particularly, of muskets. After all, if in 1647 there were 200,000 horsemen under the imperial banner, there were also no less than 40,000 infantry-men, consisting of 'match-lock men, gunners, cannoneers and rocketeers'.[28]

It is quite likely that the increasing use of artillery during the hundred

[27] Cf. H.N. Wright, *The Coinage and Metrology of the Sultans of Delhi* (Delhi, 1936), pp. 260–1; Irfan Habib, *IESHR*, IV, 1967, pp. 217–19.

[28] Lāhorī, *Bādshāhnāma*, II, p. 715.

years following the battle of Panipat in 1526, gave the Mughal army a decisive weapon against the traditional chiefs with their old cavalry retainers (of whom the Rājpūts were a characteristic illustration). Moreover, artillery gave to the towns, where alone guns and muskets could be manufactured, a new basis for political and military domination over the countryside. In so far as the Mughal ruling class was mainly urban in character,[29] it must certainly have gained as a result of the new military importance of towns.

We can thus at least identify two new sources of strength and stability that 'modern' developments gave to the Mughal polity—the silver influx, a component of the Price Revolution, and the artillery, an early product of modern technology. It is, moreover, possible that the developments in Europe were influencing ideas too, indirectly but powerfully.

Information about the Europeans was available to Akbar and his contemporaries; and this was not confined to knowledge about the Jesuits and Christianity. Abū 'l-Faẓl was aware that the Europeans had discovered the Americas, which he called *'ālam-i nau*,[30] the New World. The accounts of the time are replete with references to the technological ingenuity of the *Firangīs*, it being mentioned with pride if craftsmen at any place could manufacture articles that might compare with those of European manufacturers. As is well known, by the seventeenth century, European physicians and surgeons had established a reputation for western science; and, in a notable encounter of the two cultures, Bernier explained the theory of the circulation of blood to Dānishmand Khān.[31]

Such information, showing the lead that Europe was attaining in several branches of human activity, could not but engender questions about the finality of traditional knowledge. This question took several forms. On one side was the rational approach of Abū'l-Faẓl, who would point out that zinc, as a separate metal (a recent discovery in Asia), was not known to the ancients,[32] or would say that al-Ghazālī spoke nonsense when he condemned sciences that were not manifestly based upon the Qur'ān.[33] Then there was Dārā Shukoh and men of his stamp, who

29 See my *Mughal Nobility Under Aurangzeb*, pp. 154ff.

30 *Ā'īn-i Akbarī*, III, p. 22.

31 Bernier, *Travels in the Mogul Empire* (Bombay, 1934), pp. 324, 339.

32 *Ā'īn-i Akbarī*, I, p. 24.

33 Muḥammad Hāshim Kishmī, *Zubdat al-Maqāmāt*, Mahmud Press, Lucknow, AH 1302, p. 131.

rejected the traditional sciences, but also rejected rationality, and sought to establish an obscurantist spiritual dogma on the foundations of Comparative Religion.[34] Further to the 'right' still, there were men like Mullah Nāṣir of Burhānpūr who thought that no particular sanctity attached to the classical Islamic jurists, and what they said could be challenged by men of equal or greater learning, like himself.[35] Even Shaykh Aḥmad Sirhindī was thought by his critics to be tarnished with similar thoughts of his own superiority over the earlier interpreters.[36]

In the previous (sixteenth) century, the Mahdavī Movement had attained considerable success; and it was certainly a consciously 'revisionist' doctrine.

All these were symptoms of a cleft in the hitherto solid structure of faith in the traditional cultural heritage of Islam. It was this void that was unconsciously sought to be filled by the special position of the Mughal emperor as a spiritual guide, and the self-conscious view of the Mughal Empire as a great new polity, essentially just and humane (to the individual members of the ruling class). If this hypothesis is accepted, then we can perhaps see a dual ideological role of the Mughal Empire. On the one hand, the need of an official theory of sovereignty, and of the specific role of Mughal polity, arose because of the undermining of the traditional ideological structure from tremors originating from the remote and largely unidentified developments of the early modern world; but, in its turn, the theory cemented and strengthened the traditional culture and made the Mughal Empire its upholder and protector.

The suggestion that I should like to make is, then, that we should not treat the Mughal Empire as simply the last in the line of a succession of traditional Indian empires. It is true that its structure and institutions had deep indigenous roots. Its success also owed not a little to the genius of one man, Akbar. But the circumstances and atmosphere in which it was created were shaped by certain other factors as well that had much to do with the very events that played an important part in the origin and development of modern culture in Europe. A certain intellectual ferment was in the air in India also, stirred in unseen ways by the advance

[34] Cf. Qanungo, *Dara Shukoh* (Calcutta, 1935), pp. 78ff.

[35] Muḥammad Baqa, *Mirāt al-'ālam*, MS Aligarh; 'Abd al-Salām, 84/314, Pairaish III.

[36] S.A. Rizvi, *Muslim Revivalist Movements in Northern India in the 16th and 17th Centuries* (Agra, 1965), pp. 268–70.

of Europe; and this too contributed to the acceptance of a new ideological basis offered for the Mughal Empire.

I am not suggesting that these factors converted the Mughal Empire into a modern state. If it had some rudiments of an unwritten constitution, it did not yet claim for itself the legislative power and functions that are the hallmarks of a modern state. It was essentially the 'perfection' of a medieval polity, made possible by certain early modern developments. Though this gave it the stability and power denied to its predecessors, it still did not resolve the new contradiction inherent in the existence of a medieval polity in a world advancing towards modernity.

As I see it, this contradiction expressed itself mainly in the contrast between the sense of unity infused in the imperial ruling class, in spite of its heterogeneity, and the absence of the consciousness of such unity among the mass of the imperial subjects. In other words, the subcontinent of India had a centralized quasi-modern state without any developing sense of nationhood. It is true that 'Hindustān', a word so often used, was more than a simple geographical expression. But if it was so, this was not because of any new popular consciousness but because of its geographical correspondence with the area in which Hindu mythology had been enacted and places of pilgrimage lay scattered. This was not sufficient to overcome divisions of caste and community.

It was perhaps for this reason that the Mughal Empire proved so vulnerable to the challenges from the Marāthās, Jāts, Sikhs and Afghāns, who represented not its conventional political opponents, but forces of a new kind, involving the entry of peasant-soldiers. This is not the place to discuss how far these forces were the product of the 'agrarian crisis' of the Mughal Empire. For my present purpose what is more significant is that while no serious division occurred within the Mughal ruling class, in the face of these challenges it still proved incapable of meeting them and failed to invoke any popular support in its struggle. It seemed as if the people at large were indifferent to whether they were under an imperial or a regional regime.

Admittedly, all this is hypothesis, even speculation. But my sole purpose here is simply to suggest a sphere in which speculation may usefully be pursued, in that it may lead to our attaching fresh significance to facts hitherto not noticed, or hardly noticed at all. Then, one day, perhaps, we may really assign to the Mughal Empire its true place in history.

Chapter Nine

The Patrimonial-Bureaucratic Empire of the Mughals*

STEPHEN P. BLAKE

A number of non-specialists have used the Mughal Empire as an example of various models of state organization,[1] but no authority on Muslim India has yet attempted to place the Mughal state in a larger context, as part of a more generalized type of political organization. Depending on which aspect of the state was examined (economic, administrative, social, religious or military), the Empire was characterized as oriental, despotic, Persian, Indian, Turkish, Mongol, or some combination of these. In no instance were the implications of these terms fully spelled out, and no complete model of this traditional state was presented.[2] The lack of a

* Stephen P. Blake is Associate Professor, Department of History, St Olaf College, Northfield, MV. This paper is based partly on research in England and India underwritten by a grant from the Fulbright Fellowship Committee. The author would like to thank them for their support.

1 Compare the treatment of the Mughal Empire in the following: S.N. Eisenstadt, *The Political Systems of Empires* (New York: The Free Press, 1969); Arnold Toynbee, *A Study of History*, 12 vols, (London: Oxford Univ. Press, 1935–64), p. 7, pt. 4; Marshall G.S. Hodgson, *The Venture of Islam*, 3 vols, (Chicago and London: Univ. of Chicago Press, 1974), p. 3; Edward L. Farmer et al., *A Comparative History of Civilizations in Asia*, 2 vols, (Reading, Mass., Addison-Wesley, 1977), I; and Max Weber, *Economy and Society*, Guenther Roth and Claus Wittich (eds), 3 vols, (New York: Bedminster Press, 1968), p. 3.

2 M. Athar Ali exhibits the clearest perception of this failure in his presidential address to the 1972 meeting of the Indian History Congress, *Proceedings of the 33rd Session of the Indian History Congress* (Muzaffarpur: Indian History Congress, 1972), pp. 175–88. In the last chapter of his recent work, *Merchants and Rulers in Gujarat* (Berkeley and Los Angeles: Univ. of California Press, 1976), Michael Pearson offers a model of the political system in Gujarat. This model certainly has implications for the organization

blueprint did not mean, however, that scholars wrote about the Mughal Empire in a vacuum, without presuppositions; on the contrary, a set of unexamined assumptions which established the categories of analysis and limited the varieties of evidence lay beneath most explications of the Mughal state. The following reinterpretation is based on the belief that these assumptions were non-indigenous and anachronistic, were not supported by the Persian sources, and were the cause of widespread misunderstanding.

The source of these assumptions was the notion that the Mughal Empire was ancestor to the British Raj—and, to be sure, there were a number of ways in which the British system followed the Mughal practice. For example, like the Mughals, the British divided governmental authority into two main branches, military and revenue; they kept the basic Mughal administrative subdivisions and centralized civil power at each level in the hands of one person; and they adopted, especially after the Mutiny of 1857, the Mughal position that the state's role should be limited to collecting taxes and maintaining law and order. As a result, most specialists on the Mughal period (particularly those writing in the early part of the century) looked to the highly structured military, judicial and administrative systems of late Imperial India (*c.* 1875–1914) for clues to the organization of the Mughal state. Thus, scholars described *mansabdārs*, the officers of the Mughal army, as members of a finely graded, hierarchical system of rank and responsibility similar to that of the British army, with detailed salary schedules, promotions, demotions, bestowal of honours, regulations regarding horses and equipment, with a great gap between officers and soldiers. Mansabdārs filled almost all the posts in what was portrayed as an elaborately bureaucratic administrative system. The Empire was divided and subdivided, according to this view, into provinces, districts and subdistricts for ease of administration. At each level, military, fiscal and judicial officials operated within definite jurisdictional limits. Carefully drawn lines of authority, it was argued, linked ministers of central departments in the capital to junior officials in small towns, with each official answering to his immediate superior. These scholars seem to have understood Mughal government as a kind

of the empire at large, but Pearson does not spell them out in any detail. He restricts his analysis for the most part to western India and Gujarat.

of undeveloped forerunner of the rational, highly systematized military, administrative and legal framework of British Imperial India.[3]

THE PATRIMONIAL-BUREAUCRATIC EMPIRE

Before analysing the Mughal government, I would like to discuss briefly a model of the pre-modern state called the patrimonial-bureaucratic empire. As an ideal type, this model does not reflect the working of any actual state, but presents a catalogue of elements drawn from existing situations and ordered into a functioning but theoretical system. Just as an economy can be judged as a 'free market economy' without displaying

[3] Examples of this approach occur most frequently in the work of an earlier generation of scholars whose writings were responsible for the standard introductions to the Mughal state. See, for example, William Irvine, *The Army of the Indian Moghuls: Its Organization and Administration* (1903; rpt. New Delhi: Eurasian Publishing House Private Ltd., 1962); Ibn Hasan, *The Central Structure of the Mughal Empire* (1936; rpt. Karachi: Oxford Univ. Press, 1967); Ishtiaq Husain Qureshi, *The Administration of the Mughal Empire* (Karachi: Univ. of Karachi, 1966); A.L. Srivastava, *Akbar the Great*, 2 vols, (Agra, U.P.: Shiva Lal Agarwala and Company, 1962–67), 2; P. Saran, *The Provincial Government of the Mughals* (Allahabad, U.P., Kitabistan, 1941).

The younger historians, on the other hand, having narrowed their interests and limited their topics, have not yet begun to re-examine the larger question. While none of what I stress here is unknown to them, these scholars have not, because of their more circumscribed purview, reflected on the implications of these aspects of Mughal government for the established interpretation. They have not seen the contradiction between the patrimonial aspects of the Mughal state and the conventional description of it in the standard works. See M. Athar Ali, *The Mughal Nobility Under Aurangzeb* (Bombay: Asia Publishing House, 1968; paperback ed., 1970); and Satish Chandra, *Parties and Politics at the Mughal Court*, 2nd ed. (New Delhi: People's Publishing House, 1972). Both authors have put together detailed studies that break important new ground, but neither has looked into the impact of his work on the conventional model of the Mughal state.

Two careful, imaginative Western historians of Mughal India, John F. Richards and Michael N. Pearson, are pertinent also. Pearson's closely argued study focuses almost exclusively on western India. Richards's painstaking examination of Mughal administration in the south Indian state of Golconda, a revealing look at an often-ignored area, discusses both the patrimonial and bureaucratic aspects of the Mughal state without touching the larger issue. See *Mughal Administration in Golconda* (Oxford: Clarendon Press, 1975), pp. 75–8. Finally, a look at the new historical atlas of South Asia reveals that the older view is far from dead. The table portraying the administrative organization of the Mughal Empire is a perfect rendering of the standard interpretation. See Joseph Schwartzberg (ed.), *A Historical Atlas of South Asia* (Chicago and London: Univ. of Chicago Press, 1978), plate VI. A. 2, p. 45.

all the elements of Adam Smith's model, for example, so an empire can be termed 'patrimonial-bureaucratic' without demonstrating all the particulars of the type. Understood in this way, the model is more a suggestion, an outline, a guide, or point of departure than a final explanation of a particular historical circumstance.

In discussing the political framework of this type I draw heavily on Max Weber's work on the patrimonial state. The ruler of such a state governs on the basis of a personal, traditional authority whose model is the patriarchal family. Patrimonial domination originates in the patriarch's authority over his household; it entails obedience to a person, not an office; it depends on the reciprocal loyalty between a subject and his master; and it is limited only by the ruler's discretion. Patrimonial states arise, according to Weber, when lords and princes extend their sway over extrahousehold subjects (patrimonial masters themselves) in areas beyond the patriarchal domain. This extension involves a change of authority: from the patrimonial, which is domestic and personal, to the purely political, which is military and judicial and which must be administered by extrahousehold officials. Expansion does not limit the ruler's ambition, however. Within the larger realm, conceived as a huge household, the ruler/master tries to exercise military and judicial power in the same absolute and unrestrained way. In the description which follows I distinguish two variants within the patrimonial type of political organization. The first, the patrimonial kingdom, is the smaller of the two, and is closer in organization and government to the ideal represented by the patriarchal family. The second, the patrimonial-bureaucratic empire, is larger and more diffuse. Rulers of such empires developed a collection of strategies and techniques that allowed personal, household-dominated rule of an attenuated sort within realms of considerable area, population and complexity.

To govern successfully, a patrimonial ruler must have at his disposal a body of loyal, disciplined soldiers. Patrimonial armies were made up of troops whose primary allegiance was to an individual rather than to a dynasty or an office. In patrimonial kingdoms the military forces consisted, for the most part, of the household troops of the ruler. In patrimonial-bureaucratic empires, on the other hand, armies were large and complex. The armies required to maintain order in states of such size were too large for the imperial household to manage and support. As a result, the armies of patrimonial-bureaucratic emperors split into two groups: the private household troops of the emperor, and the soldiers of major subordinates, who made up the bulk of the army—men who were bound more to their commanders than to the emperor.

Patrimonial administration followed a similar pattern. In the limited compass of the patrimonial kingdom the private domain of the ruler was virtually coterminous with the realm itself, and there was little or no difference between the state and household officials. In patrimonial-bureaucratic empires, however, these groups were not the same. The extension of control beyond the household domain called forth extra-patrimonial officials who administered, for the most part, the collection of taxes and the settlement of a limited number of disputes. Such officials, neither dependents nor bureaucrats, worked in an organization intermediate between the household apparatus of the patrimonial kingdom and the highly bureaucratized system of the modern state. For example, patrimonial-bureaucratic officials filled positions that were loosely defined and imperfectly ordered—a situation very different from the articulated hierarchy of precisely circumscribed offices in a modern bureaucracy. Candidates for posts in patrimonial-bureaucratic administrations had to demonstrate personal qualifications—loyalty, family and position—in addition to technical qualifications such as reading and writing. Whereas modern bureaucrats are given fixed salaries in money, members of these administrations were often assigned prebends or benefices, such as rights to certain fees, taxes or goods due to the state. In a modern bureaucracy a job is a career and is the primary occupation of the jobholder; in patrimonial-bureaucratic administrations, on the other hand, office-holders served at the pleasure of the ruler and often performed tasks unrelated to their appointments. Finally, while modern bureaucrats are subject to an official, impersonal authority, patrimonial-bureaucratic emperors demanded personal loyalty and allegiance of their officials. Such rulers ignored the modern distinction between private and official, or personal and professional, and tried to make household dependents of their subordinates.

In the smallest and most intimate patrimonial kingdoms, officials received compensation for their services directly from the ruler's household—they ate at his table, clothed themselves from his wardrobe and rode horses from his stables. Beyond that, however, they had no claim on the resources of the realm. In the larger, more complex situation of the patrimonial-bureaucratic empire, on the other hand, rulers found it impossible to maintain personally all members of their expanded administrations; thus they began more and more to give officials benefices or prebends. In time this led to a situation in which the greater portion of state revenues was assigned to soldiers and officials. Since these revenues bypassed the ruler entirely, and since the assigned lands were often at considerable distances from the capital, this arrangement meant a loosening of the emperor's control over his officials. Under such conditions the strength of personal, patrimonial authority began to wane, and officials began to appropriate prebends and declare their independence.

As a result, patrimonial-bureaucratic emperors began to devise strategies that would replace, to some extent at least, the traditional sources of control. In order to maintain their hold and prevent appropriation, emperors travelled widely and frequently, renewing in countless face-to-face meetings the personal bond between master and subject on which the state was founded; they demanded of all soldiers and officials regular attendance at court and, on their departure, often required that a son or relative be left behind as hostage; they periodically rotated officials from post to post, allowing no one to keep his job for more than a few years running; they maintained a network of newswriters or intelligence gatherers outside the regular administrative structure who reported directly to them; and, finally, in an effort to check the power of subordinates, rulers of patrimonial-bureaucratic empires created provincial and district offices with overlapping responsibilities.[4]

As I turn now to an analysis of the Mughal state, it is important to remember that I have just described the political structure of an ideal type. Although one cannot expect to find a perfect patrimonial-bureaucratic image in the governmental organization of any historical state, a number of states should approximate the model more or less closely. The Mughal Empire belongs to that number,[5] as do several other roughly

[4] The most complete discussion of the patrimonial state and its variants is in Weber, *Economy and Society*, 1: 229–57, 263–4; 3: 966–72, 1006–69, 1086–92. Weber's remarks on the patrimonial-bureaucratic empire are scattered and fragmentary, and so not easy to integrate and interpret. His style is to construct pure types—the patrimonial state and the modern bureaucratic state—and contrast them. No historical state, as Weber himself points out, exactly matches either type. All present and past state systems are combinations of elements from several types; the patrimonial-bureaucratic empire is a mixture of the modern bureaucratic and patrimonial states. Actual historical examples of the model differ as they approach closer to one or the other pure type.

[5] This is, as far as I know, the first serious attempt to analyse the Mughal empire in

contemporaneous Asian states—the Ottoman Empire in Turkey, the Safavid Empire in Iran, the Tokugawa Shogunate in Japan and the Ming Empire in China.[6]

The *Āʾīn-i Akbari* (Regulations of Akbar) of Abu al-Fazl is the major text on Mughal government; it is the manual that expounds Akbar's conception of the state and his plans for ordering and administering it. The structure developed by Akbar and described in the *Āʾīn* by Abu al-Fazl endured: succeeding emperors left it pretty much alone, and it survived in its basic form down to the early eighteenth century. Most misinterpretations of the Mughal Empire stem from a misreading of the *Āʾīn.* It is not that scholars relied on inaccurate translations—most of them, in fact, knew Persian, and read the texts in the original. The misreading arose instead from the preconceptions they brought to their work. To examine the *Āʾīn* de novo, in Persian, and, as far as possible, without presuppositions, is the only way to uncover the indigenous categories of state organization.

The bulk of this essay concentrates on the details of reinterpretation. While I do not mean to imply that the Mughal state was unique, I also do not want to begin a search for origins. Such a search is often elusive and unproductive, especially when it is intended as an explanation. However, I do want to include a few lines on the Asian states that seem to have influenced, to some degree at least, the organization of the Mughal Empire.

The Mughal Emperors were Turks. Babar, the founder of the dynasty, spoke Chaghatai Turkish and descended from Timur, the great Central Asian ruler (r. 1370–1405). 'Timurid' is probably a more accurate name for the dynasty than 'Mughal' (from Mongol). As Turks, the Mughal Emperors—like the Timurid rulers before them—were influenced by both the Mongols and Persians. The Mongol state of Chinghiz Khan (r. 1206–27), much closer than the Mughal Empire to the pure patrimonial type, contributed a strong patrimonial strain. The Mongols, for example, gave Imperial officers household titles: the man in charge of one of Chinghiz's armies had the title 'cook', and some of the highest officials

terms of the patrimonial-bureaucratic model. Both Pearson, *Merchants and Rulers,* p. 62, and Peter Hardy, *The Muslims of British India* (Cambridge: Cambridge Univ. Press, 1972), pp. 12–14 mention Weber's work. Neither, however, writes at any length on the application of the model to Mughal India.

[6] See *Shahjahanabad,* ch. 7.

were given the title 'fifth-son'—Chinghiz had four natural sons and, at one time, three fifth-sons. Furthermore, a decree issued by Hulegu (son of the Grand Khan Mongke) in the mid-1250s divided government into the same three categories—household, army and empire—as did the *Ā'īn*.[7]

The Persians contributed a strong bureaucratic strain not only to the Mughals, but also to the other Turkish and Mongol states in West and Central Asia. From the time of the Sasanid Empire (*c.* AD 224–651), the Persians had a routinized system of tax collection, a well-developed, bureaucratic administrative system and a tradition of strong centralized rule under an absolute, semidivine emperor. Akbar's contribution to the patrimonial-bureaucratic empire in India was to develop, refine, and systematize the elements of state organization he had inherited from India and West and Central Asia. Both the Muslim dynasties which preceded the Mughals (collectively called the Delhi Sultanate, *c.* 1206–1526) and the earlier Hindu states such as the Mauryan Empire (*c.* 322–185 BC) exhibited aspects of patrimonial-bureaucratic organization. Akbar synthesized these elements into the coherent, rational system of government that we see described in the *Ā'īn-i Akbari*, and gave the patrimonial-bureaucratic empire in India its most systematic, fully developed, and clearly articulated form.

THE STRUCTURE OF THE MUGHAL EMPIRE

In his preface to the *Ā'īn-i Akbari*, Abu al-Fazl states that the art of governing comprises three topics: 'I shall explain the regulations [*ā'īn*] of the household [*manzil*], the army [*sipāh*], and the empire [*mulk*] since these three constitute the work of a ruler.'[8] The divisions of the text reflect

[7] Rashid al-Din, *Jami al-Tavarikh*, B. Karimi (ed.), 2 vols, (Tehran: n.p., 1959), 2: 688. I am indebted to Thomas Allsen for the reference and the information about the Mongols.

[8] Abu al-Fazl, *The A'in-i Akbari*, H. Blochmann (ed.), 2 vols, (Calcutta: Asiatic Society of Bengal, 1872–77), 1: 7; Abu al-Fazl, *The A'in-i Akbari*, H. Blochmann and H.S. Jarrett, trans., corrected and annotated by Jadunath Sarkar, 2nd edn, 3 vols, (1927–49; rpt. New Delhi: New Imperial Book Depot, 1965), 1: 9. I follow the system of transliteration in F. Steingass, *A Comprehensive Persian-English Dictionary*. In all footnotes to the *Ā'īn*, I include references to both the Persian and English editions of the text, so that interested readers may discover Blochmann's errors by comparing his translation with the original work. All translations in this paper are, of course, my own.

this view of state organization. Book One discusses the Imperial household, Book Two the army, Book Three the empire at large, Book Four Hindu religious, social and intellectual activity, and Book Five the sayings of Akbar.

Household

The dominating presence in Book One and, indeed, in the text as a whole (two of the five books centre on him) is Akbar, the emperor. A major theme in the first book, one that is treated from a variety of perspectives, is the relationship between the emperor and his subjects. Abu al-Fazl defines a ruler as a man touched by God, a person ennobled by divine inspiration: 'Royalty [*pādshāhī*] is a light from God. . . . Without a mediator it appears as a holy form to the holders of power and at the sight of it everyone bends the forehead of praise to the ground of submission.'[9] On receipt of this illumination a ruler acquires the qualities and virtues needed to govern successfully. These include trust in God, prayer and devotion, a large heart, and, first and most important, a paternal love for the people—the ideal ruler governs as a father.[10] Such a ruler—and Abu al-Fazl uses Akbar as the exemplar—is presented as an *insān-i kāmil* (perfect man), a Sufi phrase which describes a person who enjoys a special and intimate relationship with God.[11] In his massive biography of Akbar, the *Akbar Namah*, Abu al-Fazl includes a number of miraculous stories intended to illustrate the emperor's close relationship with God, and to buttress the claim that Akbar was a perfect man.

This view of Akbar as a divinely inspired patriarch, an extremely wise, just, competent and creative father of his people, is one supported by the most controversial *āʾīn* in Book One, A'in 77. 'The Regulation on Guidance' (*āʾīn-i rāhnamūnī*), mistranslated 'His Majesty as the Spiritual Guide of the People',[12] has been interpreted by the translator Heinrich

[9] Ibid., 1: 2; trans. 1: 3. For a similar statement, see Ibid., 1: 158 and trans. 1: 172.

[10] Ibid., 1: 2; 1: 3.

[11] For a discussion of the term, see *The Encyclopaedia of Islam*, 2nd. edn, s.v. 'al-insan al-kamil'. Hodgson, *Venture of Islam*, 3: 75–80; and Srivastava, *Akbar*, 2: 309 both argue that Abu al-Fazl presented Akbar in such a light throughout his writings. A'in 77 provides perhaps the best example of Abu al-Fazl's approach. See *A'in*, Blochmann (ed.), 1: 158–60; and trans. 1: 170–6.

[12] Ibid., 1: 158; trans. 1: 170.

Blochmann and others as Akbar's attempt to start a new religion called the *dīn-i ilāhī* or divine faith. As several scholars have pointed out, however, this interpretation is surely false. What Akbar almost certainly intended, as befits a perfect man, was to start a small Sufi sect with himself as *pīr* or leader.[13] A crucial phrase in A'in 77, 'regulations for the disciples' (*ā'īn-i irādat guzīnān*) was misrendered 'Ordinances of the Divine Faith' by Blochmann and was, without justification, set off from the body of the text.[14] Neither the regulations nor the ceremony of initiation described in A'in 77 would seem unusual to any member of a Sufi order.

The elaborate rules governing admission to the court and observing correct behaviour before the throne (A'ins 73–75) also support this reading of the relationship between emperor and subject. Extreme deference is the only attitude possible in the presence of an emperor who is also a perfect man. That rulers are touched by God, singled out, and called to the throne is a major theme in Abu al-Fazl's discussion of the Imperial household. Once in power a ruler is inspired by God to govern his state with the same strength, wisdom and compassion that a father employs in looking after his household.

A second theme—the mixing of household and state—surfaces in Abu al-Fazl's discussion of this first branch of government. In the Imperial household, departments dealing with purely domestic matters coexist side-by-side with departments of wider reach and greater significance. In Book One there are regulations for the harem, the wardrobe, the kitchen and the perfumery; there are also directives on the care and keeping of the emperor's elephants, horses, cows, camels and mules. Several *ā'īn* touch on matters of construction—on styles, materials and workmen. In addition to departments of a mostly personal and familial kind, there are departments whose responsibility extends beyond the care and comfort of the emperor's immediate family. Thus Book One contains regulations on the Imperial mint, the state arsenal, the department of the treasury,

13 This issue has generated a good deal of controversy. For the arguments in favour of a new religion, see ibid., trans. 1: 176–223. For the opposing and, it seems to me, more plausible view, see Srivastava, *Akbar*, 1: 303–13, 2: 311–16; and S.M. Ikram, *Muslim Civilization in India*, Ainslie T. Embree (ed.) (New York and London: Columbia Univ. Press, 1964), pp. 156–65. For a comprehensive and reliable discussion of the entire issue, see S.A.A. Rizvi, *Religious and Intellectual History of the Muslims in Akbar's Reign* (New Delhi: Munshiram Manoharlal, 1975), pp. 374–417.

14 *A'in*, Blochmann (ed.), 1: 160 and trans. 1: 175.

the use of royal seals, the symbolic prerogatives of royalty and the organization of the Imperial camp.

A look at the finances of the Imperial household indicates something of the scale of this branch of government. In 1594 the income of Akbar's household (i.e. the monies from the emperor's private lands) was about 25 per cent of total state revenues, and salaries for clerks, servants and labourers—by no means the entire dependent population of the household—amounted to nearly 9 per cent of Imperial revenues.[15] All of this suggests close similarities between the Mughal and patrimonial-bureaucratic empires. The centrality and importance of the Imperial household in the organization of Akbar's empire parallels the position of the ruler's establishment in the ideal type. Abu al-Fazl's portrayal of Akbar as a divinely aided father to his people recalls the traditional, family rooted authority of the patrimonial-bureaucratic emperor. And, finally, the inclusion of state offices and officials in the Imperial household, the combination there of personal and official, brings to mind the thwarted ambition of patrimonial-bureaucratic emperors to absorb the state into the household and to rule the realm as one great extended family.

Army

In Book Two of the *Āʾīn-i Akbari* Abu al-Fazl discusses the army, and divides this second branch of Mughal government into four classes: mansabdārs and their men, *aḥadis* (from *aḥad*, 'one'), other soldiers and infantry. Although mansabdārs are clearly preferred, and although scholars have written a good deal about them, it is well to remember that this group did not make up the whole of the Mughal army. Men with mounted followers became mansabdārs only after an interview with Akbar. In the meeting between the emperor and the applicant, Akbar had an opportunity to size up the candidate and to inquire into his background and experience. With his divinely aided insight and judgement, Akbar was, according to Abu al-Fazl, consistently able to choose superior men: 'According to his knowledge of the temper of the times . . . he

[15] In *The Agrarian System of Mughal India: 1556–1739* (Bombay, India: Asia Publishing House, 1963), p. 272, Irfan Habib estimates Akbar's private lands to have yielded about 25 per cent of total land revenues. For the salaries of servants and others, see *A'in*, Blochmann(ed.), 1: 9 and trans. 1: 12. The figure for total state revenues can be found in ibid., 1: 386 and trans. 2: 129.

evaluated many [candidates] immediately and gave them high rank at once.'[16] Akbar established sixty-six ranks, corresponding to the value of the letters in the word Allah. It is clear, however, that this division of the interval between ten and ten thousand, the high and low ranks, was mostly theoretical. Blochmann found, for example, that only thirty-three of the sixty-six possible ranks were ever actually filled during Akbar's reign.[17]

Aḥadis, the second class of the Mughal army, were single men who had no mounted military following, and so could not be given mansabdāri rank. Since they were often men of talent and birth, however, and skilled in fighting and administration, the emperor decided it was better to keep them nearby as a body of personal servants than to assign them to mansabdāri contingents. Aḥadis, like mansabdārs, had to maintain a certain number of horses in proper condition.[18]

The third class of the Mughal army included all those horsemen who were neither aḥadis nor members of a mansabdāri contingent. Since these men were usually too poor to own horses, the Mughals gave them lands or cash to buy mounts and to support themselves. In return, these cavalrymen served as extra troops for mansabdārs on campaigns and as auxiliaries for provincial authorities.[19]

The dominance of the cavalry in Mughal military thought and organization is reflected in the rag-tag character of the fourth class of the Mughal army, the footsoldiers. Of the nine groups listed under A'in 6, only one, matchlock bearers, participated in actual combat. Porters, runners, guards, gladiators, wrestlers, slaves, bearers and labourers worked as miscellaneous support personnel.[20]

The remainder of Book Two deals with other aspects of army organization: A'ins 7 and 8 establish procedures for the branding of horses, while A'in 9 outlines the regulations for mounting guard. For purposes of protecting the person and household of the ruler, the four divisions of the army were required to perform three kinds of guard duty. To staff the most visible and demanding shift, that which performed court duties and stood daily before the emperor, the army was divided into seven parts,

[16] Ibid., 1: 179 and trans. 1: 248. For another example of Akbar's penchant for making quick decisions on mansabdāri candidates see Ibid., 1: 191 and 1: 265.

[17] Ibid., trans. 1: 248–50.

[18] Ibid., 1: 187 and trans. 1: 259–60.

[19] Ibid., 1: 175, 187–8 and trans. 1: 241, 260–1.

[20] Ibid., 1: 188–90 and trans. 1: 261–4.

one for each day of the week. For the two longer shifts, the Mughal military forces were broken down into two separate and distinct divisions of twelve parts each. One shift, one-twelfth of the army, headquartered in the Imperial establishment for an entire month and the other shift, a different one-twelfth, lived with the emperor for a full year.[21]

Another group of regulations appears at first glance to have little in common with the subject matter of Book Two: A'ins 16–19 treat Akbar's charitable contributions; A'in 22 discusses feasts; A'in 23, fancy bazaars; A'in 24, marriage; and A'in 25, education. If these regulations are read carefully and in context, however, a common theme links them all: namely, the emperor's efforts to influence, order and shape the lives of his subordinates. Thus, the *ā'īns* on Akbar's gifts to the needy and deserving seem intended to give mansabdārs examples of meritorious activity.[22] The regulations on feasts and fancy bazaars are also exemplary, since feasts provide opportunities to dispense charity, and bazaars are occasions for hearing the grievances of local shopkeepers and inspecting the productions of household workshops.[23] Akbar's intention to regulate the private lives of his nobles is even more evident in the *ā'īns* covering marriage and education. In A'in 24 Akbar established rules for the size of dowries, the age of consent and the permitted degrees of consanguinity; he also appointed two officials to see that the rules were followed. Finally, in A'in 25 Akbar suggested reforms in the traditional system of education: he wanted the method of instruction simplified and its pace increased, and urged that the curriculum be expanded to include subjects of practical interest, like arithmetic, arithmetical notation, agriculture, household management, rules of government, and physiognomy in addition to the traditional religious topics.[24]

A'ins 27 and 28 cover hunting, and A'in 29, games. According to Abu al-Fazl, Akbar's motive in pursuing these activities was not primarily relaxation or diversion: hunting expeditions gave the emperor a chance to examine the condition of the people and the army, and games like chess and field hockey sharpened the reflexes, judgement and concentration of the participants.[25]

[21] Ibid., 1: 192 and trans. 1: 267–8.
[22] Ibid., 1: 197–9 and trans. 1: 276–80.
[23] Ibid., 1: 200–201 and trans. 1: 286–7.
[24] Ibid., 1: 201–2 and trans. 1: 287–89.
[25] Ibid., 1: 204–22 and trans. 1: 292–320.

It is time now to summarize Abu al-Fazl's discussion of the Mughal army. Mansabdārs, the most important of the four military divisions, received ranks and assignments only after an interview with the emperor. Acceptance into the army required no special qualifications and did not depend on heredity. Although Abu al-Fazl's table of sixty-six ranks suggests a carefully worked out system of organization, the fact that only thirty-three of these were ever used agrees with the individual and ad hoc character of other military arrangements—recruitment, promotion and assignment, for example. All mansabdārs reported directly to the ruler and not to other men of greater rank; no chain of command separated the emperor from his officer. Mansabdārs had to spend a good deal of time in the presence of the emperor. They were called to court on a change of assignment and for promotion, and they had to stand three separate guard duties in the Imperial household. The emperor apparently took advantage of these periods of proximity to meddle in their private lives: he regulated their marriages, prescribed the education of their sons and organized their leisure activities. The personnel of the Mughal army, like soldiers in patrimonial-bureaucratic empires, could not be contained within the Imperial household. As a result, the Mughal army functioned in two parts. One part was headquartered in the Imperial household. It included the aḥadis, Imperial foot-soldiers and mansabdārs who had been assigned duty at court and their contingents. The other part, on campaign or stationed in posts around the realm, comprised the mansabdārs outside court, their cavalry, and the extra horsemen and infantry assigned them.

All of this suggests an empire much closer to the patrimonial-bureaucratic than to the British Indian. It is inappropriate, it seems to me, to characterize Abu al-Fazl's discussion of mansabdārs in Book Two as the delineation of a highly bureaucratic administrative system. To describe it this way, as many scholars have done,[26] is to employ categories anachronistic and foreign to the Mughal experience. And, as I have tried to show in the discussion above, Book Two of the *Āʾīn-i Akbari* cannot bear the burden of such an interpretation. Book Two *does* seem to support the interpretation of the Mughal state as a patrimonial-bureaucratic empire. In Abu al-Fazl's discussion, the Mughal army is the adjunct of a household-dominated patrimonial-bureaucratic empire rather than the fighting arm of a highly structured, bureaucratically administered state.

26 See, for example, Srivastava, *Akbar*, 2: 218; 2: 37–41 and Qureshi, *Mughal Administration*, p. 102.

Empire

The designation of the empire as the third aspect of governance indicates a progressive widening in the range of the ruler's responsibility. A'in I of Book Three lays out the duties of the *sipāh sālār* (army commander), the man in general charge of provincial affairs. Known later as the *nāzim* or *ṣūbahdār*, this mansabdār controlled the largest body of troops in the area and was primarily responsible for keeping the peace.[27] A'in 2 discusses the major military subordinate of the sipāh sālār, the *faujdār.* This officer commanded a large body of cavalry and was supposed to maintain order in several subdivisions (*parganahs*) of the province. He was charged with not only subduing recalcitrant cultivators, but also with checking the ambitions of local revenue collectors and *jāgirdārs* (mansabdārs who had been assigned lands in lieu of cash salaries).[28] A'in 3 outlines the duties of the Imperial subordinates (*qāzi* and *mīr' adl*) responsible for the administration of justice in the provinces. The regulation does not assign these men specific posts, and they may well have had permanent positions only in large towns and cities, spending the rest of their time riding circuit and dispensing periodic justice.[29] A'in 4 takes up the duties of the *kotwāl,* the chief urban official in Mughal India, who was charged with patrolling the streets and maintaining order, collecting information on townspeople, regulating artisans and merchants, seeing that markets ran properly, and collecting taxes.[30]

A'ins 5, 6, and 7 describe the responsibilities of revenue collectors. The *'amal-guzār* (collector) was the chief fiscal officer at the subprovincial level, who, with the help of his assistants, oversaw all aspects of revenue administration in the village. He dealt directly with village officials, and mediated between them and provincial and Imperial officers. He also sent to court information on prices, local assignees, artisans, cultivators and the poor.[31] A'in 6 sets out the duties of the accountant (*bitikchī*), writer, and assistant to the 'amal-guzār. He gathered data on land tenures, sales, leases, yields, prices and taxes and made it available to the collector. In the survey of village lands, and during the assessment and collection of taxes, the bitikchī prepared a meticulous record of all holdings,

[27] *A'in,* Blochmann, ed., 1: 280–3 and trans. 2: 37–41.

[28] Ibid., 1: 283 and trans. 2: 41–2.

[29] Ibid., 1: 283; and trans. 2: 42–3.

[30] Ibid., 1: 284–5 and trans. 2: 43–5.

assessments, payments, and disbursements. After being checked by the collector, this record was sent directly to the Imperial court.[32] The second assistant of the collector, the *khizānadār* (treasurer), is considered in A'in 7; this official deposited government revenues in a secure place in or near the collector's residence. All monies received were entered in an account book and no disbursements were made without the written order of the provincial or Imperial *dīwān* (finance officer).[33]

The rest of Book Three deals with matters of land revenue. A'ins 8 through 13 consider the classification and measurement of agricultural lands. To fully understand A'ins 14 (The Nineteen Years' Rate) and 15 (The Ten Years' Settlement) it is necessary to see them in the context of Akbar's attempts to determine a fair and accurate tax on agricultural produce. Before 1579 the tax demanded of an individual cultivator was based on estimates of the size of his land, the yield on his crop and its price in the market. In 1560, in an attempt to reduce the inaccuracy and unreliability of this method, Akbar's men began collecting data on the market prices and revenue rates of various crops in the provinces of Agra, Allahabad, Oudh, Delhi, Lahore, Multan and Malwa. These figures, collected for the years through 1579, are displayed in the tables of A'in 14.[34] In 1575, still dissatisfied with the revenue system, Akbar ordered that all lands in the central Indo-Gangetic provinces revert to the *khāliṣa*, the Imperial domain. This meant that mansabdārs who had been assigned the state's share of the tax on a group of lands (the lands were called a *jāgīr* and the person so compensated a *jāgīrdār*) were henceforward to be paid in cash from the Imperial treasury. During the following five years the lands in the newly expanded Imperial domain were carefully measured, crop prices meticulously noted and the tax rates accurately determined. In 1579 a new assessment was prepared: the revenue rates for the five years prior to 1575 were added to the figures collected from 1575 to 1579, and the total divided by ten. The new assessment, the average of the rates for each crop over a ten year period, is shown for the eight provinces of the central Empire in A'in 15.[35] After these figures were established, Akbar removed a large part of the rich lands of the

31 Ibid., 1: 285–8 and trans. 2: 46–50.
32 Ibid., 1: 288 and trans. 2: 50–2.
33 Ibid., 1: 289 and trans. 2: 52–3.
34 Ibid., 1: 303–47 and trans. 2: 75–93.
35 Ibid., 1: 347–86 and trans. 2: 94–122.

central provinces from the Imperial domain and reassigned it to mansabdārs, but retained for his own household lands yielding some 25 per cent of total revenues. The remainder of A'in 15 is given over to a general account of the fifteen provinces of the empire. Included in these descriptions are revenue figures for each revenue subdivision of each district of each province.

The seven officials who made up the administrative structure described in Book Three are not presented as links in administrative chains joining individual villages—by way of subdistrict, district and provincial offices—to central departments in the capital. Rather, as we have seen, an official's responsibility often cut across several of these essentially fiscal divisions; individual men were not posted at each separate level. In such an arrangement Mughal officials, unlike modern bureaucrats, were expected to deal not only with those nearest them in the organization—immediate superiors and subordinates—but with others as well. In fact, the expectation seems to have been that most officials would report directly to the emperor. A passage in A'in 7 suggests the Mughal view: 'All of the work, from that of the sipāh sālār to that of this person [k͟hizānadār], is primarily in the charge of the emperor. And since the strength of one person is not sufficient, he appointed a deputy for each task and gave the necessary threads [of government] extra strength.'[36] A look at what modern scholars call the central level of administration lends support to the idea that the emperor took direct and personal responsibility for all facets of governance. Book Three, as we have seen, discusses only the seven officials named above; it contains nothing whatsoever on the superiors of the army-commander, collector or judge stationed at court.

It is necessary to return to the preface to find mention of these officials. There Abu al-Fazl divides the men who assist the ruler, the men of the state, into four groups. The first group, nobles of the state (*nūyīnān-i daulat*), included all high-ranking mansabdārs. As the head of this group, the *vākīl* (prime minister) was the '. . . emperor's deputy in all things concerning the empire (*mulk*) and the household (*manzil*).'[37] Accordingly, he was the one person in the Imperial entourage most concerned with the problems of the army-commander and his subordinates in the districts. Group two, friends of victory (*auliyā-i nuṣrat*),

36 Ibid., 1: 289 and trans. 2: 53.

37 Ibid., 1: 4 and trans. 1: 4–5.

included all those who dealt with the collection and disbursement of state funds. The dīwān commanded these men, and was the person in the capital most interested in the reports of the 'amal-guẕār and his assistants. Group three, companions of the emperor (*aṣḥābi-i ṣuḥbat*) included men of religion and learning. Here we find the *sadr*, to whom the provincial officials responsible for law and justice reported. Group four, servants (*arbāb-i k̲h̲idmat*), included those who worked for and waited upon the emperor and his family in the Imperial household.[38]

Book Three, like Books One and Two, describes an empire much closer to the patrimonial-bureaucratic than to the British Indian model. Although the Mughal state was too large to be absorbed into the household and administered as the emperor's private domain, the Mughal policy of dividing the realm for purposes of land revenue administration into two types—household lands and assignable lands—enabled the Mughal ruler to control a large part of state revenues personally, as did the patrimonial-bureaucratic emperor. In the area of the Imperial domain, supplementary officers from the Imperial establishment were assigned to district and subdistrict levels to help the regular officials with the actual collection of taxes. Officials at court, whose responsibilities covered both the household and the empire, directed the activities of all administrative personnel in the lands of the Imperial domain.

The second area comprised the lands assigned to mansabdārs, and ranged from a minimum of 75 per cent of the empire during the reign of Akbar to a maximum of 95 per cent during the reign of his son Jahangir. Although the extra household officials of Book Three remained in the assigned lands to oversee the activities of the mansabdārs' agents, it is clear that this part of the empire could not be controlled as closely as the household lands of the emperor. Akbar's brief resumption of assigned lands—surely in part an attempt to extend the range of authority of the Imperial establishment—illustrates an important truth about patrimonial-bureaucratic empires: the impossibility of achieving in pre-modern times a degree of control over the empire at large comparable to that exercised in the household.

The organization of officials also followed a patrimonial-bureaucratic pattern. In Mughal India men of the state were not, for the most part, allowed to specialize in either the civil or military branches of government;

[38] Ibid., 1: 4–5 and trans. 1: 6–7.

all officials came from one class, the mansabdāri, and all were deemed capable of handling both kinds of responsibility. For the Mughals, there was no clear relationship between mansabdāri rank and position in government; high-ranking officials sometimes held provincial or subprovincial posts, and middling ranks often filled central level offices in the household. For Mughal officials, promotion depended as much on being present at court for birthday, New Year's and *'Īd* (Islamic holiday) celebrations and on the quality of gifts given to the emperor, as it did on performance in office. Finally, as we saw above, Mughal officials usually reported directly to officers in the Imperial household rather than to officials of lesser responsibility outside the capital. All of this, it seems to me, argues against the prevailing interpretation of Mughal administration.

That interpretation supposes a complex system of offices arranged in a hierarchy stretching from villages to central departments, offices manned by graded and ranked officials with specific duties and responsibilities. Blochmann's decision to entitle Book Three of his translation of the *Ā'īn* 'Imperial Administration' encapsulates this entire misconceived attempt to explain the Mughal state on the model of the British Indian Empire. There is, in fact, no justification for such a heading: the Persian edition of the text uses the word mulk (empire)[39] and Book Three itself deals with the state at large—everything of interest outside the household and the army. It covers much more than 'Administration'. In the Mughal method of government there were no clear-cut lines of authority, no separate departments at successive levels of administration and no tables of organization. On the contrary, what one finds are groups of men in the Imperial household who oversaw, on behalf of the emperor, provincial and subprovincial officials, who in turn exercised military, financial or legal power within jurisdictions of varying scope.

CONTROL OF OFFICIALS

Within the smaller compass of the patrimonial kingdom, the ruler retained control by dint of personal force. Where the area and scale were restricted, and where the fiction of the state as a household approached reality, a ruler was better able to renew the ties of loyalty and devotion

[39] Ibid., 1: 265 and trans. 2: 1.

in the day-to-day job of governing. The great size of patrimonial-bureaucratic empires, however, denied emperors the advantages of such workaday intimacy. In order to prevent the appropriation of prebends or benefices, and to reinvigorate the relationship on which the empire was founded, patrimonial-bureaucratic emperors had to employ extraordinary measures: requiring attendance at court, establishing overlapping spheres of authority, transferring officials frequently, using intelligence gatherers and travelling regularly.[40] That the Mughals used all of these strategies again suggests the similarities between the patrimonial-bureaucratic model and the Mughal Empire.

As we have seen, the Mughal Emperor required regular attendance at court of all his officers. In addition to the intricate schedule of weekly, monthly and yearly visits set out in A'in 9 of Book Two, mansabdārs were expected to present themselves before the emperor on a number of other occasions: after a change in assignment, after a change in jāgīr posting, on the occasion of promotion, and, if at all possible, on days of special celebration. A second technique of patrimonial-bureaucratic control used by the Mughals was the appointment of officials with competing, cross-cutting areas of responsibility. In the provinces, the authority of the provincial governor was undercut by two other officials, the finance officer and the *ba<u>kh</u>shī* (military official). The finance officer was responsible for collecting and disbursing monies at both the provincial and subprovincial levels. No sum of consequence could be withdrawn from the provincial treasuries without his signature. In matters concerning the army, the military official encroached on the provincial governor's territory. He inspected the contingents of provincial mansabdārs, including those of the provincial governor and the finance officer, to see that horses and riders met rank requirements. At the subprovincial level a similar system of checks and balances prevailed: the army captain worked to protect villagers against unjust demands by the collector and local assignees, and the treasurer would not make payments without the authorization of the finance officer.

The Mughal emperors relied on frequent transfers to curb the independence of far-flung subordinates; no man was allowed to keep his piece of land or stay at his post for more than three or four consecutive years. This strategy was designed to prevent distant mansabdārs from making

40 Weber, *Economy and Society*, 3: 1042–4.

TABLE 1

YEARS AWAY FROM THE CAPITAL: 1556–1739*

Regnal Years	*Akbar*	*Jahangir*	*Shahjahan*	*Aurangzeb*	*Bahadur Shah*	*Farrukhsiyar*	*Muhammad Shah*	
	1556–1605	*1605–1627*	*1627–1658*	*1658–1707*	*1707–1712*	*1712–1719*	*1719–1739*	
	49 years	*22 years*	*31 years*	*49 years*	*5 years*	*7 years*	*20 years*	
5	1556–60		1630–32	1662–64	1707–12			
10	1565–67	1613–19	1635–37					
15			1638–43	1669–71				
20	1577–78		1645–48	1674–76				
25			1651–53	1679–1707				
30	1585–86							
35								
40								
45	1599–1601							
50								
Percentage of Reign Absent	10/49 20%	6/22 27%	14/31 45%	34/49 69%	5/5 100%	0/7 0%	0/20 0%	Total 69/183 38%

* The sources for this table are the chronicles of each emperor's reign. The capital city of the empire shifted several times during the period. From 1564–71 it was in Agra, from 1571–85 in Fatehpur Sikri, from 1585–98 in Lahore, from 1598–1648 in Agra and from 1648–1858 in Shahjahanabad. Only the first twenty years of Muhammad Ṣhah's reign, up to the sack of Delhi in 1739, are included. Muhammad Shah died in 1748.

alliances with local elements and building independent bases of power. Although such frequent shifts introduced a great deal of waste and uncertainty into Mughal government, Akbar and his successors thought the gain in control worth the loss in efficiency. A'in 10 of Book Two discusses the duties of the newswriter (*wāqi'-nawīs*). Although Abu al-Fazl concentrates on the duties of those men assigned to court, it is clear that newswriters were stationed in cities and towns throughout the realm, and were responsible for acquainting the emperor with the doings of the mansabdārs and local assignees in their areas.[41]

Of the strategies used by patrimonial-bureaucratic emperors to control their officials, travel was the one most heavily relied upon by Mughal rulers. Regular travel across the countryside to renew personal ties between the leader and distant subordinates was an important activity in the reigns of most emperors. Table 1 illustrates the pervasiveness of this tactic during the reigns of the seven emperors between 1556 and 1739. Even when trips of one year or less are excluded, rulers of the Mughal state spent nearly 40 per cent of their time during this approximately two hundred-year period on tour. An administrative manual written in the early eighteenth century and devoted to the reigns of Shahjahan and Aurangzeb corroborates this finding. The manual divides the reign of each emperor into two parts: settled (*istiqāmat*) and peripatetic (*safar*). Under 'settled' the manual lists the periods during which each emperor resided in the major cities of the realm; under 'peripatetic' the manual gives the itineraries of the longer journeys of each ruler.[42] A final piece of information, perhaps apocryphal, underscores the central role of travel in the life of the Imperial household. In a letter said to have been written to the emperor Muhammad Shah in the early eighteenth century, Nizam al-Mulk, the ruler of Haiderabad, referred to a curious practice among the women of the Imperial harem: the wives of the Mughal emperor, he wrote, gave birth lying on a saddle cloth.[43]

41 See *A'in*, Blochmann, ed., 1: 192–3 and *A'in*, Blochmann, trans., 1: 268–9 about newswriters at court. *A'in*, Blochmann, ed., 1: 5 and *A'in*, Blochmann, trans., 1: 7 discuss the need for spies. For such people in the provinces, see Noman Ahmad Siddiqi, *Land Revenue Administration under the Mughals: 1700–50* (Bombay: Aligarh Muslim University, 1970), p. 113.

42 'Dastur al-' Amal', Persian Manuscript Collection, Oriental 1690, British Museum, folios 98a–99b, 145a–49b.

43 *Asiastick Miscellany* (Calcutta: n.p., 1785), 1: 491.

During the period 1556–1739, an emperor would leave the capital and begin a tour for one or more of the following reasons: to hunt, to put down a rebellion, to check the administration of a province, to conquer new areas, to reconquer old ones, to visit a shrine, to attend a festival or to escape the midsummer heat of northern India. Amidst all this change and variety, however, the place and function of the emperor remained constant. No matter where he might be, city or camp, the Mughal emperor held court and conducted state business. The organization and activity of the Imperial camp illustrate the exercise of sovereignty on tour. Virtually the entire Imperial household—men, women, animals, supplies and equipment—travelled with the emperor. In addition to officers, soldiers, clerks, artists, musicians, craftsmen and merchants of the palace, the records of the Imperial record office, the money and jewels of the Imperial treasuries and the men and equipment of the mint could all be found at the Imperial camp.[44] Those princes and great nobles assigned to court accompanied the emperor, of course, along with the personnel and supplies of their establishments.

A look at the arrangement and function of tents within the enclosure of the Imperial household confirms that the Mughal emperor continued to rule on tour. The map of the Imperial establishment in the *Ā'īn-i Akbari* shows a two-storied structure with a window or balcony near the harem.[45] From this balcony in camp, as from the balcony of audience in the palace, the emperor gave audience, listening to complaints, receiving petitions and dispensing justice to anyone who chose to come. In Akbar's reign the hall of ordinary audience of the camp stood just inside the gate to the Imperial enclosure.[46] The emperor conducted the routine business of state in the hall of ordinary audience in both the camp and city; that is, he received reports and petitions, examined financial accounts, granted promotions, decided on assignments, interviewed mansabdāri candidates and inspected the products of various Imperial workshops. During the reign of Akbar the hall of special audience was set back within the Imperial

[44] For the *daftar*, see *A'in*, Blochmann, trans., 1: xxi, plate iv; for the treasuries, see Nizam al-Din Ahmad Harawi, *Tabaqat-i Akbari*, B. De and Muhammad Hidayat Husain (eds), 3 vols, (Calcutta: Asiatic Society of Bengal, 1913–40), 2: 284 and for the mint, see *A'in*, Blochmann, ed., 1: 27 and *A'in*, Blochmann, trans., 1: 16–18.

[45] Ibid., trans. 1: xxii, plates iv, xi.

[46] Ibid., I: 42 and trans. 1: 48–9.

enclosure; this secluded location indicated the importance and secrecy of matters transacted there.[47]

It is clear from this discussion that the Imperial camp was a place of significance for the state at large. The emperor's frequent and extended travels and their activities on tour have led several scholars to conclude that the Imperial camp functioned as the administrative centre of the realm during much of the Mughal period.[48] Although it is difficult to point to a great deal of indigenous, contemporary evidence on this point, a look at the inscriptions on some of the coins from Akbar's reign suggests that the Mughals held this view. Coins issued for only one or two years from small towns or villages, the work of the camp mint, carried the epithet *dār al khilāfat* (seat of sovereignty).[49] Since this same phrase was used to describe capital cities throughout the period 1556–1739,[50] it appears that the Mughals considered the Imperial camp—the temporary settlement of the emperor, princes, great nobles and their households—the seat of sovereignty of the state and the capital of the empire.

Aurangzeb, the most peripatetic of the seven emperors, stressed the importance of frequent movement. He wrote that '. . . the ruler of a kingdom should not spare himself from moving about'.[51] Elsewhere, he justified the overthrow of his father Shahjahan: 'If Shajahan had not chosen to stay in *dār al-khilāfat* [Shahjahanabad] and *mustaqqar al-*

47 Ibid., trans. 1: xxii, plate iv, p. 48.

48 See, for example, Parmeshwari Gupta, 'A Study of the Mint Towns of Akbar', in *Essays Presented to Sir Jadunath Sarkar*, Hari Ram Gupta (ed.), 2 vols, (Hoshiarpur, India: Punjab University, 1958), 2: 147; Upendra Thakur, *Mints and Minting in India* (Varanasi, U.P.: Chowkhamba Sanskrit Series Office, 1972), pp. 140–1; and Irvine, *Army of the Indian Mughals*, p. 190.

49 Gupta, 'A Study of the Mint Towns of Akbar', 2: 157; Stanley Lane Poole, *The Coins of the Mughal Emperors in the British Museum* (London: Trustees of the British Museum, 1892), pp. 24, 51; and V.P. Rode, *Catalogue of the Coins in the Central Museum, Nagpur: Coins of the Mughal Emperors* (Bombay: Government of Maharashtra, 1969), pp. 23, 38, 39, 42.

50 The epithets for Akbar's capitals illustrate the point. For Agra, see Harawi, *Tabaqat-i Akbari*, 1: 331; 2: 145, 168, 202, 227, 249, 284, 298; and Abu al-Fazl, *Akbar Namah*, Agha Ahmad Ali and Maulavi Abd al Rahim (eds), 3 vols, (Calcutta: Asiatic Society of Bengal, 1873–86), 2: 14, 45, 60, 76, 78; 3: 4, 9, 19, 21, 23, 29; for Fatehpur Sikri, see Harawi, *Tabaqat-i Akbari*, 2: 253; 256, 284, 324, 331, 362; and Abu al-Fazl, *Akbar Namah*, 2: 344, 364, 370; 3: 52, 66, 74; and for Lahore, see Harawi, *Tabaqat-i Akbari*, 2: 402, 424, 646.

51 Hamid al-Din Khan, *Ahkam-i 'Alamgiri*, Persian text with an English translation by Jadunath Sarkar (Calcutta: M.C. Sarkar and Sons, 1912), p. 14.

khilāfat [Agra], but had been constantly travelling [safar], he would not have ended up as he did. . . .'[52] The Mughal emperor kept the personal, quasi-familial ties of the patrimonial-bureaucratic empire fresh and vital by moving rapidly and frequently from one distant subordinate to another, renewing in the face-to-face contact of the court ceremonial the household bonds of loyalty, respect and devotion.

Summary and Implications

The prevailing view of the Mughal Empire has been based on the mistaken assumption that this state was a kind of unfinished, unfocused prototype of the British Indian Empire of the late nineteenth and early twentieth centuries. This assumption has caused most writers to misunderstand and misinterpret the nature and organization of the Mughal state. A more fruitful approach, one closer to indigenous ideas and more consonant with the work of other scholars on pre-modern states, is to treat the Mughal Empire as one example of the patrimonial-bureaucratic empire. A close and careful reading of the major document on Mughal government, the *Ā'īn-i Akbari* of Abu al-Fazl, not only reveals the weakness of the established interpretation, but shows as well the remarkable congruence between the state Akbar organized and the patrimonial-bureaucratic empire analysed by Weber. In its depiction of the emperor as a divinely aided patriarch, the household as the central element in government, members of the army as dependent on the emperor, the administration as a loosely structured group of men controlled by the Imperial household and travel as a significant part of the emperor's activities, the *Ā'īn-i Akbari* supports the suggestion that Akbar's state was a patrimonial-bureaucratic empire.

This view of the state has a number of implications for our understanding of Mughal India. First and most important, it alters our conception of Mughal political organization. This is obviously the basic argument of my essay; I have tried to show the new light this reinterpretation sheds on such aspects of the political system as the transfer of officials, administrative structure and the mansabdāri system. Other issues in Mughal politics—the rebellion of princes and the causes of decline, for

[52] Ibid., p. 49.

example—I have not touched upon at all. Nevertheless, it seems clear that to accept this interpretation of the empire is to accept the necessity of re-examining the entire structure of Mughal political activity.

Our understanding of other facets of Mughal culture and civilization is also affected. Urban organization is one example. From this new perspective, like in the administrative centres of patrimonial-bureaucratic empires—capital cities, provincial headquarters and the like—is seen to revolve around the resources and requirements of Imperial and noble households. Thus, in Shahjahanabad (capital of the Mughal Empire from 1648 to 1858) the palace-fortress of Shahjahan and the mansions of princes and nobles dominated social, economic and political activity.[53]

Finally, taking this view of the state highlights a hitherto neglected aspect of the Mughal economy, and enables us to see the households of emperors and great nobles as important elements in the economic organization of the empire. In administrative centres in particular, the households of great men emerge as the central productive institutions in the urban economy and as major forces in the patterns of production, exchange and consumption.

53 My book on Shahjahanabad discusses these points and those in the following paragraph in considerable detail.

Chapter Ten

State Formation and Rajput Myth in Tribal Central India*

SURAJIT SINHA

INTRODUCTION

My first field experience in anthropology was among the Ho tribe of Kolhan (Singhbhum) which has been described by various ethnographers as a fairly primitive representative of the Kolarian or the Mundari group of tribes (Dalton 1872). Following the lead given in the later reports on the Ho by Majumdar (Majumdar 1950), I was quite intrigued to find in the same group a class of people, the *manki* or chief of an area (*pir*) comprising more than a dozen villages, who lived in a commodious house, maintained a number of servants, strictly avoided all manual labour, indulged in the luxury of keeping a mistress, and so on. Although the manki shared the same clan with the average tribesmen in the surrounding villages, he and his close agnates distinctly stood apart as a class. In course of time, I came to learn that the chief of Bharbharia pir was a sort of fief-holder under the Raja of Mayurbhanj before British rule. Later on, while studying the Bhumij and the Munda of Chotanagpur, I came across similar and even more highly aristocratic strata and attendant aristocratic moods among these so-called tribal people. A little probing into these societies and a few others indicated a fairly long-standing association of these tribal groups with feudalistic states. Thus the Gond had their famous kingdom of Garha-Mandla, Deogarh and Chanda (Chatterton 1916), the Bhuiya are linked with the state of Keonjhar (Cobden-Ramsay 1910), the Munda with Chota Nagpur Raj (Dalton 1872), the Bhumij with

* Presidental Address, Section of Anthropology and Archaeology, Forty-ninth Indian Science Congress, Cuttack, 1962.

Barabhum (Dalton 1872, Risley 1891, Sinha 1957), and so on. As a matter of fact, it is hard to find any settled agricultural tribe of importance in the entire tribal belt of Central India, with the possible exception of the Santal, which has not been substantially affected by long-standing connection with feudalistic state organizations.

The most important consequence of this development is that the main body of the tribe has often been stratified into social classes, mainly in terms of differential land-holding and of the territorial extent of political dominance. This fact of stratification again has made the various segments of the once relatively equalitarian tribes eager for social upgrading. The most striking feature in these processes is that all over this vast territory of Central India, the peak point of identification of social movements among the tribes is the Rajput of north-western India which is regarded as the true representative of the traditional Kshatriya class. As a result of these social movements which have gone on for centuries, there are today Rajputs and pseudo-Rajputs of varying orders of prestige throughout this tribal tract. The highest in status are the traditional princely clans of Rajasthan belonging to the familiar solar and lunar branches and on the lowest rung are the recent entrants into the chain from the tribal upper class. In other words, state formation in the tribal belt of Central India is very largely a story of the *Rajputization* of the tribes.

Most of the early ethnographers of tribal India like Dalton, Risley, Russell and Hira Lal, and Roy, in spite of the considerable knowledge of the historical processes among the groups they studied—probably in their primary urge to record the most primitive core before they changed too far—paid somewhat inadequate attention to the complex developments which connected these tribes with the Hindu civilization. This essay is an attempt to trace the developmental processes as well as the consequences of the formation of states in tribal Central India. We shall discuss such questions as conquest vis-à-vis evolutionary theories of state formation, and investigate the techno-economic, social, military and symbolic conditions favouring the growth of the state. Our primary concern, however, will be with the consequences. We are interested in studying how the equalitarian, primitive, clan-based tribal organization has adjusted itself to centralized, hierarchic, territorially-oriented political developments, the nature of social class formation, interaction between the primitive ritual symbols of the tribe and the advanced symbols sponsored by the states and the effect of such historical processes on the minds of these people in relation to the current canvas of rapid economic and political change.

My task is difficult on account of the lack of reliable historical material in pre-British times when these kingdoms or chieftaincies actually came into being. The Moslem records on these areas are also inadequate, and the spurious long genealogies of the aspirant pseudo-Rajput tribal chieftains are often quite misleading. The archaeological ruins of Jain, Buddhist and Hindu periods, belonging approximately to the period between the eighth and twelfth centuries AD, which are sporadically scattered over this territory, seem to date considerably anterior to the formation of these tribal states. Under the circumstances, my enquiries will have to be based mainly on the structural insight gained by studying a number of contemporary or recently ruined states in the area.

I will, therefore, begin with a fairly detailed analytical description of the estate of Barabhum in the former Manbhum district of Bihar[1] in relation to the Bhumij tribe, where I have been involved in fieldwork off and on for about four years between 1950 and 1960.[2] This detailed description will be followed by brief comparative notes on some of the other feudalistic states and zemindaris in Chhattisgarh, Chotanagpur and Gondwana.

Barabhum, a Bhumij Kingdom

A Kingdom from a Tribal Base

The *pargannah* or estate of Barabhum in south Manbhum covers an area of 635 square miles and 244,733 people. It has 596 revenue villages or *mauzas* of which 20 are no longer inhabited. Of the 64 castes living in this pargannah the numerically dominant groups are: the Kurmi (71,892—30%), the Santal (40,236—16%) and the Bhumij (37,947—15%). Of these three the Bhumij are locally regarded as the earliest settlers who had cleared the virgin forests and set up villages as khuntkatti tenure-holders.

[1] Since 1 November 1957, the bulk of Manbhum has been reconstituted into the new district of Purulia in West Bengal.

[2] It gives me pleasure to put on record here the assistance received from Biman Kumar Dasgupta and Hemendra Nath Banerjee of the Anthropological Survey of India, in undertaking an over-all survey of Barabhum pargannah during 1958 and 1959.

They also nearly monopolized the offices of the village headman, *ghatwal*, and the village priest, *laya*.

When the British first came into contact with Barabhum around 1770, the Raja of Barabhum was apparently an independent king or chief owing allegiance to no superior authority (Higginson 1771). He was already claiming to be a Rajput Kshatriya and spoke an Aryan language, namely, Bengali. There are no records of Moslem or Maratha incursions into Barabhum. The earliest semi-historical reference to the Bhumij state of Barabhum is to be found in the Brahmanda section of the *Bhabishya Purana* compiled in the fifteenth or sixteenth century AD, where it is stated:

> Barabhumi is in one direction contiguous to Tungabhumi and in others to Shekha mountain; and it comprises Barabhumi, Samantabhumi and Manbhumi. This country is overspread with impenetrable forest of *shwal* and other trees . . . In the same district are numerous mountains, containing mines of copper, iron and tin. The men are mostly Rajputs, robbers by profession, irreligious and savage. They eat snakes and all sorts of fish, drink spirituous liquors and live principally by plunder or the chase. As to the women, they are, in garb, manners and appearance, more like Rakshashis than human beings. The only aspects of veneration in these countries are rude village divinities (Coupland 1911).

The prevailing myth about the origin of Barabhum Raj runs roughly as follows:

A prince from Rajputana was going on pilgrimage to Puri accompanied by his pregnant wife. On the way, near Rupsang village, in the area which later became known as Barabhum, the queen gave birth to twins without the knowledge of the king and left them by the side of a forest. A pig took pity on these babies and raised them along with her litter on her own milk. The Bhumij who belonged to the Gulgu clan rescued these babies by killing the pig. The twins became known as Svet Baraha (White Boar) and Nath Varaha (Nath, the Boar). As the boys grew up the Bhumij watched with admiration and amazement the remarkable mental and physical qualities of the boys, and were convinced of their Kshatriya parentage. The Bhumij then took the boys to the court of Raja Vikramjit of Patkum who ruled over this tract of land. It is said that, impressed by the princely courage of the brothers, Vikramjit honoured Nath Varaha with a portion of his own kingdom. This new kingdom, having a circumference of 16 *yojanas*, came to be known as Barabhum.

A slightly different version of the same legend is given by Dalton in his *Descriptive Ethnology of Bengal* (1960: 174).

It is hard to decide as to what truth can be salvaged from this myth. The legend of a Rajput prince of northern India going with his pregnant wife on pilgrimage to Puri is associated with the miraculous origin myth of a number of other states in Central India and Orissa. It is not difficult to adapt such a prevailing myth to prove Rajput ancestry for a powerful tribal chief. This particular myth, however, seems to indicate that Patkum was established earlier than Barabhum and Barabhum was perhaps, in the beginning, a feudal frontier chieftaincy under Patkum. The most significant point in this legend, nevertheless, is the tradition that the ancestors of Barabhum Raj were reared by the Bhumij of the Gulgu clan, just as the first ancestor of Chotanagpur Raj is said to have been reared by Madra Manki, the Munda chief of a *parha* (Roy 1912: 138). There is also the tradition in Barabhum, that before settling down at Barabazar, the present capital, the rajas of Barabhum had their forts (*garh*) at Pabanpur and at Bhuni. It is of interest to note that Pabanpur lies within a mile of Bhula the ossuary of the Gulgu clan. The Bhumij priests at Bhumi, where the royal goddess of Koteswari is located in a sacred grove, belong to the Gulgu clan. Again, the village of Rupsang where the twin ancestors of Barabhum Raj were discovered, is also a Gulgu clan-dominated village. These repeated associations of the royal family with the Gulgu clan lead one to suspect that the Raj family originally belonged to the Gulgu clan, which is one of the earliest and most numerically dominant of the Bhumij clans in the pargannah.

The genealogical table of the Raj family encompasses forty-one generations from the founder, Nath Varaha, to the present raja or *zemindar*. The British came to Barabhum during the reign of Vivek Narayan, the thirty-third descendant of Nath Varaha. The date of inception of the kingdom is given by tradition as 23rd Magha in the second Saka era, i.e. around the third century AD, whereas a normal ascription of twenty-five years to one generation would place the establishment of the kingdom at around 900 AD. The genealogies, however, appear to be fictitious beyond a few generations before Vivek Narayan.

There is one more important feature worth examining. Near the alleged site of the first capital of Barabhum Raj there are extensive ruins of stone architecture and images which had at one time been conjectured by Cunningham to be the ruins of the capital of King Sasanka of Bengal (Coupland 1911). There are similar associations of the originally tribal Patkum Raj with the extensive Hindu-Jain-Buddhist remains at Dulmi and of Manbazar Raj with similar ruins at Budhpur near Manbazar. The legends connecting the tribal kingdoms with these remains that indicate a higher level of civilization are clearly imaginary. But the existence of the ruins significantly sets the date of origin of these tribal kingdoms at a period later than the breakdown of the earlier extensions of Jain-Buddhist-Hindu civilizations in these hilly tracts around the end of the twelfth century AD. It thus appears that such tribal kingdoms as Barabhum, Patkum and Panchakot (or Panchet) came into being some time between the thirteenth and the sixteenth centuries AD, when we find references to them in *Bhavishya Purana* (*supra*: 5–6). Moreover, we find a reference to Bir Narain, the zemindar of Panchet in Mogul chronicles—*Padi-San-Nama*—around 1632 or 1633 (Gokhale 1918: 18–19). It is likely that the Bhumij imbibed some of the ideas associated with kingship from these outposts of Brahminical civilization.

The territorial organization that prevailed at the initial stage of British contact in Barabhum provided the Bhumij with a near monopoly of all the important positions of power and land-holding in the regional hierarchy. This included the holders of the privileged khuntkatti-cultivating tenancies, *tanbedars* or soldiers enjoying the choicest plots for cultivation; ghatwals, the headmen and tenure-holders of single villages; *sadiyals*, the chiefs of about twelve villages; *taraf sardars* or *sardar ghatwals*, chiefs of a number of sadiyals; and finally the raja or the zemindar himself. All these office holders from the ghatwal to the taraf sardar exerted considerable autonomy regarding law and order within their own jurisdictions, and seemed to enjoy this privilege hereditarily as a customary right rather than by virtue of a position granted by the king. This arrangement itself suggests that political evolution in Barabhum was not through the sudden invasion and conquest of the region by an aggressive militant immigrant group; the growth of the state appears rather as a constructive coagulation of traditional socio-political units of the Bhumij. On the other hand, from the local tradition of constant warfare among the neighbouring chieftaincies, it appears that local military pressure contributed considerably towards the kind of territorial arrangement found in Barabhum, namely the chief's directly controlled territory being surrounded and guarded on all sides by frontier fief-holders (Dent 1833)

Even in the early days of British contact with Barabhum, the raja was a patron of Brahminism (both of the Sakta and Vaishnava varieties) as is evident from numerous grants of villages to the Brahmins. The raja used to be constantly surrounded by members of the upper Hindu castes, such as the Brahmin, Chhatri, Kayastha, etc. who were his advisers in religious as well as secular matters. It is clear that as the Bhumij chiefs gained ascendancy over the territory of Barabhum they became more and more attracted to the life-style of the larger Hinduized states around them. The inevitable consequence was the invitation to an increasing number of higher caste Hindus to the posts of secular and ritual offices who helped the chiefs achieve their desired goal of gaining respectability in the eyes of the civilized (!) Rajputs chiefs around them. At what point the Raj family finally succeeded in getting out of this original Bhumij affiliation cannot be ascertained. However, the processes seem to be analogous to the ones described by Roy in connection with the Munda of Ranchi (Roy 1912: 134–49).

Apart from receiving the ritual service of respectable Brahmins, the two other crucial features that led to the severance of the tribal affiliations of the royal lineage are: (i) the creation of a flattering and miraculous myth of origin and (ii) the giving up of connections with the clan ossuary. In the case of Barabhum Raj, the link with the clan ossuary at Bhula was given up so many generations ago that it is now practically forgotten by the other clan brethren. In the case of the smaller chieftaincy of Baghmundi, the process of Rajputization has not developed so far; their Bhumij identity is still recognized by the tribal Bhumij who point out the line in the clan ossuary where the chief's ashes used to be carried even as recently as two generations ago.

A Brief Outline of the Tribal Tradition

We should say something at this point about the traditional pattern of society and culture among the Bhumij who are regarded by all competent ethnographers on the Kolarian tribes as a group closely allied to the Munda of Ranchi. As a matter of fact, the two groups freely intermarry in the border areas of Ranchi and Manbhum districts. In Manbhum, however, nearly all the Bhumij have forgotten their traditional language and now speak Bengali, the language of the Hindu immigrants. When Risley studied this tribe in the latter half of the nineteenth century, the tribe had already moved quite far towards becoming a Hindu caste and had even started employing Brahmins of an inferior status in their rites of passage (Risley 1915: 75). However, they still maintain a good deal of their original social and cultural pattern. Like the Munda of Ranchi, the Bhumij are grouped into a number of patrilineal exogamous clans or *gotras,* which are affiliated to the respective ancestral villages where the clan ossuaries are located. The clans tended to be localized around the ossuary villages. In cases where members of the clan were widely dispersed new ossuaries could be initiated for facilitating the easy burial of ashes.

Although the Bhumij have incorporated a good deal of immigrant Hindu magico-religious traditions under the influence of 'degraded' Brahmin priests and Vaishnava preceptors, they still maintain their loyalty to the traditional gods—the deities residing in the sacred grove (Jaher Budi Dessauli), spirits of hills and forests, ancestral spirits and so on. With regard to festivals also, the tribal rites like Sarhul, Jantal, Magh Puja, Buru Puja, etc. are still maintained along with participation in typical Hindu festivals like Durga Puja, Ratha Yatra and so on (Sinha 1953 and 1958).

Clan and Territory

Keeping the above background in mind, let us examine the relation between the clan and the administrative segments in the state of Barabhum. According to the Settlement Survey of 1908–13, the various *tarafs* in Barabhum contained the following number of villages:

Taraf	*Number of villages*
Gartali	120
Dubraji	10
Satrakhani	97
Dhadka	79
Panchasardari	80
Tinsoya	35
Kumaripar	110
Sarberia	48
Bangurda	17
Total	596

Of these, Gartali is the central tract south of the river Kumari under the direct control of the raja. Dubraji, a taraf of only ten villages, is for the maintenance of the eldest son of the raja. Except for the two taraf sardars of Kumaripar who claim to be Rajput Chhatris and are recognized as later immigrants to the region, all the other taraf sardars belong to the Bhumij tribe. Colonel Dalton speaks of these tenures as follows: 'Their tenures are the oldest in the country; older than the rights of their Chief, who there is every reason to suppose descends from one of the same stock originally elected to rule over them. . . .' (Nandjee 1883: paragraph 7).

In the two big tarafs of Satrakhani and Panchasardari, the taraf area was divided into a number of tracts known as *sadiyals*, under subordinate chiefs or sadiyals. Under the sadiyal were the ghatwals or village headmen who often belonged to the Bhumij tribe and usually belonged to the same lineage as that of the hereditary village priest or laya. Like the taraf sardar in relation to the raja, the sadiyals and the ghatwals enjoyed a good deal of autonomy in their respective areas. Moreover, the authority of the ghatwals, sadiyals and taraf sardars was considerably tempered by the existence of territorial councils of elders at the village, sadiyali and taraf levels where people used to meet in an equalitarian atmosphere. Within the village again, large areas of cultivable land, often of the choicest kind, used to be leased out at nominal rent to tanbedars or *paiks*, as service tenures. These tanbedars, mostly belonging to the Bhumij tribe, operated as foot soldiers under the guidance of the ghatwals, sadiyals and taraf sardars to defend the territories of the raja and for other military expeditions.

The situation is thus substantially different from that of European feudalism in which the king granted fiefs to his vassals on a contractual basis (Bloch 1961: 145–75). In Barabhum the raja and his taraf sardars are bound by irrevocable traditional ties of long standing. The existence of equalitarian councils of elders at the various levels of territorial hierarchy represents another striking contrast to European feudalism. It should be mentioned here that the relation between the chiefs and the raja was not without tension. There was an effort on the part of the raja to expand his direct control over his entire pargannah and similarly the taraf sardars also wielded their authority on the sadiyals under them.

Risley is under the impression that the four major tarafs as well as the Taraf Gartali represent the original jurisdiction of five Bhumij clans and that the chief of Gartali attained supremacy by belonging to the senior line:

'It seems to me the present distribution of the so-called *Ghatwali* tenures strongly suggests that body of Mundas divided into *Khunts* or stripes . . . settled in

Barabhum and cleared the country. There were probably as many Khunts as there are *Tarafs* and the ancestor of the present Zemindar was the head of the eldest *Khunt*. . . . In course of time the Zemindar, from the chief of the eldest *Khunt* of the Bhumij became a Hindu and called himself a Raja. . . . The present organisation of the *Ghatwals* in Barabhum corresponds so exactly to the Mundari system in Lohardaga that there can hardly be a doubt that it is the same thing under a different name. The village *Sardar* corresponds to the *Manki* of Munda *Parha*. As for the *Sardar Ghatwals* of the larger *Tarafs* it seems to me most likely that they were originally *Mankis* of outlying *Parhas* . . . (Risley 1883: paragraph 50).

The actual state of distribution of the Bhumij clans is too complicated today (it must have been more or less similar in Risley's time also) to reconstruct the mono-clanic homogeneous tracts defining the limits of tarafs as hypothesized by Risley. A total of 8,395 Bhumij families spread over 437 villages of Pargannah Barabhum are affiliated to 50 clans with 363 ossuaries. Of these, 17 clans cover the bulk of the population. Each of the four major tarafs contains more than one clan ossuary. Taraf Panchasardari, for example, contains as many as five important ossuaries belonging to five clans, leaving aside a few relatively unimportant ones. Even if we break down the data to the narrower range of sadiyali, it does not lead us to a picture of mono-clanic homogeneity. If we take up the case of a single sadiyali, namely that of Koira, we find that of the 15 villages falling within the sadiyali only 6 are dominated by the Jaru, a clan of the Sadiyal, three by the Koira, and two each by the Badda Baghra and Gulgu, respectively. At the village level, however, the tradition persists that the headman and the priest should belong to the earliest settled clan whose members enjoy a privileged monopoly over khuntkatti-cultivating tenancies. There is, therefore, some degree of idealized correspondence between the clan and the village.

Neither the chief of Barabhum nor the people at large conceive of the tarafs as the areas of particular clans. These are, at least now, regarded as land-revenue-*cum*-political jurisdictions without any reference to caste or clan, except in the matter of the caste of the chieftain. A single taraf like Panchasardari contains, besides the Bhumij with their numerous clans and still more numerous ossuaries, many other castes. Nevertheless, there is an awareness among the Bhumij that particular tracts of land (not defined in terms of taraf) within Barabhum are inhabited by the members of a particular clan. In Bhumij marriages it is still customary to address the members of the gathering in terms of clan group: 'Friends of the Jugi clan of the Jaru clan and of the Ubursandi clan! We offer you obeisance and with your permission we begin the marriage rituals'.

Although the above-mentioned concrete data on the clan–territory relationship do not lend support to Risley's hypothesis, I do not feel inclined to throw overboard his insights based on long acquaintance with the Kolarian tribes. The very fact that all the Bhumij taraf sardars invariably belong to the most or one of the most important clans in their tarafs indicates that it may not be altogether improbable that originally the tarafs were the territorial jurisdictions of the major clans, and that the present complex picture is the result of an extensive population movement in the pargannah bringing in many castes and many clans in otherwise nearly mono-clanic taraf areas.

The Economic Base

The political supremacy of the raja had the necessary support of the economy. Settled agriculture with the plough provided the necessary technological base for the inflow of surplus wealth to the raja and the hierarchy of chiefs. As the taraf sardars, who controlled nearly three-fourths of his territory, paid only token revenues to the raja, his main income was from the *khas* or directly controlled tarafs of Gartali and Dubraji. Here again it is said that formerly no cash rent used to be levied. Every farmer used to give a certain quantity of rice (*shyama chaul*), clarified butter (*shyama ghee*) and a he-goat (*shyama pantha*), to the raja on the festival of Durga Puja. This sacred festival was thus an important occasion for replenishing the royal exchequer. But the main source of income was the cultivable plots, *manjami*, that the king owned in many of the villages in his khas taraf. Very often these plots were located near an irrigation ditch (*bandh*). Each tenant had to provide one day's labour with the plough, one day's labour with the hoe and two days' labour with sickles for the cultivation of these plots. The raja had the advantage of a large supply of labourers in his khas plots. Various artisan castes like the potter, blacksmith, basket-maker, etc. contributed a quota of their wares to the king in lieu of land enjoyed without rent. In later periods we also find the king sponsoring weekly markets. The raja had additional income not only from his own khas territory but also from the tarafs, as miscellaneous benevolence on occasions such as coronations, marriages, sacred initiation ceremonies etc. in the family.

The Social Classes

The territorial distribution of power and economic interest in the land guided the major lines of social stratification in Barabhum right from the level of the raja down to the level of the Bhumij cultivator. We are already familiar with the territorially defined power hierarchy, i.e. with *political classes.* The important *social classes*, in descending order, defined in terms of ritual status were: Rajput Kshatriyas of the Namahal[3] order; inferior Rajputs of the Dashmahal order, who are still recognized as being derived from the Bhumij; the upper class or Ataisha Bhumij, who do not consume chicken or wine, who invariably take *diksha* from a Vaishnava preceptor and who consult a Brahmin priest in the rites of passage; the ordinary Bhumij or Nagadi who, though enjoying the ritual services of 'degraded' Brahmans, as do members of the Ataisha class, usually consume chicken and wine and practise widow remarriage; and last of all are the socially degraded or 'fallen' Nichu Bhumij whose degradation is often due to a breach of rules of clan exogamy or caste endogamy.

The nature of the interrelation between economic, political and ritual hierarchies in Barabhum may be presented diagrammatically, and is shown in the accompanying diagram.[4] There is a fair degree of correspondence between the three systems of hierarchies. This is particularly impressive above the territorial level of the village. Within the village level, even the landless labourer and poor cultivator share the same ritual rank as the headman of the village, whereas even a substantial cultivator may be degraded to the Nichu class for a social offence. It may also be mentioned here that besides forming a hierarchy of marriage classes, a member of a higher socio-ritual class will not accept cooked food or drinking water from a member of a lower class. A Namahal Rajput will not accept water even from a zemindar of the Dashmahal class.

[3] The Raja of Barabhum with eight royal or zemindar families such as Manbazar, Dhalbhum, Ambikanagar, Raspal, Simlapal, etc. form an intermarrying social class known as the Nine Houses or Namahal. Lower in status there is another group of royal houses belonging to smaller zemindaris in the same area. Conventionally these comprise ten zemindar families and are thus known as Dashmahal. In most of the Dashmahal groups of Rajput families such as Baghmundi, Jaipur, Jhalda and Begunkudor, their Bhumij ancestry is still remembered in the locality, though emphatically denied by these aspirant Rajput families.

[4] Information at the village level is based on our data on Madhupur village in Chandil P.S.

It may be pointed out here that within the district of Manbhum itself there is a class of Rajput Kshatriyas even higher than the Namahal order and this class is represented by Panchet and Patkum Raj families. It appears that the relative position of the various orders of so-called Rajput families has been determined mainly by two factors: the priority in their entrance to Kshatriyahood and the size of territories politically and economically controlled by them.

This hierarchic arrangement generates an atmosphere of excessive sensitiveness about one's rank and perpetual drive for higher recognition. The means to achieve these ends are:

1. The employment of Brahmins of the right kind. This can only be done by attracting Brahmins from distant lands with the promise of adequate remuneration in terms of land grants.
2. Making up, with the help of the Brahmins, a fictitious genealogy establishing a mythical connection with the illustrious Rajput clans of north-western India.
3. Ritual display of the right kind. This involves positive actions like the observation under the guidance of priests, of typical Brahminical rites of passage, such as initiation with the sacred thread, observance of Vedic rituals in marriage and funeral rites, maintenance of Hindu idols and temples and observance of festivals like Durga Puja, etc., introduction of taboos such as the avoidance of 'degrading' food like beef, pork and chicken, restriction of the freedom of womenfolk in movement and in forms of marriage, avoidance of the traditional practices of widow remarriage, levirate and marriage by elopement.
4. Marriage alliance with an already recognized Rajput Kshatriya family, often in a very poor economic position.

It has been observed that rather than ritual purification in the abstract, the crucial factors in social upgrading are the setting up of characteristic social relations, namely getting the service of a Brahmin of the right kind and marriage affiliation with a recognized Rajput family. Both of these are attainable with persistent effort and with the backing of economic and political power.

We find an excellent recent example of such upgrading in the taraf sardar family of Satrakhani in Barabhum Pargannah. Even as recently as three generations ago, these taraf sardars of a fief covering 97 villages and

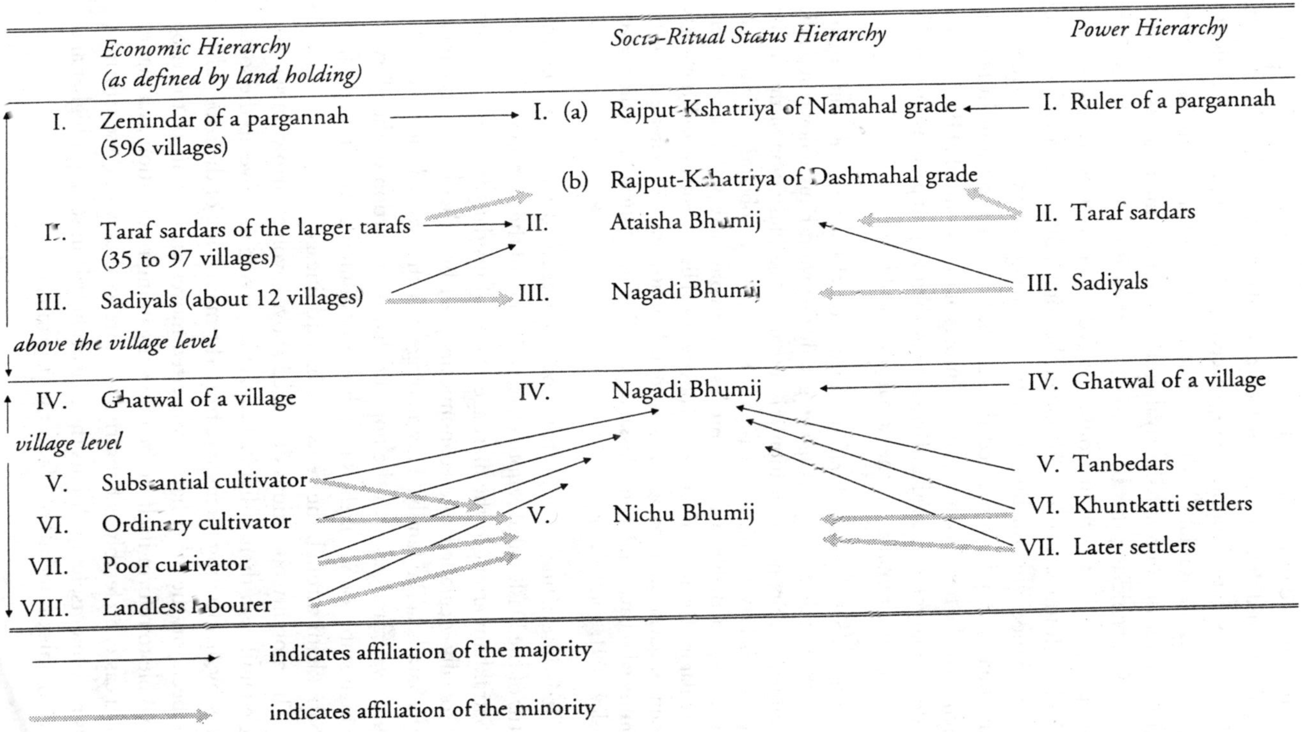
Economic Hierarchy
(as defined by land holding)
Socio-Ritual Status Hierarchy
Power Hierarchy
I. Zemindar of a pargannah (596 villages)
II. Taraf sardars of the larger tarafs (35 to 97 villages)
III. Sadiyals (about 12 villages)
above the village level
IV. Ghatwal of a village
village level
V. Substantial cultivator
VI. Ordinary cultivator
VII. Poor cultivator
VIII. Landless labourer
I. (a) Rajput-Kshatriya of Namahal grade
(b) Rajput-Kshatriya of Dashmahal grade
II. Ataisha Bhumij
III. Nagadi Bhumij
IV. Nagadi Bhumij
V. Nichu Bhumij
I. Ruler of a pargannah
II. Taraf sardars
III. Sadiyals
IV. Ghatwal of a village
V. Tanbedars
VI. Khuntkatti settlers
VII. Later settlers
indicates affiliation of the majority
indicates affiliation of the minority

over a hundred square miles, used to be regarded as Bhumij of the Ataisha class by all and their clan ossuary was at Bhula. Bharat Singh, the powerful chief of this taraf around 1880, succeeded in getting his own daughter married to the Raj family of Begunkudor which had already been raised to the level of Rajput-Kshatriyahood of the Dashmahal class. He succeeded in achieving this by alluring the then Raja of Begunkudor with the prospect that his son would succeed to his vast estate—a promise which he fulfilled later on. Although the stigma of this known history of social manoeuvre still lingers on in the lineage of the taraf sardars of Satrakhani, they have succeeded in the last three generations in making themselves be regarded as regular members of the Dashmahal Rajput class. Risley, apparently amused and irritated by their Rajput pretensions, makes the following remarks on the sardars of Satrakhani:

> . . . Manmohan Singh, of Taraf Satrakhani, now claims to be a Rajput, regardless of the fact that a few years ago his grandfather wrote himself down in public documents as Bhumij. I mention this instance as an illustration of the facility with which brevet rank as a self-made Rajput may be obtained. Manmohan Singh keeps a Brahman to support his pretensions, and professes to be very particular in all matters of ceremonial observance. His descendants will doubtless obtain unquestioning recognition as local Rajputs, and will intermarry with families who have undergone the same process of transformation as themselves (Risley 1891: vol. I, 127).

It is interesting to note that, not quite satisfied with attaining the status of the Dashmahal Rajput class, the father of the present taraf sardar of Satrakhani arranged the marriage of one of his daughters with one of the socially 'degraded' and economically poor branches of the very high status Saraikela Raj family. This marriage, which involved a lot of expenditure, was arranged with the hope of sharing a portion of the glory of the high status of Saraikela Raj, in however diluted a form it might flow to Satrakhani through the veins of a bastard lineage.

The mobility operations described above involve narrow lineages or single families in their individual capacities, trying to move up the social ladder by dissociating themselves from the main body of the tribe. There have been, on the other hand, concerted moves on the part of the tribe as a whole to reform itself in the hope of gaining recognition as a higher Hindu caste, preferably as Kshatriyas. Before we deal with these reformist mass movements, let us discuss the role of the raja in setting a higher and more complex standard of life in the pargannah.

Upgradation or Universalization of Regional Culture

Besides his political and economic roles in the pargannah the raja set down the highest standard of cultural style in the region as a patron of Brahminism and in the secular sphere as well. As many as forty-seven villages in Barabhum were presented to Brahmins of various orders as Brahmottar and Debottar grants. The raja maintained the following categories of priestly offices: Kula Purohit, Kula Guru, Chakravarti, Deogharis, Sabha Pandit and Grahacharya—all belonging to so-called 'pure' Brahmins either of the Utkal or Bengali Rarhi section. The raja had two guardian deities of importance, namely Brindabanchand (or Krishna) in the palace temple and the Tantric goddess of Chamundi, locally known as Koteswari, in the traditional sacred grove of the Bhumij at Bhuni.

The members of the Raj family, as Rajput Kshatriyas, had to go through initiation with the sacred thread and all their rites of passage were guided by the Brahmin priests of the highest order with Vedic mantras. The raja also sponsored a number of religious festivals among which Ind Parab and Durga Puja were the two most important ones. These festivals attracted people from all over the pargannah and fief-holders would come on horseback with open swords to join in the procession with the raja in the Ind Parab. Female visitors to the Ind festival would carry with them seedlings from their sacred Jawdali baskets, connected with tribal Karam festivals in their own villages. These seedlings would be thrown at the Ind posts while they were being raised, with the hope of receiving the blessings of Indra, the king of the gods, on the crops (Sinha 1958: 35). On the same day, again, villagers throughout the pargannah would plant branches of *sal* trees in their agricultural plots to invoke supernatural blessings on their agricultural operations. These are interesting cases of the meeting of the simple village traditions and the elaborate rituals of the raja. By locating the temple of his goddess, Koteswari, in the tribal sacred grove at Bhuni, or by patronizing the tribal festivals of Delde Buru in the village of Rupsang, the raja raised the importance of these local sacred sites of the respective villages to a pan-pargannah level of importance. There was a widespread belief in Barabhum that the raja ruled on behalf of the god Brindabanchand and goddess Koteswari and as such the raja shared in the divinity. The human congregation in Barabhum was thus bound by a moral order of shared sacred ideas and sentiments with the raja as the pivot.

I will now present some ideas about the secular phase of the life of the raja. The palace, which is also described as a garh or fort is bound on all sides by high walls. Within the compound itself there is a large tank where the queens enjoyed bathing in privacy. Among the many rooms in the palace are the coronation room of the raja (*patghar*), his personal room, audience room or *vaithakkhana*, the office room (*kacharimela*), a room for each of the queens, a room for the raja to retire alone when 'angry' with his wives (*gosaghar*) and so on. Among his servants were the *duari* (gatekeeper), *tel makhani* (oil massager), *dhuti kochani* (one who dresses the *dhuti* cloth), *khaoa* (food-taster, as a precaution against pöisoning), etc. Formerly it was the custom to play on the *sanai* (a type of clarinet) at intervals throughout the night for the raja's entertainment. The rajas had a flair for patronizing concubines, dancing girls and wrestlers. It was expected by the subjects that the raja would be courageous, powerful, romantic, magnificent and whimsical; he would, as befitted the standard of the true 'Rajput', be deeply devoted to the gods and also be a generous protector of his subjects.

It is of interest to note how the chiefs of the lower order imitated the ritual and secular standard of the raja in an attenuated form, cut to the size of their economic capacity. All the taraf sardars sponsored Durga Puja by making clay images of the goddess, maintained priests who were offered gifts of land, wore the sacred thread (but did not always go through an initiation rite), etc.

In the image of the raja's garh the taraf sardars used to have enclosed household compounds where the arenas of the womenfolk were sufficiently excluded from access to outsiders. These chiefs were also indulgent in the matter of keeping concubines and dancing girls.

The same image ran through, in an even more diminutive form, to the level of the village headman or ghatwal. With his limited resources he would perform Durga Puja with a small earthen pot (*ghat*) representing the goddess. He would avoid manual labour in the field but would go personally to his fields to supervise agricultural operations. The female inmates of his house could go to any house in his own village, but would never go as far as the weekly market. Even at the level of the headman, these fief-holders used to be called 'raja' by their immediate neighbours, and the lower class of peasantry, belonging to the other castes, would, half-mockingly and half-seriously, flatter even the ordinary Bhumij cultivators by calling them 'raja lok', belonging to the king's class.

The raja and the state thus set a standard for the emulation of a complex tradition which is also locally regarded as the 'Rajput tradition', strongly supporting Brahminical traits. And this percolated down to the level of the ordinary Bhumij cultivator. In this general universalization of culture, both the importation of Brahminical traits and the syncretization of the Brahminical with the local Hindu and tribal traditions, have played their parts. It should be noted that even in his eagerness for social upgrading the raja could not ignore the tribal gods and rituals and the associated priesthood.

Social Mobility of the Bhumij Masses

This leads us to examine the process of emulation of the 'Rajput' model by the ordinary Bhumij peasants through concerted mobility movements. The other taraf sardars of Barabhum did not have the economic resources of the Satrakhani (*supra*) to attract the Brahmins of a high order to come to their service and to devise a suitable myth of origin. These taraf sardars, unable to dissociate themselves from the main body of the tribe, took the initiative for the tribe as a whole to be regarded as Rajput Kshatriyas, with the support of floating Brahmin pundits of a lower order. This involved meetings of the Bhumij over a large territory, even transcending the limits of Pargannah Barabhum. The slogans raised included the following prescriptive and proscriptive elements. The prescriptions included employing Brahmin priests and Vaishnava preceptors in the rites of passage, learning to read the sacred scriptures like the *Ramayana* and *Mahabharata* and so on. The main taboos were: ploughing with the cow, drinking wine, eating chicken, marriage by elopement, widow remarriage and group-dancing by women. In these meetings they made frequent references to the 'heroic Kshatriya tradition of the past' from which they had fallen in recent years. This movement was generally successful, with occasional setbacks, between 1921 and 1947, and the Bhumij were shocked in 1951 when they were labelled as 'Scheduled Wild Tribes' in the electoral rolls. Between 1952 and 1960, however, the interest in Rajput identification waned considerably. This was partly because the leaders of the movement realized the advantages to be gained from the government by belonging to the tribal category. They also became aware that Rajput standards were no longer the norm among the people who wielded power, had money and were considered 'cultured' in their mixed social environment. When I participated in one of their meetings in June 1958, I found that the speakers only paid lip service to Kshatriyahood and the leadership had also shifted from the taraf sardar to modernized commoners with initiative. This meeting mainly outlined secular goals such as economic upliftment, employment, education, etc., and Rajputhood made a curious compromise with tribal affiliation by making a common cause with the Mundas from whom they had tried to be dissociated all these years. In this compromise they have taken the hybrid label of Bhumij Kshatriya Adivasi. I wrote in a previous paper that this secular phase of the social movement of the Bhumij did not gain as clear a grip on the minds of the Bhumij as had the Rajput Kshatriya myth (Sinha 1957). It is to be marked that it was this myth that helped the Bhumij in withstanding all the pulls of proselytizing Christian missionaries. And it is this same aspiration that kept them apart from the general trend of the pan-tribal Jharkhand movement.

While reluctantly falling in line with less Hinduized tribes like the Santal, Ho or Munda today, the Bhumij continue to carry the burden of their frustrated aspirations to be regarded as Rajputs. The Bhumij country has an atmosphere of decadent aristocracy and there is a feeling among the people of having fallen from the crest of past glory which has paralyzed their initiative in the competition with less aristocratic peasants like the Kurmi or the tribal Santal. We shall come across similar moods of frustration among a few other tribal groups in a review of the comparative material.

Comparative Notes

Before making a further analysis of the data on Barabhum estate in relation to the Bhumij tribe, let us briefly review some comparable cases in Manbhum District and then in some other areas in tribal Central India.

The Manbhum Estates

Of the revenue paying estates in the former Manbhum District, Panchet is easily the largest, both in area and in revenue demand. It includes no less than nineteen out of the thirty-nine pargannahs which make up the district area and covers 1650 square miles in Manbhum alone. With two exceptions each of the remaining pargannahs of the district constitute single estates. They range in size from a large estate like Barabhum which covers 600 square miles to a petty zemindari like Torang, barely eleven miles in extent.

As has been stated before, the zemindars of Manbhum can be classified status-wise into at least four classes, given below:

Panchet, Patkum, etc. . . . The highest class of Rajputs Barabhum, Manbhum (Manbazar), etc..Namahal Rajputs Baghmundi, Jhalda, Begunkudor, etc. Dashmahal Rajputs Torang, Matha . . . Thakur, Manki, etc. of the Ataisha Bhumij class.

Most of these estates share a number of characteristics with the Barabhum estate. Settled agriculture with the plough provides the requisite technological base for the accumulation of wealth in these zemindar families, and the frontier vassals or subordinate chiefs maintain considerable autonomy in their own territories. The villages are grouped in a hierarchic order of territorial units in terms of an increasing series of a *conventional* number of villages: 12 in the area of a Manki, 24 in the area of a Thakur, and 84, at the minimum, forming a pargannah. These conventional numbers, particularly 12 and 84, have quite a widespread distribution throughout Central India and even farther north-west in Rajasthan (Wills 1919: 213). In the largest estate of Panchet, however, the earlier systematic hierarchic arrangement has been replaced by a system of semi-military, semi-police chieftains under the direct control of the zemindar. In Patkum there used to be as late as in 1897, 12 taraf divisions as we found in Barabhum.

All these zemindars, again, like the Raja of Barabhum, are great patrons of Brahminism, through generous land grants to the Brahmins and acceptance of the ritual standards of 'Rajput Kshatriyas' under Brahmin priests, and are supposed to rule over their respective territories on behalf of a Brahminical god or goddess. Worshipping the clay image of Durga is a universal feature among these zemindars as is also the observance of the Ind or Chhata festival in which an umbrella, fixed at the top of a long pole, is raised in obeisance to the royal god.

In spite of their enthusiasm for the Sanskritization of their rituals, these zemindars continue to lend support to the worship of old tribal gods in their own territories. The chief of Baghmundi, for example, worships the tribal god Marang Buru and goddess Chuprungi as the presiding deities of the zemindar's lineage.

No information is available on the relationship between clan and traditional administrative territories in the zemindaris of Manbhum, other than those of Barabhum and Baghmundi.

The resemblance to the Munda type of clan-parha organization is most marked in the case of the Raja of Baghmundi. The Baghmundi estate is today composed of five groups of villages one of these being held directly by the zemindar himself. The other four areas as controlled by the mankis occupy 12 villages while the zemindar, in his turn, exerts direct control over 36 villages, making a conventional total of 84 villages for the pargannah of Baghmundi.

Each of these mankis belongs to the Sandil (or Ubursandi) clan of the Bhumij tribe (who are also known as Munda in this area) with their respective distinct ossuaries situated within their own jurisdiction.

The Raja of Baghmundi also belongs to the Sandil clan whose ossuary lies within a mile of his headquarters. There is a tradition in the pargannah that the four lineages of the mankis are derived from four brothers, of whom the ancestor of the manki of Suisa was the eldest. There is also the alternative legend that originally there were five brothers and that the Raj family is descended from the eldest brother.

As regards the tribal affiliation of these zemindars of Manbhum, the possibility of Munda or Bhumij ancestry is quite transparent in the cases of Torang, Baghmundi and other zemindaris of the Dashmahal group (Nandjee 1883). The origin of a few other estates in Manbhum or Manbazar Raj is associated with the Kurmi and the estates north of the Damodar with the Bhuiya castes (Coupland 1913: Chapter XI).

The Munda Raj of Chotanagpur

The case of the emergence of kingship among the Munda of Ranchi is too familiar to students of tribal ethnography of Central India through the writings of Dalton (1960: 164–8) and Roy (1912: 136–40) to need an elaborate treatment here.

The Munda, who subsist principally by settled agriculture with the plough, live in the eastern half of Ranchi. The Munda society, like the Bhumij, is organized into groups of exogamous, patrilineal, totemic clans whose members live in distinct territorial clusters around the ancestral village in which the clan ossuary is located.

Traditionally it is said that the Munda socio-political organization did not stretch very far from the jurisdiction of a clan, known as *patti* or *parha*, except for marriage negotiations. The village had its headman, *munda*, who was also often the *pahan* or the priest of the village; and the manki was at the head of a parha or patti, conventionally consisting of twelve villages. The village chief, munda, and the manki were regarded as chiefs among equals and did not get much economic remuneration on account of holding their respective offices. It has been stated by Dalton, Risley and Roy that the kingdom of Chotanagpur came into being through an agglomeration of a number of such clan-based territorial clusters.

The exact historical origin of this Raj family is wrapped in mystery. The myth which has been detailed by Dalton and Roy (Roy 1912: 136–40) ascribes the origin to the union of a serpent god Pundarik Nag (in the form of a Brahmin) with a Brahmin girl. The latter gave birth to a child near Suitambe, a village in Ranchi district, while on a pilgrimage with her husband from Banaras to Puri. Reared by Madra, a member of the Munda tribe who was also the manki of a patti, the child, who subsequently came to be known as Phani Mukut Rai, was allowed to succeed Madra to the mankiship of his patti. Later on, all the parha chiefs assembled to elect Phani Mukut Rai as their supreme chief or raja. It will be noted that this origin myth, widely prevalent throughout Chotanagpur, does not entail any mass immigration of an aggressive military group displacing the authorities of the autochthones of the area. Judging from parallels elsewhere in tribal middle India, one would naturally suspect, in line with Dalton, Risley and Roy, that the myth is a rationalization, in terms of later Brahminical elaborations connected with the Rajput myth, of the process of the internal development of Munda society leading to the emergence of kingship.

The Raj family of Chotanagpur claims to be Nagvanshi Chhatris and its members perform all the necessary rituals of the 'twice-born' Rajputs under the guidance of Brahmin priests. The extent of patronization of the Brahmins by the Raja of Chotanagpur would be apparent from the grant of nearly 134,89 square miles as privileged brahmottar, debottar and other brit grants to Brahmins (Roy 1912: Appendix xliii–xliv).

The Raja of Chotanagpur, unlike the smaller Raja of Barabhum, chose in course of time to let the more aggressive immigrant Hindus hold the bulk of service tenures or *jagirs* around his headquarters. This rudely disturbed the indigenous arrangement. However, in the outlying frontier tracts of Panch Pargannah, the relation with the subordinate fief-holders or zemindars continued to be of the traditional kind. These zemindari tenures are regarded as ancient as the Raj of Ranchi itself. And there is clear evidence that these zemindars, like the family of the Raja, were derived from the Munda community. The internal territorial organization of Tamar closely parallels that of Barabhum in that the zemindari is divided into a descending territorial hierarchy: zemindar—*thakur*—manki—munda (chief of a single village). Above the zemindar is, of course, the Raja of Chotanagpur. The chiefs of each of the above levels of territorial unit belong to a nearly endogamous social class and Brahminic and Rajput emulations increase as one moves up the hierarchy. The chiefs of various orders in the district of Ranchi are maritally connected with similar levels of chiefs in Manbhum district: the Raja of Chotanagpur with Panchet and Ichagarh zemindars, Tamar with the Dashmahal zemindars, the thakurs and mankis under Tamar with the Ataisha families of the order of manki and taraf sardar.

The Gonds and their Medieval Kingdoms

We may now take up the case of the Dravidian-speaking Gonds who had developed, around the fourteenth and fifteenth centuries, kingdoms of a much larger extent than the Munda or Bhumij kingdoms of Chotanagpur. Numbering about four million, they are thinly spread over a large territory in Central India, of whom about three million live in the state of Madhya Pradesh. The Gonds are found at various levels of economic development and acculturation—depending upon the nature of ecological isolation—over the vast stretch of their habitat. The bulk of their population is settled cultivators who use the plough, whereas the tradition of slash-and-burn cultivation is still alive among the isolated Hill Marias of Bastar.

As in the case of the Mundari tribes, Gond society is based on initiality localized totemic clans. These clans, unlike the Mundari clans, have a frequent tendency to cluster as phratries or even to be grouped into two exogamous moieties (Russell and Hira Lal 1916: III, 62–72). Stephen Fuchs observes that the two different systems of social organization, namely territorial and genealogical, merged. Thus the territorial unit of a garh was the same as the territorial unit of a clan or gotra and although clans are now quite dispersed, the clan members are aware of their original garh affiliation which guides their funeral ceremonies

(Fuchs 1960, 162–3). Fuchs further remarks: 'There is little doubt that this original territorial group system of the Gond was somewhat modified in the whole of Gondwana, and gradually developed into the present *Garh* system through the influence of the Rajput soldiers and landowners domiciled in the Gond area'. (ibid., 138).

According to Russell and Hira Lal (1916, III, 44–7) and Bishop Chatterton (1916: 9), the four independent Gond kingdoms arose in Gondwana 400 years ago more or less simultaneously, with capitals at Garha, Deogarh, Kherla and Chanda. These kingdoms lasted for nearly 400 years, accepting nominal suzerainty of the Moghuls during the reign of Akbar, and ultimately fell to the raids of the Marathas in the seventeenth century.

It is of interest to note that one semi-Rajput dynasty, the Kalachuri kings claiming to be of Haihaya descent, reigned in the territory for more than two centuries before the Gonds came into power. Their capital was at Tewar or Triari lying only four miles beyond Garha. The legend goes that Jadurai, the Gond hero who overthrew the Kalachuri raja, began by entering into the service of the Kalachuri rajas.

It was an important turning point in the history of the kingdom of Garha, when King Sangram Shah manipulated the marriage of his son Dalpat with Durgabati, the daughter of the Raja of Mahoba, a Chandel Rajput of high status. The battle between Durgabati and the Moghul viceroy of Malwa, Asaf Khan, has been fully recorded by Abul Fazl, the chronicler of Akbar's reign. It is stated there that Rani Durgabati's kingdom of Garha contained as many as 70,000 villages (compare 596 in Barabhum), and the wealth on the fall of the last Gond queen can be gauged from the fact that Asaf Khan's army looted '101 cooking pots and valuable gold coins besides jewels, gold and silver plates and images of gods'. There were also 1000 elephants.

Sleeman says about the method of government of these Gond kings, 'Under these Gond Rajas the country seems for the most part to have been distributed among feudatory chiefs, bound to attend upon the prince at his capital with a stipulated number of troops, to be employed wherever their services might be required, but to furnish little or no revenue in money. These chiefs were Gonds, and the countries they held for the support of their families and the payment of their troops and retinue little more than wild jungles . . . ' (Russell and Hira Lal 1916: III, 41). Nevertheless, there is evidence of a certain degree of development of bureaucratized, centralized machinery cutting across the principle of sub-infeudation, in the kingdoms of Garha and Chanda, the like of which we have not come across in the much smaller kingdoms in the Bhumij and Munda countries of Chotanagpur (Wills 1919: 257–8).

It may be noted at this point that the Gond rajas, like other tribal chiefs described above, became patrons of Brahminism and Brahmins, and we have already mentioned the evidence of their Rajput aspiration in the marriage of the Gond prince Dalpat with the Chandel princess Durgabati.

We find reflections of these complex developments in the socio-political structure in the elaborate development of the Lingo myth of creation which is recited by members of the Pradhan caste who served as minstrels of the Gonds, just as the Charans were the bards of the Rajputs of Rajputana. The Brahminical influence on the Gond kings is evidenced in many Hindu interpolations in the original Gond tradition by associating the cult of Lingo with Mahadeva and Parvati (Russell and Hira Lal 1916: III, 48–9).

The epic songs recited by the Pradhans fall into two classes, namely those describing the glory of the Gond rajas or Gondwani and Pandwani which is an astonishing variant of the usual stories from the *Ramayana* (Hivale 1946: 78).

Although the great Gond kingdoms perished nearly two hundred years ago, social stratification and associated aspirations to be regarded as Rajput Kshatriyas still persists. Russell and Hira Lal find two aristocratic subdivisions among the Gonds, the Raj Gonds and the Khatolas, while the Dhur Gonds or ordinary peasants are of a lower status. The Raj Gonds now rank with the Hindu cultivating castes and Brahmins accept water from them. They sometimes wear the sacred thread (Russell and Hira Lal 1916: III, 63).

Stephen Fuchs finds the following four ranked strata among the Gonds of Mandla District, from the highest to the lowest: the teetotaller Deo Gonds, the Suryavansi Raj Gonds who claim to be the descendants of Rama, the Suryavansi Deogarhi (the sun-born Gond of Deogarh) and, lastly, the Ravanvansi Gonds. The two Suryavansi Gonds are also known as Raj Gonds and assume the rank of Kshatriyas. Fuchs observes that 'recently any wealthy Gond proprietor willing to submit to Rajput caste rules could get his family admitted into the Raj Gond community' (Fuchs 1960: 190).

We find among the Raj Gonds a reform movement started about thirty years ago, for the complete absorption of the Gonds into the Hindu fold with the rank of Kshatriyas. The pamphlets enumerating the ideology and tenets of this reform movement glorify the past cultural attainments of the Gond rajas and put the blame of the present degradation of their status on the Ravanvansi Gonds who eat beef, sacrifice pigs and chicken and drink liquor. It is stated that if the Gonds could give up these 'low' habits they would be able to recover their old status. There have also been several cases when the Brahmins invested the Gonds with the sacred thread (ibid., 191–2).

This nostalgia for past glory and involvement in the Kshatriya movement reminds us very much of the case of the Bhumij. Hivale speaks of the satisfaction that the Raj Gond landlord or thakur derives from the poetical eulogies of the Pradhan bards: 'The Pradhans talk of the Great Gond Rajas and the noble and generous tribe of which his Thakur is such a shining example' (Hivale 1946: 50–1).

The Rajput Chieftaincies of Medieval and Later Chhattisgarh

Since 1905, the Chhattisgarh group of feudatory states included fourteen states under the British Government. These covered an area of 30,959 square miles and 1,618,109 people in 1901. While the majority of the states fall between 500 and 2000 square miles in area, there are also the bigger states of Surguja (6055) and Bastar (13002). These chieftains were, in most cases, subordinate to the higher chiefs such as the Raj Gond rajas of Mandla, Deogarh or Chanda or the Haihaya Rajputs of Ratanpur. Bastar alone seems to have remained intact from a very remote period without the territorial interference of a paramount power (De Brett 1909: 8–9).

Instead of reviewing the situation in each of the fourteen states, the position of the old kingdoms of Ratanpur and Raipur as well as that of the remote state of Bastar will be examined. Before doing so, we will quickly reconnoitre the histories (mixed up with legends) of the origin of some of the states.

Tribal connections with the lineage of the chieftains are most evident in the cases of Kawardha, Raigarh and Sakti where the Raj families are derived from the ancient Raj Gond rulers of Gondwana. It is widely believed in their respective regions of Korea and Jashpur that the current regimes of the Raksel Rajputs were preceded by tribal chieftaincies of the Kol and Dom tribes, respectively. Khairagarh claims descent from the Nagavansi Raja of Chotanagpur, and is thus probably related to the Munda. Besides these cases of possible on the spot growth of states, there is also evidence of conquest playing an essential role in giving shape to the present form of some of the states. The Raksel Rajputs from Palamau are believed to have conquered Surguja from the local tribal chieftains and become overlords over Udaipur, Jashpur, Korea and Changbhakar (De Brett 1909).

We will now examine the structure of traditional Chhattisgarh in the medieval period under the Haihaya Rajputs. For this we will depend principally on C.W. Wills' careful analysis of the available records on the old Rajput kingdoms of Ratanpur and Raipur (Wills 1919).

A powerful Rajput family belonging to the Chedi dynasty ruled at Tripuri near Jabalpur around the tenth century AD. A descendant of this Chedi family named Kalingaraja, settled at Tuman in modern Bilaspur district. His grandson, Ratanraja, founded Ratanpur, the then capital of Chhattisgarh. The dynasty continued to rule for some six centuries. In about the fourteenth century it split into two, the elder branch continuing at Ratanpur which was still the capital of Chhattisgarh, while the younger ruled as a semi-independent in Raipur. About the end of the sixteenth century, the rulers of Chhattisgarh acknowledged the suzerainty of the Great Moghuls and thereafter sank into complete obscurity, to be finally deposed by the Marathas around AD 1745. By comparing the past administrative system of the Chhattisgarh rulers with those of the present chieftaincies, Wills discovered the following symmetrical arrangements that used to guide the territorial organization in this area:

(a) The whole country was divided into two kingdoms—a northern kingdom with its capital at Ratanpur and a southern one with its capital at Raipur.

(b) Each kingdom or Raj was subdivided into districts known as *Garhs* or forts, conventionally supposed to be eighteen in number. The whole owed allegiance to a Rajput king.

(c) Each district or *Garh* was conventionally supposed to contain 84 villages, whence the term *Chaurasi* is derived. It was held by a *Diwan* or *Thakur*, a local chief whose power within his territory was of the widest kind.

(d) Inside the *Garh* were smaller units of *Taluqs* each conventionally supposed to contain 12 villages and therefore known as *Barhons*. Those were held by *Daos* or *Barhainihas*, minor chiefs . . .

The *Dao* was ordinarily the Headman or *Daontia* of the village where he

> resided, the other village headmen of his *Taluq* being separate *Gaontias* who acknowledged his authority. Similiarly the *Diwan* was the *Dao* of the particular *Talaq* in which his headquarters were situated while his outer *Taluqs* were allotted to chiefs of the second degree subordinate to him. Lastly the Raja kept under his direct control the Headquarters *Garh*, while the other *Garhs* of his Kingdom were allotted to the chiefs of the other rank. Sometimes the chiefs of *Garhs* were kinsmen of the Raja; minor chiefs of *Taluqs* were similarly related in some cases to the lord of the *Garh*, and the *Gaontias* in their degree were sometimes related to the chief of their *Taluq* . . . (Wills 1919: 199).

Wills was fully aware that the above was an 'ideal model' or a 'theory' and that it was nowhere exemplified in full detail. This ideal model for Chhattisgarh tallies fairly closely with our data on chieftaincies derived from Bhumij, Munda or Gond bases. This widespread uniformity in the *ideal* model of the territorial system cannot be explained away as cases of independently derived similar socio-political solution. An ideal model, expressed through such conventional numbers of territorial units—12, 84, 18, etc.—must have had widespread diffusion throughout this territory. It should be mentioned here that the conventional unit, *chaurasi* (84 villages), occurred frequently in Rajasthan, the universally acclaimed headquarters of the highest order of Rajputs (Tod 1920: I, 166).

Wills finally labels the prevailing territorial arrangement in medieval Chhattisgarh as 'feudalism superimposed on an earlier tribal base and finds it to be a great contrast to the old Hindu kingdoms which were essentially monarchical and bureaucratic (Wills 1919: 255–7).

I will end this comparative survey with the state of Bastar, the largest member of the modern Chhattisgarh group of states. With an area of nearly 14,000 square miles it has a population of only 524,721 (in 1931), working out to a density of only 34 to the square mile. Out of these, nearly 75 per cent belongs to the 'tribal' category, mostly of the Gond family, variously known in this state as Muria, Maria, Dorla and Koya.

The present ruling family of Bastar is regarded as having descended from the Kakatiyas, who were feudatories of the Chalukya kings of Warangal. Defeated by Ahmad Shah Bahmani, early in the fifteenth century, Annamdeo, the surviving brother of Raja Prataparudra, fled across the river Godavari into Bastar and set up his capital at Dantewara by subjugating the local chieftains. It is stated that portions of Bastar under these local chiefs were already feudatories of the Kakatiyas, before the coming of Annamdeo. It is said that eighteen garhs or pargannahs around Baredongar in Kondagaon were conquered by the Kakatiyas of Bastar from the Somavansi Rajput raja of Kanker. One finds the ruins of an earlier and advanced Hindu civilization at Barsur and at Dantewara under a Telugu line of Nagavansi kings who ruled these areas around the eleventh century AD. The Bastar Raj family claims descent from the Pandu king, Birabhadra of Indraprastha. The legendary nature of this claim is too obvious to need further probing.

The *khalsa* or directly controlled territory of the raja was located around Jagdalpur, the capital. This khalsa tract used to be protectively surrounded in the north, west and south by seventeen or eighteen zemindaris, among which only four survived till recent years. Of these, the Sukma zemindars are regarded as Kshatriyas, and of even greater antiquity than the Raj family of Bastar. The zemindars of Bhopalpatnam are Raj Gonds and are perhaps also of an earlier origin than the Kakatiya Raj of Bastar. In Kutru, moreover, there remain three or four sub-zemindars under the zemindars. According to Grigson, 'All these facts indicate that before Annamdeo's arrival there was a nominal suzerainty of Warangal over most of Bastar, the real authority resting with local chiefs, or in the heads of the old tribal organization that was so marked a feature of the medieval kingdoms of the eastern Central Provinces and some of the Chotanagpur and the Orissa estates' (Grigson 1949: 4). In Glasfurd's report of 1862 we find that of the 43 non-zemindari subdivisions of Bastar, 17 were called pargannahs and 26 garhs (ibid., 33). Grigson finds a fair correspondence between the territorial unit of pargannah and clan among the Hill Marias of Bastar (ibid., 288).

The most striking feature about the Bastar state is the completeness of interaction between the cults of the tribals and those of the raja. The cult of the royal goddess Danteswari, Manikeswari or Maoli has spread over wide areas in Bastar, although when she is worshipped by the local tribal priests, the rituals become necessarily simple with local non-sanskritic connotations. On the occasion of the Dussehra festival it is customary for all these village priests to bring the emblems of their gods and goddesses, and to assemble these around the emblem of the royal goddess Danteswari at Jagdalpur. On the other hand, we find the tribal log-god gaining an almost equal status in the palace cult as Danteswari by assuming the name of Patdeo. It is during the Dussehra festival, again, that the raja has to offer worship to Danteswari as her chief devotee, and on alternate days the goddess and the raja are carried in a swing on a huge chariot pulled by the Maria and Muria tribals of Bastar. The raja is practically regarded as an incarnation of Danteswari and it is believed that he rules Bastar on behalf of the goddess. Elwin mentions that the Murias believe so strongly in the divinity of the raja that 'they greatly resent the Maharaja leaving the state even for a short time. His absence means a withdrawal of divine protection from cattle, crops and people' (Elwin 1947, 183).

The raja's role as a regulator of social customs is apparent from the fact that he had the authority to auction widows and divorced women of the Sundi, Kalar, Dhobi and Panar castes. The chief could also sell the headmanship of various castes, and had the authority to upgrade the members of a low caste by conferring on them the sacred thread (De Brett 1909: 64–5). Being so vitally connected with the rule of the Kshatriya rajas, the major tribes and castes in Bastar have been drawn into a perpetual upward drive in the direction of Kshatriyahood, a feature which has become so familiar to us through the Bhumij, Munda and Gond data. Roughly, the ethnic groups of Bastar are stratified from the highest to the lowest as follows: 'True' Rajputs, Dhakars, Halbas, Bhātras, Murias, Bison-horn Marias and Hill Marias. This list, of course, does not include a number of other tribes and castes in Bastar. (See also Majumdar 1939: 106). The Hill Marias, on settling down in the plains to the south of Abujhmarh, tend to become Plain Marias. In the vicinity of Jagdalpur *tahsil*, the Bison-horn Marias wish to be identified as Murias. In the border of the Muria and the Bhatra tracts, some Murias claim recognition as Bhatras, while the Halbas wish to be regarded as full Kshatriyas of the status of the Raj family.

Discussion

I have discussed above, with a number of examples, how the various tribes of Central India such as the Bhumij, Munda and Gond have been influenced by the formation of states in their respective territories. If the enquiry had been extended into the former feudatory states of Orissa, we would have come across similar developments among the Saura, Bhuiya and Kandha.

The actual process of the formation of the states, as far as could be ascertained, has taken varied courses in the different instances discussed above. Some, like the Munda Raj of Chotanagpur, the Bhumij state of Barabhum and the Raj Gond kingdoms of Gondwana, appear to have emerged mainly through internal developments out of a tribal base. There are also cases of immigrant Rajput adventurers gaining power in the tribal tract by manoeuvring the narrow-range, clan-bound tribal chieftaincies and in a few cases, even by conquest (for example, Bastar, Surguja, Jashpur and so on). There is, however, no tradition or record of a large-scale invasion of the agriculturist tribal territory by aggressive nomads which could lend support to the typical 'conquest theory' of Gumplowicz or Oppenheimer which posits that the invasion of peasants by hordes of herdsmen is an essential historic prerequisite to the formation of a state (Oppenheimer 1914: 51–81).

Whether a particular state is primarily due to an internal growth or is the creation of an adventurous Rajput or pseudo-Rajput lineage, the final forms of the political structure of these chieftaincies in Central India look more or less alike in essential features, namely a feudalistic superstructure on a tribal base. While the immigrant adventurous Rajputs and their associates had to adjust themselves to the in situ clan-based tribal territorial system, internal developmental processes in the tribal belt, in their turn, took the form of aspirations to meet the Rajput model (at least the version that was accessible nearby) with corresponding adaptations. The widespread prevalence of certain conventional numbers such as 12, 84 and 18, in organizing the territorial segments of a state indicates a general sharing of certain ideas throughout Central India. In the absence of any definite record of the large-scale southward migration of Rajputs, this unusual spread can partly be explained through the concept of the 'stimulus diffusion' of an idea as defined by Kroeber (1948: 368–370).

Besides the conventional territorial system, a whole set of ideas such as the high position of the Rajputs in the *varna* order of the caste system, their conventional qualities of valour, chivalry and glamour, the role of the Rajputs as defenders of Brahminism and their patronization of a key symbolic festival (Dussehra, Durga Puja, and so on), have an extensive distribution as a model of social and cultural aspirations throughout Central India. In specific detail, however, the concrete Rajput models of emulation differed from area to area. I should also mention that Brahmin priests in search of new clients in the growing aristocratic strata in the tribal frontiers perhaps played a more important role in the diffusion of the Rajput model, both on the sacred and secular levels, than the Rajputs themselves.

The diffusion of the Rajput model of the state as also the indigenous developmental processes could gain ground only among those tribal groups like the Bhumij, Munda, Gond or Bhuiya, who had attained the technological level of settled agriculture. In no case do we find a shifting cultivating group like the Juang (Orissa), Hill Bhuiya (Orissa), Kharia (Manbhum) or the Hill Maria (Bastar) developing a kingship supported mainly by their primitive technique of cultivation.[5] On the other hand, it is also true that cultivation with the plough is not a *sufficient* condition for the formation of states from tribal bases, for example, the settled-farming community of Ho of Kolhan and the Santal of Santal Pargannah and the neighbouring districts. Stable occupation of a particular territory for a number of generations is perhaps another essential condition for the emergence of a state in situ. There is some evidence that the Santal had to migrate fairly quickly from their original homeland in Hazaribagh and have settled down in widely scattered blocks during the last two hundred years (Datta-Majumder 1956, 23). The core of the Ho area was much too rudely disturbed by internecine wars among feudatory chiefs surrounding Kolhan.

That the clan seemed to have initially demarcated the lower levels of territorial organization is fairly well borne out by the data in hand among the Munda, Bhumij and Gond, among whom the superstructure of the state looks like a coagulation of clan-based territories. However, once the structure of the state had come into existence, the territories seemed to be regarded, from the top at least, mainly as military-administrative units, without reference to clan or caste. In the Bhumij and Munda territories, five as a conventional number is important in territorial organization. Thus there are the five pargannahs under the Raja of Chotanagpur; the zemindari of Panchet is also know as Pancha Khunts or the 'five stripes' and Pancha Sardari or the five Sadivalis under the taraf sardars in Barabhum. This conventional number of five is often associated with the myth that the five major segments of a state, including one originally controlled

[5] It is not being suggested that cultivation with the plough is essential for the rise of kingship. Even slash-and-burn farming with the digging stick and hoe can give rise to states if there are no plough technologies to compete with in the immediate environment (for example, the Mayan, Aztec and the Inca states of Meso-America and the numerous kingdoms in Negro Africa).

by the raja, owe their respective origins to five ancestral brothers, among whom the most senior brother is the ancestor of the royal lineage proper.

Thus, the cases studied lend support to the theories of Maine and Morgan stating that the transference of the organizing principle from 'clan' to 'territory' is one of the fundamental steps in social evolution (Morgan 1878 and Maine 1888: 72–4). Links with the archaic clan organization and the principle of mythical kinship, however, still linger in the territorial organization in these states.

As regards the over-all nature of the kingdoms or chieftaincies of Central India, Wills seems to have said the last word, '. . . a system of feudalism superimposed on an earlier tribal organisation'. It should be noted, however, that the superstructure of a Rajput model par excellence of Rajputana itself has not been regarded as strictly feudal by competent historians. A.C. Layall is of the opinion that the political system of Rajputana was essentially tribal and had not fully evolved to the state of feudalism. Nowhere, he writes, had 'military tenure entirely obliterated the original tenure by blood and birthright of the clan' and that land-tenure had not become the basis of Rajput nobility; rather, 'their pure blood is the origin of their land tenure'. It is also stated by Layall that 'it is universally assumed in every clan of Rajputana, that the chief and the ruler of the state is only *primus inter pares*' (Layall 1875: 203–64).

It is also true that these kingdoms were very different from the early Hindu kingdoms of India in the plains of Magadha, Bengal, Orissa and so on. These latter governments were in the form of a centralized, monarchical system operating with an elaborate bureaucratic machinery of military, revenue and administrative officials. Such machinery practically did not develop at all among the tribal-derived states of Central India, except to a very limited extent among the large Raj Gond kingdoms of Garha-Mandla.

The most striking and important impact of state formation on the internal structure of these tribes was, of course, the stratification of the hitherto equalitarian society into social classes. Social stratification follows mainly the lines of sub-infeudation of territorial units. On the whole, power, economy (as defined in terms of land-holding) and social status have a fairly close correlation in the regional system of stratification. However, the final validation of a status is in terms of kinship (fictitious or real), marriage alliance and ritual symbols. A poor person, related by kinship and marriage to wealthy 'Rajput' families, gains considerable prestige from the right kinds of symbolic associations with the caste status of the Rajput. On the other hand, the Brahmins, who are the key social specialists in the validation of status, have been demonstrably affected by the secular lure of money and power. And this brings the status system more or less in line with the objective state of differentiation in power and economy.

If we examine the case of the Bhumij of Barabhum along with that of the Munda of Tamar, we find that both groups, after running through the equivalent lines of local hierarchy, arrive at the next higher level (Panchet-Ratu) of the scope of an all-Chotanagpur division. These superior rajas of Panchet and Ratu in their turn look up to the Rajput level of the larger chiefs of Orissa and Chhattisgarh. These latter Rajput aristocracies are aware that a still higher status is accorded to some of the Rajput clans like the Suryavansi Sesodiyas of Mewar, Rajputana, at an all-India level. It should not be imagined, however, that there is a neatly worked out and universally agreed upon status hierarchy for the Rajputs all over India, or even within central India as a whole. We are not concerned here with the numerous competing claims for a relatively high caste status within the Rajput stratum among these kingdoms. Over and above these details of status controversies there is a certain degree of general consensus among the 'Rajput' feudatory states and zemindari states of Central India as to the relative status of the various royal lineages tied in fairly stable clusters and classes of marriage alliances. Most of these look up to the Rajput princes of the solar and lunar branches in Rajputana as belonging to the highest order of Kshatriyahood. Tod writes: 'From Rama all the tribes termed Suryavansa, or "Race of the Sun", claim descent as the present princes of Mewar, Marwar and Bikaner and their numerous clans; while from the Lunar (Indu) line of Budha and Krishna, the families of Jaisalmer and Cutch . . . extending throughout the Indian desert from the Sutlej to the ocean, deduce their pedigrees' (Tod 1920: 55).

In other words, there is an hierarchic, structural and ideological (mythical) link between the ordinary tribal Munda, Bhumij or Gond farmers of Central India and the Rajputs of the highest order in north-western India. The myth of the Rajput standard of living and the structural framework of states ruled by Rajput and pseudo-Rajput lineages of various orders connects the tribal belt of Central India in a special way to the mainstream of Hindu civilization and its core of sacred lore in the form of epics and *Puranas*.

The way in which the upper strata of the tribal groups described above have been drawn to the generic Kshatriya-Rajput pool is perhaps not much different from the way in which the bulk of the now most highly esteemed Rajputs of Rajputana had been drawn into the Kshatriya fold from the original invading stocks of tribal Hunas around the sixth century AD.

Probably it would be safe to affirm that all the distinguished clan-castes of Rajasthan are descended mainly from foreigners, the 'Scythians' of Tod. The upper ranks of the invading hordes of Hunas, Gurjaras, Maitrakas, and the rest became Rajput clans . . .

Such clan-castes of foreign descent are the proud and the chivalrous Sisodiyas or Guhilots of Mewar (Smith 1958: 191).

It is in more or less the same way that the great builders of the Khajuraho temples emerged as Rajput Kshatriyas of the Chandel clans out of a tribal base (ibid., 191).

As to the cultural role of these states, they have not only propagated the standard Brahminic socio-ritual forms, but have also universalized the local tribal cults to a grand level of elaboration, providing a rich regional flavour to the cultural pattern of a kingdom.

My presentation so far may suggest a much too smooth on-going process leading the tribes into the Rajput fold. There have been occasional and significant setbacks and reversals to this generic process. Navalakha's observations on the Bhils of Banswara who were organized under indigenous chieftaincies, may be cited in this connection. The Bhils of Banswara were finally subjugated by the Guhil Rajputs during the eighteenth century. The Bhils largely retired to the hilly and wooded interiors to escape the aggressive conquerors.

The Bhils who escaped to the geographically inhospitable interiors were motivated by their urge to preserve independence; but their political structure was shattered and they were politically disintegrated . . . The Bhils eventually retreated to a comparative seclusion beyond the reach of the alien peoples and particularly of the arms of the state authority (Navalakha 1959: 37–8).

It should be made clear at this point that the tribals at the lower rungs of the social hierarchy had only feeble aspirations for identification as Rajput-Kshatriyas. Their poor economic position, more than any other factor, virtually ruled out the possibility of their ever realizing the status of Rajputs for which it was essential to 'purchase' the ritual services of

Brahmins of the right kind. There is also the fact that the Rajputized chieftains used to maintain a fairly close control over the inter-ethnic rank hierarchy in their respective territories. The various castes and tribes, in their turn, were always watchful for a possible supercession of rank claims by the groups which were traditionally considered relatively low. This partially explains the fact that the tribes and castes living within the territory of a Rajputized chieftain were able to maintain their respective ethnic identities through the centuries instead of rapidly melting into a monolithic Rajput affiliation. Thus, while the emergent state structure facilitated the upper hierarchies to attain Rajput status, the power of the same structure was directed, to a considerable extent, towards inhibiting the realization of similar aspirations by commoners. However, even the lower strata of the tribal population were not immune to the percolation of Rajput aspirations primarily generated at the aristocratic level. At appropriate moments, especially with the disintegration of the overarching, watchful state structures these latent aspirations found expression in the periodic social mobility movements in Manbhum.

Although this paper has emphasized the positive role of the state in integrating the tribals with the Hindu social system, it should also be noted that unwise oppressive policies followed by some of these chieftains occasionally hindered, or even reversed, the process. The rajas of Chotanagpur leased out to aggressive Hindu immigrants a large portion of their central domain, between the seventeenth and eighteenth centuries. This was done for immediate economic gain by dispossessing a good number of Munda headmen and khuntkatti tenants. Such an alienation with their sacred ancestral manoeuvres of Hindu money-lenders gave rise to repeated agrarian revolts between 1800 and 1900 (Roy 1912: 182–353). These uprisings were directed mainly against the upper caste Hindu immigrants and today form an essential component of the folk songs and the historic legends of the Munda. As a result, in spite of their progressive integration with Hindu society and culture, the Munda, in common with many other Kolarian tribes of Chotanagpur, maintain a residual feeling of separation and antagonism with the Hindu Diku (foreigners). This latter sentiment has been conveniently utilized by a section of the tribal leaders in Chotanagpur to build up the separatist pan-tribal Jharkhand movement.

It should also be pointed out here that the Hinduization of tribes has not been implemented through the structural medium of the states alone; a good deal of it has been achieved through the spontaneous interaction of the Hindu artisan, cultivator and sacerdotal castes with the tribals, and this has not been covered in this paper.

I have so far viewed the tribals in the orthogenetic phase[6] of the growth, spread and persistence of the traditional civilization of India. The tribes were moving up in terms of established social mechanisms and towards goals clearly defined in terms of ideational and behavioural standards. With the merger of the feudatory chieftaincies, abolition of zemindaris and rapid encroachment into tribal areas due to the secular non-Brahminical policy of the 'welfare state' of India, the image of the 'Rajput' has been fast losing its glitter; the many concrete advantages offered by the Government to the 'low' tribals is more attractive.

It is no wonder that at the last meeting of the Bhumij Kshatriyas that I attended in 1958, little enthusiasm was shown for being recognized as Rajputs or for quoting Sanskrit texts in support of such claims. The concern was more for gaining some footing in the coming General Election and for competing with the hard-headed Mahato in education and economic prosperity (Sinha 1959: 28–32).

With the unfulfilled desire for Rajput recognition still lingering in their hearts and a residue of the broken landed aristocracy yet remaining in their midst, the Bhumij and the Raj Gonds find it hard to adjust themselves to the current secular demands made upon them. These Hinduized tribals, in their aristocratic vacillations, are at a distinct disadvantage in relation to the less Hinduized groups, such as the Ho, Santal, sections of the Munda and the Gond and so on, who are building up the Adivasi movement with good secular goals, with a good feeling for the future.

I am not assuming that the general process of integration into Hindu society will come to an end with the shattering of historical state structures. 'State formation' has already achieved the historic task of hastening the dissemination of Brahminical standards and of synthesizing the latter and the tribal cults. The tribes and the Hindus already share many common elements and there exists today a wide range of contact between the tribes of Central India and the Hindu castes on the economic and administrative planes which facilitate the tempo of integration with

6 See Robert Redfield and Milton Singer, 'The Cultural Role of Cities', *Economic Development and Cultural Change*, Research Center in Economic Development and Cultural Change, University of Chicago, vol. 3, 1954, no. 1, pp. 53–73. Reprinted in *Man in India*, vol. 36, 1956, no. 3, pp. 161–94.

Hindu society. The steps through which the new (heterogenetic) phase of integrative processes moves on remains to be investigated.

This inadequately documented and somewhat speculative and cursory essay has been attempted mainly with a view to attracting the attention of my colleagues in the field of tribal ethnography to fill in the major gaps in my presentation on the tribe-Rajput continuum in relation to the general study of Indian civilization. This is also a pointer to the fact that tribes should be studied not only as ethnic isolates interacting with other ethnic groups, but also within a wide spatial framework such as a pargannah, garh or kingdom which has considerable historic continuity. This essay is also intended to stimulate an awareness in the research worker of the distinct orthogenetic and heterogenetic phases in the study of cultural transformation in tribal India.

References Cited

Bloch, Marc, *Feudal Society* (Chicago, 1961).

Chatterton, Eyre, *The Story of Gondwana* (London, 1916).

Coupland, H., *Bengal District Gazetteers: Manbhum* (Calcutta, 1911).

Dalton, E.T., *Descriptive Ethnology of Bengal*, reprinted (Calcutta, 1960) (first published in 1872).

Datta-Majumder, N., *The Santal: A Study in Culture Change* (Calcutta, 1956).

De Brett, E.A., *Central Provinces Gazetteers: Chhattisgarh Feudatory States* (Bombay, 1909).

Dent, W., *Report on Barabhum*, 1883.

Elwin, Verrier, *The Muria and Their Ghotul* (Bombay, 1947).

Fuchs, Stephen, *The Gond and the Bhumia of Eastern Mandla* (London, 1960).

Gokhale, B.K., *Final Report on the Survey and Settlement Operations in Manbhum*, 1918–25 (Patna, 1928).

Grigson, Wilfrid, *The Maria Gonds of Bastar* (London, 1949).

Higginson, *Report on Barabhum*, 1771.

Hivale, Samrao, *The Pradhans of the Upper Narbada Valley* (Bombay, 1946).

Layall, A.C., 'The Rajput States of India', *Asiatic Studies I*, 1875, pp. 203–64.

Maine, H.S., *Lectures on the Early History of Institutions* (New York, 1888).

Majumdar, D.N., 'Tribal Cultures and Acculturation', *Man in India*, vol. 19, 1939, pp. 99–173.

——*The Affairs of a Tribe* (Lucknow, 1950).

Morgan, L.H., *Ancient Society* (New York, 1878).

Nandjee, Munshi, *Report on the Ghatwali Survey in Manbhum*, 1883.

Navalakha, S.K., 'The Authority Structure Among the Bhumij and the Bhil: A Study of Historic Causations', *The Eastern Anthropologist*, vol. 13, no. 1, 1959, pp. 27–40.

Oppenheimer, Franz, *The State*, Indianapolis, 1914.

Redfield, Robert and Milton, B. Singer, 'The Cultural Role of Cities', *Economic Development and Cultural Change*, vol. 3, no. 1, 1954, pp. 53–73.

Risley, H.H., *Special Note on Barabhum*, 1883.

—— *Tribes and Castes of Bengal*, vols I and II (Calcutta, 1891).

—— *The People of India*, second edn (London, 1915).

Roy, S.C., *The Mundas and Their Country* (Calcutta, 1912).

Russell, R.V. and Hira Lal, *The Castes and Tribes of the Central Provinces of India*, vol. 3 (London, 1916).

Sinha, Surajit, 'Some Aspects of Changes in Bhumij Religion in South Manbhum', *Man in India*, vol. 33, no. 2, 1953, pp. 148–64.

—— 'The Media and Nature of Hindu-Bhumij Interaction', *Journal of the Asiatic Society of Bengal: Letters and Sciences*, vol. 23, no. 1, 1957, pp. 23–37.

—— 'Changes in the Cycle of Festivals in a Bhumij Village', *Journal of Social Research* (Ranchi, September, 1958).

—— 'Bhumij-Kshatriya Social Movement in South Manbhum', *Bulletin of the Department of Anthropology* (Calcutta), vol. 8, no. 2, 1959, pp. 9–32.

Smith, V.A., *The Oxford History of India*, third edn (Oxford, 1958).

Tod, James, *Annals and Antiquities of Rajasthan*, vol. I (London, 1920).

Wills, C.U., 'Territorial System of the Rajput Kingdoms of Mediaeval Chhattisgarh', *Journal of the Royal Asiatic Society Bengal*, vol. 15, 1919, pp. 197–262.

Annotated Bibliography

This annotated bibliography has two objectives: (i) to attempt to classify, keeping in view the approach, methodology and chronological coverage, the alphabetically arranged bibliography and (ii) to provide within this framework a brief résumé of the literature listed in the Bibliography and analysed in the introductory essay of this volume which itself is meant to be an extended bibliographical essay on the literature on the theories of the state in India, 1000–1700.

1. General

The state (its origin and development) has lost much of its nineteenth century philosophical fascination but remains a central theme of history and social science. As examples of more recent approaches to the state one may refer to standard works like S.N. Eisenstadt's (1963) and P. Anderson's (1974) studies with their respective Weberian and Marxian leanings. The most recent attempt to study the state on a worldwide comparative basis was a series of international conferences organized by J.M. Claessen and P. Skalnik, the results of which have been published in three volumes (1978, 1981, 1987). In its theoretical coverage of the subject the first volume is strongest whereas specific papers on India are published mainly in the following two volumes. During the seventies a considerably large number of new efforts to conceptualize the Indian state, its formation and kingship ideology emerged from rather specialized workshops focussing on South Asia. The reports of some of these conferences meanwhile may be regarded as standard texts in their respective fields, e.g. R. Fox (1977), J.F. Richards (1978), R.J. Moore (1979) and more recently J. Pouchepadass and H. Stern (1991). The more specific issue of late medieval state formation in India has been taken up by

F. Perlin (1985a) and S.H. Rudolf (1987) whereas S. Subrahmanyam (1986) questions the relevance of these mostly 'foreign' concepts for Indian and Southeast Asian history. Schwartzberg, the editor of the *Historical Atlas of South Asia*, offers a historical and geographical explanation of the regional and transregional state formation in South Asia (1977).

2. The Asiatic Mode of Production in the Indian Context

Since the publication of K. Wittfogel's controversial book, *Oriental Despotim* (1957), K. Marx's scattered writings on India belong to the most frequently and thoroughly scrutinized pages ever written on India as they form the basis of the concept of the APM and 'Oriental Despotism'. Except for a few studies, e.g. K.D. Erdmann's article on Marx's and Engels' perception of the Asian world (1961), the controversial debate on the application of the APM to Indian history remained primarily a Marxist concern. Whereas western Marxist historians had tried to construct a coherent concept on the basis of Marx's comments on India, Indian Marxist historians vehemently reject its applicability to Indian history. This was done most ardently by Kosambi (1956; see also R. Thapar 1992: 104) and I. Habib (1961, published 1962 and 1969), followed by D.N. Jha in his Presidential Address (1979) and recently again by R.S. Sharma (1989). The only significant though unconvincing attempt to apply the APM to Indian history comes from K. Gough (1980, 1981). Moreover A. Southall (1987) refers to her work in his strange attempt to equate his segmentary state concept with Marx's APM. The most recent thorough study by B. O'Leary (1989) may—for the time being—put an end to further futile attempts to apply the APM to Indian history even though a general sympathy with Marx's ingenious thoughts on India will remain alive [e.g. I. Habib (1985) and B. Stein in the present volume].

3. The Indian Historiographical Model

The Indian historiographical model depicting the Indian state as a strong and centrally administered unitary kingdom is best represented in the classical monographs of A.S. Altekar on the Rāṣṭrakūṭas (1st edn 1934), K.A.N. Sastri on the Cōḷas (1st edn 1935/37) and R.C. Majumdar on Bengal (1st edn 1943) and in most of the contributions to India's monumental 'national' series *History and Culture of the Indian People* (1951–1977). This historiography also produced several important studies on special aspects of the so-called 'classical' Indian state and its administration. Of particular relevance are R.K. Mookerji's *Local Government* (1st edn 1918), A.S. Altekar's work on the *State and Government in Ancient India* (1st edn 1949) and more recently D.C. Sircar's *Political and Administrative System of Ancient and Medieval India* (1974). The most recent comprehensive representation of the Indian state in classical Indological studies is H. Scharfe's *The State in Indian Tradition* (1989). Certainly it is this school that has produced the greatest number of books and articles on the Indian state and various aspects of its administration. But most of them focus on the early classical state, e.g. on the Maurya state and on related Arthaśāstra studies which are outside the scope of the present volume. So far however this school has not come forward with a systematic conceptualization of the classical and early medieval Indian state. Its regional and often communalist approach (Settar 1982) and its gazetteer-like 'compartmentalization' (Stein 1975b) of history into political, religious, social and economic history may be some of the reasons of this historiographic lacuna.

4. The Muslim States in Medieval India

An interesting introduction into the study of Muslim states in India contains the chapter 'The State' in Rizvi's second volume *The Wonder that was India* (1987: 154–95). The study of the Delhi Sultanate began under the heavy burden of the third volume of the *Cambridge History of India*, Sir Wolseley Haig's *Turks and Afghans*, published in 1928. It is nothing more than a monotonous chronicle of mainly martial events and is devoid of any attempt to define the statehood of the Sultanate. The first generation of studies on the Muslim state in medieval India in the thirties and forties appears to have been a reaction against this 'imperial' verdict as it had already come under the strong influence of W.H. Moreland's pathbreaking studies on the economic history of medieval India, culminating in his *Agrarian System of Muslim India* (1929). The early studies on the Delhi Sultanate, e.g. K.M. Ashraf's *Life and Condition of the Peoples of Hindustan* (1935), I.H. Qureshi's *The Administration of the Delhi Sultanate* (1942) and A.M. Aziz's studies (1944 and 1949) are regarded as works having made major progress and were accordingly reprinted several times. Other important contributions to the history of the Delhi Sultanate are K.M. Nizami's *Some Aspects of Religion and Politics in India During the Thirteenth Century* (1961), Mohammad Habib's collected works (1974–81) and volume five of the Comprehensive History of India, *The Delhi Sultanate* (1970), jointly edited by Habib and Nizami. However, probably due to the reasons mentioned in the Introduction, most of these writings on medieval 'Muslim' India, too, follow the contemporary Indian historiographical model of a unitary and rather monolithic state with a particularly strong emphasis on the personal authority of the Sultan and his religious legitimation. A new period of historiography of medieval India began in the late fifties with a series of more critical studies on the social fabric of the ruling elites, their agro-economic foundation, etc. In a detailed article on 'Writings on Social History of Medieval India' Satish Chandra (1977) traced the 'trends and prospects' of these new studies and their authors who meanwhile became known as the 'Aligarh School'. Satish Chandra's *Parties and Politics at the Mughal Court* (1959), Irfan Habib's *The Agrarian System of Mughal India* (1963) and Athar Ali's *The Moghul Nobility under Aurangzeb* (1966) are usually regarded as the foundation stones of this School. Apart from a large number of detailed papers on various, mainly socio-economic, aspects of the Mughal state other important works of this School are the first volume of the *Cambridge Economic History of India 1200–1750* jointly edited by Tapan Raychaudhuri and Irfan Habib (1982)— which in fact has a lot to say about the state under the Sultans and the Mughals— and Athar Ali's *Apparatus of Empire* (1985). Moreover, three series should be mentioned—*Medieval India Quarterly* (5 vols, 1950–63), *Medieval India—a Miscellany* (4 vols, 1969–75) and *Medieval India* (so far one vol., 1992)—which have been successively published by the Centre of Advanced Study in History of Aligarh Muslim University. Two excellent introductions to the major research topics of this School are Satish Chandra's introduction to his book on the Mughal court (1959: XVII–LII) and Nurul Hasan's booklet *Thoughts on Agrarian Relations in Mughal India* (1973). In a broader context Q. Ahmad's comprehensive review article 'Works on Mughal Administration' (1987) is very helpful. In recent years, however, Muzaffar Alam (1986, 1991 and forthcoming, together with Sanjay Subrahmanyam) has begun questioning several important issues of the Aligarh School, particularly its still prevailing depiction of the Mughal state as a unitary state. In his volume, *The Mughal Empire* of the New Cambridge History of India (1993) J.F. Richards repeats his criticism of the 'jagir crisis' (first expressed in his study on Golkonda 1975) which forms an important issue of the Aligarh School ever since Irfan Habib published his *Agrarian System* in 1963. For a new attempt to define the Mughal state in view of contradicting models see also D.E. Streusand, *The Formation of the Mughal Empire* (1989).

5. Indian Feudalism

The formulation of the Indian feudalism model appears to have been influenced, apart from the relevant Marxist literature, by M. Bloch's *Feudal Society* (1956) and by *Mohammed and Charlemagne*, Pirenne's classical history of Europe between the fifth and ninth centuries (Pirenne, 1939). Max Weber's concept of feudalism (1920) is referred to only by B.N.S. Yadava (1973). The basic work *Indian Feudalism* was published by R.S. Sharma in 1965. A comprehensive overview of further research on this topic is provided by the first volume of the *Indian Historical Review* (1974) and the anthology, *Feudal Social Formation in Early India*, edited by D.N. Jha (1987). V.K. Thakur's *Historiography of Indian Feudalism* (1989) is an attempt to defend Indian feudalism with familiar arguments against dissenting voices and clear rejections of the concept. D.C. Sircar's verdict ('Landlordism Confused with Feudalism', 1966) reflects the general reaction against the concept by adherents of the 'Indian historiographical model'. Far more influential than this outright rejection of anything feudal-like in Indian history were rather cautious and differentiating dissenting works like B.D. Chattopadhyaya's article on early medieval urbanism (1974) or M.R. Tarafdar's paper on trade and economy in early medieval Bengal (1978). The struggle 'Against Feudalism' (A. Rudra 1981) was elevated to a more thorough debate on the general question of the very existence of feudalism in India with H. Mukhia's Presidential Address, 'Was there Feudalism in India?' (in the present volume). It raised the debate for the first time to a truely international level which found expression in a special issue of the *Journal of Peasant*

Studies devoted to the theme, 'Feudalism and Non-European Societies', jointly published by T.J. Byres and H. Mukhia (1985). In this volume R.S. Sharma answered his critics in a paper, 'How Feudal was Indian Feudalism?' (reprinted in the present volume); again in 1993 he rebutted Southall's concept of the segmentary state and its application to Indian history by B. Stein who had hailed Mukhia's Address for his deconstruction of the feudalism concept (1985).

6. The Segmentary State

B. Stein's concept of the segmentary state in South Indian history is derived from A. Southall's *Alur Society* (1956) and was also strongly influenced by B. Subha Rao's historic archaeological-geographical study *The Personality of India* (1956) and by Y. Subbarayalu's *Political Geography of the Chola Country* (1973). The classical text of Stein's concept is his article 'The Segmentary State in South Indian History' (1977) even though he extended his concept considerably in his monograph *Peasant State and Society in Medieval South India* (1980). Stein's concept was welcomed by a few historians as 'an alternative model to the unitary state model' (G. Spencer 1983; also H. Kulke 1982, D. Shulman 1985, Dirks 1987 and Berkemer, forthcoming). But it was even more strongly criticized by a number of Indian historians, notably by R. Champakalakshmi (1981) and V. Ramaswamy (1982) and in a broader context by B.D. Chattopadhyaya in his Presidential Address (1983) reprinted in the present volume. Of particular relevance are, in this context, new structural analyses of the Chola state which differ considerably from Stein's interpretation, e.g. Y. Subbarayalu 1982 and J. Heitzman 1987 (reprinted in the present volume). Stein answered his critics for the first time in 1985 in connection with his critique of the Indian feudalism concept and again in his 'Interim Reflections' of the year 1991 (reprinted in the present volume) which was followed again by an outright attack by R.S. Sharma (1993).

7. The Patrimonial-Bureaucratic State

Max Weber formulated his concept of patrimonialism and the patrimonial-bureaucratic state in his *Economy and Society* (trans. 1978).

S. Blake applied it for the first time to the Indian context in his article, 'The Patrimonial-Bureaucratic Empire of the Mughals' (1979, repr. in the present volume). He referred to this concept again in his recent study *Shahjahanabad: The Sovereign City in Mughal India, 1639–1739* (1991). P. Hardy accepted Blake's definition of the Mughal empire as a patrimonial- bureaucratic state. He focused his paper 'Islamic Patrimonialism under the Mughals' (in German, 1987) on the personal authority of the Mughal rulers and on the extra-patrimonial bureaucracy. Recently S. Conermann (1993) has shown that the Delhi Sultanate under Muhammad Ibn Tugluq depicts all characteristics of a traditional patrimonial state whose administrative-bureaucratic capacity was still only rudimentarily developed. Influenced by Blake, B. Stein applied Weber's concept to Vijayanagara where he detected features of transition from a segmentary state to a patrimonial-bureaucratic regime (1985b and c). The more general question of the applicability of Weber's concept in the context of Indian history was taken up by J. Rösel (1986). He too subscribes to the idea of its usefulness in the context of India without however specifying a particular state or period of Indian history which could be called patrimonial-bureaucratic. However, S. Subrahmanyam in 1986 came forward with a rebuttal of this model in the Indian context.

8. 'Non-aligned' Historiography of the Indian State: A Model of Integrative State Formation

A considerably large number of historians endeavour to conceptualize the process of state formation and the state outside the above mentioned models. A common denominator of their reasoning is their awareness of socio-economic and political changes and integrative forces in early and late medieval periods though none of them follows an evolutionary paradigm nor are they striving for a chronological compartmentalization of history in terms of modes of production. B.D. Chattopadhyaya's Presidential Address on 'Political Processes and the Structure of Polity' (1983, repr. in the present volume) is as significant and exemplary for these studies as is his most recent paper 'The Making of Early Medieval India' which forms an introduction to a selection of his own articles (1993).

Another major feature of these comprehensive studies is their regional focus. Most important among these foci is South India and its Chola state in particular. Several of these contributions have already been mentioned in connection with their rebuttal of Stein's segmentary state concept. Y. Subbarayalu's studies, the first of which had strongly influenced Stein's concept (1973), are of particular relevance in defining the Chola state *vis-à-vis* K.A.N. Sastri's 'Indian historiographical model' and Stein's segmentary model. Heitzman's paper on 'State Formation in South India' (1987a, repr. in the present volume) corroborates Subbarayalu's findings of a structurally differentiated development of the Chola state. N. Karashima's detailed epigraphical studies, some of which tend to corroborate the feudal model (e.g. 1976), are now available in his collection of articles (1984 and 1992).

Trade and its organization as constituent factors of the Chola state are stressed by K.R. Hall (1980) whereas G.W. Spencer emphasizes 'politics of plunder' (1976) and expansionism (1983) as major features of the Chola state. R. Champakalakshmi contributed several papers on urbanization as yet another important aspect of early medieval South India (1979, 1986). Another attempt is H. Kulke's 'integrative model' based on his studies in Orissa, which was then further extended in his 'processural model of state formation' (in the present volume).

Whereas these studies focus on the great 'regional kingdoms' as representing the typology of the early medieval state, the 'little kingdoms' as their late medieval successor states, have become yet another focus of recent studies on pre-modern state formation in India. Originally elucidated by B. Cohn in the context of eighteenth century Benares (1962, repr. 1987) it was developed by N. Dirks in the context of Tamilnadu into a full-fledged concept of late medieval local state formation in his monograph *The Hollow Crown: Ethnohistory of an Indian Kingdom* (1987). G. Berkemer (1989 and 1991) found corroborative evidence of this concept in northern Andhra Pradesh since the early medieval period. In a very recent paper however B. Schnepel questions the validity of Dirks' concept on the basis of his studies in Koraput/Orissa (1994). The most outstanding recent study of late medieval state formation in South India is the joint work of V. Narayana Rao, D. Shulman and S. Subrahmanyam—*Symbols of Substance* (1992)—which deals with the political culture of the court and state in the Nayaka period of Tamilnadu during the sixteenth and seventeenth centuries. In many respects it may be regarded as a continuation of D. Shulman's study on early medieval kingship in Tamilnadu (1985).

Late medieval state formation in the Hindu tribal frontier region is yet another important, though still rather neglected, topic of research. An early exemplary contribution to these studies is C.U. Wills' paper on Rajput kingdoms in medieval Chhattisgarh (1920). S.C. Sinha's seminal paper on Rajputization and state formation in Central India (1962) is reprinted in this volume. Further studies on this topic are included in a recently published volume edited by S.C. Sinha (1987). The integration of tribal communities into the process of 'Hindu' state formation through ritual policies (e.g. royal patronage of tribal cults) has been the subject of some papers by H. Kulke in the context of Orissa (repr. 1993) and B. Schnepel (1992, 1994) and more recently in a paper on the Draksharama temple in Andhra Pradesh by K. Durga and S. Reddy (1992).

Temples and temple cities have often been studied as key factors of early and late medieval state formation. A major focus of these studies is again Orissa (Eschmann et al. 1978) and South India and in particular the Tanjore temple due to its unique corpus of contemporary temple inscriptions. G.W. Spencer's paper on 'Religious Networks and Royal Influence' (1969) is one of the first important contributions to these studies. B. Stein has also referred largely to Tanjore while elaborating on his concept of 'ritual sovereignty' (1977, 1980), whereas Heitzman emphasizes in a recent paper (1991) the role of the Tanjore temple as a major instrument of the rituo-political integration and economic development of the dynastic core area of the Cholas. An anthology of articles on *South Indian Temples* edited by B. Stein (1978a) includes inter alia several papers on the Vijayanagara period. Thus A. Appadurai stresses the attempt of Vijayanagara rulers to control temple cities as nodal points of royal influences through the patronage of sect leaders. A more recent study of R. Palat (1986) shows how Vijayanagara kings tried to quell popular revolts through establishing their hold over temple cities. J. Rösel underlined the importance of temple cities for the establishment of regional kingdoms in Orissa (1978). H. Kulke, too, emphasized in the Orissan context the importance of temple cities for royal legitimation and kingship ideology (1978, 1993). An anthology of papers on various aspects of *The Sacred Centre as the Focus of Political Interest*, edited by H. Bakker (1992) extends these studies to contemporary India.

Select Bibliography

(Compiled by Georg Berkemer)

ABBREVIATIONS

AES	Archive Européen de Sociologie
CIS	Contributions to Indian Sociology
CSSH	Comparative Studies in Society and History
IESHR	Indian Economic and Social History Review
IHR	Indian Historical Review
JAS	Journal of Asian Studies
JESHO	Journal of the Economic and Social History of the Orient
JIH	Journal of Indian History
JPS	Journal of Peasant Studies
JRAS	Journal of the Royal Asiatic Society
MAS	Modern Asian Studies
OHRJ	Orissa Historical Research Journal
PIHC	Proceedings of the Indian History Congress

Ahmad, Qeyamuddin, 'Work on Mughal Administration: A Survey', *IHR*, 14, 1987–88, pp. 138–73

Alam, Muzaffar, *The Crisis of Empire in Mughal North India. Awadh and the Punjab, 1707–1748* (Delhi: Oxford University Press, 1986)

—— 'Eastern India in the Early Eighteenth Century "Crisis" : Some Evidence from Bihar', *IESHR*, 28, 1991, pp. 43–71

—— (together with S. Subrahmanyam) 'State-Building in South Asia and the Mughals, 1500–1750', in Aricanli, A. Ghani and D. Ludden (eds), *The Political Economy of the Ottoman, Safavid and Mughal Empires* (forthcoming)

Ali, M. Athar, *The Mughal Nobility under Aurangzeb* (London, 1966)

—— 'The Mughal Empire in History', Presidential Address, Medieval India Section, *Indian History Congress*, 33rd Session (Muzaffarpur, Dec. 1972)

—— 'The Passing of the Empire: The Mughal Case', *MAS*, 9, 1975, pp. 385–96

—— 'Mansab and Imperial Policy under Shah Jahan', *IHR*, 3, 1976–77, pp. 99–104

—— 'Towards an Interpretation of the Mughal Empire', *JRAS*, 1978, pp. 38–49

—— 'The Pre-Colonial Social Structure and the Polity of the Mughal Empire', *PIHC*, 44, 1983, pp. 253–61

—— *The Apparatus of Empire. Awards of Ranks, Offices and Titles to the Mughal Nobility, 1574–1658* (Delhi: Oxford University Press, 1985)

—— 'The Islamic Background of Indian History—An Interpretation', *JESHO*, 32, 1989, pp. 335–45

—— 'The Mughal Polity–A Critique of "Revisionist" Approaches', *MAS*, 24, 1993, pp. 699–710

Altekar, Anant Sadashiv, *The Rāṣṭrakūṭas and Their Times* (Poone, 1934, rev. edn 1967)

—— *State and Government in Ancient India* (Benares, 1949, Delhi, 3rd edn 1972)

Anderson, Perry, *Lineages of the Absolutist State* (London, 1974)

Appadurai, Arjun, 'Kings, Sects and Temples in South India, 1350–1700', in Stein, B. (1978a), pp. 75–106

Appadurai, Arjun and Carol Breckenridge, 'The South Indian Temple: Authority, Honour and Redistribution', *CIS (N.S.)* 10, 1976, pp. 187–211

Ashraf, K.M., *Life and Conditions of the People of Hindustan*, Calcutta, Asiatic Society (*Journal of the Asiatic Society of Bengal, Letters*, 1935, pp. 103–358) 2nd. edn (New Delhi, 1970)

Aziz, Ahmad Muhammad, 'The Central Structure of the Sultanate of Delhi', in *Islamic Culture*, 18, 1944, pp. 62–83

—— *Political History and Institutions of the Early Turkish Empire of Delhi (1206–1290* AD) (Lahore, 1949, reprint Delhi, 1972)

Bakker, Hans (ed.), *The Sacred Center as the Focus of Political Interest*, Groningen Oriental Studies, vol. 6, 1992

Banerjee, A.C., *The State and Society in Northern India (1206–1526)* (Calcutta, 1982)

Berkemer, Georg, 'The "Center out There" as State Archive: The Temple of Siṃhācalam', in H. Bakker, 1992

—— *Little Kingdoms in Kalinga: Ideologie, Legitimation und Politik regionaler Eliten* (Wiesbaden, 1993)

—— Political Systems and Political Structure of Medieval South India (forthcoming)

Bhattacharya, Swapna, 'A Comparative Analysis of Landgrant Documents from Early Medieval Bengal and Germany', *Proceedings of the All India Oriental Conference*, 30th Session, 1980 (Poona: Bhandarkar Oriental Research Institute, 1982), pp. 343–50

—— *Landschenkungen und staatliche Entwicklung im frühmittelalterlichen Bengalen (5. bis 13. Jh. n. Chr.)* (Wiesbaden, 1985)

Bhattacharya, S. and R. Thapar (eds), *Situating Indian History, For Sarvepalli Gopal* (Delhi: OUP, 1986)

Biller, Jürgen, *Zur Entstehung von Herrschaft und Staat. Das Beispiel des indischen Regionalreiches von Orissa* (Freiburg, 1986)

Blake, Stephen P., 'The Patrimonial-Bureaucratic Empire of the Mughals', *JAS*, 39, 1979, pp. 77–94

—— 'The Hierarchy of Central Places in North India During the Mughal Period of Indian History', in *South Asia*, 6, 1983, pp. 1–32

—— 'Cityspace of an Imperial Capital: Shahjahanabad in 1739', in R.E. Frykenberg (ed.), *Delhi Through the Ages* (New Delhi: OUP, 1986), pp. 152–91

—— 'The Urban Economy in Pre-modern Muslim India. Shahjahanabad, 1639–1739', *MAS*, 21, 1987a, pp. 447–71

—— 'The Structure of Monetary Exchange in North India: The Provinces of Agra, Delhi, and Lahore in 1600', in *The Imperial Monetary System of Mughal India*, J.F. Richards (ed.) (Delhi: OUP, 1987b), pp. 100–36

—— 'Courtly Culture Under Babur and the Early Mughals', *JAS*, 20, 1987, pp. 49–68

—— *Shahjahanabad: The Sovereign City in Mughal India, 1639–1739* (Cambridge, 1991)

Bloch, Marc, *Feudal Society*, transl. from French by L.A. Manyon, 2 vols (London, 1961)

Byres, T.J. and Harbans Mukhia (eds), 'Feudalism and Non-European Societies', Special Issue of *JPS*, 12, nos. 2–3 (London, 1985)

Chakrabarti, Ranabhir, 'Monarchs, Merchants and a Maṭha in Northern Konkan (*c.* 900–1053 AD)', *IESHR*, 27, 1990, pp. 189–208

Champakalakshmi, R., 'Growth of Urban Centres in South India: Kuḍamūkku-Palaiyārai, the Twin-City of the Coḷas', *Studies in History*, 1, 1979, pp. 1–29

—— 'Peasant State and Society in Medieval South India: A Review Article', *IESHR*, 18, 1981, pp. 411–27

—— 'Urbanization in Early Medieval Tamil Nadu', in Bhattacharya, S. and R. Thapar, 1986, pp. 34–105

Chandra, Satish, *Parties and Politics at the Mughal Court* (Calcutta, 1959)

—— 'Writings on Social History of Medieval India: Trends and Prospects', *IHR*, 3, 1976–77, pp. 267–85

—— *Medieval India: Society, the Jagirdari Crisis and the Village* (Delhi, 1982)

Chattopadhyaya, Brajadulal, 'Irrigation in Early Medieval Rajasthan', *JESHO*, 16, 1973, pp. 298–316

—— 'Trade and Urban Centres in Early Medieval North India', *IHR*, 1, 1974, pp. 203–19

—— 'Origin of the Rajputs: The Political, Economic and Social Processes in Early Medieval Rajasthan', *IHR*, 3, 1976, pp. 59–82

—— 'Political Processes and the Structure of Polity in Early Medieval India', Presidential Address, Ancient India Section, *Indian History Congress*, 44th Session (Burdwan, Dec. 1983)

—— 'Markets and Merchants in Early Medieval Rajasthan', *Social Science Probings*, 2, 1985, pp. 413–40

—— 'Urban Centers in Early Medieval India: An Overview', in Bhattacharya, S. and R. Thapar, 1986, pp. 8–33

—— *Aspects of Rural Settlements and Rural Society in Early Medieval India* (Calcutta, 1990)

—— *The Making of Early Medieval India* (Delhi: OUP, 1994)

—— 'State and Economy in North India: 4th Century to 12th Century AD', in R. Thapar (ed.), *Recent Perspectives of Early Indian History* (Bombay, 1995), pp. 320–57

Claessen, H.J.M. and P. Skalnik (eds), *The Early State* (The Hague, 1978)

—— *The Study of the State* (The Hague, 1981)

Claessen, H.J.M. and P. Van de Velde (eds), *Early State Dynamics* (Leiden, 1987)

Cohn, Bernard S., 'Political Systems and Political Structures in Eighteenth-Century India: The Banaras Region', *Journal of the American Oriental Society*, 82, 1962, pp. 312–20

—— 'African Models and Indian Histories', in Richard G. Fox, 1977, pp. 90–113 (reprinted in Cohn, 1987), pp. 200–23

—— *An Anthropologist among the Historians and Other Essays* (Delhi: OUP, 1987)

Conermann, Stephan, *Die Beschreibung Indiens in der 'Riḥla' des Ibn Baṭṭūṭa, Aspekte einer herrschaftsoziologischen Einordnung des Delhi-Sultanates unter Muḥammad Ibn Tuğluq* (Berlin, 1993)

—— *Patrimonialism in Pre-Mughal Muslim India. A Case Study* (forthcoming)

Coulborn, Rushton (ed.), *Feudalism in History* (Princeton, 1956)

—— 'Feudalism, Brahmanism, and the Intrusion of Islam upon Indian History, *CSSH*, 10, 1968, pp. 356–74

Dallapiccola, Anna Libera and S. Zingel-Avé Lallemant (eds), *Vijayanagara—City and Empire*, 2 vols (Stuttgart, 1985)

Dash, Gaganendra, 'The Evolution of Priestly Power: 1, the Gaṅgavaṃśa Period;

2, the Sūryavaṃśa Period', in A.C. Eschmann, H. Kulke and G.C. Tripathi, 1978, pp. 157–68; 209–22

Day, Upendra Nath, *Administrative System of Delhi Sultanate (1206–1413 AD)* (Allahabad, 1965)

Deyell, John S., *Living without Silver. The Monetary History of Early Medieval North India* (Delhi: OUP, 1990)

Digby, Simon, *Warhorse and Elephant in the Delhi Sultanate; a Study in Military Supplies* (Oxford: OUP, 1971)

Dirks, Nicholas B., 'The Pasts of a Pāḷaiyakārar: The Ethnohistory of a South Indian Little King', *JAS*, 41, 1982, pp. 655–83

—— *The Hollow Crown, Ethnohistory of an Indian Kingdom* (Cambridge, 1987)

Durga, P.S. Kanaka and Y.A. Sudhakar Reddy, 'Kings, Temples and Legitimation of Autochthonous Communities, A Case Study of a South Indian Temple', *JESHO*, 35, 1992, pp. 144–66

Duverger, M. (ed.), *Le concept d'empire* (Paris, 1980)

Eaton, Richard M., 'Islamisierung im spätmittelalterlichen Bengalen', in Schluchter, W. (ed.), *Max Webers Sicht des Islams* (Frankfurt, 1987), pp. 156–79

Eisenstadt, Shmuel N., *The Political System of Empires* (New York, 1963)

Erdmann, Karl Dietrich, 'Die asiatische Welt im Denken von Karl Marx und Friedrich Engels', in Erdmann, K.D., *Geschichte, Politik und Pädagogik, Aufsätze und Reden* (Stuttgart, 1961), pp. 149–82

Eschmann, Anncharlott, Hermann Kulke and Gaya Charan Tripathi (eds), *The Cult of Jagannath and the Regional Tradition of Orissa* (New Delhi: Manohar, 1978)

Filliozat, V., *Vijayanagara Empire* (New Delhi, 1977).

Fox, R.G. (ed.), *Realm and Region in Traditional India* (New Delhi, 1977)

Fritz, J. and G. Michell, *City of Victory—Vijayanagara* (New York, 1991)

Frykenberg, Robert Eric (ed.), *Land Control and Social Structure in Indian History* (Madison, 1969)

Frykenberg R. and P. Kolenda, (eds), *Studies in South India: An Anthology of Recent Research and Scholarship* (Madras/New Delhi, 1985)

Fukazawa, Hiroshi, *The Medieval Deccan. Peasants, Social Systems and States. Sixteenth to Eighteenth Centuries* (New Delhi: OUP, 1991)

Gopal, K.K., 'The Assembly of Samantas in Early Medieval India', *JIH*, 42, 1964, pp. 241–50

Gopal, L., 'Sāmanta—Its Varying Significance in Ancient India', *JRAS*, 5, 1963a, pp. 21–37

—— 'On Feudal Polity in Ancient India', *JIH*, 41, 1963b, pp. 405–13

—— 'Quasi-manorial Rights in Ancient India', *JESHO*, 6, 1963c, pp. 296–308

Gough, Kathleen, 'Modes of Production in Southern India', *Economic and Political Weekly*, Annual Number, Feb. 1980, pp. 337–64

—— *Rural Society in Southeast India* (Cambridge, 1981)

Guha, Amalendu, 'Tribalism to Feudalism in Assam, 1600–1750', *IHR*, 1, 1974, pp. 65–76 (reprinted in D.N. Jha, 1987, pp. 145–65)

—— 'The Ahom Political System: An Enquiry into State Formation in Medieval Assam: 1228–1800', in S.C. Sinha, 1987, pp. 143–76

Gunawardana, R.A.L.H., 'The Analysis of Pre-Colonial Social Formations in Asia in the Writings of Karl Marx', in *IHR*, 2, 1976, pp. 365–88

Habib, Irfan, *The Agrarian System of Mughal India, 1556–1707* (Bombay, 1963)

—— 'The Mansab System, 1595–1637', *PIHC* (Patiala, 1967), pp. 221–42

—— 'An Examination of Wittfogel's Theory of 'Oriental Despotism', in K.S. Lal (ed.), *Studies in Asian History, Proceedings of the Asian History Congress, 1961* (London, 1969), pp. 378–92

—— 'Problems of Marxist Historical Analysis', in *Science and Human Progress, Essays in Honour of the Late Prof. D.D. Kosambi* (Bombay, 1974), pp. 34–47

—— 'Classifying Pre-Colonial India', in T.J. Byres and H. Mukhia, 1985, pp. 44–53

Habib, Muhammad, together with K.A. Nizami, *A Comprehensive History of India*, vol. V: *The Delhi Sultanate* (New Delhi, 1970).

—— *Politics and Society During the Early Medieval Period: Collected Papers of Professor Muhammad Habib*, 2 vols, K.A. Nizami (ed.) (New Delhi, 1974–81)

Hall, Kenneth R., *Trade and Statecraft in the Age of the Cōḷas* (New Delhi, 1980)

—— 'Peasant State and Society in Chola Times. A View from the Tiruvidaimarudur Urban Complex', *IESHR*, 18, 1981, pp. 393–410

Hall, Kenneth R. and George Spencer, 'The Economy of Kaṇchipuram, a Sacred Center in Early South India', *Journal of Urban History*, 6, 1980, pp. 127ff

Hardy, Peter, 'The Growth of Authority over a Conquered Political Elite: The Early Delhi Sultanate as a Possible Case Study', in J.F. Richards, 1978, pp. 192–214

—— 'The Authority of Muslim Kings in Medieval India', *Puruṣārtha*, 9, 1986, pp. 37–55

—— 'Islamischer Patrimonialismus: Die Mogulherrschaft', in W. Schluchter (ed.), *Max Webers Sicht des Islams* (Frankfurt, 1987), pp. 190–216

Hasan, S. Nurul, 'Zamindars under the Mughals', in Frykenberg, R.E., 1969, pp. 17–32

—— *Thoughts on Agrarian Relations in Mughal India* (New Delhi, 1973)

Heitzman, James, 'Early Buddhism, Trade and Empire', in K. Kennedy and G. Possehl (eds), *Studies in Archaeology and Palaeoanthropology of Asia* (New Delhi: OUP, 1984a), pp. 121–37

—— 'Segments, Centralization and Modes of Production in the Cola State', Paper presented to the 13th Annual Conference on South Asia, Madison, Wisconsin, 1984b

—— 'Socio-Economic Formations in Premodern South Asia: Case Studies and Methodology', *JPS*, 13, 1985a, pp. 47–60

—— Gifts of Power: Temples, Politics and Economy in Medieval South India, Ph.D. Dissertation, University of Pennsylvania, 1985b

—— 'Temple, Landholding and Village Geography in the Chola Period: Reconstruction through Inscriptions (together with S. Rajagopal)', *Tamil Civilizations*, 3, no. 2/3, 1985c, pp. 6–31

—— 'State Formation in South India, 850–1280', *IESHR*, 24, 1987a, pp. 44–61

—— 'Temple Urbanism in Medieval South India', *JAS*, 46, 1987b, pp. 791–826

—— 'Ritual Polity and Economy: The Transactional Network of an Imperial Temple in Medieval South India', *JESHO*, 34, 1991, pp. 23–54

Inden, Ronald, 'Hierarchies of Kings in Medieval India', in T.N. Madan (ed.), *Way of Life: King, Householder, Renouncer, Essays in Honour of Louis Dumont* (New Delhi, 1982), pp. 99–125

Jaiswal, Suvira, 'Caste in the Socio-Economic Framework of Early India', Presidential Address, Ancient Indian Section, *Indian History Congress*, 38th Session (Bhubaneswar: Dec. 1977)

—— 'Studies in Early Indian Social History: Trends and Possibilities', *IHR*, 6, 1979, pp. 1–63

Jha, D.N., 'Temples as Landed Magnates in Early Medieval South India (*c.* AD 700–1300)', in R.S. Sharma and V. Jha, 1974, pp. 202–16

—— 'Early Indian Feudalism: A Historiographical Critique', Presidential Address, Ancient India Session, *Indian History Congress*, 40th Session, Waltair: Dec. 1979

—— 'Relevance of "Peasant State and Society" to Pallava-Coḷa Times', *IHR*, 8, 1981, pp. 74–94

—— *Economy and Society in Early India. Issues and Paradigms* (New Delhi, 1993)

—— (ed.), *Feudal Social Formation in Early India* (Delhi, 1987)

Kantowsky, D. (ed.), *Recent Research on Max Weber's Studies of Hinduism* (München, 1986)

Karashima, Noboru, 'Nayakas as Lease-holders of Temple Land', *JESHO*, 19, 1976, pp. 227–32 (reprinted in Karashima, 1984) pp. 159–65

—— *South Indian History and Society, Studies from Inscriptions AD 850–1800* (Delhi: OUP, 1984)

—— *Towards a New Formation. South Indian Society under Vijayanagar Rule* (New Delhi: OUP, 1992)

Kennedy, R., 'The King in Early South India as Chieftain and Emperor', *IHR*, 3, 1976, pp. 1–15

Kolff, D.H.A., *Naukar, Rajput and Sepoy. The Ethnohistory of the Military Labour Market in Hindustan, 1450–1850* (Cambridge, 1990)

Kosambi, D.D., *An Introduction to the Study of Indian History* (Bombay, 1956a)

—— 'On the Development of Feudalism in India', *Annals of the Bhandarkar Oriental Research Institute*, 36, 1956b, pp. 258–69

—— 'Origins of Feudalism in Kashmir', *Journal of the Bombay Branch of the Royal Asiatic Society*, 31/32, 1956c, pp. 108–20

—— 'Indian Feudal Trade Charters', *JESHO*, 2, 1959, pp. 281–93

D.D. Kosambi Commemoration Committee, *Prof. D.D. Kosambi Commemoration Volume*, Varanasi, Kosambi Commemoration Committee (Banaras Hindu University, 1974)

Science and Human Progress, Essays in Honour of the Late D.D. Kosambi (Bombay, 1974)

Krishnaswami, A., *Tamil Country under Vijayanagura* (Annamalainagar, 1964)

Kulke, Hermann, 'Kshatriyaization and Social Change. A Study in Orissa Setting', in S. Devadas Pillai, *Aspects of Changing India: Studies in the Honour of Prof. S.G. Ghurye* (Bombay, 1976), pp. 398–409

—— 'Royal Temple Policy and the Structure of Medieval Hindu Kingdoms', in A.C. Eschmann, H. Kulke and G.C. Tripathi, 1978, pp. 125–38

—— 'Early State Formation and Royal Legitimation in Tribal Areas of Eastern India', in Rupert R. Moser and Mohan K. Gautam (eds), *Aspects of Tribal Life in South Asia, 1: Strategy and Survival* (Bern, 1978b), pp. 29–37

—— *Jagannātha-Kult und Gajapati-Königtum. Ein Beitrag zur Geschichte religiöser Legitimation hinduistischer Herrscher* (Wiesbaden, 1979)

—— 'Legitimation and Town-Planning in the Feudatory States of Central Orissa', in idem 1993, pp. 93–113

—— 'Fragmentation and Segmentation versus Integration? Reflections on the Concepts of Indian Feudalism and the Segmentary State in Indian History, *Studies in History*, 4, 1982, pp. 237–63

—— 'The Early and the Imperial Kingdom in Southeast Asian History', in D.G. Marr and A.C. Milner (eds), *Southeast Asia in the 9th to 14th Centuries* (Singapore, 1986)

—— 'Die indische Debatte über asiatische Produktionsweise und indischen Feudalismus', in H. Bookmann and K. Jürgensen (eds), *Nachdenken über die Geschichte. Gedenkschrift für K.D. Erdmann* (Neumünster, 1991), pp. 305–20

—— *Kings and Cults. State Formation and Legitimation in India and Southeast Asia* (New Delhi: Manohar 1993)

—— 'Some Observations on the Political Functions of the Copper-Plate Grants in Early Medieval India', in B. Kölver (ed.), *The State, the Law and Administration in Classical India* (Munich, 1977), pp. 237–43

Ludden, David, *Peasant History of South India* (Princeton, 1985)

Mahalingam, Teralundur Venkatarama, *Administration and Social Life under Vijayanagara*, 2 vols (Madras, 1940)

—— 'Genesis and Nature of Feudalism Under the Pallavas of Kānchī', in S.K. Maity and U. Thakur (eds), *Indological Studies, Prof. D.C. Sircar Commemoration Volume* (New Delhi, 1987), pp. 89–96

Mahapatra, L.K. 'Ex-Princely States of Orissa: Mayurbhanj, Keonjhar and Bonai', in Surajit Sinha, 1987, pp. 1–51

Maity, S.K., 'Medieval Feudalism and Manorialism *versus* Ancient Indian Landed Economy', in D.C. Sircar, 1966b, pp. 100–17

Majumdar, R.C., *History of Medieval Bengal* (Calcutta, 1973)

Mitra, S.K., 'Feudalism in India', in D.C. Sircar, 1966b, pp. 51–7

Mookherji, Radhakamund, *Local Government in Ancient India* (Delhi, 1958 rev. edn)

Moore, R.J. (ed.), *Tradition and Politics in India* (New Delhi, 1979)

Moosvi, Shireen, 'The Evolution of the Mansab System under Akbar until 1596–7', *JRAS*, 1981, pp. 173–85

—— *The Economy of the Mughal Empire c. 1595. A Statistical Study* (Delhi: OUP, 1987)

Moreland, W.H., *The Agrarian System of Moslem India* (Cambridge, 1929)

Morrison, B.M., *Political Centers and Cultural Regions in Early Bengal* (Tuscon, 1970)

Mukhia, Harbans, *Historians and Historiography during the Reign of Akbar* (New Delhi, 1976)

—— Was There Feudalism in Indian History? Presidential Address, Medieval Section, *Indian History Congress*, 40th Session, Waltair, Dec. 1979a

—— 'Maurice Dobb's Explanation of the Decline of Feudalism in Western Europe—A Critique', *IHR*, 6, 1979b, pp. 154–84

—— 'Peasant Production and Medieval Indian Society', in T.J. Byres and H. Mukhia, 1985, pp. 228–51

—— *Perspectives on Medieval History* (Delhi, 1993)

Nandi, Ramendra Nath, 'Growth of Rural Economy in Early Feudal India', Presidential Address, Ancient India Section, *Indian History Congress*, 45th Session, Annamalai, Dec. 1984a

—— 'Feudalization of State in Medieval South India', in *Social Science Probings*, 1, 1984b, pp. 33–59

Nigam, S.B.P., *Nobility under the Delhi Sultanate* (Delhi, 1968)

Nilakantha Sastri, K.A., *The Cōḷas* (Madras, 1955)

Nizami, Khaliq Ahmad, *Some Aspects of Religion and Politics in India during the Thirteenth Century* (Delhi, 1961)

—— *State and Culture in Medieval India* (New Delhi, 1985)

Njammasch, Marlene, *Untersuchungen zur Genesis des Feudalismus in Indien* (Berlin, 1984)

O'Leary, Brenden, *The Asiatic Mode of Production: Oriental Despotism, Historical Materialism and Indian History* (Oxford, 1989)

Palat, Ravi, 'Popular Revolts and the State in India: A Study of the Vijayanagara Empire (1360–1565)', *Bijtragen tot de Taal, Land- en Volkenkunde*, no. 142, 1986, pp. 128–44

—— 'The Vijayanagara Empire, Re-Integration of the Agrarian Order of Medieval South India, 1336–1565', in H.J.M. Claessen and P. Van de Velde, 1987, pp. 170–86

Panda, Shishir Kumar, *Herrschaft und Verwaltung im östlichen Indien unter den späten Gangas (ca. 1038–1434)* (Stuttgart, 1986)

—— *Medieval Orissa. A Socio-Economic Study* (New Delhi, 1991)

—— 'From Kingdom to Empire. A Study of the Medieval State of Orissa under the Later Eastern Gaṅgas', AD 1038–1434', *IHR*, 17, 1993, pp. 149–60

Pearson, Michael, *Merchants and Rulers in Gujarat* (Berkeley/Los Angeles, 1976)

Perlin, Frank, 'The Pre-Colonial Indian State in History and Epistemology. A Reconstruction of Societal Formation in the Western Deccan from the Fifteenth to the Early Nineteenth Century', in H.J.M. Claessen and P. Skalnik, 1981, pp. 275–302

—— 'State Formation Reconsidered', II, *MAS*, 19, 1985a, pp. 415–80

—— 'Concepts of Order and Comparison, with a Diversion on Counter Ideologies and Corporate Institutions in Late Pre-Colonial India', *JPS* 12, 2/3, 1985b, pp. 87–165

Pirenne, Henri, *Mohammad and Charlemagne* (London, 1939)

Pouchepadass, J. and H. Stern (eds), *From Kingship to State. The Political in the Anthropology and History of the Indian World* (Paris, 1991). (Collection Puruṣārtha 13)

Prakash, Buddha, 'The Genesis and Character of Landed Aristocracy in Ancient India', *JFSHO*, 14, 1971, pp. 196–220

Prakash, Om, *Early Indian Land Grants and State Economy* (Allahabad, 1988)

—— *Conceptualization and History* (Allahabad, 1992)

Qureshi, Ishtaq Husain, *The Administration of the Sultanate of Delhi* (Lahore, 1942, 5th rev. edn, New Delhi, 1971)

Ramaswamy, Vijaya, 'Peasant State and Society in Medieval South India—A Review Article', *Studies in History*, 4, 1982, pp. 307–19

Rao, Velcheru, David Shulman and Sanjay Subrahmanyam, *Symbols of Substance, Court and State in Nāyaka Period Tamil Nadu* (Delhi: OUP, 1992)

Raychaudhuri, Tapan and Irfan Habib, *The Cambridge History of India*, vol. 1: *c.* 1200–*c.* 1750 (Cambridge, 1982)

Richards, J.F. (ed.), *Kingship and Authority in South Asia* (Madison, 1978)

—— *Mughal Administration in Golkonda* (Delhi: OUP, 1975)

—— *The Mughal Empire*, The New Cambridge History of India, vol. I.5, (Cambridge, 1993)

Rizvi, S.A.A. *The Wonder that was India, Volume II. A Survey of the History and Culture of the Indian Subcontinent from the Coming of the Muslims to the British Conquest, 1200–1700* (London, 1987)

Rösel, Jakob, 'Über die Bedeutung von Tempelstädten für Entsehen und Bestand des Regionalreiches Orissa', *Internationales Asienforum*, 9, 1978, pp. 41–58

—— 'Max Weber and the Patrimonial State', in D. Kantowsky, 1986, pp. 117–52

Rothermund, Dietmar, 'Feudalism in India', in D. Rothermund, *The Phases of Indian Nationalism and Other Essays* (Delhi, 1970), pp. 165–78

Rudra, Ashok, 'Against Feudalism', *Economic and Political Weekly*, 16, 1981, pp. 2133–46

Rudolph, Lloyd and Susanne H. Rudolph, 'The Subcontinental Empire and the Regional Kingdom in Indian State Formation', in Paul Wallace (ed.), *Region and Nation in India* (New Delhi: OUP, 1985), pp. 40–59

Rudolph, Susanne H., 'Presidential Address: State Formation in Asia—Prolegomenon to a Comparative Study', *JAS*, 46, 1987, pp. 731–46

Sarkar, J.N., *Mughal Administration*, (reprint Bombay, 1972)

Scharfe, Hartmut, *The State in Indian Tradition*, Handbuch der Orientalistik, II, 3, 2 (Leiden, 1989)

Schnepel, Burkhart, 'The Nandapur Suryavamshis. Origin and Consolidation of a South Orissan Kingdom', *OHRJ*, 1992, 170–99

—— 'Little Kingdoms Reconsidered', Occasional Papers of the Dept. of Anthropology, Nr. 5, Utkal University (Bhubaneswar, 1994)

—— 'Durga and the King. Ethnohistorical Aspects of the Politico-Ritual Life in a South Orissan Jungle Kingdom', in *Journal of the Royal Anthropological Institute (Man)*, 1, 1995, pp. 145–66

Schwartzberg, Joseph E., 'The Evolution of Regional Power Configurations in the Indian Subcontinent', in R.G. Fox, 1977, pp. 197–233

Seneviratne, Sudarshan D.S., 'Kalinga and Andhra: The Process of Secondary State Formation', in H.J.M. Claessen and P. Skalnik, 1981, pp. 317–38

Settar, S., 'Twentieth Century in Ancient India', Presidential Address, Ancient India Section, *Indian History Congress*, 43rd Session (Kurukshetra, Dec. 1982)

Sharma, Ram Sharan, 'Origins of Feudalism in India (*c.* AD 400–650)', *JESHO*, 1, 1957, pp. 297–328

—— *Aspects of Political Ideas and Institutions in Ancient India*, Delhi: 1959 (3rd rev. edn Delhi, 1991)

—— 'Landgrants to Vassals and Officials in Northern India *c.* AD 1000–1200', *JESHO*, 4, 1961, pp. 70–105

—— *Indian Feudalism, c. 300–1200* (Calcutta, 1965)

—— 'Decay of Gangetic Towns in Gupta and Post-Gupta Times', *JIH*, 50, 1973, pp. 135–50

—— 'Problem of Transition from Ancient to Medieval in Indian History', *IHR*, 1, 1974a, pp. 1–9

—— 'Methods and Problems of the Study of Feudalism in Early Medieval India', *IHR*, 1, 1974b, pp. 81–4

—— 'Indian Feudalism Re-touched', *IHR*, 2, 1974c, pp. 320–30

—— 'The Kali-Age: A Period of Social Crisis', in S.N. Mukherjee (ed.), *History and Thought, Essays in Honour of A.L. Basham* (Calcutta, 1982), pp. 186–203

—— 'How Feudal was Indian Feudalism?', in T.J. Byres and H. Mukhia, 1985, pp. 19–43

—— *Urban Decay in India 300–1000* (New Delhi, 1987)

—— 'Problems of Peasant Protest in Early Medieval India (*c.* 500– *c.* 1000)', *Social Scientist*, 16, no. 9, 1988, pp. 3–16

—— 'The Segmentary State and the Indian Experience', *IHR*, 16, 1993, pp. 81–110

Sharma, R.S. and V. Jha (eds), *Indian Society: Historical Probings, In Memory of D.D. Kosambi* (New Delhi, 1974)

Sharma, S.R., *Mughal Government and Administration* (Bombay, 1951)

Sherwani, Haroon Khan and P.M. Joshi (eds), *History of Medieval Deccan (1295–1724)*, 2 vols (Hyderabad, 1973–74)

Shrimali, K.M. 'Political Organization of Northern India', in R.S. Sharma and K.M. Shrimali (eds), *A Comprehensive History of India*, vol. IV, pt. 1, New Delhi, 1992, pp. 728–39; 758–72

—— 'Reflections on Recent Perceptions of Early Medieval India', Presidential Address, Section IV: Historiography, *Andhra Pradesh Historical Congress*, 18th Session, Tenali 1994

Shulman, David Dean, 'On South Indian Bandits and Kings', *IESHR*, 17, 1980, pp. 283–306

—— *The King and the Clown in South Indian Myth and Poetry* (Princeton, 1985)

Shulman, David Dean and S. Subrahmanyam, 'The Men who would be King? The Politics of Expansion in Early Seventeenth-Century Northern Tamilnadu', *MAS*, 24, 1990, pp. 225–48

Singh, Chetan, 'Centre and Periphery in the Mughal State: The Case of the Seventeenth-Century Panjab', *MAS*, 22, 1988, pp. 299–318

Singh, Suresh K., 'A Study of State Formation among Tribal Communities', in R.S. Sharma and V. Jha, 1974, pp. 317–36

Singh, Upinder, 'Kings, Brahmanas and Temples in Orissa: An Epigraphic Study (300–1147 AD)', unpublished Ph.D. dissertation, McGill University, Montreal, 1990

Sinha, Surajit C., 'State Formation and Rajput Myth in Tribal Central India', *Man in India*, 42, 1962, pp. 35–80

—— (ed.), *Tribal Polities and State Systems in Pre-Colonial Eastern and North Eastern India* (New Delhi, 1987)

Sircar, Dines Chandra, 'Landlordism Confused with Feudalism', in D.C. Sircar, 1966b, pp. 57–61, 1966a

—— (ed.), *Land System and Feudalism in Ancient India* (Calcutta, 1966b)

—— *Landlordism and Tenancy in Ancient and Medieval India as Revealed by Epigraphical Resources* (Lucknow, 1969)

—— *Political and Administrative System of Ancient and Medieval India* (Delhi, 1973)

Sitaraman, B., N. Karashima and Y. Subbarayalu, 'A List of Tamil Inscriptions of the Cola Dynasty', *Journal of Asian and African Studies*, Tokyo, 11, 1976, pp. 87–181

Sontheimer, Günther-D., *Pastoral Deities in Western India* (New York, 1989)

Southall, Aidan, *Alur Society: A Study in Processes and Types of Domination* (Cambridge, 1956)

—— 'The Segmentary State in Africa and Asia', *CSSH*, 30, 1987, pp. 52–82

Spencer, George, W., 'Religious Networks and Royal Influence in Eleventh-Century South India', *JESHO*, 12, 1969, pp. 42–56

—— 'Royal Initiative under Rajaraja I', *IESHR*, 7, 1970, pp. 431–42

—— 'The Politics of Plunder: The Cholas in Eleventh-Century Ceylon', *JAS*, 35, 1976, pp. 405–19

—— *The Politics of Expansion. The Chola Conquest of Sri Lanka and Sri Vijaya* (Madras, 1983)

Spencer, George W. and Kenneth R. Hall, 'Toward an Analysis of Dynastic Hinterlands: The Imperial Cholas of 11th Century South India', *Asian Profile*, 2, 1974, pp. 51–62

Stein, Burton, The Tirupati Temple: An Economic Study of a Medieval South Indian Temple, Ph.D. thesis, Dept. of History, Univ. of Chicago, 1958

—— 'The Economic Function of a South Indian Temple', *JAS*, 19, 1959–60, pp. 163–76

—— 'The State, the Temple and Agricultural Development. A Study in Medieval South India', *Economic and Political Weekly*, 13, 1961, pp. 179–89

—— 'Integration of the Agrarian System of South India', in R.E. Frykenberg, 1969, pp. 175–213

—— (ed.), *Essays on South India*, Honolulu, 1975a

—— 'The State and the Agrarian Order in Medieval South India: A Historiographical Critique', in B. Stein, 1975a, pp. 64–91, 1975b

—— 'The Segmentary State in South Indian History', in R.G. Fox, 1977, pp. 3–51

—— (ed.), *South Indian Temples; An Analytical Reconsideration*, published as a supplemental volume of *IESHR*, 14, 1977 and reprinted by Vikas (Delhi, 1978a)

——'Temples in Tamil Country, 1300–1750 AD, in Stein, 1978a, pp. 11–45, 1978b

—— *Peasant State and Society in Medieval South India* (Delhi: OUP, 1980)

—— 'Mahānavami: Medieval and Modern Kingly Ritual in South India', in B.L. Smith (ed.), *Essays on Gupta Culture* (Delhi, 1983), pp. 67–90

—— *All the King's Mana: Papers on Medieval South Indian History* (Madras, 1984)

—— 'Politics, Peasants and the Deconstruction of Feudalism in Medieval India', in T.J. Byres and H. Mukhia, 1985, pp. 54–86, 1985a

—— 'Vijayanagara and the Transition to Patrimonial Systems', in A.L. Dallapiccola and S. Zingel-Avé Lallemant, 1985, vol. 1, pp. 73–87, 1985b

—— 'Reapproaching Vijayanagara', in R. Frykenberg and P. Kolenda (eds), 1985c, pp. 31–50

—— State Formation and Economy Reconsidered, I, *MAS*, 19, 1985d, pp. 387–413

—— *Vijayanagara*, The New Cambridge History of India, vol. 1.2 (Cambridge, 1989)

—— 'The Segmentary State: Interim Reflections', in J. Pouchepadass and H. Stern, 1991, pp. 217–38

—— 'Patronage and Vijayanagara Religious Foundations', in Barbara Stoler Miller (ed.), *The Powers of Art: Patronage in Indian Culture* (New Delhi: OUP, 1992A)

—— 'The Politicized Temples of Southern India', in Hans Bakker (ed.), *The Sacred Centre as the Focus of Political Interest*, Groningen Oriental Series, vol. 6 (Groningen, 1992b), pp. 163–78

—— 'Communities, States and "Classical" India', in B. Kölver (ed.), *Law, State and Society in Classical India*, (Munich, forthcoming)

Stern, Henri, 'Power in Traditional India: Territory, Caste and Kinship in Rajasthan', in R.G. Fox, 1977, pp. 52–89

Streusand, Douglas, *The Formation of the Mughal Empire* (Delhi: OUP, 1989)

Subba Rao, Bendapuli, *The Personality of India: A Study of the Development of Material Culture of India and Pakistan* (Baroda, 1956)
Subbarayalu, Y., *The Political Geography of the Chola Country* (Madras, 1973)
—— 'The Cola State', in *Studies in History*, 4, 1982, pp. 269–306
—— 'The Cola State and the Agrarian Order—Some Clarifications', paper presented to the Seminar on 'The State in Pre-Colonial South India', Centre for Historical Studies (Jawaharlal Nehru University, 1989)
Subrahmanyam, Sanjay, 'Aspects of State Formation in South India and Southeast Asia', 1550–1650, *IESHR*, 23, 1986, pp. 358–77
Subrahmanyam, Sanjay and C.A. Bayly, 'Portfolio Capitalists and Political Economy of Early Modern India', *IESHR*, 25, 1988, pp. 401–24
Subrahmanyam, Sanjay and David Shulman, 'The Men who would be King? The Politics of Expansion in Early Seventeenth-Century Northern Tamilnadu', *MAS*, 24, 1990, pp. 225–48
Talbot, Cynthia, 'Temples, Donors and Gifts: Patterns of Patronage in Thirteenth-Century South India', *JAS*, 50, 1991, pp. 308–40
Tambiah, Stanley J., *World Conqueror and World Renouncer* (Cambridge, 1976)
Tarafdar, M.R., 'Trade and Economy in Early Medieval Bengal', *IHR*, 4, 1978, pp. 24–286; reprinted in Jha, D.N., 1987, 1978, pp. 220–38
Thakur, Vijay Kumar, 'Trade and Towns in Early Medieval Bengal', (*c*. AD 600–1200), *JESHO*, 30, 1987, pp. 196–220
—— *Historiography of Indian Feudalism. Towards a Model of Early Medieval Indian Economy, c.* AD 600–1000 (Patna, 1989)
Thapar, Romila, *A History of India*, vol. 1 (Harmondsworth, 1966)
—— 'State Formation in Early India', *International Social Science Journal*, 1980, pp. 655–69
—— 'The State as Empire', in H.J.M. Claessen and P. Skalnik, 1981, pp. 409–26
—— *From Lineage to State. Social Formations in the Mid-First Millennium* BC *in the Ganges Valley* (Bombay, 1984)
—— 'The Contribution of D.D. Kosambi to Indology', in: idem, *Interpreting Early India* (Delhi: OUP, 1992), pp. 89–113
—— *Cultural Transaction and Early India: Tradition and Patronage* (Delhi: OUP, 1994)
—— (ed.), *Recent Perspectives of Early Indian History* (Bombay: Popular Prakashan, 1994)
Thorner, Daniel, 'Feudalism in India', in R. Coulborn, 1956, pp. 133–50
Voyce, M.B., 'The Control of the King over Temples in Ancient India', *Archív Orientální*. 51, 1983, pp. 310–26
Weber, Max, *Economy and Society, an Outline of Interpretative Sociology*, translated and edited by G. Roth and C. Wittich, Berkeley, 1978

Wills, Cecil, 'The Territorial System of the Rajput Kingdoms of Medieval Chhattisgarh', *Journal and Proceedings of the Asiatic Society of Bengal (N.S.)*, 15, 1920, pp. 197–262

Wink, André, 'Sovereignty and Universal Dominion in South Asia', *IESHR*, 21, 1984, pp. 265–92

—— *Al-Hind. The Making of the Indo-Islamic World, vol. 1: Early Medieval Expansion of Islam, 7th–11th Century* (Leiden, 1990)

Wittfogel, Karl, *Oriental Despotism. A Comparative Study of Total Power* (Yale University, 1957)

Wojtilla, Gyula, 'Rural Expansion in Early Medieval India. A Linguistic Assessment', *Altorientalische Forschungen*, 18, 1991, pp. 163–9

Yadava, B.N.S., *Society and Culture in North India in the Twelfth Century* (Allahabad, 1973)

—— The Problem of the Emergence of Feudal Relations in Early India, Presidential Address, Ancient India Section, *Indian History Congress*, 41st Session, Bombay, Dec. 1980

Ziegler, Norman P., 'Some Notes on Rajpūt Loyalties During the Mughal Period', in J.F. Richards, 1978, pp. 215–51